The Limits of Settler Colonial Reconciliation

Sarah Maddison · Tom Clark
Ravi de Costa
Editors

The Limits of Settler Colonial Reconciliation

Non-Indigenous People and the Responsibility to Engage

Springer

Editors
Sarah Maddison
School of Social and Political Sciences
University of Melbourne
Melbourne, VIC
Australia

Tom Clark
Victoria University
Melbourne, VIC
Australia

Ravi de Costa
York University
Toronto, ON
Canada

ISBN 978-981-10-2653-9 ISBN 978-981-10-2654-6 (eBook)
DOI 10.1007/978-981-10-2654-6

Library of Congress Control Number: 2016950913

Printed on acid-free paper

This Springer imprint is published by Springer Nature
The registered company is Springer Nature Singapore Pte Ltd.
The registered company address is: 152 Beach Road, #22-06/08 Gateway East, Singapore 189721, Singapore

Contents

Editors and Contributors

About the Editors

Sarah Maddison is an associate professor in the School of Social and Political Sciences at the University of Melbourne. In 2015, Sarah published a new book *Conflict Transformation and Reconciliation* (Routledge) based on research in South Africa, Northern Ireland, Australia, and Guatemala. Her other recent books include *Black Politics* (2009), *Beyond White Guilt* (2011), *Unsettling the Settler State* (coedited with Morgan Brigg, 2011), and *The Women's Movement in Protest, Institutions and the Internet*, (coedited with Marian Sawer 2014).

Tom Clark is an associate professor in the College of Arts at Victoria University (Melbourne). He is currently serving as Secretary General of the International federation for Modern Languages and Literatures and as president of the Australasian Universities Languages and Literature Association. His long-term teaching and research focus on the poetics of public rhetoric have led to his involvement with Sarah Maddison and Ravi de Costa in research into non-Indigenous attitudes and identities in Australia and Canada. Previous research includes his 2012 book, *Stay on Message: Poetry and Truthfulness in Political Speech* (ASP).

Ravi de Costa is an associate professor and associate dean for research in the Faculty of Environmental Studies at York University, Toronto. He has written on the politics of reconciliation in Australia and Canada, as well as on treaty-making, the global Indigenous movement and the UN Declaration on the Rights of Indigenous Peoples. His previous work includes *A higher authority: Indigenous transnationalism and Australia* (UNSW Press, 2006).

Contributors

Jon Altman Alfred Deakin Institute for Citizenship and Globalisation, Deakin University, Melbourne, Australia

Thalia Anthony University of Technology, Sydney, Australia

Kerry A. Bailey McMaster University, Hamilton, Canada

Adam J. Barker University of Leicester, Leicester, UK

Emma Battell Lowman University of Hertfordshire, Hatfield, UK

Tom Clark Victoria University, Melbourne, Australia

Ravi de Costa York University, Toronto, Canada

Jeffrey S. Denis McMaster University, Hamilton, Canada

Sasha Henriss-Anderssen Victoria University, Melbourne, Australia

Adrian Little University of Melbourne, Parkville, Australia

Alissa Macoun University of Queensland, Brisbane, Australia

Sarah Maddison University of Melbourne, Parkville, Australia

Ry Moran Canadian National Centre for Truth and Reconciliation, University of Manitoba, Winnipeg, Canada

Yin Paradies Deakin University, Burwood, Australia

Joanna R. Quinn University of Western Ontario, London, Canada

Peter Read Australian National University, Acton, Australia

Angélique Stastny University of Melbourne, Parkville, Australia

Elizabeth Strakosch University of Queensland, St Lucia, Australia

Lorenzo Veracini Swinburne University of Technology, Melbourne, Australia

Chapter 1
Non-Indigenous People and the Limits of Settler Colonial Reconciliation

Tom Clark, Ravi de Costa and Sarah Maddison

Abstract This chapter sets the context for this volume's concern with the conceptual, attitudinal, and political limits to policies and practices of reconciliation in settler colonial societies. It explains the complex and interconnected focuses of the book as a whole and sets the notion of a non-Indigenous 'responsibility to engage' in a broader context of theory and research, Australian, Canadian, and globally. The chapter maps the continuities and contestations evident among the book's following 15 chapters, and outlines an overall contribution to an operational understanding of reconciliation as an historically critical problem.

Keywords Reconciliation · Settler colonialism · Engagement · Politics · Non-Indigenous responsibility · Non-Indigenous people · Interdisciplinary research methods

Everywhere we turn we see conflicting narratives about the possibilities of better relations between Indigenous and settler peoples. Patient efforts to support Indigenous acts of self-determination compete with indifference and hostility towards Indigenous peoples' alleged failure to stop being 'the problem'; serious undertakings are derailed by debate about the merits of the 'symbolic' versus the imperative for more 'practical' reforms.

Much of what has been studied in this field has been state-led attempts to refashion these relations and their effects: researchers analyse institutions and policies; we critique ideologies; and we parse the language and patterns of com-

T. Clark (✉)
Victoria University, Melbourne, Australia
e-mail: Tom.clark@vu.edu.au

R. de Costa
York University, Toronto, Canada
e-mail: rdc@yorku.ca

S. Maddison
University of Melbourne, Parkville, Australia
e-mail: Sarah.maddison@unimelb.edu.au

S. Maddison et al. (eds.), *The limits of settler colonial reconciliation*,
DOI 10.1007/978-981-10-2654-6_1

munication. As scholars of reconciliation we have studied a range of community-led projects, from the work of radical activists to church groups and others in 'the reconciliation movement'. In all of this we search for signs of hope and promise, but more often we despair at the new ways in which colonial assumptions are able to reproduce themselves in policy and in practice.

This dynamic—of hope turning to despair in the face of colonial intractability—is a key thematic in the field of reconciliation. The extent to which it has played out over the last two decades and more has hardened positions. The proximity of efforts at reconciliation to the challenges of the wider public policy domain in Indigenous affairs has more often tainted reconciliation in the eyes of Indigenous and settler publics than provided energy and momentum. True believers maintain that efforts such as constitutional reform can move the nation from symbolic to substantive change; opponents are confirmed in their belief that such changes are irrelevant, counter-productive or unjustified. Indigenous skeptics and their non-Indigenous allies find these moves beside the point, while a large body of the population remains disinterested and unengaged.

Our own efforts in this project, both as co-editors and as collaborators, have been to find 'pathways' to reconciliation. The metaphor implies a journey through known obstacles, such that we might chart a course for our communities to follow. But this formulation of the challenges of Indigenous-settler colonial relations retains a teleological quality that obliges us to tackle the question, 'how will we know when we are reconciled?'

Thinking Reconciliation in a Settler Colonial Society

The field of reconciliation studies is replete with efforts to define what is meant by reconciliation. As a political concept, reconciliation emerged first in societies transitioning from periods of authoritarian rule or civil war, and has since been applied to efforts in settler colonial societies still grappling with historical wrongs, including Australia and Canada (Bashir and Kymlicka 2008: 3–4). In recent decades, reconciliation has become a commonplace term expressing a regulatory ideal in political discourse (Christodoulidis and Veitch 2007: 3), moving over time from 'the seminary and the academy into public policy' (Hamber and Kelly 2009: 286).

Although there have now been some decades of effort collected under the rubric of reconciliation, there remains a significant lack of agreement about its meaning. Much research has attempted to further define the concept in an effort to 'boil it down' to an agreed policy framework (Renner 2012: 55). Despite such efforts, however, and despite the huge political and economic capital being expended on reconciliation-promoting projects around the world, there remains a broad inability to either understand reconciliation or 'confront its multitudinous and sometimes contradictory relationships' (Daly and Sarkin 2007: 4).

But although this situation may at times be confusing, it is not necessarily problematic. As Andrew Schaap (2005: 13) suggests, there are advantages to the continuing conceptual ambiguity of reconciliation, as by 'accommodating multiple meanings' the idea also 'provides a common vocabulary within which citizens may contest the terms and possibilities of their political association.' The alternative—pursuing a definitional consensus—would have the effect of containing reconciliation discourse, effectively limiting how it might be communicated and understood and therefore where and how it might be practiced. In settler colonial societies, where reconciliation actors in both government and civil society daily confront the limits of what may be possible, retaining the capacity to debate the meaning of reconciliation itself continues to be important.

For that reason, this volume does not advance a single definition of what reconciliation might mean. In the chapters that follow several authors continue to pursue critical discussions about what it is we expect from our communal lives in the paradigm of settler colonialism, confronting the possibilities and limitations of reconciliation in settler societies. In this book that theoretical turn starts with the contributions of Strakosch, Veracini, and Macoun, although it also finds an operational intensity in this volume's chapters by Anthony and by Read.

What marks the contributions to this volume is our shared focus on the challenges particular to reconciliation in settler colonial societies, specifically Australia and Canada. The common thread of this conversation is concern about the persistence of an assimilationist agenda that is contained within reconciliation's premises. How do we escape the colonial desire to shape indigeneity in its own image? Mapping the inherent and emergent limits and possibilities of reconciliation in settler colonial societies seems key if we are to be effective scholars, to participate in movements and contribute to social changes that overcome colonial desire. We need to be candid about what we know and be scrupulously careful about how we know it. This involves colonial and settler colonial histories at multiple scales; it involves the vigorous institutional dissection of political science; studies of education, culture and language; and imaginative forays into critical and normative theory; it involves comparative work across settler societies.

In Australia, for example, the settler colonial limits of the formal reconciliation process were abundantly clear from the outset. The Australian process was widely criticised for its 'intense resistance' to any decolonising action, which denied Aboriginal and Torres Strait Islander peoples in Australia the opportunity to pursue their claims regarding colonial injustice properly, providing them with 'a right to be incorporated into the Australian nation but not a right to refuse' (Short 2005: 274). Many Aboriginal and Torres Strait Islander people have been openly hostile to the concept of reconciliation, conscious that the formal ten-year process was offered as a consolation for the Hawke government's failure to deliver on their promise of national land rights and a treaty (Gunstone 2009: 45). As Kevin Gilbert expressed with force (quoted in Mudrooroo 1995: 228):

> What are we to reconcile ourselves to? To a holocaust, to massacre, to the removal of us from our land, from the taking of our land? The reconciliation process can achieve nothing because it does not at the end of the day promise justice.

Irene Watson (2007: 20) has asked similar questions, wondering:

> … what does reconciliation really mean? Will it provide homes for the homeless, food for the hungry, land for the dispossessed, language and culture for those hungry to revive from stolen and dispossessed spaces? How can you become reconciled with a state and its citizens who have not yet acknowledged your humanity, let alone your status as the first peoples of this conquered land?

As Damien Short (2008: 162) has argued, from the outset reconciliation in Australia placed a 'colonial ceiling' on Indigenous aspirations by emphasising nation-building and national unity over sovereignty or the negotiation of a treaty. Indeed, the Australian reconciliation process remained extremely tightly controlled and managed within political boundaries acceptable to the settler colonial state, a situation that seems likely to replicate itself in the current campaign for Indigenous 'recognition' in the Australian Constitution. Aspects of this political circumscription are the perceived 'stakes' in Australia's still-brewing debate about constitutional recognition addressed in Little's chapter.

Visibility, Invisibility, and Relations of Reconciliation

A politics of reconciliation challenges settler colonial states to deal with the problems of visibility and invisibility, of what and who is legible and to what end. These concerns, and the relations that underpin them, are multiple and layered. For the bulk of colonial history Indigenous peoples were, to most settlers, invisible, and for most the realities of Indigenous lives today still remain invisible. While Aboriginal and Torres Strait Islander cultures and peoples have a higher public profile now, they are often simply positioned within a blandly agreeable multiculturalism of food and sport, kept banal precisely in order to avoid confronting these troubling questions; either that or they are deemed to be radicals and ratbags, by definition ungrateful and 'inauthentic'—concerns addressed by Read in his chapter. The focus groups and interviews described in the 'Methodology' appendix to this collection tapped into the imaginative frameworks that sustain both these lines of thinking. By contrast, settler peoples have had a limited but powerful visibility. We have not until recently talked in national or mainstream discussions about 'non-Indigenous peoples' as a significant category or identity in settler societies. The 'problem' has always been located as Aboriginal or Indigenous, obscuring the fundamental roles and power of settler institutions and values.

The central logic of settler colonialism has long been understood as one of elimination and absorption into the settler society (Wolfe 1999). Indeed, the places that settler societies have in mind for Indigenous peoples are almost never those they have defined themselves, meaning reconciliation has usually set off on the wrong foot. This a priori certainty that we already know Indigenous peoples has severely affected our relations to Indigenous forms of leadership and practices of governance. Each national government in Australia at least since the 1960s has tried to create an Indigenous political interlocutor it finds amenable to its own agenda, cursing it in the eyes of both most Aboriginal and Torres Strait Islander people and the following government.

In some senses the mainstream political argument is simply about how much difference political parties are willing to engage with, variations that have more to do with the slight ideological variations between the settler left and right. As Macoun and Strakosch (2013) have quite rightly pointed out, however, even progressive political actors are drawn into the settler fantasy of white benevolence and colonial completion, despite their aspiration to virtue. Accounting for Indigenous differences still requires making Indigenous people accountable for their differences. Settler reconciliation projects in Australia never take seriously the right of Aboriginal and Torres Strait Islander peoples not to engage with us at all, or to do so on their own, very selective terms.

Somewhat differently in Canada, the colonial schism persists between an imposed administrative system now devolved into neoliberal self-management, and classical forms of Indigenous governance that have always persisted or are now resurgent. Some worry about the persistence of internalised inferiority among Indigenous peoples, with Indigenous scholars, in particular those in the 'Victoria school' of Indigenous radicalism (see for example Coulthard 2014; Simpson 2014), having tried to address this consequence of colonialism as part of a politics of resurgence. However, these varied political forms and positions with their attendant institutions have necessarily occupied different positions in relation to state-led reforms in Indigenous affairs, particularly those that imagine new relations as the key to improvements in the circumstances of Indigenous peoples. In settler societies, the art of consultation across cultures seems to have been lost, or perhaps it was never really known. If there are to be better futures then settler peoples have much to do if they are to come to terms with the complex realities of Indigenous polities.

One of the ways the research underpinning this volume seeks to inform reconciliation projects is to examine what Indigenous peoples and non-Indigenous peoples think about each other and the problems presented by racism, colonialism, identity and inequality in contemporary societies. Thinking about Indigenous-non-Indigenous relationships in this way is perhaps closest to popular understanding of reconciliation, pointing to the ways in which reconciliation aspires to engage with the contemporary relational manifestations of historical wounds and injustice (see Maddison 2015). Indeed, the very concept of reconciliation is based on the idea that a stable and legitimate political order is only possible if the psychological sources of conflict—'the residues of violence and death that linger long after open hostilities have ceased' (Hutchison and Bleiker 2013: 81)—are engaged. John Paul Lederach (2005: 34–35) suggests that relational concerns are at the centre of reconciliation efforts, with the goal of allowing people to imagine themselves in relationship with one another, creating a new social context in which cycles of violence might be broken. Lederach (2005: 85) maintains that relational engagement is key to reconciliation, enabling people to see 'spaces of intersection, both those that exist and those that can be created'.

Yet in settler colonial societies, reconciliation scholars and activist organisations find persistent evidence of the daily racism faced by Indigenous peoples; and, more alarmingly, the openness of non-Indigenous peoples in reporting their own discriminatory and anti-reconciliation views. In his chapter in this volume Paradies in particular illuminates the limits of what may be made possible through harnessing contemporary attitudes. Maddison and Stastny's chapter draws on focus group data to reveal the pitfalls of generalised education projects as well of the limits to attitudinal change evident through the creation of curricula or other strategies that simply address ignorance but do not appear to change attitudes or power relations.

But as Paradies suggests, awareness of white privilege seems to be an important correlate to a positive attitude to Aboriginal and Torres Strait Islander people and reconciliation. The question then is how to build such an awareness by drawing on what Rita Dhamoon has called settler privilege or settler complicity. Research underpinning this volume suggests that a hyperdetermined 'us' versus 'them' marks our language in all discussions in this field, revealing the embedded ideological commitments of settler nationalism. As the chapter by Stastny, Henriss-Anderssen and Clark makes clear, this has profound consequences for how non-Indigenous peoples can ever participate in discussions and policy about colonialism and social justice, not defining themselves as 'against' or simply 'not' Indigenous peoples but as in some ways as 'with'. This chapter raises the disconcerting possibility—which is as problematic for opponents of reconciliation of the right and the left as for its supporters—that strategically working with this incumbent pronoun system may contribute more productively to a discourse about the scope for changing Indigenous and non-Indigenous relations than attempts to annul or replace it.

Small but sincere efforts at imagining alternative ways for non-Indigenous peoples to understand themselves may have unforeseen policy implications. That is a clear warning in the chapters by Moran and by Denis and Bailey. For example, white affinity groups have proliferated since the emergence of formal reconciliation policies, often among groups with prior forms of organisation such as in churches or environmental movements. Such projects, like truth and reconciliation, have found significant reservoirs of support among non-Indigenous peoples and public institutions. However, it is these that are most subject to criticisms about the reproduction of colonial relations, the spectacle of reliving Indigenous peoples' suffering through testimonies or a culture of healing that exposes Indigenous communities to further well-meaning intervention. More often than not these processes have done little more than gesture at the colonial destruction of Indigenous polities, legal orders, economies and territories.

Among more radical activists, there is a growing attention to the possibilities of thinking how to live on Indigenous land without being colonial. Adam Barker and Emma Battell Lowman's chapter develops Taiaiake Alfred's (2005) concept of a 'clearing'—a concept that also finds some resonance in Strakosch's discussion of 'the middle thing.' The clearing offers more than a spatial metaphor; it seeks to describe a specific anticolonial geography replete with new possibilities for engagement. What would the clearing look like in the real world of politics? What are the political effects of such space? How do metaphors work to help us reimagine cultural and political reality?

Perhaps more than anything, this exploration of the non-Indigenous role in reconciliation efforts begins with the idea of 'bad settlers', or those who start failing at being settlers by contemplating and alternative political relationship with Indigenous peoples. On the one hand such an orientation seems a minimal requirement of anti-colonial allies to refuse to support the ongoing assumptions and practices of settlement. But what are the conditions for this to be distinctive from the more general task of being a critical person? On the other hand, it elides the fact that settler liberal democracy is a paramount failure in its own terms as a potential universal ground for postcolonial justice. Could these actors be a vanguard for new engagements and forms of justice? What are the potential effects of a strategy that privileges one form of settler knowing and learning? We need to be very clear about the terms in which we categorise our own positions within and against colonialism.

Research with self-identified 'allies' shows how these can be 'strikingly disconnected' from wider movements for decolonisation. Within such groups, we can see a wide diversity of views about what reconciliation is. 'Allyship' as a self-reflexive identity would presumably be highly variable; it may be 'conditional'. Even for those who take a more radical perspective, there is variation among those who see non-Indigenous peoples needing to take a more or less passive role, whether 'we' actively engage in work on ourselves, or we 'take direction' from Indigenous peoples.

Scholars have begun to do more work with these groups but most of these possibilities for solidarity or allyship are conceived of within explicitly activist spaces and contexts, such as providing food and supplies or working at camps in struggles over land, and of course in universities. In these settings there is a possibility, perhaps even an obligation to examine the basic foundations and assumptions of colonialism. It is less clear what allyship might mean in a highly structured and regulated context, like a hospital or a supermarket or a large corporation.

What is revealed by a broad examination of the range of positions of non-Indigenous peoples in settler societies is that we need to work more effectively with those not currently or sufficiently engaged. Not only do we require better forms of training for small or specific groups but also better large-scale communication: in both contexts we should be able to test out the positive correlation between an understanding of white or settler privilege and a substantive interest in reconciliation, for example. On the other hand, we need to figure out how to manage the variety of positions of those who already see themselves as having some sort of engagement: Among the diverse group of people who see themselves as already politicised on an issue, if we cannot cultivate agreement on the fundamental 'problem' or goals, then at least we might be able to encourage cooperative and productive work.

Within these problematics of settler self-recognition lies the fraught challenge of moving to collective action. A spectrum of delegation to embodiment, articulated previously by Clark and de Costa (REF) is one we might use to understand how individuals think of whose responsibility it is to engage, to act and change the colonial arrangements and relationships. For that to happen, collective bodies may need to respond in ways that do not foreclose new individual or local forms.

The challenge of moving to collective action is further complicated by the dynamics of ongoing migration into settler colonial nation-states. The coherence of a settler identity in the contemporary moment is very much under discussion, if mainly in more radical activist and academic settings. Whether or not it is possible to see migrants/refugees as settlers using an idea of 'political descent', reconciliation projects will need to be continually aware of the implications of framing the issues in crudely binary ways.

The Limits of Settler Colonial Policy

Given the persistence of national efforts such as constitutional reform or 'recognition,' we have further questions to consider. It seems almost bizarre that a nation-state like Australia, barely past its 200th birthday, should be considering whether to recognise Indigenous peoples and cultures who trace their histories for tens of millennia. Constitutional recognition could have the virtue of drawing attention to the felonious origins of Australia's original possession of the continent. But the latent colonial instincts make one wonder whether there is value in a project that emphasises the 'self-recognition' of the privileges of settler colonialism and its consequences for Indigenous peoples as a way to diminish the burden placed on the latter, that they be amenable to non-Indigenous recognisers, to be recognisable in existing and unthreatening forms. This is a central concern of the chapter by de Costa.

A further and related question is the invisibility of conflict. Most of settler society does not see the violence and vulnerability that many Indigenous peoples experience. When they do—and typically this occurs under states of emergency imposed by settler societies—these situations are absolutely not allowed to be understood as the inevitable product of colonialism. This limited, contrived understanding of Indigenous life weakens reconciliation projects by placing the burden on Indigenous peoples to deal with their own problems, or to be subject to further state interventions. Indigenous peoples by contrast, are unlikely to become more widely and deeply interested in reconciling with societies that sporadically pay them attention only to see their suffering as an inherent failing of their cultures and capacities.

One recurring approach has been that of transitional justice, a scholarly and institutional movement for overcoming conflict and building good relations. Some of its tools have been used in the countries under examination here, but can we think of transitional justice when thinking of longer settler colonial history not marked by a historical rupture that we now wish to close? Is 'transition' truly a pathway to transformation or substantive change, or will Indigenous peoples always be further colonised by transitions in which they are subordinate actors? Quinn's chapter, in particular, helps us to untangle some of the structural possibilities and dominant motives in addressing such questions.

We remain, however, far from clear on the matters that need to be on the table. A division in discussions about reconciliation is often between those who emphasise or are content with the symbolic, the psychological, the educational and the cultural, on the one hand, and those committed to structural transformation on the other. But transformation of what and which structures? This very distinction between the 'symbolic' and the 'practical,' or between culture and substance, or (in an earlier jargon) between superstructure and base, has always been deeply troubling for political ontology, because the symbolic necessarily is the practical and vice versa. In politics, words are deeds and deeds are words.

Many would say that extensions of land ownership to Indigenous peoples and the varied economies based on land are tantalising possibilities for a reconciliation that has substance. However, colonialism has also created environmental disadvantage: Indigenous people are not getting their land back in the state they had it taken away from them. Moreover, the politics of this disadvantaging has become entrenched in institutions of native title and comprehensive claims in settler states, systems that have strong colonial imperatives of settling and managing Indigenous difference and dynamism. In any case, where does this strategy leave the millions of Indigenous peoples who cannot prove their 'title' and 'claims' within the assumed sovereignty of colonial states? As Altman's chapter canvasses, land and hybrid economies may offer little for urban Indigenous peoples; they may also be ways that settler states forego their obligations to those who do have economic opportunities based on traditional cultures or on development rights over lands and resources.

It remains to be asked, at what level are we looking for the potential for reconciliation? The concept remains infused with a register of healing and feeling, making the personal and intimate dimensions of reconciliation seem plausible. As we proceed, however, we must certainly be aware of 'what is at stake' in our desire to do good, to have meaningful relations with peoples who might well be suspicious of us and our motives, who may see little need or value in an interpersonal, intercultural engagement. Much of what has characterised reconciliation has been top-down, politically-formulated ideas of unified political community—the ongoing dream of progressive settlers as taken up by political elites. We can see the cleavage between the personal and the national in discussions about treaties in Canada for example. For many settlers, if they are aware of treaties, it is as historical forms of national completion, a necessary and possibly unfortunate way that the colonial state ensured access first to resources and then also to lands for settlement. Another possibility is for non-Indigenous peoples to see themselves as 'treaty persons', perhaps another form of 'political descent', that is a daily obligation for those living on treaties territory (most of Canada) to be learning across that space, about the obligations the treaties give rise to.

What if this is an incommensurable problem? What if the project of a just unity across the differences of colonialism might actually be a philosophical error? We need to problematize what might be an Indigenous response—for example, 'What makes you think we want your sympathy?' Similarly, the 'talking past' that goes on in the engagement is a critical problem reproduced in numerous state- and community-led projects: the failure to acknowledge and manage the radical pluralism of contemporary Indigenous and settler worlds.

And yet we do see individuals and communities who appear to have found mutually intelligible ways to live, work and survive together. Being in mutual intelligibility may be a quality of self-reflection. What is the impact of my work on others? The quality of our relationship might then become the barometer (from ontological to axiological). Thus it offers a relational assessment of the value of our work. Is incommensurability a concern borne of prior commitments about what culture and difference are, a response informed by an understanding of the perennial violence of succeeding colonial 'best practices' in Indigenous affairs, or an anxiety about the possibility of us identifying and working towards something that might be good for other, different human communities?

Throughout this discussion many weary of visions of grandeur, but secretly thirst for bold transformation. Our sense of a common future barely escapes the life of the current government. Settler futurity exists in a perpetual present, with no plans other than to cling nervously to its privileges. With futurity here as with teleology earlier in this Introduction, so much remains ambiguous, for better and for worse. Both the goal and the possible pathways to it remain profoundly uncertain.

Arrangement

This book arises from a symposium convened in Melbourne during April 2016. The symposium brought together scholars and policy professionals working in Australia, Canada, and the United Kingdom. It explored concepts and practices of reconciliation, considering their specific application in the context of Australia and of other nations that have undergone reconciliation processes.

Much like the symposium, this book brings together and complements current research approaches to the problems of responsibility and engagement between Aboriginal and non-Aboriginal peoples. Contributors ask high-order conceptual questions about definition (*What is the nature of reconciliation?*), situational frame (*Is Australia a unique case?*), and evidence base (*How can we gauge the adequacy or otherwise of any given intervention towards reconciliation?*). Above all, they grapple with a question that sits between ethics and agency: *What responsibility might non-Indigenous Australians share to engage with reconciliation, and with the matters that need reconciling?*

The work here is interdisciplinary, by which we mean it involves contributions from people working in a range of fields. While the authors are all academic researchers, the work is intended to speak beyond the university research system, consciously framed to be of use to interested professionals who are actively involved in the reconciliation processes we discuss.

We have arranged the following chapters into groupings that reflect broad lines of philosophical approach to the central problems, more than disciplinary background or research method. Those groupings form the three parts of this book:

1. Conceptualising the limits of settler colonial reconciliation.
2. Testing the limits of settler colonial relationships.
3. The politics and policy of settler colonial reconciliation.

There is a final point to make on the research background. This Introduction and the three chapters that the editors and their associates have contributed to this volume all arise from a research project substantially funded by the Australian Research Council. That project has involved eight focus group discussions with non-Indigenous people at four locations around Australia, as well as follow-up interviews on a one-to-one basis with six of the focus group participants. That project was directly informed by comparable research undertaken earlier in Canada, with funding support from the Social Sciences and Humanities Research Council in that country. It greatly informed our efforts to convene the workshop that has led to this book in turn. These points of relevance to the collection as a whole mean we feel obliged to account for the project and its methodology in an appendix to this book.

One of the standout features of that research, as well as of the discussions at our workshop in April 2016, was the difficulty of aligning the question of a non-Indigenous responsibility to engage with complex political understandings of history. As Read's chapter reminds, the past dispenses an ongoing colonial legacy that countries like Australia can engage with or ignore, at their pleasure and peril simultaneously. Non-Indigenous participants in our Australian focus groups and interviews made clear—as have innumerable other sources—that arguments focused on the morality or justice of the past lack sufficient impetus to provoke any widespread non-Indigenous engagement. It does not automatically follow that arguments focused on the pragmatic workability of the future will overcome that reluctance to engage, but they are at least not precluded from willing consideration in the same way. Past-facing rationales have no clear prospects for political traction.

And so here, once again, we are confronted with the structural, ideational, and relational limits to thinking and practicing reconciliation in settler colonial societies. We cannot pretend that this collection offers concrete suggestions of breaching these limits or transforming Indigenous-non-Indigenous relations. If nothing else, this book confirms that policies instantiated in the hope of such outcomes are fundamentally naïve. Our hope, however, is that the theory, data and insight collected here will provide stimulus for new thought, reflection and dialogue on what these limits mean for all of us who—willingly or otherwise—share the histories, territories, harms and responsibilities of contemporary settler colonial societies.

References

Alfred, T. (2005). *Wasase: Indigenous pathways to action and freedom*. Peterborough, ON: Broadview Press.

Bashir, B., & Kymlicka, W. (2008). Introduction: Struggles for inclusion and reconciliation in modern democracies. In B. Bashir & W. Kymlicka (Eds.), *The politics of reconciliation in multicultural societies* (pp. 1–24). Oxford: Oxford University Press.

Christodoulidis, E., & Veitch, S. (2007). Introduction. In S. Veitch (Ed.), *Law and the politics of reconciliation* (pp. 1–8). Aldershot: Ashgate Publishing Ltd.

Coulthard, G. (2014). *Red skin, white masks: Rejecting the colonial politics of recognition*. Minneapolis: University of Minnesota Press.

Daly, E., & Sarkin, J. (2007). *Reconciliation in divided societies: Finding common ground*. Philadelphia: University of Pennsylvania Press.

Gunstone, A. (2009). *Unfinished business: The Australian formal reconciliation process* (2nd ed.). Melbourne: Australian Scholarly Publishing.

Hamber, B., & Kelly, G. (2009). Beyond coexistence: Towards a working definition of reconciliation. In J. R. Quinn (Ed.), *Reconciliation(s): Transnational justice in postconflict societies* (pp. 286–310). Montreal: Mcgill-Queen's University Press.

Hutchison, E., & Bleiker, R. (2013). Reconciliation. In R. Mac Ginty (Ed.), *The Routledge handbook of peacebuilding* (pp. 81–91). Abington: Routledge.

Lederach, J. P. (2005). *The moral imagination: The art and soul of building peace*. New York: Oxford University Press.

Macoun, A., & Strakosch, E. (2013). The ethical demands of settler colonial theory. *Settler Colonial Studies, 3*(3–4), 426–443.

Maddison, S. (2015). *Conflict transformation and reconciliation: Multi-level challenges in deeply divided societies*. Abington: Routledge.

Mudrooroo, (1995). *Us mob: History, culture, struggle. An introduction to Indigenous Australia*. Sydney: Harper Collins Publishers.

Renner, J. (2012). A discourse theoretical approach to transitional justice ideals: Conceptualising 'reconciliation' as an empty universal in times of political transition. In N. Palmer, P. Clark, & D. Granville (Eds.), *Critical perspectives in transitional justice* (pp. 51–71). Cambridge: Intersentia Publishing.

Schaap, A. (2005). *Political reconciliation*. London: Routledge.

Short, D. (2005). Reconciliation and the problem of internal colonisation. *Journal of Intercultural studies, 26*(3), 267–282.

Short, D. (2008). *Reconciliation and colonial power: Indigenous rights in Australia*. Aldershot: Ashgate.

Simpson, A. (2014). *Mohawk interruptus: Political life across the borders of settler states*. Durham: Duke University Press.

Watson, I. (2007). Settled and unsettled spaces: Are we free to roam? In A. Moreton-Robinson (Ed.), *Sovereign subjects: Indigenous sovereignty matters* (pp. 15–32). Crows Nest: Allen and Unwin.

Wolfe, P. (1999). *Settler colonialism and the transformation of anthropology: The politics and poetics of an ethnographic event*. London: Cassell.

Part I
Conceptualising the Limits of Settler Colonial Reconciliation

Chapter 2
Beyond Colonial Completion: Arendt, Settler Colonialism and the End of Politics

Elizabeth Strakosch

Abstract As many have argued, the Western political theory tradition tends to justify settler colonialism and erase its ongoing effects. However, this chapter suggests that we can draw on resources from within that tradition to challenge problematic settler colonial dynamics, which can prevent us as settlers from engaging in genuine political dialogue with Indigenous peoples. As an example, I show how Arendt helps us rethink traditional settler visions of 'decolonisation', which are deeply entwined with the drive to colonial completion and the erasure of Indigenous political independence. While her overall body of work has a complex relationship to settler colonialism, she offers an important critique of political projects that paradoxically seek to end politics once and for all. Most importantly, she reinstates political action as a positive enduring condition, and offers an account of politics as the good life rather than as pathway to the good life. This allow us to move the political task facing Indigenous and settler relations from 'fixing the problem' Indigenous people pose for us and for the dominant state towards fostering a productive but uncomfortable political coexistence. However, she can only help us to see the need for deep encounter with Indigenous people and worlds. At this point a different and more deeply dialogic conversation must begin.

Keywords Settler colonialism · Indigenous critical theory · Hannah Arendt · Jacques Ranciere · Western political theory · Reconciliation

> Thus our tradition of political philosophy, unhappily and fatefully, and from its very beginning, has deprived political affairs, that is, those activities concerning the common public realm that comes into being wherever men live together, of all dignity of their own. In Aristotelian terms, politics is a means to an end; it has no end in and by itself. More than that, the proper end of politics is in a way its opposite, namely, nonparticipation in political affairs (Arendt, The Promise of Politics 2005: 82–83).

> Politics is the art of suppressing the political (Ranciere, On the Shores of Politics 1992: 11)

E. Strakosch (✉)
University of Queensland, St Lucia, Australia
e-mail: e.strakosch@uq.edu.au

S. Maddison et al. (eds.), *The limits of settler colonial reconciliation*,
DOI 10.1007/978-981-10-2654-6_2

As a political formation, settler colonialism constantly works to dissolve its own colonial status. At an abstract level, settlers imagine that the beginning of settler society coincides exactly with the end of Aboriginal society.[1] At the moment of arrival, one society gives way to another and we are relieved of the burden of being colonisers. On the ground, however, we have always acknowledged a more or less violent overlap. If colonialism itself is understood as the simultaneous occupation of a single land area by both Indigenous and settler political societies, then settlers have always known colonialism to be problematic. However, its existence is justified by its temporary status. Eventually, Indigenous societies will give way completely to settler societies, or else combine with them in ways that legitimise and complete settler sovereign institutions. Therefore, as Macoun and I have argued elsewhere (2012: 53), 'the eventual legitimacy and stability of the settler-colonial project is always-already assumed. Through this a priori assumption, settler colonialism is able to entrench and sustain itself on the basis of its eventual demise'. This outcome is presented as constantly deferred and delayed, but ultimately unavoidable; there is no question that two political societies are unable to coexist in one place and that those concerned will seek an end to this coexistence. Settler colonialism assumes the inevitability of its own colonising actions in such a circumstance.

As an academic field, settler colonial studies tracks this drive towards colonial completion, but can also reproduce its assumptions (Snelgrove et al. 2015; Macoun and Strakosch 2013; Svirsky 2016). It tends to suggest that settlers by their very 'settlerness' will seek possession of all land, and that the settler state—because of its liberal statehood—will seek to naturalise its claim to be the sole legitimate political authority in an area. Settlers will not 'go home', as in Algeria, nor can they ever achieve the task of ending colonialism through Indigenous dissolution. As Svirsky (2016) argues, settler colonialism only exists because Indigenous societies continue to resist and survive. Without this dynamic colonialism would have ended long ago. Therefore, foundational settler colonial studies scholar Lorenzo Veracini (2011: 211) observes that 'the decolonisation of settler colonialism needs to be imagined before it is practised, and this has proved especially challenging'. There is no ending from within settler colonial and liberal logics—this political formation is trapped in its own tragic and permanent incompletion. So how do we as settler scholars theorise the end of the settler colonial story? This chapter begins with this question, but moves beyond it to consider the problems with understanding this political relationship in the terms of one party to that relationship.

I suggest that settlers cannot and should not imagine decolonisation on our own. In fact, we cannot even imagine colonisation on our own: 'indigenous people must be central to any theorisations of the conditions of postcoloniality, empire and

[1]In the popular settler understanding, for example, the instant Captain James Cook claimed sovereignty and radical land title in 1788 all Aboriginal sovereignty was immediately extinguished (Reynolds 1992). Recent scholarship has shown that the actual legal and political assertion of sovereignty was much slower and more fragmented, following more closely the actual extension of settlement and the ability to enforce settler criminal jurisdiction (Ford 2011).

death-dealing regimes that arise out of indigenous lands' (Byrd 2011: xiv). This is an argument already articulated by a number of critical Indigenous and non-Indigenous scholars (Byrd 2011; Simpson 2014; Battell-Lowman and Barker 2015). Transformation must be imagined and acted together by both parties in the relationship, so we cannot form a blueprint in advance. Only as we begin to act beyond the logics of liberal settler colonialism can we start the process of imagining decolonisation; we as non-Indigenous societies cannot yet envisage this process and its endpoint because we have not yet had genuine political conversations with Indigenous societies. There may be no 'resolution' in the sense that non-Indigenous political actors long for—an ending to our problematic status, a dissolving of political difference, a securing of settler futures (Tuck and Yang 2012). As Australian Aboriginal scholar Lyndon Murphy articulated in response to constant student questions about the 'solution' to the 'problem', neither side knows what might emerge from a deep negotiation about political possibilities because this negotiation remains a long way off.

If the space of this conversation is a shared political space, then we as settlers regularly believe ourselves to be operating within it. But while official initiatives such as reconciliation, constitutional recognition and apology aim to be mechanisms of encounter and resolution, in many ways they are products of our own understandings of the political, which overlay this shared space. In this chapter I explore the notion of the political as a 'middle thing' that both parties reach for, yet as one that is currently overdetermined by the frameworks and needs of settler selves. That is, we imagine we are in conversation, but this conversation is held with an imagined other rather than with the 'Aboriginal polity that already exists' (Murphy 2000). As a polity, we see ourselves formulating transformative strategies, but these remain our solutions to our problems. We see ourselves engaging in profound political debates about possible ways forward, but these 'good colonist/bad colonist' debates remain circumscribed by liberal categories. The middle thing becomes suppressed, not by potentially incommensurate understandings of what is acceptable and politically possible, but by the dominance of one understanding, which preconfigures political possibilities. To truly enter into that shared space is to 'attend to what is irreconcilable within settler colonial relations' (Tuck and Yang 2012: 4) rather than to force reconciliations. It involves countenancing the exposure rather than the securing of our unsettled political and social identities in this place. Most challengingly, it is to begin a conversation without a clear idea of its direction, and to enter into a politics that is potentially without end.

In this first section of the chapter, I outline the settler dynamics that tend to condition our understanding of political transformation and can foreclose genuine conversations with Indigenous societies. Settler colonialism's ultimate preoccupation with its problematic colonial status (whether this status is acknowledged or denied) means that many political initiatives seek colonial completion. What even the most progressive settler state currently asks for and offers in an imagined settler-Indigenous exchange is the final (re)founding of settler sovereignty. Put another way, it offers inclusion *as* decolonisation, not a choice between inclusion *or* decolonisation as material and political redistribution (and certainly not inclusion *and* decolonisation). Therefore debates that do exist in the public space remain largely between settler approaches rather than between settler and Indigenous peoples. There are clearly battles between conservatives and progressives over the reality of past violence, the need for social and cultural recognition and the status of the current nation-state. Yet these are ultimately different pathways to arriving at a similar point, and share common assumptions. I then consider the notion of politics as a 'middle thing' that is created by the presence of alternative orders and projects, but which is bypassed in favour of this ongoing setter conversation within our own frameworks.

In the second part of the chapter, I aim to use the work of Arendt to both deepen the analysis and to challenge these settler colonial dynamics. I draw from her work on the nature of the political to argue that this settler colonial drive towards colonial completion reflects a much longer political theoretical tradition. Since Plato, Arendt argues, politics has been seen as a means to an end and, since Marx, as existing in order to exhaust itself and leave us with the more desirable 'administration of things' (Engels quoted in Kohn 2005: ix). Instead, Arendt rearticulates political action as a good in itself, rather than as a pathway to the good. She locates us all in the field of the political, and as already responsible for violent, oppressive political structures we find ourselves within. We can and must make judgments, and take political action, but must do so in concert with others and hence in ways that cannot be determined in advance. The uncertainty of politics is the result of human freedom and plurality; this understanding of the promise of politics can help us to enter into settler-Indigenous political conversations without attempting to predetermine them.

In using Arendt in this way, I do not seek 'solutions' to our current problematic relationships from within the Western tradition. Instead, I raise the possibility of looking within this tradition to find counter-currents that push us towards a deeper encounter with Indigenous societies. Arendt on her own cannot do this. As others have shown, she herself argues for the legitimacy of settler colonialism in Zionist and other contexts. She does so both directly—framing it as the replacement of a non-political society by a political one—and indirectly (to the extent that she links full humanity and political participation) as the replacement of a less human society by a more human one. Her valorisation of the state is also problematic here. Nonetheless, she articulates and becomes part of a longer thread that contests Western understandings of politics as an instrumental process (Ranciere challenges and develops these ideas; see also Schaap 2011). An engagement with Arendt can be one part of a longer and more complicated process of finding the version of ourselves that is capable of entering into a deeper encounter and more meaningful dialogue.

The Settler Drive to Colonial Completion

Settler institutions are driven by a logic of elimination that targets Indigenous political difference. Patrick Wolfe argues that the logic of elimination works to replace Indigenous people on their land, and to naturalise this replacement (1999, 2006). In some settler colonial contexts such as Israel, the work of replacing Indigenous people on their land continues street by street; questions of political legitimacy are important but in some ways secondary to this practical process. However, in the contemporary Anglophone liberal nation-state, with extensive physical dispossession already underway, the second half of this logic becomes more salient as the state seeks to legitimise its claim to full possession to both external and internal constituencies.[2] Historical colonial sovereignty may have established its imperatives incrementally and in practical ways; it is not necessarily the case that settler projects begin with a clear plan for absolute physical and political possession and work towards this in an intentional way (Ford 2011; Ford and Rowse 2012; see discussion in Veracini 2010). However, the contemporary formulation of liberal Western nation-state sovereignty emphasises the indivisibility, consent-based legitimacy and universal character of a territorial state. This leads to a contemporary settler colonial desire to establish absolute sovereignty and ingest or destroy Indigenous political difference. The enactment of settler state jurisdiction was historically partial and remains so, but the persistence of the modern unified sovereign imaginary continues to drive present political activities. Contemporary settler colonialism as a destructive force upon Indigenous lives operates precisely in this gap between the partial reality of settler sovereignty and the impossible and increasingly inadequate political imperative that this sovereignty must constitute and exhaust the political.

In seeking to naturalise their existence as the sole legitimate authority over a particular area, settler states mobilise different political strategies. These can include entering into highly sophisticated forms of political engagement with Indigenous people that recognise some kinds of land ownership, past colonial violence and Indigenous culture in exchange for an extinguishment of political difference and legitimisation of the status quo. For example, official reconciliation processes are underway (or stalled) in many settler colonial contexts such as Australia and Canada. While these may facilitate important grassroots conversations and opportunities for healing, in their current limited forms they remain driven by assumptions about 'moving on' from a colonial past to a post-colonial present. As Nehiyaw activist Erica Lee (2016) argues:

---

[2]While in the contemporary Anglophone world, the logic of elimination is less focused on the possession of land as physical resource, this dimension of the settler colonial encounter continues to manifest itself in the present, especially around struggles over land that was previously economically marginal (such as the 'northern regions' attached to many settler colonies—Alaska, the Australian Northern Territory, and Nunavut). Such land may not have previously been the object of comprehensive settler attempts at dispossession, but if new technologies or economies lead to it becoming more economically desirable then new strategies of economic and physical dispossession are mobilised. Such changing settler valuations of land can therefore create Indigenous estates recognised by the settler legal and political system that this system later seeks to dissolve. The settler colonial project may not necessarily seek to possess *all* land in this sense, although it may eventually calculate this to be in its interests and do so. But, once it takes the form of the contemporary liberal nation-state, the settler project will necessarily seek to dissolve substantive Indigenous political difference.

> it seems that with any idea of reconciliation I've heard, there is an unspoken requirement of Indigenous forgiveness and Indigenous consent to continued occupation… The real task of reconciliation, however, is not in Canada waiting around to be forgiven for colonialism so business can carry on as usual; it is for Canadians to end the ongoing colonial violence that still suffocates Indigenous lives.

However, if non-Indigenous polities engage in a more direct conversation with these challenging Indigenous perspectives, then it is possible to reimagine 'reconciliation as the restoration of good relations. Restoring good relations requires fundamentally breaking with a vastly unjust world to a focus on how we relate to each other and the world around us… Reconciliation is the realization of worlds that should have been' (Lee 2016). This suggests that reconciliation processes are not inevitably colonising in and of themselves, but only to the extent they are driven by a limited, state focused agenda to 'resolve' colonial tensions without addressing colonial structures themselves (or to the extent they remain ideological rather than truly political; Schaap 2008).

To take another example, treaty is a long-standing tool of colonial regimes, and functions to recognise Indigenous political difference in the same moment that it absorbs that difference into the general pool of state sovereignty. Aboriginal sovereignty, in this formulation, is 'given up' and cannot be re-extracted, and thus the state is finally (re)founded once and for all. This is therefore a mechanism of extinguishment of political difference, and a means to colonial completion. McHugh (1997) argues that this understanding of treaties is not necessarily shared by all Indigenous parties, who might see them as mechanisms to facilitate ongoing negotiations to combine different sovereignties that continue to be held by each party. There are important spaces for renegotiation and political change created by these tools, but to the extent they remain driven and determined by the settler state they continue to seek to dissolve Indigenous political difference.

As Australian Aboriginal scholar Morrissey argues, this political difference is 'an embodied sovereignty which cannot be lost as long as Aboriginals assert it' (Morrisey 2007: 72; Moreton-Robinson 2015). It arises both from the alternative forms of political organisation practiced in Indigenous cultures—'the Aboriginal polity that already exists' (Murphy 2000)—and from the fact that these Indigenous jurisdictions were in place prior to the founding acts of the settler polity. As Veracini (2010) emphasises, sovereignty is brought with settlers rather than being constituted through genuine interaction with Indigenous people or local circumstances. It is therefore disrupted by and unable to account for political existences already in situ but must deny them while working to dissolve them, or else declare them to be immediately ended by the founding of the new polity, or else acknowledge them in order to immediately attempt to incorporate them (or all three together). And yet, precisely because of the absolute nature of contemporary state sovereignty claims, the settler polity is constantly prevented by independent Indigenous political existence from being fully itself. The flip side of colonisation being a structure rather than an event is that settler sovereignty is a performance claiming to be an essence.

This leads to the peculiar and complicated temporality of settler colonialism. At one level, it is a clear linear narrative of a movement from an (Indigenous) past to a more civilised, unified (settler) future. Once this future arrives, it is no longer only settler, but a universal shared future. However, at another level the temporal narrative constantly circles back on itself. It at once declares sovereignty to be already complete, posits an inevitable future of sovereign completion (implicitly acknowledging current incompletion), and works in the present to bring about that future. This is a form of political fantasy, which does more than simply assert the convergence of political stories and political realities. If you confront the fantasy of completed settler sovereignty with the contradictory reality of Aboriginal sovereignty, this fantasy will not dissolve. Instead it will animate its agents to pursue the extinction of Aboriginal sovereignty with a renewed intensity. Misrecognition might be susceptible to a challenge from reality, but fantasy will use this challenge to more intensively pursue its desires.

This complicated manoeuvre is illustrated by Australian debates about constitutional recognition. Both major political parties support the move to recognition. In the second reading speeches given by then Prime Minister Gillard and Opposition Leader Tony Abbott, both articulate a strange notion of colonialism as already complete, but needing to be completed. Our nation-state already exists as a unified thing, but must be made fully itself. For example: 'among the 128 sections of the Constitution, there is no acknowledgement of Australia's First Peoples… Or the unhealed wound that even now lies open at the heart of our national story' (Gillard 2013). Or, 'Until we acknowledge this we will be an incomplete nation and a torn people' (Abbott 2013). But how can the territorially sovereign state be torn if it was never whole? At what moment was the wound created that now needs repair? Was there ever a moment in which the body politic existed without a wound? In a linear narrative, the body politic would be awaiting embodiment and its constitution as a unified subject. But in settler colonial temporalities, the settler state asserts its completion even as it seeks to enact it, declares that colonialism is past even as it seeks to end it, and denies Indigenous difference even as it confronts and seeks to manage it.

I suggest that this settler colonial dynamic is particularly powerful in suppressing a genuine political conversation with Indigenous peoples and political orders. It admits interaction only in the context of, and to the extent that it contributes to, the resolution of our problematic settler colonial status via the legitimation of the current order. Because this resolution can involve inclusion and recognition of Indigenous people as well as exclusion, both progressive and conservative approaches are invested in this process of dissolving Indigenous political difference. The drive towards colonial completion thus easily becomes confused and conflated with a process of decolonisation. But while both colonial completion and decolonisation involve the 'end' of colonial relations, they do so for very different reasons and with very different effects. Most importantly for this chapter, the settler pursuit of the 'vanishing endpoint' of settler colonialism frames the Indigenous-settler political relationship as inherently temporary (Strakosch and Macoun 2012). It is a relationship that should be engaged and acknowledged to the extent that it allows us to 'settle' political differences and create a unified political order (that is, to the extent that it dissolves the settler-Indigenous political relationship). But while we regularly deny that we are in a relationship with Indigenous people, or seek to end that relationship, it remains a constant feature of our world. In its conflictual and irresolvable character, it generates important political possibilities.

Settler Politics and Its Occupation of the Middle Ground

> Every city has these two irreducible components, ever virtually at war, ever present and represented to each other through the names they adopt and the principles with which they identify themselves, which they make their own: liberty (eleutheria) for the mass of the poor, virtue (arête) for the small number of the rich. Thus do rich and poor constantly grasp the common thing, the middle thing, in the pincers … of material interests and imaginary investments (Ranciere, On the Shores of Politics, 1992: 13).

I take this quote out of context. In its original setting, it refers to the divisions between rich and poor in Aristotle's imagined *polis*. The middle thing is the realm of moderate politics that becomes compressed between two irreconcilable forces. The categories cannot be erased or combined, as no magic can ever make someone rich and poor at the same time. It is in fact the presence of both which creates the space of the political, 'which is, in modern terms, the art of putting up with what cannot be reconciled, of tolerating the existence alongside the rich of the poor, who can no longer be thrown overboard' (Ranciere 1992: 14). However, Ranciere argues, Aristotle seeks to pacify and secure this centre by making it coincide with an ideal middle class able to operate beyond the desires of each extreme.

I reread this quote in the context of contemporary settler-Indigenous political relationships. In this context, it highlights how the space of the political is produced by the encounter of two different and hierarchically positioned parties. Both reach for the middle thing that is produced between them, in order to pursue different goals that are themselves constituted by the encounter. For settlers, the presence of Indigenous peoples we have clearly dispossessed, but who cannot be eliminated or expelled from the territory, exposes our own status and privilege. We seek to act in the middle space to demonstrate virtue and to cultivate honour—but these political goals constitute 'imaginary investments' in our own legitimised identities and in creating a world that no longer reflects back to us our conflict with the disenfranchised. Even the attempts to complete sovereignty, discussed above, are in the end 'imaginary investments' in political stories about the nature of our collective identities. Indigenous societies, on the other hand, seek material redress and liberation. Their struggle is a concrete one for actual freedom and change (decolonisation is not a metaphor; Coulthard 2014). So the middle thing is brought into being by the conflict, but becomes what either side seeks to grasp in order to articulate and transform this conflict in their own ways.

The quote highlights the often very different ways that each party reaches towards political transformation, and what they imagine this transformation to be. Read together with settler colonial theory, it illuminates the field within which non-Indigenous struggles for political change take place. It places us in relationship with Indigenous people, albeit in a highly unequal power relationship, and reveals our politics as a particular kind of politics that derives from our position. Our politics is not coincident with all political struggles in this place and is animated by a subjective investment in becoming natural. It suggests that our political tendencies will be towards:

- The metaphorical rather than the actual
- The ethical rather than the economic
- Our status rather than the distribution of statuses
- 'Voluntarism' or choice in engaging the political as an act of virtue (rather than, say, as inescapable or a necessity for survival)
- Being good rather than doing good (see Macoun, this volume).

To engage for virtue's sake is to engage to the extent to which that virtue is recognised and enhanced. This cannot ground a politics of liberation that tears down hierarchies because it is conditioned by those hierarchies and by the politics of privilege itself (only in conditions of unjust privilege can virtue and public legitimacy become the ultimate political goals). It does not allow us to 'cross over' and become part of, or even to politically identify ourselves with, Indigenous struggles for material and cultural survival.[3]

But this quote does not thereby foreclose political possibility. It illuminates the necessary existence of a fragile but shared space that exists precisely because of this political difference, and which we as settlers cannot erase. The middle thing generated in our encounter is not so much the site of resolution, but the site where settler colonial conflict itself is understood, represented and contested. It is the political interface—brought into being by our shared history—rather than the outcome of that history (for example, the distributions of resources, land and institutional recognition). The goals of political action in this shared space are not themselves necessarily shared, and may indeed be incommensurable—but the encounter of these incommensurable frameworks will nonetheless continue to constitute this middle thing. It is, as I suggest later in this chapter, a site with the potential to facilitate new forms of action.

But while this space always exists, it is often misunderstood and suppressed. In the case of settler colonial interaction, it is suppressed by the dominance of one party's understanding of the nature of the conflict. For unlike Aristotle's rich, settlers have the privilege *and the numbers* to concrete over the middle thing with their political preoccupations—to occupy that space and claim to be resolving the

---

[3]That is, we as settlers may be involved in these struggles, but we cannot use this to ground our political identities or 'opt out' of our own political history and status. All too easily, this goal of transforming our own political identities becomes the most important part of our collaborations with Indigenous people.

conflict in the interests of both parties. What is significant is not that Western settlers have their own understanding of the issues and the appropriate resolution, it is that they (mis)take this for a shared understanding and so for the middle thing. Thus, for example, the liberal settler state becomes positioned not as a settler institution that is implicated as party to the conflict, but as neutral arbiter between settlers and Indigenous peoples, and as the necessary site of colonial resolution (Alfred 1999; 2005). From a settler colonial perspective, any interaction with Indigenous societies should take place within settler political frameworks because these are already assumed to be universal. To some extent this perspective may recognise the existence of a cultural interface (Nakata 2007), but cultural difference is separated from political difference; while the former can sometimes be engaged the latter is denied. Yet, as Alfred argues, this separation is a form of violence: 'politics matters: the imposition of Western governance structures and the denial of indigenous ones continue to have profoundly harmful effects on indigenous people. Land, culture, and government are inseparable in traditional philosophies; each depends on the others' (Alfred 1999: 2). The middle thing is thus the result of the ongoing coexistence of two political orders in one place, the very circumstance that Western political societies see as the most impossible and undesirable of conditions. The middle thing exists *despite* settler colonial claims that it cannot; it already exposes our political stories as partial and inadequate.[4]

The Political as a Site of Change

To speak about politics as the fragile shared space that creates genuine possibilities for new pathways is to fetishise it to a degree, or at least to frame it in a particular and limited way. In a deeper, more Foucauldian sense, politics is clearly all around us, and is central to our constitution of ourselves as settler colonial societies and subjects. To frame politics as a specific place that is not reducible to the social or the economic is to engage with a specifically Western vision of the political as a site of change. This is a conscious attempt to stretch as well as critique Western traditions, finding currents and gaps that prepare us to engage better with political difference in a settler colonial context. As I suggest below, working with this tradition allows us to challenge its dominant account of politics as secondary, collapsible and driven by external goals, which facilitates the drive to colonial completion.

Not just settler colonialism itself, but our current academic understandings of settler colonialism can also evacuate the space of productive politics and leave us with a sense of colonial fatalism. In certain registers, settler colonial theory presents

[4]In fact, settler colonialism itself is a politically impossible condition on its own terms, to the extent that it is the period of overlap of two political societies in one place, and therefore must dissolve itself to bring reality into line with liberal political logic. See discussion on fantasy and colonial completion above.

interaction between Indigenous and non-Indigenous people as already determined and negated by the deeper colonial structures that bind us. This can reduce *all* politics to a function of a structural colonialism, rather than just *settler* politics (seminal settler colonial theorist Patrick Wolfe has been labelled as 'very much a structuralist stuck in a poststructuralist world', see Cavanagh 2012: 19). When, for example, settler colonialism is presented as a primarily economic relationship with a political and cultural superstructure, then real change must come from transformations in this economic base. The problem, as Macoun and I have argued elsewhere, is that settler colonial analysis emphasises structural continuity. Unlike Marxism accounts of capitalism, it 'does not give an account of… a transformed future, or of the conditions for settler colonialism's demise' (Macoun and Strakosch 2013: 435). The only political pathway forward in this context would be to show how structural transformation is ultimately inevitable (say through the intensification of conflictual dynamics) or to represent settlers as also structurally dispossessed by settler colonial regimes (so to reposition them as political subjects struggling alongside Indigenous people for liberation).

The problem of settler political possibilities is important. How and why can non-Indigenous people engage with Indigenous people and orders at the limits of our own frameworks that are partly constituted by our current relationships with them? It is the current arrangements that allow us to substitute our politics for a shared politics, and it is this substitution that prevents these arrangements from being rearranged. Are we not trapped in an endless circle? One important response would be to emphasise the role that personal affective relationships play in exposing our political frameworks as partisan, violent and inadequate and creating change (see Barker and Battell-Lowman, this volume). Acknowledging this as crucially important, however, I pursue a different pathway, by seeking to recuperate Western notions of the political as a site of freedom. I consider Arendt's notion of the political as a space: firstly, where genuine political judgement and action is possible; and secondly, as a site of possible new beginnings that emerge out of the interaction between irreducible human plurality. In this sense, our political actions can never be fully reduced to our material conditions.

To emphasise the existence of a suppressed 'middle thing' is therefore to say (perhaps controversially) that Western settlers do not need to stop being ourselves in order to engage in genuine political interaction. We do not need to 'become Indigenous', or to transcend our own identities. I doubt whether this is possible, and the constant attempt to construct ourselves as neutral transcendent subjects is one of the 'settler moves to innocence' so persuasively identified by Tuck and Yang (2012) among others. Rather, we need to challenge the aspects of our own identities which prevent us from locating ourselves as particular (Western settler) subjects, and from understanding that we are always already in relationship with Indigenous peoples. Some may argue that the universal claims and possessive dimensions of Western identity are so central that they cannot be challenged without overthrowing these identities themselves (see, for example, Moreton-Robinson on the possessive logic of white patriarchal sovereignty 2015). That is, the Western settler self will never meet an Indigenous person as that person actually is, they will only ever deal with a fantasy. This fantasy subject is in fact the settler subject in their own primitive past, and is capable of being dispossessed in order to ground the property regimes of the present white subject. This is a strong objection, and my response is grounded in optimism that if the political interface is genuinely engaged by recuperating the promise of the political in Western thinking, other aspects of Western identity can be called into question and transformed in the process of deep political engagement.

Arendt and Colonialism

> She had no choice but to think apart from traditional categories—ohne Gelander ("without bannisters"), as she used to say—if she were to succeed in bringing to light an evil that was unknown and could not have been known within the tradition (Kohn 2005: xiii).

The writing of Hannah Arendt is not a natural place to look for decolonising resources. She is increasingly criticised for her particular validation of settler colonialism, as well as for her general endorsement of the universal value of the Western political tradition (Moses 2011, 2013; Lederman 2016). While Arendt challenges *imperialism* (which she understands to be the domination of one human society by another human society), she often endorses *colonialism* (which is framed as one human society's occupation of space held by another, less than human society). This, of course, is a version of the long-term mainstream justification for colonialism; Arendt gives it a particular political inflection by defining humanness in terms of political action and judgment. For her, such action and judgment, which arise between human beings rather than in isolation, are enabled by a secure state that creates a vibrant public sphere. Where societies do not have this sort of state, Arendt believes, they do not have the possibility and habit of acting politically and thus in a fully human way. The extension of a state through colonialism could therefore be seen as a project of progress and improvement (again, in line with wider settler colonial narratives).

This argument about humanness and political action, it should be added, was turned against multiple groups. At points Arendt is critical of what she saw as the Jewish people's failure to judge and act appropriately during the Holocaust, and linked this to their long history of being stateless (Arendt 1963). On the other hand, she is also critical of Israel's behaviour as a state; for example, she argues that during the trial of Eichmann the Israeli state sought revenge rather than the exercise of appropriate public judgment. Nonetheless, as Lederman (2016) has recently pointed out, she does not contest the right of Israel to establish itself on Palestinian land, and uses a version of the common argument that Jews 'made the desert bloom' by mixing their labour effectively with it. She presents many societies, including Palestinian and African societies, as dominated by nature and therefore not fully human in their failure to create a human world. Whether Arendt's position on settler colonialism negates the possibility of working with other aspects of her thinking is debatable—and is not dissimilar to the deeper question of the value of working with the broader Western political theory tradition given its settler colonial effects.

Arendt is therefore an interesting figure in the Western political theoretical tradition to the extent that she is both within and outside it. She endorses the basic categories of Western political thought—especially notions of republicanism, judgment and freedom—and remains convinced of the value of the modern Western political project (Benhabib 2003). However, she offers a profound critique of this tradition, and its contemporary derailments. Writing in the wake of the Jewish Holocaust, she suggests that current ways of thinking are unable to explain this catastrophe, and in fact actively contributed to it. She therefore criticises and reconceptualises the elements of the Western tradition that have sustained violent political orders. This approach seems to me to resonate with our Anglophone settler colonial contexts, and with the feeling that our current political frameworks are not adequate. While appearing to function as sites of resistance and debate they fail to transform stubbornly persistent injustices. Her contribution is her insistence that we must rethink the Western tradition when in the presence of intolerable political realities rather than iron over these realities in its name.

Colonial Completion and the End of Politics

Arendt's writings on the status of politics arose out of her previous analysis of totalitarianism, which she felt had failed to account for latent totalitarianism of Marxist thought itself (Arendt 1951). Published posthumously as 'The Promise of Politics' (2005), this second work argues that Marxism pushed to its logical conclusion the contempt of politics inherent in previous Western thinking.

Plato initiated this contempt by seeking to place political arrangements in the service of higher philosophical truths. In his city-state ruled by philosopher kings, politics was tolerated to the extent that it was necessary to maintain life and facilitate the realm of philosophy (Arendt 2005: 5–39). However, it should always be subordinate to this realm, and structured according to philosophical principles rather than according to its own immanent logics:

> Thus our tradition of political philosophy, unhappily and fatefully, and from its very beginning, has deprived political affairs, that is, those activities concerning the common public realm that comes into being wherever men live together, of all dignity of their own. In Aristotelian terms, politics is a means to an end; it has no end in and by itself. More than that, the proper end of politics is in a way its opposite, namely, nonparticipation in political affairs (Arendt 2005: 82–83).

The outlines of this attitude to politics have remained intact throughout the centuries because of the 'insulation shown by our tradition from its beginning against all political experiences that did not fit into its framework' (2005: 47). However, to the extent that the proper aim of politics was to facilitate and reflect non-political philosophical truths, the post-Platonic tradition saw it as a contemptible but permanent feature of human life.

Arendt argues that Marx consummates this tradition by dispensing with politics altogether. Again, politics is put in the service of an ideal that lies beyond itself. However, in reaching this ideal the political will exhaust itself and release us into a post-political world where we can concern ourselves with "the administration of things" rather than the negotiation of our relationships. Politics is not just secondary, it is temporary and indicates the presence of an undesirable state. If there is politics, there is a problem; its presence means we have not reached our goals. In Marxism, 'permanence [of the public realm] is seen as an obstacle by which the force of development, which in its most elementary form is the development of man's productive capacities, is constantly arrested and hindered' (2005: 89–90).

In the post-Marxist Western world, politics has been put in the service of apolitical ideals and is tolerated only to the extent that it drives us towards these ideals. By presenting politics as a means to an end, we justify all manner of violence and harm in our political present in the name of ending politics once and for all. This reduction of politics to an instrumental realm leads directly to totalitarianism and genocide. Significantly, it means we have also lost the space to challenge these violent political orders. In understanding politics as instrumental and as necessarily working towards predetermined goals, we evacuate the space of *true* politics—the only space where we can judge and resist totalitarianism. True politics occurs in the always unpredictable and spontaneous interaction between humans in their irreducible differences. It cannot know its ends in advance, or it is rendered apolitical and even antipolitical. True politics is not there to achieve human freedom, it *is* human freedom:

> the only standards of judgment with any degree of dependability are in no sense handed down from above but emerge from human plurality, *the* condition of politics. Political judgment is not a matter of knowledge, pseudoknowledge, or speculative thought. It does not eliminate risk but affirms human freedom and the world that free people share with one another. Or rather, it establishes the *reality* of human freedom in a common world (Kohn 2005: xi)

Thus, we as Western subjects arrive in the present with a deep assumption that the end of politics is the end of politics. That is, the purpose of politics is to close itself down once and for all, to ground the polity definitively and release us finally into the 'administration of things'.

These arguments are fascinating in themselves, and say a great deal that is relevant to our contemporary Western world where 'politics' is an increasingly negative word. However, I raise them here because they resonate in a particularly powerful way with our approach to settler-Indigenous issues in Australia and other settler colonial contexts. Resonating with Arendt's account of Western politics, the goal of settler colonialism lies beyond itself—to progress, to improve, to possess. This has justified all kinds of violence, depredation and dispossession in the name of a higher goal. More significantly for this paper, the goal of contemporary settler colonial *politics* also lies beyond itself, in the desire to close down political relations between Indigenous and settler selves once and for all. As Macoun and I argue elsewhere:

> The transformative event is positioned as part of an inevitable and inescapable trajectory (although it may be consistently deferred or delayed). In this way, the eventual legitimacy and stability of the settler-colonial project is always-already assumed (2012).

At one level, we can see the Platonic distrust of politics in the Australian tendency to deal with settler-Indigenous issues in the policy register—we would rather 'administer things' than negotiate relationships. This tendency has been amplified in recent decades; ongoing policy failures have led to increasingly technical performance measurement frameworks such as Close the Gap and to constant criticism of the ways political imperatives derail 'evidence based policy' (Patridge 2013).

At a deeper level, settler colonial frameworks tend to imagine politics as at best a temporary necessity to achieve a settled, apolitical future. We can see our contemporary political debates in terms of two approaches to politics—both of which are laden with distrust. In his development of Arendt's argument regarding the status of politics, French thinker Jacques Ranciere (1992) identifies these moves as 'the promise' and 'the anti-promise'. In the progressive register, politics is seen as a necessary step towards resolving Indigenous-settler issues once and for all. This is the act of the promise: a declaration that we will pursue a higher ideal and for this reason only will launch ourselves into politics in the present. This promise is dangerous, '[f]or the paradox of the undertaking is that hauling politics onto the solid ground of knowledge and courage entails a return to the isles of refoundation; it means crossing the sea once more and surrendering the shepherds' resurrected city to the whims of tides and mariners' (Ranciere 1992: 2). In the name of a final (re)foundation, we undertake to venture into the waters of politics and trust our political leaders to carry us safely to the other side.

Progressive non-Indigenous perspectives, while embracing political processes such as reconciliation, apology or treaty, often implicitly do so in the name of ending politics and creating a unified political community. Our nation-state, they argue, was founded illegitimately and without recognition of Indigenous existence. This existence must now be recognised and 'dealt with' so that the foundation can be complete and we can move forward as an inclusive Australian nation. There is a sense here of an incomplete project—the political work of foundation was begun but never completed. We stopped the work of politics before it had truly completed itself and become unnecessary. Thus in Rudd's 2007 apology to the Stolen Generations:

> The time has now come for the nation to turn a new page in Australia's history by righting the wrongs of the past and so moving forward with confidence to the future … For the future we take heart; resolving that this new page in the history of our great continent can now be written … We today take this first step by acknowledging the past and laying claim to a future that embraces all Australians.

By apologising we enter into a completely new phase. We are released from a past that has captured us in the present and finally enter into a delayed and non-colonial future ('excess is the essence of the promise', Ranciere 1992: 5). Thus the progressive promise endorses the vision of the proper role of politics as completing itself and erasing the need for ongoing political relationship.

The second mode has become more salient in the disillusioned 21st century world. This is the anti-promise, based on an assumption that 'the original evil was the promise itself: the gesture which propels the telos of community, whose splintered parts rain back down like murderous stones' (Ranciere 1992: 5). The anti-promise is the determination never to re-enter the political world and risk the fracturing of unity in the uncertainty and divisions of politics. This is reflected in the conservative position on settler-Indigenous conflict. From this position, such conflict has been resolved in the past, leading to a united nation and state that is already fully legitimated. Politics has done its work, and the reopening of political discussions can only *create* politics where there was none before. This unleashing of politics is undesirable. The Howard government, for example, in responding to the report of Reconciliation Australia (and effectively closing down the reconciliation process) argued that '[t]he Council's draft legislation would impose a potentially divisive, protracted (at least 12 years) and inconclusive process on the nation… rather than offering closure, pursuit of a treaty would be a recipe for ongoing disputation and litigation' (Commonwealth 2002: 19). Again, '[t]he Government's position on a treaty is that such a legally enforceable instrument, as between sovereign states, would be divisive, would undermine the concept of a single Australian nation, would create legal uncertainty and future disputation' (Commonwealth 2002: 23). Here politics creates indefinite uncertainty where there is already closure. We are already in the era of the administration of things and should remain there. At its worst, the return of politics brings the prospect of sovereign division, even the spectre of sovereign collapse. We see again how politics is positioned as a problematic state; this is reflected in the Howard government's constant labelling of ATSIC as 'politicised' and 'too little concerned with delivering real outcomes for indigenous people' (Howard and Vanstone 2004).

Conclusion

What possibilities are opened up if we join Arendt in recuperating the positive dimensions of politics? Arendt herself did not deny the difficulty of politics to the extent that it forces us to exercise our judgment as mature human beings. We cannot rely on preformed goals or authorities, for 'politics is not like the nursery' (1963). In a settler colonial context, this means deciding to live with our anxieties rather than seeking to resolve them through colonial completion. Only with a much more profound tolerance of (or even appreciation for) uncertainty can we truly enter upon a shared and truly political negotiation of pathways forward, that Arendt says must be grounded in human freedom, and the outcomes of which can never be known in advance.

However, in return for this tolerance we access a genuine site of change, to the extent that the '"miracle" of political action is *ontologically* rooted in humankind, not as a unique species but as a plurality of unique beginnings' (Kohn xxxiii). It is in the interaction between this plurality that new possibilities emerge, which we could never have imagined in isolation. Settler colonialism cannot imagine its own end, though it continually fantasises about it. We know then that its transformation can only come from beyond itself—we ourselves sense that we have exhausted the utility of unilateral, predetermined goals that will orient us in the 'right' direction. While it sounds truistic, settler colonialism cannot create post-settler colonial futures. Politics offers us a way to engage as ourselves, but beyond ourselves.

To seek to act in the shared space of politics (the middle thing) is not to *share* our politics. Such an engagement, it is worth emphasising once more, cannot presume commensurability between settler and Indigenous political frameworks, desires and goals. As Tuck and Yang (2012: 28–36) argue:

> the opportunities for solidarity lie in what is incommensurable rather than what is common… The answers will not emerge from friendly understanding, and indeed require a dangerous understanding of uncommonality that un-coalesces coalition politics - moves that may feel very unfriendly. But we will find out the answers as we get there… The Native futures, the lives to be lived once the settler nation is gone - these are the unwritten possibilities made possible by an ethic of incommensurability.

But to be part of this process of mutual imagination, we as settlers must first give up the fundamental desire to attach these futures to the project of legitimising our current privileges once and for all.

References

Abbott, T. (2013). *Speech to the Australian parliament in favour of the Act of Recognition Bill.* Feb 13 2013.

Alfred, T. (1999). *Peace, power, righteousness: An indigenous manifesto.* Don Mills, Ontario: Oxford University Press.

Alfred, T. (2005). Sovereignty. In J. Barker (Ed.), *Sovereignty matters: Locations of contestation and possibility in indigenous struggles for self-determination.* Lincoln: University of Nebraska Press.

Arendt, H. (1951). *The origins of totalitarianism.* New York: Penguin.

Arendt, H. (1963). *Eichmann in Jerusalem: A report on the banality of evil.* New York: Penguin.

Arendt, H. (2005). *The promise of politics.* New York: Schocken.

Battell-Lowman, E., & Barker, A. (2015). *Settler: Identity and colonialism in 21st century Canada.* Black Point, Nova Scotia: Fernwood.

Benhabib, S. (2003). *The reluctant modernism of Hannah Arendt.* Lanham: Rowman and Littlefield.

Byrd, J. (2011). *The transit of empire: Indigenous critiques of colonialism.* Minneapolis: University of Minnesota Press.

Cavanagh, E. (2012). History, time and the Indigenist critique. *Arena Journal, 37*(38), 16–39.

Commonwealth of Australia. (2002). *Commonwealth government response to the council for aboriginal reconciliation final report.* Canberra: Government of the Commonwealth of Australia.

Coulthard, G. (2014). *Red skin/white masks: Rejecting the colonial politics of recognition*. Minneapolis: University of Minnesota Press.

Ford, L. (2011). *Settler sovereignty: Jurisdiction and Indigenous people in America and Australia, 1788–1836*. Cambridge, MA: Harvard University Press.

Ford, L., & Rowse, T. (Eds.). (2012). *Between indigenous and settler governance*. London: Routledge.

Gillard, J. (2013). *Speech to the Australian parliament in favour of the Act of Recognition Bill*. Feb 13 2013.

Howard, J., & Vanstone, A. (2004). *Joint press conference parliament house*. Canberra. Accessed January 25, 2007. www.pm.gov.au/media/Interview/2004/Interview795.cfm.

Kohn, J. (2005). Introduction. In *The promise of politics*. New York: Schocken.

Lederman, S. (2016). Making the desert bloom: Hannah Arendt and Zionist discourse. *The European Legacy: Toward New Paradigms, 21*, 393–407.

Lee, E. (2016). Reconciling in the apocalypse. *The Monitor* 1 March. Accessed June 12, 2016. https://www.policyalternatives.ca/publications/monitor/reconciling-apocalypse.

Macoun, A., & Strakosch, E. (2013). The ethical demands of settler colonial theory. *Settler Colonial Studies, 3*, 426–443.

McHugh, P. (1997). Crown-tribe relations: Contractualism and coexistence in an intercultural context. In G. Davis, B. Sullivan, & A. Yeatman (Eds.), *The new contractualism?* Melbourne: Macmillan.

Moreton-Robinson, A. (2015). *The white possessive: Property, power and indigenous sovereignty*. Minneapolis: University of Minnesota Press.

Morrisey, P. (2007). Dancing with shadows: Erasing aboriginal self and sovereignty. In A. Moreton-Robinson (Ed.), *Sovereign subjects: Indigenous sovereignty matters*. Crows Nest: Allen & Unwin.

Moses, D. (2011). Hannah Arendt, imperialisms and the holocaust. In Volker Langbehn & Mohammad Salama (Eds.), *Arendt and empire*. New York: Columbia.

Moses, D. (2013). Das römische Gespräch in a New Key: Hannah *Arendt*, Genocide, and the Defense of Republican Civilization. *Journal of Modern History, 85*(4), 867–913.

Murphy, L. (2000). *Who's Afraid of the Dark? Australia's Administration in Aboriginal affairs'*. Brisbane: Centre for Public Administration, University of Queensland.

Nakata, M. (2007). The cultural interface. *The Australian Journal of Indigenous Education, 36*, 7–14.

Patridge, E. (2013). Caught in the same frame? The language of evidence-based policy in debates about the Australian government 'intervention' into Northern Territory Aboriginal Communities. *Social Policy and Administration, 47*(4), 399–415.

Ranciere, J. (1992). *On the shores of politics*. London: Verso.

Reynolds, H. (1992). *The law of the land*. Camberwell: Penguin.

Schaap, A. (2008). Reconciliation as ideology and politics. *Constellations: An International Journal of Critical and Democratic Theory, 15*(2), 249–264.

Schaap, A. (2011). Hannah Arendt and the philosophical repression of politics. In Jean-Philippe Deranty & Alison Ross (Eds.), *Jacques Rancière in the contemporary scene: The philosophy of radical equality*. London: Continuum.

Simpson, A. (2014). *Mohawk interruptus: Political life across the borders of settler states*. Durham: Duke University Press.

Snelgrove, C., Dhamoon, R., & Corntassel, J. (2015). Unsettling settler colonialism: The discourse and politics of settlers, and solidarity with indigenous nations. *Decolonization: Indigeneity, Education Society, 3*(2), 1–32.

Strakosch, E., & Macoun, A. (2012). The vanishing endpoint of settler colonialism. *Arena Journal, 37*(38), 40–62.

Svirsky, M. (2016). Resistance is a structure not an event. *Settler Colonial Studies*. Published online March 7, 2016.

Tuck, E., & Yang, K. W. (2012). Decolonization is not a metaphor. *Decolonization: Indigeneity, Education & Society, 1*, 1–40.

Veracini, L. (2010). *Settler colonialism: A theoretical approach*. Houndmills, Basingstoke: Palgrave Macmillan.

Veracini, L. (2011). Telling the end of the settler colonial story. In F. Bateman & L. Pilkington (Eds.), *Studies in settler colonialism: Politics, identity and culture*. Basingstoke: Palgrave Macmillan.

Wolfe, P. (1999). *Settler colonialism and the transformation of anthropology*. London: Cassell.

Wolfe, P. (2006). Settler colonialism and the elimination of the native. *Journal of Genocide Research*, *8*, 387–409.

Chapter 3
Facing the Settler Colonial Present

Lorenzo Veracini

Abstract This chapter focuses on a specific mode of domination and its contemporary manifestations. It outlines what is here defined as the global settler colonial present: a predicament fundamentally characterised by a logic of elimination and containment rather than exploitation. This appraisal of a developing dispensation is offered as a reminder of the need to develop indigenous-nonindigenous alliances.

Keywords Dispossession · Primitive accumulation · Settler colonialism · Indigenous peoples · Logic of elimination

Introduction

One of the founding statements of settler colonial studies as an autonomous scholarly field, a field that has consolidated in the last two decades, is that 'settler invasion is a structure, not an event' (Wolfe 1999: 163). Patrick Wolfe's invitation was to look for settler colonialism in the ongoing subjection of indigenous peoples in the settler societies. The contemporary settler polities, he noted in a passage that was quoted several times, have been 'impervious to regime change' (Wolfe 2006: 402). It was an Australian-produced response to the consolidation and global spread of postcolonial studies as discourse and method (quite interestingly, postcolonial studies was also originally an Australian intellectual export; see Ashcroft et al. 1989).

My recent work exceeds Wolfe's invitation and looks for settler colonial structures beyond the contemporary polities established by settlers during the age of the 'settler revolution' (Belich 2009) and controlled by their political descendants.[1]

[1]The notion of 'political descent' constitutes my rejoinder to ongoing contestations regarding the advisability of seeing migrants and 'people of colour' as 'settlers': yes, one can be a settler on indigenous land even if her ancestors were forcibly moved or displaced as colonised subalterns and did not establish the political regimes of the settler societies to come.

L. Veracini (✉)
Swinburne University of Technology, Melbourne, Australia
e-mail: lveracini@swin.edu.au

S. Maddison et al. (eds.), *The limits of settler colonial reconciliation*,
DOI 10.1007/978-981-10-2654-6_3

After all, it is a collection of former settler colonies that eventually became the uncontested global hegemon (see Adas 2001). My most recent book argues that settler colonialism as a specific mode of domination has gone global and fundamentally defines the present (Veracini 2015). In this chapter I focus on the need to understand (and on the urgency to respond) to a new reality.

This chapter emphasises a growing commonality of dispossession. A commonality between indigenous and non-indigenous dispossessions affects crucially non-Indigenous responsibility to engage in reconciliation and indigenous-led struggles. Of course, commonality does not mean identity and I am not suggesting that 'we' are actually becoming 'indigenous'. I remain a migrant and a settler on indigenous land. But it seems important to note that we are increasingly being subjected to a mode of domination that treats us *like* indigenous peoples. 'Responsibility' literally means having thought things through, being responsive. Focusing on a growing crisis and a convergence of interests offers important opportunities for responsible resistance and reconciliation.

Settler Colonial Studies and the Settler Colonial Present

My work proceeds alongside that of others. A number of influential interventions have recently and not so recently drawn attention to the 'new' phenomena characterising current global dispensations. Even if the specific terminology of settler colonial studies was not used in these contexts, Naomi Klein, for example, noted that the 'redundant' are growing in numbers and are no longer even useful as an industrial reserve army (Klein 2007), while in *The New Imperialism* David Harvey concluded that accumulation by dispossession has 'moved to the fore as the primary contradiction within the imperialist organisation of capitalist accumulation' (2003: 172). This latter intuition has proved seminal and many have noted that 'accumulation by dispossession' is informing new practices of capitalist accumulation. Others have observed that the wage relation is being paralleled by proliferating forms of unwaged labour in the context of what has been defined as the 'political economy of promise' (see Allegri et al. 2015; on the 'wage-earning society' and its crisis see, for example, Castel 2003; Beck 2000). At the same time, as remarked by Sasskia Sassen, 'expulsions' of all sorts are more and more characterising the global present (2014). Who are the 'expelled'? Many constituencies in distinct settings; this is a global trend:

> I use the term 'expelled' to describe a diversity of conditions. They include the growing numbers of the abjectly poor, of the displaced in poor countries who are warehoused in formal and informal refugee camps, of the minoritized and persecuted in rich countries who are warehoused in prisons, of workers whose bodies are destroyed on the job and rendered useless at far too young an age, of able-bodied 'surplus populations' warehoused in ghettoes and slums. My argument is that this massive expulsion is actually signaling a deeper systemic transformation, one documented in bits and pieces in multiple specialized

studies but not quite narrated as an overarching dynamic that is taking us into a new phase of global capitalism (Sassen 2013: 198).

The working poor are growing in number almost everywhere; reproducing labour power is no longer a priority. Like indigenous peoples facing a settler colonial onslaught, the 'expelled' are marked as worthless. The 'systemic transformation' produces modalities of domination that look like settler colonialism.

A number of recent interventions have also emphasised the contemporary global relevance of settler colonialism as a specific mode of domination. Australian-based anthropologist Ghassan Hage has referred to the globalisation of a 'late colonial settler condition' and of 'the settler-colonial ethos' (Hage 2015, 2016). Wolfe and David Lloyd have explicitly linked contemporary neoliberal orders and settler colonialisms as compatible and reciprocally reinforcing modes of domination (Lloyd and Wolfe 2015). This approach emerges beyond Australian-based research, or work engaged in conversation with it. In a recent *Critical Inquiry* article Mahmood Mamdani deploys very similar ideas and language (Mamdani 2015). He does not cite settler colonial studies, but that a very influential public intellectual autonomously reached the same conclusions about the relationship between past and present settler colonialisms seems significant. More generally, while *terra nullius* as doctrine and practice in international relations is staging a remarkable comeback, think of land grabbing in Africa and elsewhere for example (see Geisler 2013; Hendlin 2014), and while *terra nullius* in its various formulations is inherent to settler colonialism as a mode of domination (see Fitzmaurice 2007), these predicaments are not new. A type of dispossession that is fundamentally informed by a 'logic of elimination' or containment rather than exploitation (see Wolfe 2006) is what indigenous peoples facing expanding settler colonial regimes have always had to deal with.

The very collective existence of the indigenous peoples of the earth, the 'evanescent' races, as one nineteenth century commentator influentially put it (Pearson 1893), is fundamentally marked by a purported failure to reproduce. Representations of disappearing indigeneity have proved resilient beyond the nineteenth century and remain widely held. The definition provided by the 2007 UN declaration on the Rights of Indigenous Peoples confirms it: being indigenous today is primarily about being collectively endangered. A corollary to this approach is to note that unlike other dispossessed populations, the indigenous peoples of the locales witnessing the 'explosive' establishment of settler colonial orders in the nineteenth century (see Belich 2009) were not the subject of proletarianisation processes. Historian Jürgen Osterhammel recently reiterated this widespread notion in his acclaimed *The Transformation of the World*: 'Here and there [in North America, but this passage is in a section dealing with settler colonialism as a global phenomenon] we come across Indian cowboys, but not an Indian proletariat' (2014: 336). Indeed, indigenous peoples were in the main not turned by processes of capitalist articulation and/or subsumption into providers of colonised labour and/or captive consumers of metropolitan goods. The logic of elimination is incompatible with the practice of subsumption.

What was needed was their land, not their labour, as Wolfe seminally pointed out (even though their labour could be used for a while and in particular conditions). If colonialism's outcome is at base an unequal relationship between coloniser and colonised that is reproduced through time, the outcome of settler colonialism is at base a particular socio-political body that reproduces *in the place* of another (that is, a sociopolitical body that is in time able to extinguish the unequal relation originally constituting coloniser and colonised). It is in this sense that that I have elsewhere theorised colonialism and settler colonialism as antithetical modes of domination that co-penetrate and co-define each other (Veracini 2010).

It is in the context of this analytical frame that the notion of a global settler colonial present can be sustained; as Sassen has also noted, the contemporary multiplication of various forms of labour is not concerned with the reproduction of labour power (Sassen 2014; see also Mezzadra and Neilson 2013). A 'new' capitalist global dispensation that does not seem to take the reproduction of labour as a priority brings the historical experience of indigenous peoples facing the settler colonial onslaught to the fore.

This suggestion is not unprecedented, and while many have pointed out that the Zapatista insurgency may provide a new model of revolutionary action against neoliberal orders, that the Zapatistas constitute an *indigenous* model, and that their insurgency was ostensibly aimed at resisting the extension of the economic regimes of *settler* North America should be emphasised. Klein's most recent work confirms the newly acquired centrality of indigenous transnational struggles, which is a remarkable reversal, if one considers that indigenous collectives were typically characterised by an intractable marginality (those who sought to engage with them programmatically did so in deliberate attempts to operate at the margins). Klein's *This Changes Everything* (2014) is indeed premised on the intuition that the struggles of indigenous peoples have become crucial to informing and sustaining resistance in the settler colonial present. These struggles may offer the opportunity to craft the 'pathways' to reconciliation that are mentioned in the introduction to this volume.

Settler Colonialism and Accumulation Without Reproduction

Modes of domination that reproduce the structuring dynamics of historical settler colonialism in the global present are highly visible.[2] The 'sovereign effects' of financial capital, for example, which has now acquired an unprecedented capacity

[2]It seems important to stress that this argument is premised on an analogy. It refers not to the current occurrence of actual settler colonialism as a mode of domination but to a similarity in relationships. In this context, the eliminatory logic that typically characterises settler colonialism is replicated by contemporary modalities of domination. It is a fraught situation and an analogical rather than direct correspondence fundamentally limits the possibilities of indigenous-nonindigenous alliances. There is no assumption of a shared consciousness here.

to dictate policies 'from above', can be read as one such manifestation. These processes are often referred to as instances of ongoing 'primitive accumulation', and their violent character does supersede the 'silent compulsion of economic relations' (Marx 1976: 899). But settler colonialism as a mode of domination producing specific social formations and primitive accumulation are intimately related (for a compelling outline of the relationship linking settler colonialism and primitive accumulation see Brown 2014). Gabriel Piterberg and I sketch this relation in a recent *Journal of Global History* article: primitive accumulaton was 'discovered' by Marx through Edward Gibbon Wakefield's reflection on the ways in which the availability of 'free' lands in settler colonial contexts was undoing the previous separation of workers from their means of subsistence and rendering unworkable what Wakefield had called 'capitalist civilisation' (Piterberg and Veracini 2015). Marx, after all, approached capitalism's 'secret' in *Capital*'s 33rd chapter by looking at the settler colonies, not the industrialised cores of the developing global economy. He assumed that the indigenous peoples of these colonies had already disappeared, but while this failure should not be repeated, keeping the fate of indigenous peoples vis-à-vis expanding settler orders in mind enables an original reframing of primitive accumulation. One point that the debates over the 'new' enclosures (see, for example, de Angelis 2004) have failed to address is that they are referring to a *very particular* type of primitive accumulation. It may be called accumulation without reproduction.

Primitive accumulation is a process that is typically seen as equally designed to force people into the wage relation as well as to enable the appropriation of land and resources (see Nichols 2015). This is so whether one agrees with the orthodox school and sees it as a historically given process or whether, on the contrary, one sees it as an ongoing predicament. Marx saw the creation of a waged labour force as a necessary precondition of capital accumulation (and so had Wakefield, a serial founder of settler colonies, as well as a perspicacious observer of their developments), but indigenous peoples under settler colonialism are typically forced into reservations, not into selling their labour; their labour remains a secondary consideration. To use Theodor Herzl's expression, indigenous peoples should be 'spirited' across the border by way of 'procuring employment' elsewhere (he was also a founder of settler colonies; when he confessed this to his diary he was still thinking about Argentina as a suitable location for Zionist endeavours). In other words, indigenous peoples should be worked across the frontier, not worked to be worked again. This should be done 'circumspectly', Herzl had added, producing a subdued variation on the typically settler colonial theme of 'Manifest Destiny' (1960: 88).

While there is no more explicit synthesis of accumulation without reproduction, of a type of accumulation that is originary and final at once, the distinction between 'disposable labor' and 'disposable populations' should be brought to the fore. Citing *Capital* while observing simultaneous processes of primitive accumulation and settler colonisation in nineteenth century Japan, Katsuya Hirano recently expanded on this point:

> Disposable labor 'forms an element of the floating surplus population'; some of these individuals emigrate and thus follow the flow of capital. Disposable labor therefore becomes either a 'constant latent surplus population' in the countryside passively waiting to be employed by capitalists in cities or a 'stagnant population' that 'offers capital an inexhaustible reservoir of disposable laborpower'. [...] In short, the disposability of the industrial reserve army of labor does not point to the workers' sentence to death but to the state in which they are kept alive so that they remain available and functional as a cheap commodity for capitalists to purchase and exploit. On the contrary, the dispensability of an indigenous population implies its absolute redundancy (Hirano 2015: 209).

This distinction is crucial: under settler colonialism biopolitics becomes 'thanatopolitics', and the biopolitical governance of bodies linked to the extraction of surplus value out of naked life becomes a circumstance where surplus value is no longer the primary concern.

Focusing on a related aspect of this distinction, indigenous and Marxist Canadian scholar Glen Coulthard argued a similar point when he noted that indigenous peoples are subjected to space-based processes of accumulation while other workers are subjected to time-based forms of exploitation (i.e., the theft of time, or surplus value; see Coulthard 2010: 81). That contemporary forms of accumulation by dispossession involve primarily the appropriation of physical and symbolic public space, that these dispossessions typically operate through a denial of access, and that, as its etymology suggest, access is especially about space should also be noted ('access' comes from *ad*—'to', 'toward', 'at'—and *cēdō*—'move', 'yield').

Robert Nichols has recently called for taking space seriously while talking about primitive accumulation. He begins by offering crucial background information before turning to the issue of land. Revisionist accounts of primitive accumulation, Nichols notes, have 'exploded in the past decade or so' (Nichols 2015: 20). This explosion resulted in:

> a certain conceptual shattering, throwing forth a range of ambiguously related companion concepts such as 'accumulation by displacement', 'dispossession by displacement', 'accumulation by encroachment', and 'accumulation by denial'. Perhaps most influentially, David Harvey speaks of 'accumulation by dispossession'. While offered as a synonym for primitive accumulation, in Harvey's rendering 'accumulation by dispossession' is essentially a stand-in for privatization: 'the transfer of productive public assets from the state to private companies', especially as a result of the supposed over-accumulation of capital in neoliberal times. The category is thus shorn from any connection to the transition debates or, indeed, from any particular connection to land (Nichols 2015: 20).

Nichols, on the contrary, intends to focus on land and notes how recent work on primitive accumulation and exploitation has shifted the temporal framework provided in *Capital* (i.e., the 'stages' of capitalist development) to a spatial one. He summarises: 'we are no longer operating with a distinction between mature capital and its prehistory, but with a distinction between core and periphery' (Nichols 2015: 21). Following on from this spatial turn, he then recommends: 'rather than adopting a general expansion of the category of primitive accumulation, we are better served by reworking the [Marxian] notion of *Enteignung*', 'a 'narrower and more precise term' than primitive accumulation.

> *Enteignung* [...] comes closer to grasping the original intent of the revisionist theories of primitive accumulation: naming a form of violence distinct from the silent compulsion of exploitation. Rather than working with a distinction between general and primitive accumulation, then, I commend working with a distinction between exploitation and dispossession (Nichols 2015: 22).

Enteignung, dispossession, is what we face.[3] But drawing a fundamental distinction between exploitation and dispossession is not only about violence versus silent compulsion; it is also about the distinction separating colonialism and settler colonialism as distinct modes of domination. Capitalism 'disrupts or disturbs our orientation in space, our place-based relations', Nichols concludes (2015: 25), but denial of access and settler colonialism are both primarily focused with the suppression of 'place-based' relations (on indigenous life as essentially a form of 'place-based resistance', see Alfred and Corntassel 2005). Nichols' argument is compatible with the appraisal of the settler colonial present: while it is 'possible to recast dispossession as a distinct category of violent transformation independent of the processes of proletarianization and market formation', this dispossession is 'constitutive and contemporary' (Nichols 2015: 25, 27).

Dispossession is not concerned with reproduction. The 'new enclosures', refer to 'any process in which private property is created through a violent gesture of appropriation' (Mezzadra and Neilson 2013: 295). But while rent extraction is certainly on the rise globally, the need for an industrial reserve army is no longer as strategic as it used to be (see Harvey 2003). We are all increasingly required to work, but wages are less and less meant to recreate us as labour, to allow us to live healthy lives, to pay for shelter, to purchase medical care and education. For all that, one can borrow (if one can borrow), but rent extraction (and debt is ultimately about rent) is famously uninterested in reproduction, as Marx's analysis of the contradiction pitting the industrial bourgeoisie and the landed aristocracy outlines: the latter's command over land and its determination to extract rent redistributes surplus value by forcing industrialists to pay higher wages and sustain the reproduction of labour (see Felli 2014: 270–271).

Debates pitting Harvey's notion of 'accumulation by dispossession' against Giovanni Arrighi's 'accumulation without dispossession' (see Arrighi 2007) are compelling, but do not consider the question of reproduction. My suggestion is that putative 'accumulation without dispossession' in China and accumulation by dispossession elsewhere produce 'accumulation without reproduction' globally, and that accumulation without reproduction is ultimately as good a definition of settler colonialism as a specific mode of domination as any. The surplus populations that are to be warehoused and contained *look like* indigenous people (even though, in the case of Palestine, where warehousing technologies are developed and tested, they actually *are* indigenous peoples; on warehousing, see Klein 2007, on 'global Palestine', see Collins 2011).

---

[3] I use the expansive first person advisedly (and so I did in the introduction to this chapter): these are genuinely global trends, the middle classes are shrinking, and warehousing is a fast developing technology.

But the global settler colonial present can be detected beyond a failure to focus on the reproduction of labour power. The manifest inability of facing the reality of climate change despite international attempts to extract rent out of present and future destruction, for example, brings the long-term reproduction of the very conditions of possibility for capitalist accumulation into question (see Felli 2014). The growing relevance of an 'ecological debt' can be most productively approached within a settler colonial studies paradigm. After all, recurrent narratives of successful settlement in the 'New Worlds' are inherently premised on efficient climate change adaptation. Premised on foundational displacements, settler colonialisms are ultimately and especially about changing climate, about moving from one country to another, and, conversely, about practicing localised versions of 'ecological imperialism' (Griffiths and Robin 1997). But there is more: not only settler colonialism is about changing climates, climate change will in turn produce new settler colonialisms in a coming 'age of unsettlement' (Fry 2011). Some will move as refugees, others will move endowed with a constituent capacity. Like the settlers of old, the latter will understand their movement as charged with an inherent sovereign capacity.

The current neoliberal regime 'indigenises' us in unprecedented ways. It is an exogenous dispossessory regime that penetrates into the relationships we entertain with others, with our places, and with ourselves. The recent emergence of 'solastalgia', a form of depression linked to the perception of a changing environment could be mentioned here. Connected to environmental changes that challenge 'a person's sense of place and identity and can lead to depression' (see Kenyon 2015, who cites work by Glenn Albrecht and research published in *The Lancet*'s 2015 Health and Climate Change Report), solastalgia is something many indigenous peoples around the world would know very well.[4]

What Is to Be Done?

There are limits to this mode of accumulation. Settler colonialism may be a 'structure', but structures can be torn down. True, the redundant populations are increasing, but so are the effects of an overaccumulation crisis becoming more and more visible. Financial bubbles, a generalised fall in commodity prices, and permanently anaemic economic growth are signals that accumulation without reproduction is unsustainable in the long term. An unprecedented flow of refugees moving towards Europe demonstrates that the global disposable populations will not accept the new dispensation without resisting.

This mode of domination in the 'creditocratic' age indigenises us because it does not recognise or suppresses our sovereign collective capabilities as it appropriates

---

[4]'Nostalgia' itself, after all, was once a neologism. It is significant that as a concept it emerged in the late eighteenth century during an age of revolution and unprecedented upheaval.

whatever secondary 'commons' we may still hold (on 'creditocracy', see Ross 2013). It wants what we have but is not interested in reproducing us as labour. It does not demand that we sell it in exchange for wages; some of us may still do but this is no longer the main point. Debt, it should be remembered, was one crucial way in which indigenous peoples globally were dispossessed of their lands (see Banner 2007). But rent extraction now, like rent extraction then for the indigenous peoples that 'escaped' proletarianisation and forced or servile labour, no longer diverts surplus value. It used to, but no longer does so. The contradiction pitting rent and industrial capital no longer subsists because the latter does not need to worry about reproduction.

If these observations are only partially correct, formulating a response should become a priority. As indebtedness and undersconsumption/overcapitalisation move centre stage (see, for example, Joseph 2014), settler colonialism as a mode of domination should enter the analytical frame. After all, Wakefield had proposed settler colonialism as a way out of what he had interpreted as an unprecedented overcapitalisation crisis (he was especially concerned about the falling rate of profits, see Piterberg and Veracini 2015, something that should sound familiar to observers of the current conjuncture). It is perhaps no accident that neoliberal rhetorical stances are now routinely used in relation to indigenous peoples: neglect of collective obligations towards indigenous constituencies, after all, can be framed in the language of self-reliance and self-determination (see Altman 2010; Bessire 2014; Strakosch 2015). Let's not forget that in important ways neoliberal orders are implicitly already settler colonial: if the ultimate product (if not the method) of settler colonial processes is the state, a moment marked by the 'closing' of the frontier, the current 'abdication' of the state in order to pursue and defend private property begs the question of a possible return to 'frontier' arrangements (see Sugg 2015).[5]

It is perhaps no accident that, as the Black Lives Matter movement of 2015 in the United States has brought to our attention, current repressive strategies actually conform to a 'logic of elimination' rather than one of exploitation (see Lytle Hernandez forthcoming). The blog post that started the movement, its foundational text, stated: 'stop saying we are not surprised. that's a damn shame in itself. I continue to be surprised at how little Black lives matter. And I will continue that. stop giving up on black life [sic]' (Garza cited in Cobb 2016). Surprise is necessarily premised on the perception of a new circumstance, and it is significant that Alicia Garza's call was not concerned with a lack of equality but with a disregard of life itself.

In a recent *Jacobin* piece Donna Murch addressed the affinities and divergences characterising current and past repressions and, conversely, but as part of the same rhetorical structure, between current and past resistances. There is a tension between locating recent events in a long history of racial repression and the need to emphasise the inherent novelty of current repressive paradigms (a current refrain in

[5]Even the dramatic 'ngoisation' of the structures of international governance can be seen as part of this pattern (see Choudry and Kapoor 2013). As NGOs compensate for the apparent failure of the postcolonial state, they become a constituent part of the global settler present in a growing assemblage of stateless 'frontiers'.

relation to Black Lives Matter is that it is 'not your grandfather's civil-rights movement'; see Cobb 2016). The very notion of a 'new' Jim Crow encapsulates this tension (on the 'new' Jim Crow as a type of racial control designed to 'decimate', that is, to eliminate, see Alexander 2012). Murch is analysing a new dispensation and uses the 'u' word: the links with the past are undeniable, she talks about an 'inheritance', but what is before us is 'unprecedented':

> It might even be said that the events of the past year have helped distinguish the post-civil-rights generations from iconic baby boomers, because the months of mass protest announced what many of us feel is the most pressing domestic political crisis of our time: the emergence of a massive edifice of policing, surveillance, prisons, and punishment that is unprecedented in both US and global history (Murch 2015).

What makes this 'edifice' unprecedented is that it is a 'massive state-building project'. The metaphors used here are especially significant: 'edifices' and 'buildings' are structures, and this system of domination is not just epiphenomenally unprecedented, it is structurally so. Murch continues: it is 'known alternately as mass incarceration, the new Jim Crow, the prison-industrial complex, or more simply […] "the world's most advanced police state,"' and 'has become a defining feature of our times' (Murch 2015). Discontinuity prevails; the logic of elimination prevails.

Murch's genealogy of the new dispensation is convincing. She knows where the eliminatory paradigm is coming from (it is a response to the revolutionary transformation and demands that emerged in the 1960s), but a defining feature of this 'state' is that it is not aiming at sustaining an unequal relation, as it once did. It is now aiming at *discontinuing* that relation. That state (i.e., the US) is not a colonial state (for example, a state busy dispensing a type of internal colonialism); that state is a settler colonial state. It always was, but only against Indians; now it is aiming at discontinuing relations with other constituencies as well, and is treating Black people more and more *like* Indians. Busy developing and testing various forms of mass warehousing and containment (and killing, of course), the current mode of domination is shaped by elimination. This is, after all, the substantive difference between the 'old' and the 'new' Jim Crow: the carceral state aims to supersede the racial relation by unilaterally discontinuing it, not to manage it by preserving its inequality. In this sense, the politics of 'colorblindness' and the new Jim Crow are reciprocally sustaining projects (both imagine a future when there is no relation, not even an unequal one).

As settler colonial studies has emphasised time and again, assimilation is elimination. Patrick Wolfe concludes his recent *Traces of History* by noting that emancipation and assimilation are ultimately antithetical 'strategic alternatives' that produce radically different racial formations. 'Emancipation is a way not to assimilate', he summarises, 'where assimilation denies the existence of difference, emancipation preserves liability for it' (Wolfe 2016: 101). But the fact that racial assimilation (in American parlance: 'absorption') was not tried vis-à-vis former slaves after emancipation does not mean that it could not be selectively enacted for their descendants in the era of colorblindness. In the end, one is faced with a choice: either black lives matter or they are matter (that is, matter to be brutalised and exploited in accordance with a previous paradigm or, more ominously, to be contained and/or disposed). The defining feature of our times is settler colonialism.

Linking the current enclosures with historical ones in the 'New Worlds' should be prioritised: after all, the new regime produces a renewed acceleration in the *contemporary* dispossession of indigenous communities too (see Goldstein 2014). Expressing solidarity with indigenous struggles is now in the interest of indigenous/non-indigenous assemblages. There is a substantive difference with past resistances. This is where the opportunities for effective organising may lie despite the obvious limits of a solidarity that is premised on analogy. But while indigenous peoples in the settler societies and in the colonising metropoles have had at different times non-indigenous allies at least since the 1830s, the latter supported indigenous causes out of their ethical stances and have generally proved unreliable.

On the contrary, a solidarity that is premised on self-interest (and self-preservation) is likely to be more reliable than a type of paternalist philanthropy that is focused on the next world or other forms of solidarity premised on the inequality between provider and beneficiary (see Olesen 2004).[6] Indigenous leadership is now crucial to thinking everybody's response. Good settlers must become bad settlers. Reconciliation as a concept may remain variously defined in multiple settings but a tactical ability to ally would be invariably propaedeutic. As the editors of this volume conclude, 'relational engagement' must be 'at the centre of reconciliation efforts'. Allyship is one crucial prerequisite of reconciliation. A joint struggle that is premised on an understanding of everybody's substantial interest in reconciliation would be one way of pushing against the institutional limits of settler colonial politics.

Conclusion

We are facing a dispossessory regime that is new and yet not entirely unprecedented. Sassen detects a 'shift from the complex to the elementary' (2013: 199), a move towards modalities of extractive exploitation that capitalism had abandoned long ago. This return brings settler colonialism, surplus populations and 'empty' lands, back to the fore:

> inside capitalism itself we can characterize the relation of advanced to traditional capitalism as one marked by predatory dynamics rather than merely evolution, development, or progress. At its most extreme this can mean immiseration and exclusion of growing numbers of people who cease being of value as workers and consumers. But it also means that traditional petty bourgeoisies and traditional national bourgeoisies cease being of value (2013: 200).

[6] Thomas Olsen categorises various possible types of solidarities: 'political', 'rights', 'material', and 'global' solidarity. Only the last one is not premised on inequality and 'emphasizes similarities' while 'acknowledging' differences (Olesen 2004: 259). Chandra Talpade Mohanty (2003: 502–505) similarly advocates for 'deep solidarity': a type of solidarity that is 'noncolonizing' and can be established across power imbalances.

Indigenous peoples facing expanding settler colonialisms were neither workers nor consumers (or national bourgeoisies). Her conclusion is entitled 'The Expulsion of People and the Incorporation of Terrain'. As noted, this is as good a definition of settler colonialism as a mode of domination as any (Sassen 2013: 200–201).

A reminder that accumulation by dispossession is not unprecedented is also offered by Paula Chakravartty and Denise Ferreira da Silva in a compelling intervention aptly entitled 'Accumulation, Dispossession and Debt' (2012). They have the forcibly and violently extracted labour of historically colonised peoples in mind, and they are right vis-à-vis Harvey who does not, but as they do not distinguish between colonialism and settler colonialism as distinct modes of domination producing radically different social formations, they do not consider the new absolute disposability of populations.

Kalyan Sanyal insists that primitive accumulation actively creates absolutely redundant surplus populations that remain permanently outside of capitalist relations.[7] But in postcolonial conditions they cannot be abandoned to perish like they used to; they must be managed (Sanyal 2014). The contemporary governance of capital, however, is now free from the earlier imperatives of political legitimation and more and more segments of the global population are being 'indigenized' rather than taken care of in a 'need economy' and are now increasingly subject to mechanisms of elimination and containment. While Sanyal does not refer to very recent neoliberal excesses (Sassen, however, does) and focuses on a locale that is eminently not settler colonial, all these scholars do not use the language of settler colonial studies.

But they may. If primitive accumulation separates us from our livelihoods with the purpose of recreating us as labour, and if capitalist accumulation extracts surplus value from commodified labour (and if the need economy is reduced in the context of neoliberal practice), we have no way of accounting for the present condition unless we consider the operation of settler colonialism as a specific mode of domination. It is here that the dialectical relationship entwining colonialism and settler colonialism becomes heuristically crucial to understanding the global present: if colonialism and imperialism appropriate markets and labour for the purpose of exploitation and exclusive exploitation respectively, settler colonialism merely appropriates. It does not desire indigenous labour; it simply wishes indigenous people to vanish. Disposable populations: accumulation without reproduction.

[7]It is significant that Partha Chatterjee's 'Foreword' to Sanyal's book explicitly mentions the 'millions of dispossessed peasants who migrated to the settler colonies' as one of the no longer existing outlets for the absolutely redundant (Chatterjee 2014: 12). Settler colonialism as a mode of domination was simultaneously one global result of processes of primitive accumulation and a crucial driver of them.

References

Adas, M. (2001). From Settler colony to global hegemon: Integrating the exceptionalist narrative of the American experience into world history. *The American Historical Review, 106*(5), 1692–1720.

Alexander, M. (2012). *The new Jim Crow: Mass incarceration in the age of colorblindness*. New York: New Press.

Alfred, T., & Corntassel, J. (2005). Being indigenous: Resurgences against contemporary colonialism. *Government and Opposition, 40*(4), 597–614.

Allegri, G., et al. (2015). *Economia politica della promessa*. Roma: Manifestolibri.

Altman, J. (2010). What future for remote Indigenous Australia? Economic hybridity and the neoliberal turn. In J. Altman & M. Hinkson (Eds.), *Culture crisis: Anthropology and politics in aboriginal Australia*. Sydney: UNSW Press.

Arrighi, G. (2007). *Adam smith in Beijing: Lineages of the twenty-first century*. New York: Verso.

Ashcroft, B., Griffiths, G., & Tiffin, H. (1989). *The empire writes back: Theory and practice in post-colonial literatures*. London: Routledge.

Banner, S. (2007). *How the Indians lost their land: Law and power on the frontier*. Cambridge, MA: Belknap Press.

Beck, U. (2000). *The brave new world of work*. Cambridge: Polity.

Belich, J. (2009). *Replenishing the earth: The settler revolution and the rise of the anglo-world, 1783–1939*. Oxford: Oxford University Press.

Bessire, L. (2014). The rise of indigenous hypermarginality: Native culture as a neoliberal politics of life. *Current Anthropology, 55*(3), 276–295.

Brown, N. A. (2014). The Logic of Settler Accumulation in a Landscape of Perpetual Vanishing. *Settler Colonial Studies, 4*(1), 1–26.

Castel, R. (2003). *From manual workers to wage laborers: Transformation of the social question*. New Brunswick, NJ: Transaction Publishers.

Chakravartty, P., & da Silva, D. F. (2012). Accumulation, dispossession and debt: The racial logic of global capitalism; an introduction. *American Quarterly, 64*(3), 361–385.

Chatterjee, P. (2014). Foreword. In K. Sanyal (Ed.), *Rethinking capitalist development: Primitive accumulation, governmentality and post-colonial capitalism* (pp. 9–16). London: Routledge.

Choudry, A., & Kapoor, D. (2013). *NGOization: Complicity, contradictions and prospects*. London: Zed Books.

Cobb, J. (2016, March 14). *The matter of black lives: A new kind of movement found its moment. What will its future be?* The New Yorker. http://www.newyorker.com/magazine/2016/03/14/where-is-black-lives-matter-headed. Accessed March 11, 2016.

Collins, J. (2011). *Global palestine*. New York: Columbia University Press.

Coulthard, G. S. (2010). Place against empire: Understanding indigenous anti-colonialism. *Affinities, 4*(2), 79–83.

de Angelis, M. (2004). Separating the doing and the deed: Capital and the continuous character of enclosures. *Historical Materialism, 12*(2), 57–87.

Felli, R. (2014). On climate rent. *Historical Materialism, 22*(3–4), 251–280.

Fitzmaurice, A. (2007). The geneology of *Terra Nullius*. *Australian Historical Studies, 38*(129), 1–15.

Fry, T. (2011). Urban futures in the age of unsettlement. *Futures, 43*, 432–439.

Geisler, C. (2013). New *Terra Nullius* narratives and the gentrification of africa's "empty lands". *Journal of World Systems Research, 18*(1), 15–29.

Goldstein, A. (2014). Finance and foreclosure in the colonial present. *Radical History Review, 118*, 42–63.

Griffiths, T., & Robin, L. (Eds.). (1997). *Ecology and empire: Environmental history of settler societies*. Seattle: University of Washington Press.

Hage, G. (2015). *Alter-politics: Critical anthropology and the radical imagination*. Melbourne: Melbourne University Press.

Hage, G. (2016). 'État de siège: A dying domesticating colonialism?' *American Ethnologist*.
Harvey, D. (2003). *The new imperialism*. Oxford: Oxford University Press.
Hendlin, Y. H. (2014). From *Terra Nullius* to *Terra Communis*: Reconsidering Wild Land in an Era of Conservation and Indigenous Rights. *Environmental Philosophy, 11*(2), 141–174.
Herzl, T. (1960). *The complete diaries of theodor herzl*. New York: Herzl Press.
Hirano, K. (2015). Thanatopolitics in the making of Japan's Hokkaido: Settler colonialism and primitive accumulation. *Critical Historical Studies*, 191–218.
Joseph, M. (2014). *Debt to society: Accounting for life under capitalism*. Minneapolis: University of Minnesota Press.
Kenyon, G. (2015, November 2). Have you ever felt "solastalgia"?' *BBC News*. http://www.bbc.com/future/story/20151030-have-you-ever-felt-solastalgia Accessed November 02, 2015.
Klein, N. (2007). *The shock doctrine: The rise of disaster capitalism*. Melbourne: Penguin.
Klein, N. (2014). *This changes everything*. New York: Simon & Schuster.
Lloyd, D., & Wolfe, P. (2015). Settler colonial logics and the neoliberal regime. *Settler Colonial Studies,*. doi:10.1080/2201473X.2015.1035361.
Lytle Hernandez, K. (2016, forthcoming) *City of inmates: Conquest and the rise of human caging in Los Angeles*.
Mamdani, M. (2015). Settler colonialism: Now and then. *Critical Inquiry, 41*, 1–19.
Marx, K. (1976[1867]). *Capital*. New York: Penguin Books.
Mezzadra, S., & Neilson, B. (2013). *Border as method, or the multiplication of labor*. Durham, NC: Duke University Press.
Mohanty, C. T. (2003). "Under western eyes" revisited: Feminist solidarity through anticapitalist struggles. *Signs, 28*(2), 499–535.
Murch, D. (2015, August 5). Ferguson's inheritance. *Jacobin*. https://www.jacobinmag.com/2015/08/ferguson-police-black-lives-matter/ Accessed November 18, 2015.
Nichols, R. (2015). Disaggregating primitive accumulation. *Radical Philosophy, 194*, 18–28.
Olesen, T. (2004). Globalizing the Zapatistas: from Third World solidarity to global solidarity? *Third World Quarterly, 25*(1), 255–267.
Osterhammel, J. (2014). *The transformation of the world: A global history of the nineteenth century*. Princeton, NJ: Princeton University Press.
Pearson, C. (1893). *National life and character: A forecast*. London: Macmillan & Co.
Piterberg, G., & Veracini, L. (2015). Wakefield, marx and the world turned inside out. *Journal of Global History, 10*(3), 457–478.
Ross, A. (2013). *Creditocracy and the case for debt refusal*. New York: OR Books.
Sanyal, K. (2014). *Rethinking capitalist development: Primitive accumulation, governmentality and post-colonial capitalism*. London: Routledge.
Sassen, S. (2013). Expelled: Humans in capitalism's deepening crisis. *Journal of World-Systems Research, 19*(2), 198–201.
Sassen, S. (2014). *Expulsions*. Cambridge, MA: Harvard University Press.
Strakosch, E. (2015). *Neoliberal indigenous policy: Settler colonialism in the 'post-welfare' state*. Houndmills: Palgrave.
Sugg, K. (2015). The walking dead: Late liberalism and masculine subjection in apocalypse fictions. *Journal of American Studies, 49*(4), 793–811.
Veracini, L. (2010). *Settler colonialism: A theoretical overview*. Houndmills: Palgrave Macmillan.
Veracini, L. (2015). *The Settler colonial present*. Houndmills: Palgrave Macmillan.
Wolfe, P. (1999). *Settler colonialism and the transformation of anthropology: The politics and poetics of an ethnographic event*. London: Cassell.
Wolfe, P. (2006). Settler colonialism and the elimination of the native. *Journal of Genocide Research, 8*(4), 387–409.
Wolfe, P. (2016). *Traces of history: Elementary structures of race*. London: Verso.

Chapter 4
Two Kinds of Recognition: The Politics of Engagement in Settler Societies

Ravi de Costa

Abstract Advocates of the recognition of Indigenous peoples conflate two distinct claims. On the one hand, they seek to validate the cultural differences of Indigenous peoples, such as language or prior occupation. On the other, they call on dominant states and societies to reform their own institutions and recognise their own failings, with implications that may go far beyond those for Indigenous peoples specifically. The chapter explores this distinction using rationales for recognition in the Australian constitutional debate as well as in the Final Report of the Truth and Reconciliation Commission of Canada.

Keywords Recognition · Identity · Constitutional reform · Australia · Canada

Introduction

> The Australian people do not wish to recognise me for who I am – with all that this brings – and it is the Australian people whom the politicians fear. The Australian people know that their success is built on the taking of the land, in making the country their own, which they did at the expense of so many languages and ceremonies and songlines – and people – now destroyed. They worry about what has been done for them and on their behalf, and they know that reconciliation requires much more than just words (Yunupingu 2016).

What is recognition? Why is it such a political imperative? Influential scholarship has suggested that the 'good' of recognition is limited to cultural and psychological effects; it has little value for 'transformation' and in fact can hold in place structures that maintain material inequalities. As such, the turn in recent decades from class struggles to identity politics—'from redistribution to recognition' in the writing of Nancy Fraser—is often lamented.

R. de Costa (✉)
York University, Toronto, Canada
e-mail: rdc@yorku.ca

S. Maddison et al. (eds.), *The limits of settler colonial reconciliation*,
DOI 10.1007/978-981-10-2654-6_4

But this literature largely assumes that recognition concerns those events in which a dominant actor 'recognises' a subordinate or oppressed actor: an act to recognise a marginalised Other. A formal campaign such as a constitutional referendum to define and entrench the status of the subordinated community (as in some way special and worthy of consideration) might exemplify this. Much debate then concerns the consequences of acts of recognition for the subordinated community, its subsequent possibilities: does recognition reify that identity, for example?

However, another dimension of recognition is possible, one that emerges, for example, in the context of processes of historical inquiry into events that have *already* shaped the possibilities of subordinated communities, particularly those in which a dominant society has attempted to erase a subordinate community or remake it in its own image. Such an act of recognition by a dominant community is then less about the (inherent or prior or ongoing) identity and status of the subordinate community, than about what was done to it and what that means about the identity or character of the dominant community. Though it is rarely referred to as such, arguably, this other strand is a form of *self-recognition* as much as it is one of *recognition of the Other*.

In many instances these two kinds of recognition are intertwined, even co-produced. However, this chapter explores the two as distinct political possibilities, by considering recent events in the politics of recognition of two settler societies, Australia and Canada, noting arguments against narrow and symbolic practices of recognition and those that have a strictly 'psychological' imperative. We need to beware, some authors insist, the perils of assuming that mere recognition of cultural difference will produce in the Other an improved esteem and outlook that is significant for them.

The chapter explores the critique in light of recent determined public efforts to move from the symbolic or cultural to the material and substantive. In the sections on Australia and Canada, I examine the contemporary politics of recognition, focusing largely on the arguments being made explicitly and implicitly about *why* there should be forms of recognition. The structure of these moments are necessarily different—the one a campaign for constitutional change, the other a response to a national inquiry—but they invoke similar lines of reasoning as claims for recognition: they ask settler peoples to recognise not only the distinctiveness of Indigeneity but also the accumulated effects of settler societies' actions on Indigenous life. The paper offers in conclusion a better articulation of the distinctions as well as relationship between the two dimensions of contemporary recognition politics. I also examine potential and actual pathways between symbolic and material change. Might we imagine or even glimpse in such a rearticulated politics the way back, 'from recognition to redistribution'? However, I first examine recent debates about the merits or otherwise of recognition itself.

Recognition

> Recognition presupposes a subject of recognition (the recognizer) and an object (the recognized) (Stanford 2013).

Since the 'rise in "identity politics"' (Gitlin 1993), academic debate has flourished about what has been gained and what lost. Much of this discussion can be seen in the literature on 'recognition', including work by Charles Taylor and Axel Honneth. Both writers sought to defend the political turn to identity politics as movements to address the harm inherent in the misrecognition of particular minority groups, those harmful to self-esteem and sense of personhood. Taylor called recognition 'a vital human need' (Taylor 1992). Honneth described recognition as an essential element of human cognition itself, one that plays a crucial role in a psychologically healthy life (Honneth 1995).

In self-identified 'multicultural' societies and certainly in the settler-states, these goals of recognition have informed numerous policy measures vis-à-vis cultural and other minorities. However, more recent scholarship has systematically argued against such politics of recognition, largely by arguing that the kinds of recognition on offer not only do not lead to substantive material change for cultural minorities who are frequently marginalised socially and economically but actually reinforce structures and paradigms of domination.

A recent volume (Eisenberg et al. 2014) centres these issues in the North American context, putting the two arguments clearly: 'subaltern agency does not depend on the validation of dominant groups' (Williams 2014: 16); and 'state recognition practices have often been a vehicle for sustaining structures of domination over Indigenous peoples' (2014: 5). Particularly with regard to state recognition of Indigenous identities, recognition strategies can be inherently essentialist, obscuring the fact that cultures depend for their coherence as much on their dynamism and ability to change as on the continuity of cultural practices. Williams (2014: 7) invokes James Scott's notion of 'seeing like a state': recognition makes groups 'legible by delineating the boundaries of their membership and to render them governable by defining the acceptable limits for the expression of group aspirations and identities'.

Reflecting for a moment on recent recognitions of Indigenous peoples reveals the entrenchment of a dyad between the state or society on the one hand and a generalised block of Indigenous peoples on the other, the homogenising categories of Indigenous or Aboriginal peoples, effacing the actual linguistic, geographic and other distinctions within this category. Does this enable structural injustice to be addressed more effectively or not? In a settler political and legal order, where cultural difference is the basis of recognition, can such homogenisation serve to deny not just the specific claims per se but the distinct *forms of relationship* that particular Indigenous nations have, to their own territories, identities and languages?

Coulthard's (2014a: 169) study of the post-war politics of his own Dene nation observes a 'productive capacity of colonial power to construct conciliatory indigenous subjectivities through the scripted exchange of recognition'. He wants to question 'the affirmative relationship between recognition and freedom drawn by many defenders of identity/difference politics on the grounds that such a politics has proven incapable of transforming the generative material conditions that often foreclose the realisation of self-determination in the lives of ordinary citizens.' (2014a: 149) The political theorist Singh (2014: 57) goes so far as to suggest that

> cultural claims themselves cannot present any deep challenge to the economic or political spheres or what might be called the material structures of society… (they are) self-regarding claims on the part of those who make them simply to be able to live their own lives as they see fit. These claims do not aim towards any greater social transformation or to make any contribution to the broader principles or norms of society. Culture here is subordinated to liberal-democratic norms, principles, and institutions that are themselves treated as acultural and universal.

On this basis, Singh and others distinguish between recognition 'from above' or 'from below'. From above, it is very much the statist approach: 'recognition is something that is owed to cultural groups as a means to some other higher universal good, such as individual autonomy … dignity … respect … or participatory parity' (2014: 49). From below, we need to think of recognition 'as an irreducible dimension of all relations of power and governance. All such relations involve norms of mutual recognition by which the actors involved recognize themselves and each other in any number of ways' (2014: 50). Singh wants to break down the dominant/subordinate dyad of contemporary recognition, focusing instead on 'the infinite multiplicity of forms of recognition and struggles over recognition that occur in all realms of social life—from the most public to the most private, the most powerful to the most subalternised—and to provincialise the statist, liberal-democratic form of recognition (recognition from above) as only one form among many (always shifting) forms of recognition' (2014: 51).

Trudy Gover observes 'collateral' forms of inter-tribal recognition, against the 'bilateral' recognition in which the state is the main locus of authority; such phenomena not only help shift identity processes away from positivist regimes such as descent and blood quanta, they support the 'capacity of Indigenous peoples to form and maintain communities in the face of dramatic political, demographic and cultural upheaval and to do so by drawing on their relationships with each other.' (Gover 2014: 219–220) And, if it is to have emancipatory potential, Williams argues that 'the politics of recognition (must become) a process of self-definition' (2014: 12). Coulthard calls for acts of 'self-recognition'. In his recent book *Red Skin, White Masks*, he sets out a politics of self-recognition, from below, an Indigenous vision denoted as 'Indigenous resurgence', which is 'at its core a *prefigurative* politics—the methods of decolonization prefigure its aims.' (Coulthard 2014b: 159).

However, while prefigurative and autonomist recognitions 'from and to below' remain critical, even Singh acknowledges the necessity for cultural and other minorities to continue to engage with the state and with dominant societies on numerous critical questions: 'to address deep-seated disparities of structural power and the constraining effects these have on micro-political change, … to design, configure, and maintain the stability of social institutions and large-scale forms of action coordination, and … to respond to acute, complex, and protracted conflicts and atrocities when they arise' (Singh 2014: 68). In so doing, they must have forms of standing vis-à-vis the state and society.

If we are to retain a commitment to the politics of recognition, the challenge then is to identify paths back 'from recognition to redistribution', to invert Nancy Fraser's formulation (Fraser and Honneth 2003). Fraser herself sought to recast 'recognition': no longer is it about acknowledging inherent or essential cultural differences but rather disparities in social status (Fraser and Honneth 2003: 29). Jung (2014: 24) provides a different inflection of this shift as it affects Indigenous peoples:

> The moral force of Indigenous politics rests not in cultural distinctiveness but, rather, in the way that aboriginal identities have been shaped and distorted by state policies that have raced, classed, and ethnicised this population and by the persistent interactions among such categories. It is structural injustice, in its multiple and abiding manifestations, rather than cultural difference, that establishes the moral force of indigenous politics.

Without 'validation' in the forms of apologies or other formal acts and statements of recognition, how are we to ground 'concrete measures to eliminate arbitrary cultural biases in public institutions or to dismantle structures of material inequality'? (Williams 2014: 16). With this question in mind, I think we need to think more about the actors involved, taking up Singh's ideas of 'provincialising the state', disaggregating the 'dominant' order that is reflexively posited as that which recognises.

Jeremy Webber (2014: 62–68) explains the ethical task that should direct us towards reconsideration of how all our identities are composed and the fundamental sources of value in our lives:

> …the politics of cultural diversity from below is taken up as a challenge to individuals, groups, and communities to build, from the ground up, (a) lived, practical orientation toward diversity … not a problem to be managed by the state in accordance with meta-norms but, rather as a challenge to individuals and communities to build radically pluralistic cultures of politics that incorporate an aspectival awareness and appreciation of differences, an understanding of the material relations that engender and/or exacerbate tensions across differences, and practices of trust building and cooperation across difference.

This better describes many contemporary political projects of recognition, at least in settler societies. While the state is plainly still engaged, its variegation and complexity has been exposed by more nuanced claims for and settings of recognition. Even more significant is the growing role of non-state actors, of civil society and the community at large as agents of recognition. As we will see, 'calls to action' that are aimed at Law Societies, universities, municipalities or school boards, are not necessarily best understood within the basic dyadic structure of recognition posited at the outset. Campaigns for constitutional reform, treaties or other fundamental changes may also succeed by building on such constellations of recognition, rather than reinforcing a dyad that is abstracted from real life.

Australia: The Campaign for Constitutional Recognition

Observing the Constitutional reform debate in Australia, several observers have noted how strange it is that a 200-year-old nation is being asked to 'recognise' the existence of peoples and cultures whose presence has been continuous for over 40,000 years. In this section, I review current arguments *for recognition* in Australia, as framed in the campaign for a constitutional referendum. This focus helps reveal the two dimensions of recognition clearly. The arguments revolve predominantly on a dyad of the Australian state/government/people (the recogniser) and a generalised category of Aboriginal Australians, (the 'community of the recognised' in the words of Davis 2016). However, both dimensions implicitly call on Australians to embrace forms of self-recognition, specifically the repudiation of several features of their existing political order as enshrined in the Constitution. In this section, I review briefly the timeline leading to the current campaign for recognition and then sort out the lines of argument and distinctive rationales for each.

The pre-history of formal recognition in Australia is lengthy, going back at least to the 1970s. Neville Bonner's 1975 resolution in the Senate[1] called for acceptance of prior occupancy and the payment of compensation through a representative body of some sort: 'an all Aboriginal and Torres Strait Islander statutory body empowered to administer such a compensation for dispossession fund, *for the survival of fellow Aborigines and Torres Strait Islanders*' (Commonwealth Parliamentary Debates 1975, emphasis added). In 1979 the elected National Aboriginal Conference and a group of well-known non-Aboriginal people, calling themselves the Aboriginal Treaty Committee, both called for a treaty, adopting language commonplace in the other formerly British settler colonies.

Later that year the High Court ruled in a case brought by Aboriginal activist Paul Coe that there was no longer an Aboriginal nation that could exercise sovereignty. And by the early 1980s, the term 'treaty' had been supplanted by *makarrata*, a term in the Yolngu language denoting a 'cessation of hostilities'. The Australian Senate conducted a review of the issue and laid out several options for an agreement between Indigenous Australians and the state. But it was overtaken by the election of a new government that had a different agenda, focusing on a national land rights regime and the creation of an Aboriginal elected advisory body. In 1988, Australian Aboriginal groups presented Prime Minister Bob Hawke with the Barunga Statement, a document calling for the recognition and protection of their cultural rights, self-determination and control of lands, compensation for loss of lands, and negotiation of a 'Treaty or Compact recognising our prior ownership, continued occupation and sovereignty' (Central and Northern Land Councils, 'The Barunga Statement', reproduced in Tickner 2001: 40–41).

Hawke promised to respond by beginning national treaty negotiations but his failure to do so led to the Treaty '88 campaign which embarrassed the government

[1]Neville Bonner was an Indigenous politician and Australian Senator, the first Indigenous member of the Parliament of Australia.

during its national celebration of Australia's Bicentennial in 1988 (Treaty '88 Campaign 1988), and by the start of the 1990s, the idea of an agreement had been subsumed by 'reconciliation'. The Council for Aboriginal Reconciliation (CAR) worked with a very different mandate that did not prioritise formal agreement; its overarching goal of national unity and identity ran counter to the idea of recognition of a distinctive Indigenous history and presence. In 1999 the recently-elected conservative Coalition government advanced the only concrete proposal to amend the Constitution as part of a campaign for republicanism, providing for the limited recognition of Indigenous Australians in a non-binding constitutional preamble written by then Prime Minister John Howard. That proposal was decisively defeated at the polls.

The 2007 Federal Election saw a promise by the outgoing Liberal prime minister to hold a constitutional referendum 'recognising' Indigenous Australians. The then Opposition leader, Kevin Rudd, agreed, committing his party to such a referendum should they win government. Rudd's Labor successor as PM, Julia Gillard actually began the formal process, appointing an Expert Panel in 2010 to conduct extensive consultations with Aboriginal and Torres Strait Islander communities and non-Indigenous people and present a proposal for Constitutional Reform. In the 2012 report of the Expert Panel the subject and object of recognition became clearer. Its recommendations break down into the two guiding categories suggested at the outset of this paper: recognition of an Other, and recognition of aspects of the Self. In reaching these recommendations several rationales emerge consistently in the Expert Panel report, including the political opportunity presented by 'current multiparty support' and a chance to enable Indigenous peoples to benefit from Australian democracy and prosperity:

> Constitutional recognition of the cultures, languages and heritage of Aboriginal and Torres Strait Islander peoples would *declare an important truth* in Australian history, and assist in *sustaining their cultures and languages* into the future. Constitutional recognition would help *improve the self-esteem and dignity* of Aboriginal and Torres Strait Islander people, and provide *a better framework for the governance of the nation* (Expert Panel on Constitutional Recognition of Indigenous Australians 2012: 11, emphasis added).

The Panel also examined the reasoning of those who made submissions, setting the most commonly put reasons for supporting constitutional recognition as follows:

1. Aboriginal and Torres Strait Islander peoples occupy a unique position in Australian society as the first peoples and original custodians of the land, and therefore should have special recognition in the Constitution;
2. Aboriginal and Torres Strait Islander peoples should be guaranteed equality before the law, and the Constitution should be free from racially discriminatory clauses;
3. Constitutional recognition of Aboriginal and Torres Strait Islander peoples is overdue;
4. Constitutional recognition will more accurately reflect Australia's history and national identity; and

5. Recognising Aboriginal and Torres Strait Islander peoples in the Constitution is important for recognising and protecting their unique cultures. (Expert Panel on Constitutional Recognition of Indigenous Australians 2012: 68; numbers added).

Reasons 1 and 5 are clearly motivated by a desire to recognise the difference of the Other; reason 2 expresses a recognition of Self and simultaneously a desire to change; reasons 3 and 4 might best be understood as conflating the two forms of recognition: that 'we' really are one complex and diverse people that contains within it Indigenous difference and that recognising that truth is 'overdue'.

With these in mind, the Panel recommended forms of recognition that endorsed these distinctions: 'Recognition of Aboriginal and Torres Strait Islander peoples', their prior occupation and continuing culture, and their distinctiveness to be contained in a new Section 51A, somewhat counter-intuitively conferring additional powers on government, 'to make laws for the peace, order and good government of the Commonwealth with respect to Aboriginal and Torres Strait Islander peoples'. Similarly, it calls for a new Section 127A, recognising Indigenous languages as the 'original Australian languages'.

But the Panel's other recommendations are less recognitions of an Other than acknowledgements of the Australian reality of racial discrimination: what the dominant Australian state and society did to Indigenous peoples, its exclusions and denials of them and the structures that enabled these. The Panel called for: the removal of Section 25 (which envisages disqualification from voting rights of particular 'races'); the removal of Section 51(xxvi), which gives the Commonwealth the power to make special laws for the people of any 'race'; and the introduction of a new Section 116A, prohibiting racial discrimination, while allowing laws that help any particular 'group' overcome disadvantage.

These latter recognitions are of the flaws in the dominant community's cultural, political and legal order, its histories of racist policy and its anachronism now. One cannot really have this second dimension of recognition without the first, the possibility of a cultural difference that suffered such discrimination and now needs both redress and positive validation. But it is distinctive in that it produces reasoning and requires elaboration that pulls in different directions. It also invites actions that would have wider effects than respecting the special differences of Indigenous peoples.

Indeed, it may be that addressing the discriminatory traditions and structures of the Australian polity are actually the more decisive goals of Indigenous Australians in the recognition debate (Davis 2016). As Co-Chair of the Expert Panel, Mark Leibler, observed of the Panel's consultations with Indigenous peoples, at 'every single consultation that we held, there was a reference to substantive recognition—"We want substantive recognition." What did that mean? It turned out that substantive recognition means something to preclude racial discrimination' (Joint Select Committee on Constitutional Recognition of Aboriginal and Torres Strait Islander Peoples 2015).

In December 2013 in response to the Expert Panel report, the Australian Parliament created a Joint Select Committee on Constitutional Recognition of

Aboriginal and Torres Strait Islander Peoples, 'to inquire into and report on steps that can be taken to progress towards a successful referendum on Indigenous constitutional recognition'. The Parliamentary committee's summary view, set out in the Interim Report of July 2014, re-inscribed three key features of a referendum question that would likely be successful:

- recognise Aboriginal and Torres Strait Islander peoples as the first peoples of Australia;
- preserve the Commonwealth's power to make laws with respect to Aboriginal and Torres Strait Islander peoples; and
- in making laws under such a power, prevent the Commonwealth from discriminating against Aboriginal and Torres Strait Islander peoples.

That is, to recognise the difference of the Other; to maintain power over the Other; but to restrain that power with an obligation not to discriminate. The latter criterion would restrain and renovate the Self. In addition, the Committee's Final Report in 2015 identified 'the following issues as being significant motivating factors for constitutional recognition: the strong view that constitutional recognition of Aboriginal and Torres Strait Islander peoples would be a way to complete the Constitution; there should be constitutional recognition of the historical fact that Aboriginal and Torres Strait Islander peoples have lived on the continent now known as Australia for tens of thousands of years; the timing of the referendum, noting the important symbolic connections that could be drawn from holding the referendum close to the anniversary of the 1967 referendum in which Aboriginal and Torres Strait Islander peoples were counted in the census; and that the proposal must have the support of Aboriginal and Torres Strait Islander peoples' (2015: 7). Put succinctly: a desire for completion; the need to recognise a 'historical fact'; and the symbolic opportunity of an Anniversary of 1967.

Parallel to the political and formal parliamentary process that began in 2007 and seeking to influence it, numerous influential figures and organisations began developing positions and campaigning for some form of recognition. Galarrwuy Yunupingu,[2] for example, told then Aboriginal Affairs Minister Mal Brough that he 'wanted constitutional recognition, to bring my people in from the cold, bring us into the nation' (Yunupingu 2008). The national organisation You Me Unity published a discussion paper in 2011 setting out two reasons for supporting constitutional recognition. The first was to 'more truly reflect the lives and values of Australians today … who we are as a nation' (2011: 10). In this rationale, the object of difference or Other is actually (more truly) a subset of who we are or have become. The second was to eliminate powers that could discriminate against particular races.

The peak body for Indigenous peoples, the National Congress of Australia's First Peoples endorsed the Expert Panel's recommendations completely, framing its

[2]Galarrwuy Yunupingu is leader of the Gumatj clan and an eminent Indigenous figure from East Arnhem Land in the Northern Territory.

rationale as 're-righting the rule book' (2013, sic). Its materials are aimed at Indigenous peoples directly, adopting an overt 'fair go' message and pointing out that the Constitution says nothing about 'who we are' as a people.'

However, some advocates also drew implications that an act of recognition would contribute to better social or economic outcomes for Indigenous peoples. A facile equation was sometimes drawn between the psychological and symbolic dimensions of recognition and unspecified material benefits and changes but there are also those making more substantive arguments.

The major civil society organisation now campaigning for recognition is Recognise. Their platform reproduces and refines earlier arguments about why it is important to recognise Indigenous peoples in the Constitution. Briefly these are to 'complete the constitutional task of securing equality' that was left unfinished after the 1967 referendum, removing those sections that still allow racial discrimination; to reunite or complete the Australian 'family', that became estranged at the nation's 'birth', an act that will also 'unite Australians, giving us greater shared pride and deeper connection with our country's impressive Indigenous heritage and cultures'; and also 'to protect against the loss of our unique Indigenous cultures for future generations'.

Recognise is also notable in its explicit attempt to connect symbolic or formal recognition with material benefits for Indigenous peoples. The 'Recognise Health Initiative' appears to be a direct response to arguments about the allegedly fruitless quality of symbolic action in a political culture that self-consciously privileges the practical or pragmatic. While much of the connection is asserted rather than demonstrated, it would seem that a social determinants of health framework lies in the background: strong correlations between human health and other indicators, including self and other perceptions of one's own status, are now well established, and the Recognise Health initiative endorses these and implicitly argues that constitutional recognition will lead to improvements in those other indicators.

The health professional organisations' submissions to the Expert Panel move somewhat further. For example the Australian and New Zealand College of Psychiatrists (2015) submitted that:

> Recognition would have a positive effect on the self-esteem of Aboriginal and Torres Strait Islander peoples. It would also benefit all Australians and work to reinforce the collective national pride in the longevity of Aboriginal and Torres Strait Islander heritage, culture and history. As well as addressing a national wound, it would make a significant contribution to the lives, health and wellbeing of many individuals, families and communities.

However, of the material reviewed here, far greater attention has been given to discussing the necessary steps that have to be taken to produce a successful referendum, or with the possible consequences of certain forms of recognition, than with the reasons for recognition itself. Frequently the rationale for recognition conflates the two forms: The rhetoric of many advocates foregrounds an appreciation of Indigenous difference, that is of the Other, when the arguments that are put forward are largely about removing racist powers in Australia, or a recognition of the flaws of the Self. Public opinion and commentary suggests that the former is less contentious than the latter. But as noted, it would seem that for Indigenous peoples, the price of their participation in constitutional reform is that the Australian state and society recognise its own structural failings with regard to racism.

Canada: The Recognition of Injustice as Grounds for Action

Debate in Indigenous affairs in Canada has in recent years been markedly influenced by the work of the Truth and Reconciliation Commission (TRC) of Canada, an inquiry into the history and legacy of the Indian Residential Schools (IRS) system. Over its 130-year history, from Confederation in 1867 until 1996, about 150,000 Aboriginal children were placed, with varying degrees of coercion, in 130 residential schools across the country. These schools were usually distant from the children's communities, were starved of funds, badly run and in many instances bred neglect and abuse, psychological, physical and sexual (Milloy 1999; Miller 1996; TRC Final Report 2015). Rather than arising as an act of government policy, the TRC was mandated as one piece of a settlement to an unprecedented class action of over 11,000 survivors of the IRS system. Institutionally, it is something of a hybrid form, with some of the features of a national inquiry and some of a community education campaign, though it had no formal or legal powers.

The TRC's Final Report was cannily issued in two stages, in June and December of 2015, both before and after the October 2015 federal election. This obliged the major political parties to formally respond in their campaign platforms to the June report, which included the recommendations, with two of the three main parties promising to implement these in toto. With one of those parties, the Liberals being elected to govern and whose Prime Minister has made repeated and emotive invocations of his government's responsibility to act, Indigenous policy is now frequently described as being a response to the TRC.

Indeed, the TRC very deliberately pointed its findings towards substantive and diverse policy change, in its 'Calls to Action' (TRC 2015). Going far beyond the task of informing Canadians about the dismal history of the IRS system and its ongoing effects for Indigenous communities and individuals, these recommendations 'call on' numerous distinct governmental and non-governmental actors to take specific measures on issues within their domain. However, the overall thrust of the TRC's work has been to insist, in the words of Chief Commissioner of the TRC, Sinclair (2015) that, 'Reconciliation is not an aboriginal problem, it is a Canadian problem. It involves all of us.'

Indeed Sinclair has been especially articulate on this theme. His vision of a Canada is one in which recognition of the Self comes in the same effort as recognition of the Other, work that is built on 'the central truth … that there is a relationship between aboriginal people and everyone who has come here, from 1492 to today' and that continued immigration will mean that the French and

English settlers who colonised Canada will soon be a minority, 'the aboriginal people of the future' (quoted in Ibbitson 2015). At the launch of the report in June 2015, he explained, 'I really don't care if you feel responsible for the past. The real question is do you feel a sense of responsibility for the future because that's what this is all about.'

In this section I review the TRC's 'Calls to Action' to examine further the dyad set out at the beginning of the chapter. Given space limitations, this is a schematic overview of the 94 separate recommendations, but this is nonetheless revealing of the complex interplay of the two forms of recognition at stake. Secondarily, I consider some initial responses and the reasoning underlying them, to chart out the connections between symbolic and substantive change.

Elsewhere I have suggested that the operation of the TRC revealed a specific potential for mobilising social change among 'individuals, communities or institutions that already recognise a need to engage' (de Costa, in press). I have suggested that it is through an awareness of one's own personal history, or an institutional recognition of policy failure in law, education or health, for example, that this motivation is activated. However, I have also suggested that the TRC is less effective in instigating change beyond public bodies or individuals who have such prior orientations. Examining the Calls to Action and early responses offers an opportunity to test this argument.

The Calls are set out under two high-level headings: 'Legacy' and 'Reconciliation'. These accord broadly with the two themes in the TRC's mandate: to acknowledge the past, ensuring the safety of and respect for survivors, both witnessing their stories and commemorating former students and their families; and to 'Promote awareness and public education of Canadians about the IRS system and its impacts'. The first deals with the consequences of colonialism, the second attempts to construct a new common future for Indigenous and settler peoples. Each is then broken down in specific fields.

The 42 calls to action under 'Legacy' are divided by five subheadings, mapping distinct areas of public policy: child welfare; education; language and culture; health; and justice. 'Reconciliation', by contrast, has numerous subheadings bracketing 52 calls to action, ranging from the obligations arising under specific legal instruments (like UNDRIP or the 1763 Royal Proclamation), to a series of areas of public life all captured in the format 'reconciliation and…': Museums, media, sport, and business among others.

Recognising the legacies of the IRS system involves recognising both the specific denials of Indigenous peoples and cultures, as well as recognising the general injustices of a system that disproportionately affected Indigenous peoples. We can see this for example in the various recommendations made under Child Welfare. Recommendation 4 explicitly requires government to legislate for and fund an Indigenous realm: 'Affirm the right of Aboriginal governments to establish and maintain their own child-welfare agencies.' As the Final Report makes clear, in the post-war period, the rationale of child protection became imbricated with the logic underlying the IRS system itself, a situation that persists: 'Aboriginal children are still being separated from their families and communities and placed in the care of child welfare agencies. Like the schools, child welfare agencies are underfunded, often culturally inappropriate, and, far too often, put Aboriginal children in unsafe situations. The child welfare system is the residential school system of our day' (TRC Final Report Volume 5, 2015: 4). This Call to Action is, at its core, a recognition that the difference of Indigenous peoples cannot be respected in a universal child welfare system.

By contrast, recommendation 3 calls on all governments to fully implement 'Jordan's principle',[3] a measure designed to address the jurisdictional buck-passing that frequently denies Indigenous children and families of essential services because of the constitutional reservation of powers for the federal government over Indigenous peoples under Section 91(24), while general powers over child welfare and education are held by the provinces. This Call to Action addresses the specific 'difference' experienced by Indigenous peoples in Canada because of arbitrary administrative arrangements established in the colonial era.

Similarly, recommendation 6 calls for the repeal of Section 43 of the Criminal Code of Canada, the so-called 'spanking law': 'Every schoolteacher, parent or person standing in the place of a parent is justified in using force by way of correction toward a pupil or child, as the case may be, who is under his care, if the force does not exceed what is reasonable under the circumstances.' As the TRC Final Report points out, the circumstances of Residential Schools were far from reasonable: 'It was based on racist assumptions about the intellectual and cultural inferiority of Aboriginal people—the belief that Aboriginal children were incapable of attaining anything more than a rudimentary elementary-level or vocational education… In their mission to 'civilize' and Christianise, the school staff relied on corporal punishment to discipline their students. That punishment often crossed the line into physical abuse' (TRC 2015: 144).

In this case, the Call to Action responds to the ways that Indigenous difference becomes entangled with legal and administrative systems that applied generally but which affected Indigenous peoples disproportionately because of the matrix of colonial impositions by which 'reasonableness' became a racialised construction. Non-Indigenous peoples might well think of this Call to Action as a form of self-recognition; though they would benefit Indigenous peoples to a great extent, it offers another vision of society, in which corporal punishment and the assumptions about learning and behaviour underlying it are anachronistic.

Similarly, the Calls to Action under the heading 'Reconciliation' draw on the two forms of recognition in ways that are intertwined. Under recommendation 45, dealing with the implications of the Royal Proclamation of 1763, the TRC calls on the government of Canada to operate on the basis of a fundamental acknowledgement of the difference of the Other, a respect for distinct Indigenous nations: 'Renew or establish Treaty relationships based on principles of mutual recognition,

---

[3]Jordan's Principle is the argument advanced by Indigenous child welfare activists of putting children's interests first in jurisdictional disputes over payment for government services provided to First Nations children between Canadian governments.

mutual respect, and shared responsibility for maintaining those relationships into the future.' In the same recommendation, Canada is asked to disavow a fundamental tenet of the colonial project, of its own foundation, specifically to 'Repudiate concepts used to justify European sovereignty over Indigenous lands and peoples such as the Doctrine of Discovery and terra nullius.'

We need to look also at non-state parties that have been 'called upon' by the TRC to act in specific ways. An excellent example is the system that trains and oversees the training of legal professionals in Canada, both law schools and their accrediting law societies; these are cited at several points of the Calls to Action. Recommendations 27 and 28 call on them directly:

> 27. We call upon the Federation of Law Societies of Canada to ensure that lawyers receive appropriate cultural competency training, which includes the history and legacy of residential schools, the United Nations Declaration on the Rights of Indigenous Peoples, Treaties and Aboriginal rights, Indigenous law, and Aboriginal– Crown relations. This will require skills-based training in intercultural competency, conflict resolution, human rights, and anti-racism.
>
> 28. We call upon law schools in Canada to require all law students to take a course in Aboriginal people and the law, which includes the history and legacy of residential schools, the United Nations Declaration on the Rights of Indigenous Peoples, Treaties and Aboriginal rights, Indigenous law, and Aboriginal–Crown relations. This will require skills-based training in intercultural competency, conflict resolution, human rights, and antiracism.

There is considerable debate underway about whether a single course is indeed the appropriate way to implement this goal but many law schools or societies in Canada have publicly acknowledged the Calls and indicated they are formulating their response. Taken together these two Calls to Action imply the failure of the legal system to serve Indigenous peoples justly; the Final Report puts this bluntly: first, the 'Canadian legal system failed to provide justice' to those who had suffered abuse in the schools, often revictimising survivors; and more fundamentally, 'the residential school experience lies at the root of the current over-incarceration of Aboriginal people. Traumatised by their school experiences, many succumbed to addictions and found themselves among the disproportionate number of Aboriginal people who come into conflict with the law.' Though the background of these Calls is in the differential experience of Indigenous peoples with the law, they require a reordering of the basic premises of legal education for all.

By contrast, recommendation 50 obliges government to support the flourishing of an Indigenous realm of law, comprising the myriad distinct Indigenous legal traditions in Canada: 'fund the establishment of Indigenous law institutes for the development, use, and understanding of Indigenous laws and access to justice in accordance with the unique cultures of Aboriginal peoples in Canada'. Jeremy Webber, the Dean of the Law School at the University of Victoria, has written eloquently on its implications and possibilities:

> That recommendation calls urgently for institutional structures that can deepen our knowledge of Indigenous legal traditions, develop our comprehension of Indigenous institutions, and explore how those traditions might be worked with and built upon today. It

> calls upon us to recognize Indigenous legal traditions as sources of normative insight in their own right, possessing traction within Indigenous communities today, which deserve our focused attention. That recommendation too requires law schools to respond. We need to bring to Indigenous laws the kind of seriousness that we bring to non-Indigenous law, so that Indigenous law students can learn to reason with their traditions with the rigour and soundness that we require all our students to bring to non-Indigenous law. They need to have skills to know how to access their law, understand it, work with it, assess its multiple interpretations, and function within its institutions. And we and they need to develop modes of translation between Indigenous and non-Indigenous institutions, so that non-Indigenous institutions can relate intelligibly to Indigenous modes of governance and structures can be established that mediate sensibly among our various legal traditions (Webber 2014).

How law schools and other actors substantively respond to these calls to action remains to be seen. Changing curricula, like passing federal legislation, cannot be done rapidly. But we see in the calls themselves a complex use of the two forms of recognition as necessary features of a response to the IRS system and its far-reaching effects on Canadian society. The background for these proposals is clearly the reality of Indigenous difference—the reason for the IRS system in the first place and the particular impacts it has had on Indigenous peoples—but the implications go well beyond this, turning back on Canadian state and society to demand a reconfiguration of its most basic premises and structures.

Conclusion

The chapter set out to review the orthodox understanding of recognition, and to identify forms of politics constructed as acts of recognition of the Other, suggesting that they are perhaps better understood as forms of self-recognition. While much of the politics under review is narrated as forms of justice for Indigenous peoples, the specific changes that are being contemplated appear to call on non-Indigenous peoples to restrain and refashion their own institutions, behaviours and even identities.

It seems evident that, although we might analytically distinguish between these two, in the public mind and political arena these are deeply and necessarily interconnected: the origin stories of racially discriminatory institutions and policies are usually in fear and denial of specific cultural Others. This is plainly true of Indigenous-settler politics in Australia and Canada and this conflation underpins the specific forms of discrimination both in the Australian constitution and the generational failure of Canadian policy and institutions. However, being clearer about the two forms offers clarity about specific arguments for recognition and their supporting campaigns.

For example, the focus on formal projects for reconciliation and recognition—both its apparent benefits and detriments—is built on the now questionable belief in the inherently transformative quality of historical revelation, that dominant societies will make substantive change simply upon presentation of the facts of colonialism. Not surprisingly, a growing Indigenous interest in resuming treaty negotiations in

Australia bypasses this knowledge = social change argument. Davis (2016) has written recently that 'Treaty *is* recognition' and observed 'a growing preference for recognition in an agreement outside the written Constitution' (Davis 2016).

Reading further into the TRC's Calls to Action invites the thought that it is in the move to acts of self-recognition that the true purposes of reconciliation might be realised. In earlier work drawing on focus groups in both countries, we have wondered about why and how settler or non-Indigenous people can go beyond a generic sympathy towards Indigenous concerns to adopt a posture that sees their own interests as bound up with Indigenous aspirations (de Costa and Clark 2013, 2016. See also Clark et al. in this volume). It may be helpful to think of these potentials as forms of self-recognition.

While the chapter is too preliminary an inquiry to offer formal conclusions, it may be worth exploring further a possible correlation between significant forms of *self-recognition* and material changes for Indigenous peoples or other cultural minorities, material changes that appear less consistent with acts that are limited to recognitions of the Other. If even partly true, in debates where Indigenous difference is contentious or misunderstood, a focus on self-recognition may actually prove more productive for Indigenous interests. What I have called here 'calls to self-recognition' are really the grounds for self-restraint through the restructuring of the colonial institutions of settler states: those established for the security, order and prosperity of settler societies, which had both intended and unintended consequences on the distinctive cultures and identities of Indigenous peoples.

References

Commonwealth Parliamentary Debates. (1975). *Senate Hansard*, 20 February. http://parlinfo.aph.gov.au/parlInfo/search/display/display.w3p;query=Id%3A%22hansard80%2Fhansards80%2F1975-02-20%2F0154%22. Accessed July 31, 2016.

Coulthard, G. (2014a). *Red skin, white masks: Rejecting the colonial politics of recognition*. Minneapolis, MN: University of Minnesota Press.

Coulthard, G. (2014b). Place against empire: The Dene nation, land claims, and the politics of recognition in the North. In A. Eisenberg, J. Webber, G. Coulthard, & A. Boisselle (Eds.), *Recognition versus self-determination: Dilemmas of emancipatory politics* (pp. 147–173). Vancouver, BC: UBC Press.

Davis, M. (2016). Seeking a settlement. *The Monthly* (July). https://www.themonthly.com.au/issue/2016/july/1467295200/megan-davis/seeking-settlement. Accessed July 26, 2016.

de Costa, R. (in press). Discursive institutions in non-transitional societies: The Truth and Reconciliation Commission of Canada. *International Political Science Review*.

de Costa, R., & Clark, T. (2016). On the responsibility to engage: Non-indigenous peoples in settler states. *Settler Colonial Studies, 6*(3), 191–208.

Eisenberg, A., Webber, J., Coulthard, G., & Boisselle, A. (Eds.). (2014). *Recognition versus self-determination: Dilemmas of emancipatory politics*. Vancouver, BC: UBC Press.

Fraser, N., & Honneth, A. (2003). *Redistribution or recognition?* Verso, London: A Political-philosophical exchange.

Gitlin, T. (1993). The Rise of "Identity Politics". *Dissent-New York* p. 172.
Gover, K. (2014). Inter-indigenous recognition and the cultural production of indigeneity in the Western Settler States. In A. Eisenberg, J. Webber, G. Coulthard, & A. Boisselle (Eds.), *Recognition versus self-determination: Dilemmas of emancipatory politics* (pp. 201–224). Vancouver, BC: UBC Press.
Honneth, A. (1995). *The struggle for recognition: The moral grammar of social conflicts*. Cambridge: Polity Press.
Ibbitson, J. (2015). Justice Murray Sinclair's Challenge for Canada as It Seeks Reconciliation. *The Globe and Mail*, (June 5) http://www.theglobeandmail.com/news/politics/justice-murray-sinclairs-challenge-for-canada-as-it-seeks-reconciliation/article24833535/. Accessed March 16, 2016.
Joint Select Committee on Constitutional Recognition of Aboriginal and Torres Strait Islander Peoples. (2015). *Joint Select Committee on Constitutional Recognition of Aboriginal and Torres Strait Islander Peoples*. Final Report (June). http://www.aph.gov.au/Parliamentary_Business/Committees/Joint/Constitutional_Recognition_of_Aboriginal_and_Torres_Strait_Islander_Peoples/Constitutional_Recognition/Final_Report. Accessed March 16, 2016.
Jung, C. (2014). Race, class, and ethnicity in the History of Mexican Indigenous politics. In A. Eisenberg, J. Webber, G. Coulthard, & A. Boisselle (Eds.), *Recognition versus self-determination: Dilemmas of emancipatory politics* (pp. 21–46). Vancouver, BC: UBC Press.
Miller, J. R. (1996). *Shingwauk's vision: A history of native residential schools*. Toronto: University of Toronto Press.
Milloy, J. S. (1999). *A national crime: The Canadian government and the residential school system, 1879–1986*. Winnipeg: University of Manitoba Press.
National Congress of Australia's First Peoples. (2013). *Re-right the rulebook*. http://nationalcongress.com.au/wp-content/uploads/2013/06/Rewrite-the-Rulebook.pdf. Accessed March 16, 2016.
Royal Australian and New Zealand College of Psychiatrists. (2015). Position Statement 68. Recognition of Aboriginal and Torres Strait Islander peoples in the Australian Constitution. https://www.ranzcp.org/Files/Resources/College_Statements/Position_Statements/ps68-pdf.aspx. Accessed March 16, 2016.
Sinclair, M. (2015) Speech at Launch of TRC Final Report. Ottawa, ON. http://www.cbc.ca/radio/asithappens/as-it-happens-tuesday-edition-1.3096950/reconciliation-is-not-an-aboriginal-problem-it-is-a-canadian-problem-it-involves-all-of-us-1.3097253. Accessed March 16, 2016.
Singh, Jakeet. (2014). Recognition and self-determination: Approaches from above and below. In A. Eisenberg, J. Webber, G. Coulthard, & A. Boisselle (Eds.), *Recognition versus self-Determination: Dilemmas of emancipatory politics* (pp. 47–74). Vancouver, BC: UBC Press.
Tickner, R. E. (2001). *Taking a stand: Land rights to reconciliation*. Crows Nest, NSW: Allen & Unwin.
Treaty '88 Campaign. (1988). Aboriginal sovereignty—Never ceded. *Australian Historical Studies., 91*, 1–2.
Truth and Reconciliation Commission of Canada. (2015). *Final Report*. http://www.trc.ca/websites/trcinstitution/index.php?p=890. Accessed March 16, 2016.
Webber, J. (2014). The generosity of toleration. In A. Eisenberg, J. Webber, G. Coulthard, & A. Boisselle (Eds.), *Recognition versus self-determination: Dilemmas of emancipatory politics* (pp. 269–292). Vancouver, BC: UBC Press.
Webber, J. (2016). 'The Law Schools and the Future of Indigenous Law in Canada. http://www.slaw.ca/2015/08/04/the-law-schools-and-the-future-of-indigenous-law-in-canada/. Accessed March 16, 2016.

Williams, M. (2014). Introduction: On the use and abuse of recognition in politics. In A. Eisenberg, J. Webber, G. Coulthard, & A. Boisselle (Eds.), *Recognition versus self-determination: Dilemmas of emancipatory politics* (pp. 3–18). Vancouver, BC: UBC Press.

You Me Unity. (2011). A national conversation about Aboriginal and Torres Strait Islander Constitutional Recognition. Text. *Australian Policy Online*, May 20. http://apo.org.au/resource/national-conversation-about-aboriginal-and-torres-strait-islander-constitutional. Accessed March 16, 2016.

Yunupingu, G. (2008). Tradition, truth and tomorrow. *The Monthly* (December). https://www.themonthly.com.au/issue/2008/december/1268179150/galarrwuy-yunupingu/tradition-truth-tomorrow. Accessed March 16, 2016.

Yunupingu, G. (2016). Rom Watangu. *The Monthly* (July). https://www.themonthly.com.au/issue/2016/july/1467295200/galarrwuy-yunupingu/rom-watangu. Accessed July 26, 2016.

Chapter 5
With Whom Do We Reconcile?

Peter Read

Abstract I investigate here the historical circumstances that since 1900 have created at least three kinds of Australian Indigenous people. The first are those, often of lighter complexion, whose forebears' identity was frequently challenged by white officials utilizing conflicting definitions of Aboriginality, and later by other Aborigines. The second group is that of the stolen generations, some of whom were not aware, as children, of their Aboriginal identity at all. The third section comprises those of more secure identity whose family identity has remained unchallenged. These sections of the Aboriginal community, especially the first and the third, are sometimes in serious conflict. Non-aborigines looking for a role in reconciliation are seriously handicapped by failing to understand this very wide diversity of Aboriginal historical experience. We cannot begin serious reconciliation until we understand with whom we think we are reconciling.

Keywords Identity · Part-Aborigines · Legislation · Aboriginal history · Reserves

Introduction

On 20 February 2016 the national newspaper *The Weekend Australian* ran an article, 'Push for Aboriginal ID tests'. It related how an allegedly Aboriginal leader had been disqualified from her Indigenous-specific and senior position in a State government department. Evidently advising the Federal Court on the matter, two prominent Aboriginal leaders Warren Mundine and Stephen Hagan maintained that 'the existing system to approve claims of Aboriginality was outdated and being rorted. …You can go to any town in the nation with a significant indigenous population and you'll see not one, but 'numerous white blackfellas claiming Aboriginality to get jobs and benefits that should go to our people. …We need a

P. Read (✉)
Australian National University, Acton, Australia
e-mail: peter.read@anu.edu.au

S. Maddison et al. (eds.), *The limits of settler colonial reconciliation*,
DOI 10.1007/978-981-10-2654-6_5

system that tests these claims so there is no chance of rorting and to ensure targeted taxpayer funds and jobs go to indigenous people' (*Weekend Australian* 2016).

The *Weekend Australian*, in common with much non-Aboriginal commentary on Aboriginal identity generally, made it seem easy—both to detect 'rorters' and for those asserting their Aboriginal descent to formally and legally establish their identity.

But in fact it is not at all easy. What I propose now is to investigate these questions at some historical length to explode these misconceptions. After more than forty years of working as a historian of Aboriginal Australia, it is clear to me that most non-Indigenous people do not hold anything of a full picture of Indigenous life since 1788. We have a general idea, drawing on oral history, tertiary studies, movies and TV programs; and of course Aboriginal people understand intuitively that theirs has been a very painful history indeed. Yet the purpose of this chapter is not to explore the painful past, but rather to illustrate the extraordinary variety of Indigenous historical experience that can and should contribute to our understanding of the 'white blackfellers', if that term means anything at all. It is my belief that we non-Aboriginal people cannot contribute much to reconciliation until we understand that variety of experience.

Conflicting Definitions

As usual, non-Aboriginal Australia is the root cause of most of the confusion. Imagine this situation in 1935: One morning a fair-skinned Australian of part-Indigenous descent, living on a legally designated Aboriginal Reserve, is ejected from a NSW rural hotel because he is, by one of the current definitions, an Aboriginal. When he asserts that he is Maori, he is allowed to remain. The hotel doesn't want trouble either (Ingram and Read 1984). He returns to his home on the reserve where he finds himself refused entry because, according to another definition (interpreted by the manager) he is not Aboriginal (APA 1909/1918). He protests that this is his home, that his wife lives inside the reserve fence, and that his children attend the reserve school. He tries to remove his children but is told he cannot do that because they are Aboriginal—they must be, the manager reasons, to be able to live on the reserve! He walks alone to the next town to sleep in the park where, apprehended for being an Aboriginal vagrant without obvious means of support, he is escorted by the police to the local Aboriginal reserve where he is received, although grudgingly, by its manager. It seems that he has become Aboriginal during the afternoon.

One morning in 1936, delaying his exit too late from a corner of the town where men gather at dawn looking for a job, this man is apprehended, under a new (1936) definition of Aboriginality, under what amounts to suspicion of his being Aboriginal and ordered out of town (APA 1936). When World War II breaks out he tries to enlist but is told he cannot do so because he is Aboriginal. He goes interstate and joins up there as a non-Aboriginal soldier. After the war he tries to travel overseas but is told he cannot leave without a passport for which he must apply for permission from the Aborigines Protection Board. He tries to gain entrance to his town's Returned Servicemen's Club but is prohibited from doing so—even though he is a returned serviceman—because he is Aboriginal. His son, though supposed, under the National (Military) Service Act of 1964, to be exempt from compulsory military service because he is Aboriginal, is ordered by a magistrate to register for compulsory National Service even though he was in every other respect defined as Aboriginal (Jordens 1989).

In 1972 one of his younger children is called to the school office to be told he is to receive an Aboriginal Study Grant. A class teacher, and a fair few of the students, demand of him,'What gives you the right to call yourself Aboriginal?' (Radoll 2016a). In 1984 the student graduates with a Bachelor of Commerce, but is asked by people who don't know him how he can call himself Aboriginal when he has a university degree (Perkins 2001). He joins the NSW Public Service in an Indigenous-designated position, and applies for an Aboriginal Housing Loan. The loan is granted, but several months later his identity is challenged. 'Outed' as a 'white blackfeller' because of insufficient genealogical evidence of his identity, he is forced to resign from his Aboriginal-designated position.

The Whole Community is Non-aboriginal

The far-reaching consequences of constantly manipulated definitions of Aboriginality were not confined to individuals. Whole communities suffered. In 1924, utilising the 1918 definition of Aboriginality that excluded everyone except people of the full and half-descent (this is, 'full-bloods' and 'half-castes'), the NSW Aborigines Protection Board argued that it was not responsible for the 'dark people' camping on the outskirts, it seemed, of every town in the state, and about whom every white citizen seemed to be complaining. Bitter confrontations with town councils throughout NSW in the 1920s soon brought this specious nonsense to ruin: everyone in every town knew perfectly well who was Aboriginal, not by consulting the family trees but by skin colour, association and place of abode. The camps, irrespective of any hastily constructed legislation, clearly held Aboriginal people. The legal maze might be described as farcical were it not for the fact that in every confrontation between town council and Aborigines Protection Board in the 1920s, the Aborigines were caught in the cruel crossfire of definitions.

Thus in 1923 in Condobolin, in the mid-west of NSW, the Town Council was becoming increasingly concerned at the number of Aboriginal people camping on the outskirts of what had been regarded, until now, as a safe town for Aborigines to gather. At a fiery Council meeting an alderman lugubriously asserted, 'The blacks are getting thicker in the town'. The Board, trying to apply the 1918 definition of Aborigines as 'half-castes' and 'full-bloods' only, replied that it was sorry, but most of the people in the blacks camp were not its responsibility. Contrary to appearances, association and place of abode, they were not Aborigines! Council exploded, the Board climbed down. But not before Council resolved, in a chilling phrase, that 'necessary action' be taken to remove any Aboriginal people camping in the vicinity of the showground and the railway trucking yards. Where were they to go? The number of safe towns was diminishing very rapidly (Condobolin Council Minutes 1923–1924). In any country town, whether one associated with reserve, town camp or riverbank people, it was never easy to conceal one's identity. The only alternative for anyone who wished and was able to do so, was to travel to Sydney and disappear (Read 1988: 169–174).

Associating with other Aboriginal people in the cities did little to reinforce a secure identity. Soon the bush people would encounter those who are known as the Sydney 'Traditional Custodians', members of the Darug and Gundungurra, Gweagal, Gai-Mariagal, Guringai, Dharawal and Darkinjung peoples, those who had grown up in their own country, though frequently in the suburbs. Many were people who thought of themselves as Aboriginal, but while they had had not necessarily had their identity denied, had never had it absolutely confirmed.

The biggest Aboriginal population, the Darug, clustered in their own country in western Sydney. In 1900 the two biggest Darug town camps were an area known as 'Colebee's land', close to the old Blacktown Institution site established for Aboriginal children by Governor Macquarie in 1814, and at Rooty Hill, on nearby suburban land owned by the Darug identity William Locke. Locke allowed his farming block to be used as an urban town camp for his relatives' cottages and humpies, and a base for Aboriginal Inland Mission activities, and as an Aborigines Protection Board ration distribution point.

Here daily life was decidedly insecure. In 1908 in Rooty Hill two children died of influenza after heavy rains. Concerned about community health, Board officials removed at least six children to private homes or the United Aborigines Mission institution at Bomaderry. Threatened, in poor health and persecuted, the people began to leave. The tin mission church closed in 1910. To re-signify what everyone already knew to be the dangerously impermanent nature of town camps, the remaining members of William Locke's family, and others, were finally evicted from the site in 1920.

Where were they to go? Some vanished into the farming communities up and down the river, some moved to the inner city suburbs. Many chose the other large town camp familiar to them, at this time mainly occupied by Gundangara (south western Sydney) families, just outside Katoomba, called the Gully. Until about 1905, Katoomba had seemed to be a safe town for Aborigines: but as the refugee population of the Gully grew, so in proportion grew hostile official interference. Rapidly it became unsafe in the Gully as well. Seven children of one family were removed in 1905. By 1958, no less than 27 Aboriginal children had been removed from the Gully. Threats of child removal could be as deadly as separation itself. Even in the 1950s parents might be told that if they did not leave the Gully, their children would be taken (Read 2015; Johnson 2007). Colin Locke's parents, ordered out by the Katoomba Shire council, settled in the water catchment area of Blackheath up the road with several related Darug families. 'If the white government car comes', his mother told him, 'grab your brothers, run into the bush, and don't stop running' (Locke 2016).

We can understand now why an urban identity, never as secure as in the managed reserves in the interior, could be further weakened by voluntary dis-association. Let us track some other ways in which identity might slide.

Conscious of the stain of Aboriginality in the wider community, some people of fair complexion, wishing to get ahead and lacking the imposed collective identity of reserve life, settled incognito in other parts of Sydney. They began to stay out of the sun, wear big hats, cover their ankles, and say nothing about their grandparents. They intended to leave their Aboriginality behind, and did so. In the end they came to represent only a question mark in the Aboriginal family genealogies.

Much more commonly, though, a fading urban identity was more incipient and in some ways circumstantial. In the 1930s and 1940s, working class suburbs like Balmain, Glebe and Botany were areas of enormous ethnic diversity in which Aboriginality, or any other ethnicity, simply was not thought to be important. The Dharawal (south eastern coastal) woman Margaret Slowgrove, growing up in Botany in the 1940s, knew of her descent, but an ethnic identity was irrelevant in a dockside community that included Malays, Maoris, Chinese, Torres Strait Islanders, Japanese, South Sea Islanders, Filipinos and Lascars.[1](Slowgrove and Maber 2016; Hedges and Lewis 2016).

Shame brought a very low concept of self-worth. Adopted into a white family, as a child Pam Young used to 'walk under the water drains to the city and go and get the groceries at Woolworths and Waltons, always walking, come back, go under the water drains and walk to my [adopting] parents' place. It was safer for me to do that because I was so ashamed of my colour and my identity' (Young 2016).

Association, even linguistically, was hazardous. Frances Bodkin recalls speaking Dharawal at home only at night when the blinds were drawn (Bodkin 2016). Carol Cooper believes that her parents at Katoomba were ordered never to lock their doors to enable the police to enter at any time to check if English was being spoken (Cooper 2013). Even showing an interest in an Aboriginal identity might be discouraged within the family. June McGrath, who in 2012 was the President of the NSW Link Up Corporation, grew up in Bexley. All her life, she says, her sisters put her down for 'daring' to identify as Aboriginal (McGrath 2016). As a child in Brisbane, Pat Eatock was ordered to play on the other 'black' side of the divided school playground after her father, of obviously Aboriginal descent, came to visit the school. Twenty-five years later, living in a Housing Commission house in Mt Pritchard, near Liverpool, she casually revealed her Indigenous descent to her neighbour, who promptly told her to leave the house, refusing permission for her son to continue to play with Eatock's son (Eatock 2016). Karen Maber, of Dharawal descent, studied in her primary school in Kogarah just hard enough to keep herself in the middle of the class roll, and sat as far out of sight as possible, at

[1]Margaret Slowgrove and Karen Maber, 'The track to grandma's', video interview, historyofaboriginalsydney.edu.au; see other videos also by Mrs Slowgrove and Maber 2016).

the back. 'I really loved school. But I didn't want to come first in anything. Too much attention … I would rather not do well or I'd have to go up to get a certificate.' She kept her Aboriginality to herself until the class, watching a documentary, accused the filmed Aboriginal people of cruelty. Upset, she confided her identity to her teacher. 'Don't worry dear,' was the reply, 'Nobody will know.' Karen carries the hurt to this day (Maber 2016). Peter Radoll received a hard time from both teachers and other boys at Colyton High School after he received his first Aboriginal Studies Grant cheque in the 1980s (Radoll 2016b). His mother, at length acquiring loan funds from the Western Sydney Foundation for Aboriginal Affairs to buy a house, entered the Bank of New South Wales at St Mary's to transfer the purchase funds to her account, to find the manager refusing to allow the procedure: she could not be Aboriginal, he declared, she was not dark enough (Radoll 2016c). The Gai-Mariagal elder Dennis Foley recalled that his uncles could fish all day with a rod or line in the Terrigal lagoon, but as fast as an Indigenous fishing spear appeared, so did someone try to prevent its use or to move the fishermen on (Foley 2001). The historian of the Gully, Dianne Johnson, observed the maxim that has guided Aboriginal people in all of Sydney, and much of urban Australia: 'The need for most of them to blend in, accompanied by their reluctance to put themselves forward unduly, is still paramount. These are survival skills instilled in them with childhood' (Johnson 2007: 121).

Survival skills implied not necessarily denial but simply a failure to mention an Indigenous descent to anybody who did not need to know. They meant discouraging one's relatives from visiting, and especially from camping on the lawn. No hanging your washing on the fence, throwing your empties about, leaving a broken down car in the street, shouting loudly, sleeping in the back yard on a wire bed frame, cooking in a camp oven, or using a car seat as an armchair. That's what blackfellers do. Keep the yard and inside the house immaculate, try to make it the best in the street. That's what whitefellers do. Conscious of the tensions in belonging, the generation of children in Katoomba were taught little by their parents, and learned not to ask questions.

> Sharyn Halls: One of my Dad's (Lenny McNally's) main things, doing things in the proper way. 'Keep your mouth shut and act white' … And when Dad made my brother Lenny and I not to talk to any of our relatives in the late 1950s, that's exactly what we did. We did not talk or have any contact with anyone who had Aboriginal blood. It was dangerous and he knew that we could have been taken away … You just kept your mouth shut to protect your family and you denied everything. You watch, you listen, you learn. That's what he said.
>
> Ann McNally [Sharyn's sister-in-law] Keep your mouth shut and act white. That was his big thing. He was so particular. Even going to their place for dinner! I'd go there for dinner even as an adult, you'd get whacked over the knuckles if you had your elbows on the table or of you left the lid off something…
>
> Mary: I was completely washed white (Johnson 2007).

Nor should we imagine that it is easy to turn the tide simply to declare one's identity openly. The Sydney Darug man Chris Tobin,

> People need to be encouraged, and I get that people don't put their hand up to say they're Aboriginal, I really do, gosh, who wants an argument. You can tell [people] you're Macedonian, you tell them you're Croatian or whatever, no one's going to give you an argument, but gosh you tell someone you're Aboriginal: 'No you're not!' Jesus—all right, well. So I certainly think the generation before us, they [didn't] want to have that argument with their friends thank you very much, so they just keep quiet. I love that today in our world ... that you can proudly be an Aboriginal person, the Darug community's very accepting, that's a huge step I think. (Tobin 2016)

A long-lost, then newly discovered, identity can produce some odd anomalies: In Sydney, the elder sister of an eighty year old man (whose name I leave anonymous here) dies in 2007. Discovering some genealogical papers in the usual post-burial clean-up, and curious about the obscure birthplaces of certain ancestors, the man dimly recalls, seventy years earlier, being told not to play with a boomerang lying about the house. With the help of friends, Trove and Ancestry.com, he discovers an Aboriginal connection—and is delighted![2] A local historian calls him the missing link in a genealogical puzzle. The district Reconciliation Group is overjoyed. They invite him to their meetings and call him Uncle. Within a year Uncle is presenting thirty Welcome to Countries a year at everything from school fetes to Sorry Day.[3] Non-Aborigines love him because he is so polite, so lacking in resentment compared to the sometimes uncooperative local Aborigines whose memories are very long.

Children Losing Identity

Child Welfare legislation was manipulated ruthlessly to arrange that children should fall into its net. I again cite instances from the NSW Legislation but examples can be drawn from any Australian state.

In 1883, when the Aborigines Protection Board is formed, it possesses no legal powers to remove children as 'Aborigines'. It has to fill its childrens' dormitory at Warangesda on the Murrumbidgee River by stick and carrot: stick, such as stopping food to those who will not allow their children to go to the Aboriginal children's dormitory; and carrot—by allowing parents who permit them to go into the dormitory to stay on the reserve. Parents who want to leave without their children are offered free rail passes. If they insist on taking their children with them, they are warned that they thereby render them liable for prosecution under the Neglected Children and Juvenile Offenders Act of 1905, and may be removed from them (APA Regulations 1914; Neglected Children Act 1905).

---

[2]Trove is an on-line newspaper-searching facility offered by the National Library of Australia.

[3]'Welcome to Country' is a short address that may be given at any ceremony from a national gathering to a school fete, in which a local Aboriginal representative welcomes visitors on behalf of ancestors past and present.

But in 1909 a simple charge of being a neglected child was clumsy and unreliable since a magistrate could simply declare a child not to be neglected, and release her. So in 1909 the definition of Aboriginality was amended so that Aborigines were now to be 'persons having an admixture of Aboriginal blood who had applied for rations or were living on a reserve' (APA 1909a, b). The problem now arose that parents not living on the reserve and who had not applied for rations were technically not Aborigines and ought to be prevented from entering—yet the Board wanted their children. Reserve managers with meagre budgets were reluctant to admit such parents even when ordered by the constable, especially if they were thought to be troublemakers. This wider, 1909 definition, based on the twin pillars of descent and circumstance, soon was found unworkable since if children were Aboriginal then so, clearly, were their parents. Such parents could demand entrance to a reserve just at the moment when station managers were under orders from Sydney to reduce every possible cost by not taking in, feeding and housing any new arrivals. So in 1912, in another clumsy correction, the definition was widened to include 'quadroons' and 'octoroons', that is, people with one Aboriginal grand parent or an Aboriginal great-grandparent, a dragnet which might, as late as 1960, have included half the population of an average country town! But in 1909 a Magistrate might still decline to co-operate with the local Board official, if a child before him did not look uncontrollable or ill-nourished (Lyons 1981). So in 1915 yet another definition was tried. In the re-formulation, Aboriginal children were *by definition* deemed to be neglected if their 'moral or physical welfare' was threatened. (APA 1909/1915) No appearance before a potentially uncooperative magistrate was necessary. The problem remained that adults whom the government wished to designate 'non-Aborigines' still remained living on the reserves claiming rations. In 1918, as we have already seen in Condobolin, the NSW legislative draftsman tried yet another tack to make Aboriginality much more restricted by simply contracting the Board's control only to 'half-castes' and 'full-bloods' and excluding 'quadroons' (having an Aboriginal grandparent) and 'octoroons' (having an Aboriginal great-grandparent (APA 1909/1918). The disadvantage of that, from the viewpoint of the authorities, was that children living in an Aboriginal camp or clearly of Aboriginal descent might not legally be apprehended. How to get round that? Head Office suggested to its officers that when they identified an Aboriginal child whom they wanted to remove (by the 'eyesight' definition rather than that of the Statute book) then they should try to persuade their counterpart officer in the Department of Child Welfare to formally register the child as white and have him or her received into the state welfare homes like Mittagong rather than the Aboriginal Homes like Cootamundra (former officer, pers. comm. 1981). That served the dual aims of faster assimilation and saving Departmental money. Alternatively, the child might be offered for adoption as non-Aboriginal, even though she had been initially removed *because* she was an Aboriginal child living with Aboriginal parents within an Aboriginal extended family on an Aboriginal reserve. The adopting parents might be told the child was Asian or southern European—which again served the dual aims of faster assimilation and money saved.

The implications of such definition-bending on today's controversies will now be becoming obvious. An adult did not, of course, know under which Regulation or Amendment or Statute that he had been judged, as a child, to be non-Aboriginal. Aboriginal parents were not told that their baby had been actually committed as a non-Aboriginal Ward of the State and was even now being offered for adoption as an Indian! Nor did their child. The consequences of growing up in ignorance of one's identity and history carried consequences for decades and through later generations.

Here are two instances of how the contradictory and cynically manipulated legislation might affect identity for decades and through several generations. In 1980, some 60 years after the legislation, an Aboriginal welfare worker applied to the state institution at Mittagong to speak with the Aboriginal children to be told there was none. Entry obtained at length from the NSW Youth and Community Services Minister Frank Walker, she met with no less than 30 Aboriginal children, some of whom denied their Aboriginality despite their appearance, while another screamed at the sight of the dark-skinned worker (Attending Officer, pers. comm., 1994). A second example: It was not unusual for a little child who had been removed as a toddler, to be recognized decades later in one of the urban areas that Aboriginal people frequented, such as Redfern (Sydney) or Fitzroy (Melbourne). One was Joy Williams, fostered at birth in 1942, born to her mother Doretta who had been herself declared a State Ward in 1926. Back on the Cowra reserve, Joy's aunties and uncles heard the news that Joy had been spotted in Sydney, pondered her absence and surmised—'She must be too flash, no longer wanting to associate with her own family'. They did not realise that their lost child knew neither her birthplace nor her mother's name nor her genetic descent, and in any case was too frightened to return. 'What if my family rejects me?' Joy asked herself. It was so hard to imagine life on the other side (Read 2009).

In 1980 Oomera Edwards and I established the organization Link-Up Aboriginal Corporation to reunite the removed children, now adults, with their families.[4] Several had only recently discovered they were Aboriginal rather than Indian or Maori. Among the clients who came to us wishing to meet their family and re-embrace their Aboriginality we found much apprehension and fear. Among the communities with whom we reunited our clients we found joy, but frequently a complete lack of comprehension of the pressures their lost children had experienced *not* to identify. Joy William's reunion, for example, was joyful but tense, and her relations with the Cowra reserve remained forever brittle (Read 2009). Through Link-Up and by other means, the Stolen Generations adults, lost for so long in the big cities, asked plaintively

[4]Link-Up (NSW) Aboriginal Corporation is now in its thirty sixth year and been modelled in several other states. More than 4000 clients have returned to their families through its agency.

For my spirit and culture to be as one
I must go back to where it all begun
The child of one must be taken in hand
And shown through her ancestral land
Where the old people will heal her heart
As her culture she becomes a part (McLeod 2005).

A Confident and Unchallengeable Identity

From the middle 1940s, another large section of the Aboriginal rural community, those of secure and proud identity, were leaving their traditional country to gather in ever-increasing numbers in suburbs close to the CBD of every state capital. They wanted work. In Sydney they settled near the factories in Redfern, Alexandria, Newtown and Mascot. Soon they were to meet and mix with the Sydney traditional custodians of a less secure identity, plus the people described above whose skin colour had historically made them most vulnerable to the manipulation of the legal definitions of Aboriginality.

Whence arose such confidence shared by the 1940s migrants? Consider this incident in 1893 on the Warangesda managed reserve on the Murrumbidgee. The manager confided in the station diary:

> There was another bother with MRS SWIFT today. She openly accuses FANNY HELAND of being enceinte [pregnant] & told the girls in the Dorm they ought all to laugh at her & while she was at the washtub yesterday called her a sulky looking pig. FANNY came & told manager this AM & when she spoke to MRS SWIFT she said it was all false, that she did not use any such expression. The manager asked her if she had ever said of NANCY MURRAY that she was a Chinese looking thing. Which she indignantly denied but Buckley said he heard her use the expression and FANNY HELAND says she heard her call NANCY a yellow Chinaman. And called the manager a hypocrite and that all the whites were a lot of hypocrites. After the bother MRS SWIFT poked her tongue at Fanny and made faces at her. NANCY MURRAY says she said to the girls in the Dorm she would put the people against the manager, & as far as the manager has been able to find has not done so[5](Warangesda Diary 1884).

The extract shows the ready potential for a quarrel to escalate into an 'us against them' mentality that served to reinforce identity through a consciousness of difference. The imposition of salaried managers and punitive regulations on reserves served only to heighten resentment of the Whites through a strong and cohesive collective identity. Seventy years later this sense of togetherness against the world was crystalized by Les Coe of the Erambie managed reserve at Cowra, summarising his contempt for managerial authority

> That's right, go into your house, look under your bloody bed. Wife could be in bed or something like that. Jeez they were bastards some of them. They tried to come into my

[5]Warangesda Manager's Mission Diary, 7 June 1984, typescript in National Library of Australia.

> place when I was living there. I jobbed a couple of the bloody police. I stopped them from coming in. 'If you want to talk to me, talk to me out the bloody door.' Any excuse at all, you know, just to stand over you all the bloody time. Didn't treat you like people, but treated you like bloody mongrel dogs (Coe and Read 1984).

Nobody much railed like that in Sydney. Except on the La Perouse reserve, Sydney Aborigines had no experience of reserve management—or managers! Fortunately for them they were unaffected by the kind of confrontation quoted above; but—in the terms of this essay—they were unfortunate in not having an aggressive solidarity imposed on them. In the cities, they endured the daily insults, challenges and punishments not for *being* Aboriginal, but for openly *asserting* their Indigenous identity.

Run forward 20 years, to 1960 where in the west the traditional Sydney custodians are being swamped by Aborigines from the bush. In these developing western suburbs a secret army of knowledge holders is forming. These bush people are sure of who they are, though unsure how their identity will be received by their neighbours and workmates. Dennis Foley, a Gai-Mariagal man growing up at Chester Hill, could identify house after house occupied in the 1960s by Aboriginal families. There were dozens—as many, in fact, as made up a typical reserve! Identity, though, was not a matter of announcing one's tribe or language group to the world. It was enough to answer the question, 'Are you Aboriginal', with a belligerent 'Yeah' (Or 'no') 'What of it?' until the questioners identified themselves as sympathetic (Foley 2016a). Like an unseen army, an Indigenous identity remained strong among the secret sharers. The Aborigines of the western suburbs knew or guessed who was Aboriginal, but kept the knowledge underground. It was a different identity to today's identity, but it was recognizable and genuine. Yet because it was not openly asserted, Sydney Aborigines living in other suburbs might not know identity outside their own district. 'I've been living here since the 1970s and I've never heard of that family'.

We have at last arrived at the three point nexus that lies at the root of the current Aboriginal identity crisis. The first, as have seen, are the Traditional Custodians joined by those people who have always assumed themselves to be Aboriginal, but whose identity cannot be firmly established either geographically and genealogically. The second is occupied by the stolen generations, anxious to re-connect, conscious of their ignorance, unsure of their place, sometimes only recently aware of their descent. The third are those whose identity is assured, either with a strong rural or urban history who lead the Indigenous attack upon 'rorters' and 'white blackfellers'.

Identities in Conflict

Nowhere was the division clearer than when Sally Morgan published her best-selling autobiography *My Place* in 1987. Morgan recounted how as an adult she finally discovered her Indigenous descent, the meaning of years of silence, the ambiguous behavior of her aunts. Non-Aboriginal readers embraced it enthusiastically. Aborigines, generally, did not. The long-time political activist Jackie Huggins wrote

> The greatest weakness of *My Place*, is that it presents Aboriginality as something that can be easily understood by a white audience and white literary world. It therefore represents an act of passing which is a horrendous crime in Aboriginal circles: 'We vindictively remember those who have passed and… can never forget nor forgive these traitors'. Sally and her mother and grandmother have cooperated with the enemy (Docker 1998; Huggins 1993).

A second example of the long legacy of definition-bending to destabilise and divide communities, lay potent in the 1983 *NSW Aboriginal Land Rights Act* (*ALRA* 1983). Local Aboriginal Land Councils were to be created out of Aboriginal populations in defined areas. Such was the lack of confidence to openly identify that sometimes the first lists of membership contained no individuals at all from the land of the actual language group on which the council was formed. Dennis Foley explained why not:

> [I]n the 1980s, urban Aborigines people were not fully conversant with the new opportunities that the Act bestowed upon them, nor savvy enough about the workings of the new legal system. There came a lag in the granting of these opportunities and in local resolution as to how to respond to them (Foley 2007).

The legislation, well-intentioned as it may have been, was rooted in more than a century of cynical legalistic meddling. It carried the potential for much distress.

The deadly three part nexus was soon reflected in the transactions of some of the Land Councils. Majority urban membership came from the self-confident, bush people, secure of identity, knowing absolutely who they were. Particularly before the formal Apology of Prime Minister Rudd to the Stolen Generations in 2007, they did not understand why the stolen children were unsure of who they were. Nor did they understand the initial reluctance of the local descent groups to push themselves forward, or how they had culturally survived by keeping their heads down and their identity clandestine. Some were contemptuous of the necessary urban survival skills practised and refined for many decades.

The deadly fault in the *Land Rights Act* was that, instead of encompassing all the Aboriginal people of the district, it could be used by the majority membership—those of secure and unchallenged identity—to prevent the registration of Aboriginal people *without* the rural reserve experience, that is to say, to prevent the registration of stolen generations, local descent groups and urban Traditional Custodians and those whose genealogies were uncertain. At least one Local Aboriginal Land Council declared that it refused to recognise not just individuals but whole extended families of claimants. The Deerubbin Council (Hawkesbury River Local Aboriginal Land Council) asserted its right under the *Aboriginal Land Rights Act* to represent all Aboriginal people living in the area, irrespective of their place of origin. In 2012 its website claimed to support 'genuine assertions and respectful recognition of traditional ownership (and formal recognition of native title) wherever they occur'. Then followed the caveat:

> Deerubbin LALC [Local Aboriginal Land Council] is skeptical, however, that there are Aboriginal people alive who credibly lay claim to traditional ownership of the area (Deerubbin LALC 2013).

A Darug elder Colin Workman commented

> We were the only nation to have been invaded twice .... First by Cook when he got here, second by the Indigenous people of the rest of Australia (Workman 2006).

An Identity Test?

Hagan and Mundine maintained that 'you can go to any town in the nation with a significant indigenous population and you'll see not one, but numerous white blackfellas claiming Aboriginality to get jobs and benefits that should go to our people. ...We need a system that tests these claims.' We may well ask, at the end of this discussion, who are 'our people'? For as long as elderly people have no birth record, or family genealogies are lost or concealed, or family knowledge is truncated by the arbitrary removal of whole communities, and while many hundreds of stolen children know very little of their family history—it is hard to see what sort of a test this could be.

Sometimes it needs an Aboriginal historian to really grasp the tensions felt by her forebears. Here Queenslander Judy Wickes muses on why her grandfather chose to apply for a Certificate of Exemption, in effect to abandon his heritage and discard his older relatives so that his descendants might have a better chance in the world of the whitefellers:

> For my grandfather, the decision to apply for the certificate of exemption must have been a difficult one to make. Choosing to either to live 'under the Act' or fend for himself and his family in the wider community was something that he had to consider carefully. I wonder if I could have gone down the same road as my grandfather and grandmother in 1926, and been as brave, progressive and enterprising as they? Today, however, I can see their reasoning, concerning what they wanted to achieve for their future and have seen the loss and heartache resulting from gaining the certificate of exemption, [i.e. the consequent loss of the family's Aboriginal identity] would he have taken the same road again? Nevertheless, it seems clear that he insisted his daughter and my mother, Gwen, always be conscious of the rules and regulations pertaining to the certificate of exemption, and the consequences for her family if they were not obeyed. (Wickes 2010)

Australians need a much deeper historical knowledge of why Aboriginal Australia is as divided as it is. We cannot arbitrarily decide with whom we should negotiate. Our part should be to provide the information that will help the Aboriginal community leaders come to their own best decision.

References

ALRA. (1983). *Aboriginal Land Rights Act* (NSW) 1983, 42 of 1983

APA. (1909). *Aborigines Protection Act* 1909 (NSW) ss 3(8), 1; *Aborigines Protection Act,* Amendment No. 32.

APA (1909/1915) APA. (1909), s, 13 (a) as Amended APA Amending Act 1915 ss 2(1) (a) 4 as amended by Aborigines Protection (Amending) Act 1918 s 2 (1) (a); *as Amended 1918* ss 2(1) (a), 4

APA (1909/1918) APA. (1909), s, 13 (a) as Amended APA Amending Act 1915 ss 2(1) (a) 4 as amended by Aborigines Protection (Amending) Act 1918 s 2 (1) (a); as Amended 1918 ss 2(1) (a)

APA, Regulations and Instructions issued to station managers, 1914–1924, Records of the Aboriginal Protection and Welfare Boards, State Archives of NSW.

Bodkin, F. (2016). 'I was told we spoke Spanish', video interview, historyofaboriginalsydney.edu.au. Accessed 15 Feb 2016

Coe, L., & Read, P. (Eds.). (1984). *Down there with me on the Cowra Mission* (p. 74). London: Pergamon.

Cooper, C. (2013). Interview with Julia Torpey, Katoomba.

Deerubbin Local Aboriginal Land Council, www.deerubbin.org.au/Final-CLBP-290609.pdf. Accessed 5 Oct 2013.

Docker, J. (1998). 'Recasting Sally Morgan's *My Place*: The fictionality of identity and the phenomenology of the converso', http://press.anu.edu.au/wpcontent/uploads/2011/02/4_docker_hr1_1998.pdf)

Eatock, P. (2016). 'We never spoke again', video interview, historyofaboriginalsydney.edu.au. Accessed 15 Feb 2016.

Foley, D. (2007). What has native title done for the urban Koori in New South Wales who is a Traditional Custodian? In B. Smith & F. Morphy (Eds.), *The Social effects of native title recognition, translation, coexistence* (Vol. Centre for Aboriginal Economic Research Monograph 27, pp. 166–179). Canberra: ANU Epress.

Foley, D. (2001). Interview, Narrabeen.

Foley, D. (2016). 'From Redfern to Chester Hill', video interview, historyofaboriginalsydney.edu.au. Accessed 15 February 2016.

Huggins, J. (1993). Always was always will be. *Australian Historical Studies, 100*, 459–466.

Hedges, M., & Lewis, C. (2016). 'Evading the authorities'; video, historyofaboriginalsydney.edu.au. Accessed 15 Feb 2016.

Ingram, L., & Read, P. (1984). *Down there with me on the Cowra Mission* (p. 145). Sydney: Pergamon.

Johnson, D. (2007). *Sacred waters. The story of the blue mountains gully traditional owners* (Vol. 121, pp. 148–150). Sydney: Halstead Press.

Jordens, A.-M. (1989). An administrative nightmare. Aboriginal Conscription 1965–72. *Aboriginal History, 13*, 121–134.

Lyons, M. (1981). Interview by author.

Locke, C. (2016). 'Catchment Kids', video interview, historyofaboriginalsydney.edu.au. Accessed 15 Feb 2016.

Maber, K. (2016). 'Memories of Kogarah Primary School', video interview, historyofaboriginalsydney.edu.au, Accessed 15 Feb 2016.

McGrath, J. (2016). 'I'm so proud', video interview, historyofaboriginalsydney.edu.au, Accessed 15 Feb 2016.

McLeod. (2005). 'The yearning of my soul'. In J.J. Williams, (ed.), *Love, life and pain*, Link Up (NSW) Aboriginal Corp., Sydney, 2007, 34.

Minutes (1923–4). APA Minutes of Meetings, and Condobolin Municipal Council meeting reports in *Lachlander*.

Neglected Children and Juvenile Offenders Act. (1905) (NSW) s 5, definition of 'neglected child'.

Perkins, C. (2001). Personal communication
Radoll, P. (2016a). 'My uncles gave me complete freedom', video interview, historyofaboriginalsydney.edu.au. Accessed 15 Feb. 2016.
Radoll, P. (2016b). 'It was here that I realized that I was different', video interview, historyofaboriginalsydney.edu.au. Accessed 15 Feb 2016.
Radoll, P. (2016c). 'The downside of owning an Aboriginal House', video interview, historyofaboriginalsydney.edu.au. Accessed 15 Feb 2016.
Read, P. (1988). *A hundred years war, 1998* (pp. 69–74). Canberra: ANU Press.
Read, P. (2009). *Tripping over feathers. Scenes in the life of Joy Janaka Wiradjuri Williams. A stolen generations narrative*. Perth: UWA Press.
Read, P. (2015). Dispossession is a legitimate experience. In Ann McGrath & Mary-Anne Jebb (Eds.), *Long history deep time* (pp. 124–125). Canberra: ANU Press and Aboriginal History Inc.
Slowgrove, M, & Maber, K. (2016). 'The track to grandma's', video interview, historyofaboriginalsydney.edu.au; see other videos also by Mrs Slowgrove.
Tobin, C. (2016). 'It takes a lot of courage to identify', video interview, historyofaboriginalsydney.edu.au
Warangesda Manager's Mission Diary. (1884). 7 June 1984 typescript in National Library of Australia.
Weekend Australian. (2016). 20–21 February 2016, 1.
Wickes, J. (2010). 'Never really heard of it': the certificate of exemption and lost identity. In F. Peters-Little, A. Haebich, & P. Read (Eds.), *Aboriginal biography and autobiography, aboriginal history* (pp. 73–91). Canberra: ANU Epress.
Workman, C. (2006). 'We were invaded twice', video interview, historyofaboriginalsydney.edu.au. Accessed 15 Feb 2016.
Young, P. (2016). 'No more a little shame job', video interview, historyofaboriginalsydney.edu.au. Accessed 15 Feb 2016.

Part II
Testing the Limits of Settler Colonial Relationships

Chapter 6
Colonising White Innocence: Complicity and Critical Encounters

Alissa Macoun

Abstract This paper argues that white settler researchers seeking to engage with Indigenous sovereignty or contribute to antiracist and decolonising struggles should approach these critical encounters with and through awareness of our complicity in ongoing racism and colonialism, which involves appreciating our locations and limits. A discourse of colonizing white innocence circulates in policy, academic and other spaces to reinforce and obscure progressive white investments in maintaining power relationships generated by ongoing colonising racist violence through presenting particular individuals, groups and institutions as non-problematic, and so not complicit in historical and contemporary violence. This foundational assumption allows white settlers to assume that our contributions are benevolent or in the interests of Indigenous people and that we ourselves transcend our own locations within racist and colonising systems of rule, in so doing emphasising our legitimacy and authority in relation to Indigenous people. Complicity establishes both a political responsibility and an intellectual imperative to understand and contest systems of domination in which we are enmeshed through deliberate respectful engagements with those who have experiences, knowledges and forms of authority that we do not and cannot possess.

An ethic of incommensurability, which guides moves that unsettle innocence, stands in contrast to aims of reconciliation, which motivate settler moves to innocence. Reconciliation is about rescuing settler normalcy, about rescuing a settler future. Reconciliation is concerned with questions of *what will decolonisation look like? What will happen after abolition? What will be the consequences of decolonisation for the settler?* Incommensurability acknowledges that these questions need not, and perhaps cannot, be answered in order for decolonisation to exist as a framework.

A. Macoun (✉)
University of Queensland, Brisbane, Australia
e-mail: a.macoun@uq.edu.au

S. Maddison et al. (eds.), *The limits of settler colonial reconciliation*,
DOI 10.1007/978-981-10-2654-6_6

> We want to say, first, that decolonisation is not obliged to answer those questions - decolonisation is not accountable to settlers, or settler futurity. Decolonisation is accountable to Indigenous sovereignty (Tuck and Yang 2012: 35).

> Assuming one's criticality can be a way of not admitting one's complicity. I think complicity is a starting point. We are implicated in the worlds that we critique; being critical does not suspend any such implication (Ahmed 2013).

Some white progressives interested in justice for Indigenous peoples tend to see our great political challenge to be mobilising the goodwill of other non-Indigenous people; sharing what we know and believe in order to turn those that are uneducated or unwilling or inactive into allies willing to add the strength of their numbers to Indigenous struggles. We imagine our work to be dealing with the impact of a violent and misguided colonial past, sometimes apologising for the role of our ancestors and institutions in that history, and repairing the damage caused by our predecessors in order to build a future founded in equality and justice.

This story is powerful and appealing. From the reconciliation movement to Rudd's apology, it is a story white progressives tell often. Often we're our own protagonists, but sometimes Indigenous people are allowed speaking parts. We can cling tightly to this story, even—and perhaps especially—when we can see its limits. In this chapter, I want to explore some political limits of this story.

Every person in Australia is always-already engaged with and in race-based colonial systems of rule and what many of us consider to be problematic political relationships; some of us have more opportunities to ignore or evade this reality than others. No politically pure or righteous way of being, acting or thinking as a white person or non-Indigenous person can exempt us from our political context, even though it is a context we collectively create, recreate, and may hope to change.

We declare ourselves innocent when we assume that non-Indigenous people are basically benevolent bystanders to racism and colonialism, just requiring additional information or education in order to do good. We declare ourselves innocent when we assume that we educated white progressives are fundamentally different from other non-Indigenous people, the solution to a problem that lies in the hearts and minds of others rather than in our own institutions, knowledges, and practices. We declare ourselves innocent when we acknowledge a racist colonial past but assume a separation between this past and our racist colonial present. We declare ourselves innocent when we see ourselves as agents of progressive futurity and not also of colonial institutions and racial power.

As Moreton-Robinson (2000a, 2004) demonstrates, the project of recuperating individual and collective white virtue is not just the preserve of conservatives, nationalists, or obvious colonial apologists. Progressives too are often invested in particular kinds of stories about the colonial project, and its eventual completion and conclusion through benevolent white acts (Strakosch and Macoun 2012). As others have noted, white settlers who identify as critical thinkers or progressives can be particularly invested in being good people, in doing good things, in engaging with destructive histories or problematic power structures, and thus most invested in our own innocence (Nicoll 2000; Ahmed 2004).

While a range of discursive strategies may emphasise white virtue—it is possible to consider claims to religious, civilizational, or economic worthiness and superiority in this vein, for example—I argue that one of many ways white virtue is recuperated and preserved is through a construction of colonising white innocence. In this paper particularly, I am interested in exploring some ways that claims to innocence in relation to racial and colonial oppression might shape the critical academic and political contributions of progressive white settlers when we seek to engage with Indigenous sovereignty or contribute to antiracist and decolonising struggles.[1]

First, I outline a number of premises and assumptions informing this work, and define the concept of colonising white innocence. I demonstrate the persistent deployment of colonising white innocence (particularly claims to benevolence and transcendence) in recent Australian policy discourses, and ways that this construction provides legitimacy and authority to the settler state. I then question whether processes that I have critiqued at a policy level may also operate as foundational assumptions in my own and other critical academic work, allowing white settler researchers to assert legitimacy and authority in relation to Indigenous people. This is not a confessional, although I use myself and my own work as a heuristic; rather, it is a located argument in favour of limits and in favour of complicity. I argue white settler researchers should approach critical encounters with and through our complicity in ongoing white colonialism, and that this involves attempting to appreciate our own political and epistemological limits.

I am not posing solutions to the violent colonial relationships that continue to form the foundation of Australian political community or offering strong prescriptions on what other non-Indigenous people must do. This isn't because I am wedded to a bleak future—in fact, I think it possible there could be many paths in many places through which better futures and relationships could be formed. My project here is significantly more modest however; to grapple with the conflicts we are engaged in, to try and understand them and how they perpetuate, and to think about strategies for keeping these conflicts visible in the face of ongoing white attempts to erase, suppress or even to transcend them.

[1]There are a lot of 'we' statements in this chapter, which speak to my own racial and political location. This is consistent with the focus of this paper on political and academic responsibilities and relationships that I have and share with others in broadly similar locations, although it is not intended to imply that all readers share this positioning.

Categories, Languages, Premises and Promises

While all non-Indigenous people in Australia are tied to the fiction of terra nullius, whites are granted kinds of belonging to and within colonial categories that are not available or available only in mitigated forms to non-white others (Moreton-Robinson 2003; Hage 2000). Speaking about colonialism without speaking about race allows those of us who are white to evade our greater benefit from and connection to colonialism. Speaking about race without speaking about colonialism can default to a multiculturalism that naturalises the state and its institutions, erases Indigenous sovereignty and incommensurability and reduces our ability to understand and contest systems of race that perform colonialism's work (Moreton-Robinson 2015: 47–61; Singh 2007).

An emphasis on the way settler colonialism's global political categories are embodied, experienced and enacted in racialised and locally specific forms may additionally help counter tendencies to imbue settler colonialism as an analytic with a neutral descriptive authority, despite the location of this framework as a body of raced knowledge emerging from and authorised by white institutions and academic practices (see Macoun and Strakosch 2013; Snelgrove et al. 2014). This underlines the importance of engaging with Indigenous and other knowledges that may operate from different ontological premises and so may know paths to different kinds of political futures (Coburn et al 2013). This is also crucial in attending to both colonialism's impact and attribution (we live colonialism, we are agents in colonial struggles, we do it differently depending on our locations and embodiments). However, settler colonialism's emphasis on the material political and economic drivers of white colonialism and the political relationships it generates reflects the entrenched and structural nature of systems within which we operate and illuminates political interests that non-Indigenous people bring to relationships with Indigenous peoples (see Wolfe 2001, 2006; Veracini 2008, 2010, 2011; Strakosch and Macoun 2012).

In thinking through these issues, I'm going to be inelegantly and non-canonically moving around within and between disciplinary languages and literatures. Additionally, while using multiple descriptors can sound awkward, I am not sure how else to capture the densities and specificities of systems of race and colonialism as well as ways in which they are intertwined and mutually reinforcing. Hopefully any incoherence in focus is outweighed by what is gained in nuance. As subjects, we are embedded in and engaged in creating, recreating and resisting multiple complex, interrelated and mutually reinforcing political processes and systems that overlap but do not fully constitute or replicate each other. I don't presume to offer a theory of race or settler colonialism or of the relation between the two—save to say that colonialism is not the same as race, but that neither could exist or be understood without the other. For the moment, I am drawing on these literatures and analytics as lenses or prisms which enable certain kinds of (in)sight.

There is a small, eclectic but insightful body of work engaged with race or colonialism that address the way constructions of innocence enable ongoing violence. James Baldwin (1970) identified not an innocence but an ignorance "not merely phenomenal, but sacred" which allows whites to "take refuge in their whiteness" and so "allow millions of people to be slaughtered in their name." White ignorance, in Baldwin's conception, is cultivated to allow whites to avoid seeing the ways that capitalism and perversions of American democracy result in victimisation and slaughter by cultivating a sinister distance between whites, their own honour and the rest of humanity. Ross (1990) argues that 'two rhetorical themes interwoven within the rhetorical tapestry of race' in the American legal context are an 'insistence on the innocence of contemporary whites' twinned with a black abstraction which involves 'the refusal to depict blacks in any real and vividly drawn social context.' In Ross' conception, like Baldwin's, a presumption that whites are not knowing or culpable depends upon a refusal to engage with the humanity of black people and the details of their lives.

A rhetorical insistence on white innocence takes on a different kind of inflection viewed through the lens of settler colonialism. Irene Watson (2009) has argued that the Australian state continues to pursue legitimacy by violently re-enacting its colonial foundation within a masquerade that this process is beneficial for Aboriginal people. Veracini (2008: 370) has argued that settler colonial societies operate through combining an aggressive drive to eradicate Indigenous people with the simultaneous disavowal of this violence. Mackey (1998, 1999) notes white innocence is mobilised through narratives of nationhood that emphasise national progress, tolerance, and inclusion. Tuck and Yang (2012) identify innocence as not merely a rhetorical insistence or an emphasis but a discursive manoeuvre often undertaken by progressives in settler colonial contexts. Tuck and Yang (2012: 10) are concerned with what they label 'settler moves to innocence' in purportedly decolonising endeavours, noting the ways that settlers manage to maintain progressive identities while deferring the materiality of decolonisation as a political project:

> Settler moves to innocence are those strategies or positionings that attempt to relieve the settler of feelings of guilt or responsibility without giving up land or power or privilege, without having to change much at all. In fact, settler scholars may gain professional kudos or a boost in their reputations for being so sensitive or self-aware. Yet settler moves to innocence are hollow, they only serve the settler.

Razack has used the term white settler innocence to describe 'the notion that European settlers merely settled and developed the land' (2002: 5). I am using a similar concept more expansively, as I think the construction operates more extensively and pervasively than Razack's definition implies.

I use the term colonising white innocence to describe a construction of whites as non-problematic and not implicated in either historical or contemporary violence. This construction preserves and sustains white virtue through legitimising and eliding white investments in maintaining power relationships generated by ongoing colonising racist violence. It can thus be understood as simultaneously enabling and erasing ongoing colonial violence. It circulates discursively (in the media, in institutions, in legal and policy frameworks, in cultural production or academic work) in the service of what Moreton-Robinson (2004) has termed the possessive logic of patriarchal white sovereignty. As outlined briefly above, I understand colonising white innocence to be one of many ways that white virtue is recuperated and preserved.

As innocence as a discursive strategy legitimises and elides white investments in maintaining power relationships generated by ongoing colonising racist violence, I argue it is necessary to resist this process through a focus on the continuing nature of racist colonial systems and relationships. If innocence is mobilised to support claims to white virtue and thus further narratives of settler colonial completion, then Ahmed's (2013) call to engage with complicity as '[w]e are implicated in the worlds that we critique' may be particularly pressing. In resisting what Tuck and Yang (2012: 10) describe as the 'settler desire to be made innocent, to find some mercy or relief in face of the relentlessness of settler guilt and haunting,' this becomes a process of refusing to allow ongoing systems of racist colonial violence or Indigenous and other resistances or alternatives to this violence to be made invisible, of refusing narratives that say we are at peace and keeping the conflict in view (Little and McMillan 2016).

I use the term complicity while acknowledging that it, like settler, is far too passive to capture the many ways we continue to perpetrate the violence of racism and colonialism. In positioning complicity rather than guilt in opposition to innocence, I am attempting to highlight personal and systemic implication rather than white emotion (however central white emotions may be to the way these issues are addressed or not addressed—see Maddison 2011: 15–22). While I am arguing that it isn't possible to understand or transcend our current political systems without a deep appreciation of our own continuing complicity in them and of the implications of this complicity for political action, this is not particularly an argument in favour of the affective response of white guilt. Maddison (2011) argues that white guilt is a problem and to be avoided; affective responses to our collective guilt about colonialism have rendered white Australians unable to do the adaptive work involved moving past our colonial history and achieving more just and united relationships. I share Maddison's view that it is necessary to move away from the self-centredness and paralysis of white guilt into more critical, active and meaningful engagements with colonialism and race. However, as Ahmed (2004) notes, a turn towards more agential anti-racist identities does not always result in less white self-centredness:

> The shift from the critique of white guilt to this claim to a proud anti-racism is not a necessary one. But it is a telling shift. The white response to the Black critique of shame and guilt has enabled here a 'turn' towards pride, which is not then a turn away from the white subject and towards something else, but another way of 're-turning' to the white subject.

So, to some extent, in agreeing with Ahmed that complicity should be the starting point for critical encounters, I am advocating an awareness of complicity among white settlers and the ways that we are located within whiteness and coloniality in the hope that this may ultimately assist us to effect a necessary political turn away from the white subject.

Colonising White Innocence as a Policy Dynamic

My primary research has involved examining racially charged Australian Indigenous policy discourses that legitimise colonising institutions and practices. The authoritarian spectacle of the Northern Territory Intervention, the technical rationalities of the Close the Gap process, and the inclusive politics mobilised by campaigns for constitutional recognition ostensibly address diverse policy problems and operate through different problematisations of Aboriginal peoples. These approaches are, however, made comprehensible through a reasonably coherent set of non-Indigenous political aspirations and investments in the virtue and legitimacy of settler institutions. Colonising white innocence reinforces and obscures these investments in maintaining power relationships generated by ongoing colonising violence.

The Northern Territory Emergency Response (or Intervention) was announced in June 2007 as the latest in a long Australian history of colonial child-saving projects. It operated through a set of authoritarian and paternalist policy measures imposed without consultation on Aboriginal people and communities (see Altman 2007; Altman and Hinkson 2007). The need to save the Aboriginal child was the primary basis upon which the program was justified. Rebecca Stringer (2007: 1) identifies a transactional politics operating 'by which the federal government extracts from disempowered children the power to act unilaterally upon and within their communities.' The state was depicted as a heroic protector and the morally charged tone of debates constructed opponents as politicised, complicit or morally deficient, allowing the Commonwealth and its agents to position themselves as acting for and alongside abused of Aboriginal children.

I have argued elsewhere (Macoun 2011) that this manoeuvre was facilitated through a depiction of the state as unknowing; unaware of abuse that has been enabled and perpetuated through white Australian innocence and an Aboriginal silence. Abuse is constructed as recently revealed, occurring without the knowledge—and by thus without the participation—of the state and its agents. Indigenous Affairs Minister Mal Brough (2007) argued that the *Little Children are Sacred* report made settlers aware of child abuse when it 'revealed a terrible situation.' Similarly, for his Shadow Minister Jenny Macklin (2007), 'horrific levels of child abuse that have now been made public really do require urgent action.' Frequent comparisons between the emergency of child abuse and a natural disaster exacerbate this process, as Baird (2008: 295) notes, constructing events as happening suddenly, outside of history, and as the result of natural rather than political actors. This construction relies on the erasure of several high profile government reports and significant activism by Aboriginal people and others over the preceding decade (Davis 2007). It also erases the role of the Australian state in servicing, regulating and policing NT Aboriginal communities, which has been more extensive than in comparable settler colonial jurisdictions such as Canada and the United States.

The discourse of Indigenous pathology that Moreton-Robinson (2009) identifies is evident in this debate, in the nature of the measures proposed, and in the imposition of this agenda without consultation with Aboriginal people and communities. Aboriginality and Aboriginal culture is why children require rescue. The unknowing settler state in this framing is not and cannot be implicated in enabling, initiating or perpetuating abuse; colonising white innocence both erases the state's implication in existing colonial relationships and morally authorises their continuation—in this case, arguably their escalation into a newly militarised and even more aggressively assimilationist form. This fundamental settler self-identification remained strikingly similar (as did the policy measures themselves) when the policy program was rebranded under subsequent ALP governments into an exercise in addressing disadvantage and improving health outcomes, and an agenda for broader cultural and economic integration intended to achieve Stronger Futures.

While the deployment of colonising white innocence is particularly striking in its authoritarian mode, as in early articulations of the Intervention, this construction circulates as effectively in more technocratic or ostensibly inclusive policy frames. The Closing the Gap program, which presents in a more technical mode, is concerned with the pursuit of statistical equality for Indigenous Australians against a range of indicators (particularly to do with disadvantage, health and life expectancy). As Pholi et al. (2009) note:

> Performance measurement in Closing the Gap requires a range of baseline data on what is *wrong* with Indigenous people. Deficit data then forms the basis of what is *known* about Indigenous people. This in turn sets the strategic goals for action to *fix* Indigenous people. Because the deficits are clearly situated within Indigenous Australians, progress is measured by the extent to which Indigenous Australians change for the better, thus insulating existing institutions, systems and power structures from an expectation to change

Colonising white innocence allows settler health and lifestyle indicators to be framed as neutral and Indigenous people as deficient, unruly, ungrateful or unhealthy subjects of white benevolence. The impacts of colonialism and institutional racism in shaping health outcomes among Indigenous peoples are widely acknowledged (see for example Paradies et al. 2008; Bourassa et al. 2004), but these outcomes are transformed here into an argument for the escalation of assimilation and the desirability of white settler futures. Speeches by Australian Prime Ministers from both sides of politics about the progress of Closing the Gap demonstrate how adeptly this rhetoric of deficit can be deployed to legitimise settler sovereignty and futurity (see for example Gilliard 2011; Abbott 2014).

The 'Recognise' campaign is framed in a more liberal and inclusive mode. It seeks public support for constitutional amendments changing or deleting racially specific powers allocated to the Commonwealth in the Australian constitution and inserting sections acknowledging Aboriginal peoples and languages. This is described as having both symbolic benefits and a material impact on Indigenous people (Recognise 2016). Mainstream political support for recognition has been explicitly framed around the need to act virtuously in the present to separate a racially non-discriminatory future from a problematic colonial past:

> An acknowledgement of Aboriginal people as the first Australians would complete our Constitution rather than change it.... Done well, such an amendment could be a unifying and liberating moment ....
>
> As Australians, our inclination is always to give three cheers for our country. We now accept, though, that for Aboriginal people, our settled history has never been a golden age. In this area, the challenge is not so much to live up to the past but, more often than not, to live it down. The challenge is not to be worthy of our predecessors but to be better than them. For all the good that was done in the past, these are our best days yet with better days still to come (Abbott 2013)

White benevolence must be mobilised in order to move from colonial complicity to a more neutral constitution which has the capacity to transcend the categories of race and coloniality that shaped its framing. What is not subject to debate is the capacity of the constitution to become neutral—to transcend the fundamental political relationships upon which it is based. The alternatives available to Indigenous peoples become a continued state of racist non-recognition and exclusion, or inclusion within white settler structures that deny their whiteness and their continuing coloniality—formally recognising Indigenous peoples at the same moment they are declared properties or precursors of a settler nation into which they have been successfully incorporated.

Central to each of these different policy manoeuvres is a constructed and colonising white innocence. In each of these examples, colonising white innocence operates to perpetuate the colonial project and declare it finished, while at the same time insisting upon the fundamental virtue of contemporary colonisers. There are a number of implications of this analysis. Policies presented as neutral or benevolent are almost axiomatically doing some kind of colonising work. This is not to say that all colonising policies are morally, materially and politically equivalent; differences in policy approaches have significant and substantial consequences—particularly for those Indigenous people whose lives are made the subjects of state policy. The insights this analysis provides do not substitute for a thorough evaluation of policy or an appreciation of how policy is experienced. I don't argue that differences in settler colonial policy approaches don't matter, just that it is important to consider and understand the similarities that also exist. Differences in policy articulation or effects are not the same as settler benevolence and we should not pretend that these measures exhaust the available political possibilities (even if this may be convenient for those of us who benefit from ongoing colonial domination).

The state has been and continues to be a party to racialized colonial conflict; colonising white innocence allows contemporary institutions to deny this fact, to continue generating authoritative problematisations of Indigenous others and to present continued domination as a necessary or benevolent solution. Policy narratives tend to cast the state and its agents as heroic protagonists (Luke 1997: 359). Colonising white innocence additionally imbues the state with the capacity to transcend its location in whiteness and coloniality by erasing the contribution of past and continuing practices to contemporary policy problems or in authorising the state's claim to be or to become a neutral and benign arbiter. This further reinforces white settler narratives about the capacity of liberal institutions to resolve colonialism and Indigenous difference (Strakosch 2015). These discourses exemplify the ways that Indigenous policy in multiple political framings can evidence Wolfe's (2006) logic of elimination—it simultaneously attempts to eliminate independent Indigenous territorial and political life outside settler structures, and to legitimise its replacement. While it may yet be possible for white settler institutions to engage with Indigenous peoples in ways that don't problematize, seek to coerce, or eliminate, these engagements cannot occur while colonising white innocence allows the state to continue maintaining its benevolence, its neutrality or transcendent qualities, and ultimately its authority over Indigenous people and peoples.

Colonising White Innocence: In Academic and Critical Spaces

So, if these are some things that colonising white innocence does and means in the realm of policy, this leaves me with a range of problems and questions about what it might also do and mean for me in the spaces of my own work and political life. Scholarship in race and colonialism emphasises connections between political and socioeconomic structures, institutional activities or processes, sets of ideas and fantasies, cultural productions, lifestyles, and the way these are embodied and enacted by located subjects (Moreton-Robinson 2000a; Wolfe 2006; Veracini 2011). Elizabeth Strakosch and I have reflected on the tendency of academics to apply our own theories about settler colonialism selectively and to excuse ourselves and our work from our own insights (Macoun and Strakosch 2013). So, it follows that I should also carefully consider the ways that I might be investing in colonising white innocence and in refusing to fully consider my own complicity with systems and structures I critique and describe.

I am not offering an exhaustive list of the ways that colonising white innocence might operate in political and academic work, but rather considering what some assumptions and strategies critiqued above in policy terms may look like transposed into and onto other fields and encounters. There are two principle claims to innocence I want to consider and reflect further upon. The first of these is the assumption that we and our work are fundamentally benevolent, the second is that we are capable of neutrality or transcending the power relationships we critique and describe.

As I have demonstrated above, policy narratives tell stories about the fundamental benevolence of the white settler state and its agents in addressing the problematic situation or nature of Indigenous people. The problems, these narratives confirm, are Indigenous in origin; the solutions are provided by white settler agents acting in Indigenous interests; if a relationship is countenanced between white settler institutions and the problems to be addressed, it is one that policy directed by the state will now address or overcome. I think it possible that many white settlers tell or are told similar stories about our academic and political work: we are benevolent actors in another's interest; it is necessary for us to act and possibly to lead action or reveal new ground in order to address the problematic situation or nature of Indigenous people. This is despite what we know about the disciplining and problematising impact of academic scrutiny, and the contributions of our disciplines, academic institutions, and epistemological frameworks to enabling and facilitating European colonial projects (Smith 1999; Moreton-Robinson 2011, 2013).

Like many white settlers, I imagine my own political and academic work of various kinds to be reasonably benign if not benevolent. This is a sentiment that is frequently reinforced by other whites; as Nicoll (2000) notes, virtue and goodness is automatically attributed by whites to other whites engaging with race or with Indigenous people. Tuck and Yang (2012: 10) identify in the quote above that 'settler scholars may gain professional kudos or a boost in their reputations for being so sensitive or self-aware' when we discuss race or colonialism (a sentiment not extended to Indigenous people or other people of colour in discussions of these same systems). This attribution of benevolence is not universal: white scholars working on race or colonialism may be understood by white peers as politicised or disloyal; we may encounter other difficulties working on issues that institutions and colleagues wish to avoid; we may be seen as dangerously misguided. However, work by whites in fields like race, colonialism or Indigenous studies is perceived as imbued with moral meaning in a way that working in other fields such as creek rehabilitation or data security, for example, may not be. I may do good work or work well in another field, but work in this field appears to somehow reflect on my own innate goodness (or lack thereof).

My benevolence and thus innocence is often discursively reinforced by others, even when I am contesting systems of domination that serve white settler interests or identifying my own implication and participation in these systems. It is a short step to automatically assuming my own benevolence or criticality, because systems of domination are bad and in contesting them I am, I am told, good. Moreton-Robinson (Moreton-Robinson 2000b: 350) has noted that 'recognising white race privilege often means for white feminists that you know about your privilege, you have dealt with it by writing about it, so you can move on'; in this way, knowledge of race can be proclaimed in order to maintain a position of innocence in relation to race. Criticality can thus become both automatically assumed and proof of benevolence, and as Sara Ahmed (2012, 2013) notes, function as an identity or ego ideal allowing me to evade or suspend my own complicity in the world I critique (see also Nicoll 2000). This allows white settlers to make ourselves the subjects and heroes of our own stories, even when our actual contributions may be experienced negatively or profoundly ambivalently by Indigenous peoples—as have been the bulk of white settler contributions to Indigenous peoples' lives and struggles.

Further, just as I have assumed my work to be reasonably benign, so I have often assumed my engagements with Indigenous people and my concern to contest systems of colonial and racial domination are harmonious with other political commitments and interests. However it is not necessarily the case that affirming a range of broad social justice goals or achieving a more critical comprehension of the world around me will in itself achieve decolonial or antiracist ends. As Tuck and Yang (2012: 9, 21) point out:

> The absorption of decolonisation by settler social justice frameworks is one way the settler, disturbed by her own settler status, tries to escape or contain the unbearable searchlight of complicity, of having harmed others just by being one's self. The desire to reconcile is just as relentless as the desire to disappear the Native; it is a desire to not have to deal with this (Indian) problem anymore.... [C]onsider how the pursuit of critical consciousness, the pursuit of social justice through a critical enlightenment, can also be settler moves to innocence - diversions, distractions, which relieve the settler of feelings of guilt or responsibility, and conceal the need to give up land or power or privilege.

An assumption of critical academic benevolence functions similarly to the assumption of benevolence sustaining colonising white innocence in state policy approaches: to authorise white settler contributions to discussions of the problems of Indigenous people; to position these contributions as authoritative, necessary and required; and to erase or obscure the ways in which we are a problem to be addressed rather than necessarily a solution.

The second assumption through which colonising white innocence functions relates to epistemological rather than moral capacity, and concerns the claim that I and other white settlers have the capacity to transcend our own locations and achieve objectivity in evaluating political systems and relationships. The policy discourses outlined above see the settler state and its agents positioned through colonising white innocence as a natural and legitimate authority capable of transcending and addressing problems and conflicts, but white settlers can position ourselves similarly in academic and political spaces. In some ways, this assumption of transcendence is a natural extension of the ideas about benevolence outlined above; if critical academic engagement with racial and colonial systems can be morally redemptive—can make me good—it can also allow me to transcend my own location within, benefit from, and contribution to the systems I describe. This is not to say that my identity or embodiment is a destiny I cannot see outside or beyond, just that it remains the place from which and the lens through which I see; even when I find injustice intolerable and commit myself to decolonial and antiracist ends, I do this as a white settler with sets of experiences and relationships and knowledges profoundly shaped by the meanings this embodiment has in our political and socioeconomic systems.

When white settlers write or act as though our own embodiment does not shape or delimit what and how we know as well as what it is possible for us to know, we claim disembodied and objective knowledge in ways that are only available through racialised knowledges and subject positions that understand whiteness and settlerness as neutral and disinterested (Tuhiwai Smith 1999; Nicoll 2000; Moreton-Robinson 2000a, 2011). As Moreton-Robinson (2000a: 350) notes:

> Not all knowledge is known, chosen, nor actively or happily acquired. In academic institutions where patriarchal whiteness is pervasive, race privilege blinds white feminist academics to their racial embodiment. If experience is an active way of knowing (even if it is not made explicit), and the situated knower is always a participant in the social she is discovering—what happens when the subject's experience blinds her to the social in which she is participating? There is no imperative for white women to acknowledge, own, and change their complicity in racial domination, because the mind/body split works to position 'race' as extrinsic to the subject. Their anti-racist practice, as an intellectual engagement, is evidence of their compassion, but systemic racism is not experienced as subject/knowers.

The move to neutrality and transcendence of perspective is a move generally only available to whites, as Nicoll (2000) notes, and is a move through which white settler academics claim and maintain dominance. It depends upon a number of privileges: we are able to assume that other white settlers will see our academic work describing race or colonialism as transcending experience and thus forming theory rather than data, memoir or polemic; to draw on academic sources and canons to support our work that are also understood as theory rather than political texts or folk traditions; and to operate within knowledge systems that generally reflect the ontological bases of our culture and traditions rather than those designed to perpetuate epistemic violence and colonise (see further Smith 1999: 19–78; Connell 2007: 104; Moreton-Robinson 2011, 2013).

In addition to the unequal distribution of privileges bestowed by white claims to neutrality and transcendence, these claims further allow us to continue perpetrating and legitimising colonial violence by reinforcing white authority over the way Indigenous people are known, the way political systems and processes are understood, and in fact over the entire space of our encounters with Indigenous people (Macoun and Strakosch 2013). As Strakosch (2015) has noted in relation to recent Indigenous policy literatures, claiming to analyse and synthesise binaries with a neutral descriptive power in fact offers a position of authority over this field that delimits what is analytically and politically possible. It is not an uncommon settler colonial trick to assert settler sovereignty and wage colonial conflicts while posturing as a neutral arbiter of this conflict (see also Muldoon 2008).

To claim that my work and other work by white settler scholars could in and by itself overcome our location within messy and complex white colonial systems—in order to offer either benevolent or objective analysis of these systems or politically progressive paths out of them—is bound up not only in colonising white innocence but in the same enlightenment commitments to perpetual progress and settler futurity that have driven colonial projects (see Smith 1999: 19–78). Indigenous people in this framing may be identified as capable of providing great insight about their experiences and cultures but these are, not coincidentally, located in a past it is assumed must be transcended; the future involves a naturalisation and legitimation of settlers, their institutions, and belief systems—even if in modified in form to fit new environments; settler reason is required to achieve the critical purchase necessary to harmonise these movements and achieve proper perspective. Ahmed (2004) observes that:

> What we might remember is that to be against something is precisely not to be in a position of transcendence: to be against something is, after all, to be in an intimate relation with that which one is against. To be anti 'this' or anti 'that' only makes sense if 'this' or 'that' exists. The messy work of 'againstness' might even help remind us that the work of critique does not mean the transcendence of the object of our critique; indeed, critique *might even be dependent on non-transcendence*.

Claims to transcendence or objectivity are power evasive and, in refusing to engage with the power relations and structures shaping the position of the white settler subject, reinforce the political projects and processes through which this subject comes into being.

Messy Complicities and Diffuse Conclusions

If white settler scholars hope to avoid deploying our work to recuperate our virtue through colonising claims to innocence, the discursive strategies I have outlined above should be challenged and rejected by in favour of approaches that are consistent with—and draw upon—our implication in the systems and processes we describe.

There are some obvious but fairly limited conclusions I want to make arising from these considerations. The first and most obvious implication of the arguments I have made is this; once I accept that I am complicit and not innocent, not benevolent or acting in Indigenous interests, or capable of knowing the world objectively and transcending the systems of domination in which I participate and am implicated, a range of claims become problematic. It is not possible for me to make knowledge claims about Indigenous people, what is best for Indigenous people or what the future should or will look like that do not rely upon engaging with the leadership and knowledge of Indigenous people. Since we are bound together in colonialism, this means it is similarly not possible for me to make knowledge claims about colonialism, undoing colonialism, or what Indigenous or non-Indigenous people should do that also do not rely upon engaging with the leadership and knowledge of Indigenous people.

Framing critical encounters through a lens of complicity leaves us with both a political responsibility and a critical intellectual imperative to understand and contest systems of domination in which we are enmeshed, their operations and their effects through deliberate respectful engagements with those who have experiences, knowledges and forms of authority that we do not. This requires not just a politics of ceremonial citation in our scholarship, but a more profound understanding that as white settler scholars we are always-already in political and knowledge relationships with Indigenous peoples—and these relationships are mostly not good.

I do not argue that it is impossible for white settlers to usefully critique racism and colonialism or to make contributions to resistant movements compatibly with our other political goals—simply that given the dynamics outlined above, it might be prudent to start from refutable presumptions that our pursuits of social justice or critical enlightenment will not necessarily achieve this end, and that Indigenous people will not automatically experience us as benevolent. This is not to say that we can't achieve progressive ends or do work that contributes productively to Indigenous struggles—but it does mean we need to think more carefully about our own investments, about the measure of our work, and who will judge what might constitute a useful contribution.

Similarly, just as white settlers may seek to avoid colonising white innocence by starting from the presumption that our work is not benevolent, so it might also consider it to always be profoundly limited. Perhaps refusing to deploy colonising white innocence in academic work might involve working from the basis that our knowledges—whatever they may be—are always partial and particular, our positions personally inflected and our perspectives interested. This seems compatible with Nicoll's (2000) argument that white people know Indigenous sovereignty exists because they cannot know it; that the only way for her to engage with Indigenous sovereignty is through her embodied standpoint as a queer, white woman, conscious of relationships and the limits of her knowledge. Even for those without a strong commitment to standpoint based research, this proposition may at the very least have a practical benefit of working against white settlers' continued ability to deploy the power of our institutions to continue to objectify and define Indigenous peoples and interests.

Tuck and Yang (2012: 28) argue that '[o]pportunities for solidarity lie in what is incommensurable rather than what is common,' advocating 'an ethic of incommensurability, which recognises what is distinct, what is sovereign.' Acknowledging the limited nature of our knowledges and ability to know in order to build solidarity through an ethic of incommensurability may involve relinquishing the idea that visions of the future should form the guiding parameters of our political work. This is a significant shift in political focus from a future orientation in our narratives (about a time when a gap is closed, when Australians are reconciled or when systemic decolonisation is imagined or achieved) to more limited engagements with the embodied nature, effects and practices of the systems in which we are enmeshed. Ahmed (2004) argues that:

> race, like sex, is sticky; it sticks to us, or we become 'us' as an effect of how it sticks even when we think we are beyond it. Beginning to live with that stickiness, to think it, feel it, do it, is about creating a space to deal with the effects of racism. We need to deal with the effects of racism in a way that is better.

This process may or may not lead to the kind of beloved community built through an appreciation of difference, personal encounters, activism in solidarity and located experiences of racism that hooks (1995) imagines. It may however help begin to counter the rhetorical theme of black abstraction that Ross (1990) notes, which allows whites and our systems to think about black people in ways that are disconnected from the realities and humanity of black lives.

I cannot use even these limited prescriptions to move myself to innocence however; seeking engagements in whatever form—reading critical Indigenous academic work, engaging in political activism led by Indigenous people, talking with Indigenous colleagues and friends—are not in themselves a guarantee that I am making myself useful (and not remaking myself as innocent). To engage and make judgements about my conduct and my conscience remains my responsibility even if I impose upon the generosity and knowledge of Indigenous people (including knowledges of whiteness and settlerness) and seek their guidance in this endeavour. To defer the responsibility of understanding and articulating my political responsibilities to Indigenous people or to other thinkers and activists could also operate as a move to preserve my own innocence; to authorisations or alibis in prescriptions about how to be good. In some ways, a focus on general principles rather than specific strategies is useful precisely in order to avoid these easy evasions and deployments of innocence. Prescriptions may be less helpful here than effective starting points: to reject colonising white innocence; accept that we are (at least) complicit; that we do not possess virtue; that we generally constitute problems not solutions. If innocence is not possible, material realities involving decolonised futures may well be, although there is no guarantee that these futures will be invested in settlers feeling good. As Tuck and Yang (2012: 36) note:

> To fully enact an ethic of incommensurability means relinquishing settler futurity, abandoning the hope that settlers may one day be commensurable to Native peoples... Decolonisation offers a different perspective to human and civil rights based approaches to justice, an unsettling one, rather than a complementary one. Decolonisation is not an 'and.' It is an elsewhere.

References

Abbott, T. (2013). Address to the Sydney Institute. Sydney, NSW, 15 March 2013. Available from http://www.liberal.org.au/latest-news/2013/03/15/tony-abbott-address-sydney-institute-sydney. Accessed 6 April 2016.

Abbott, T. (2014). 'Ministerial Statements Closing the Gap: Prime Minister's Report 2014' *Hansard of Debates - House of Representatives*. 12 February 2014. http://parlinfo.aph.gov.au/parlInfo/download/chamber/hansardr/d5f2441d-bbaa-47cd-9b30-b2e54878e868/toc_pdf/House%20of%20Representatives_2014_02_12_2184_Official.pdf;fileType=application%2Fpdf#search=%22chamber/hansardr/d5f2441d-bbaa-47cd-9b30-b2e54878e868/0000%22. Accessed 6 April 2016.

Ahmed, S. (2004). Declarations of whiteness: The non-performativity of anti-racism. *borderlands, 3*(2).

Ahmed, S. (2012). *On being included: Racism and diversity in institutional life*. Durham: Duke University Press.

Ahmed, S. (2013). Critical racism/critical sexism. *Feminist Killjoys*. http://feministkilljoys.com/2013/12/19/critical-racismcritical-sexism/. Accessed 6 April 2016.

Altman, J. C. (2007). *The Howard government's Northern Territory intervention: Are neo-paternalism and indigenous development compatible*. Acton: Australian National University, Centre for Aboriginal Economic Policy Research.

Altman, J. C., & Hinkson, M. (Eds.). (2007). *Coercive reconciliation: Stabilise, normalise, exit Aboriginal Australia*. Melbourne: Arena Publications.

Baird, B. (2008). Child politics, feminist analyses. *Australian Feminist Studies, 23*(57), 291–305.

Baldwin, J. (1970). *An open letter to my sister, Miss Angela Davis*. New York: Committee to Free Angela Davis.

Bourassa, C., McKay-McNabb, K., & Hampton, M. (2004). Racism, sexism and colonialism: The impact on the health of Aboriginal women in Canada. *Canadian Woman Studies, 24*(1).

Brough, M. (2007). Acting to make a safer, better life for Aboriginal children: Message from the Minister for Aboriginal Affairs. In *Northern Territory Emergency Response,* 18 August 2007. FaCSIA (Publication Reference 0635R), Australian Government.

Coburn, E., Moreton-Robinson, A., Sefa Dei, G., & Stewart-Harawira, M. (2013). Unspeakable things: Indigenous research and social science. *Socio. La nouvelle revue des sciences sociales, 2*, 331–348.

Connell, R. (2007). *Southern theory*. Crows Nest, NSW: Allen & Unwin.

Davis, M. (2007). Aboriginal or institutional silence: A brief comment on the National Emergency Response to the Anderson Wild Report. *Indigenous Law Bulletin, 6*(29), 2–3.

Gilliard, J. (2011). Ministerial statement—Indigenous affairs.' *Hansard of Debates—House of Representatives*. 9 February 2011. http://parlinfo.aph.gov.au/parlInfo/download/chamber/hansardr/2011-02-09/toc_pdf/7924-4.pdf;fileType=application%2Fpdf#search=%22chamber/hansardr/2011-02-09/0000%22. Accessed 6 April 2016.

Hage, G. (2000). *White nation: Fantasies of white supremacy in a multicultural society*. New York & London: Routledge.

hooks, B. (1995). Beloved community: A world without racism. *Killing rage: Ending racism*. New York: Henry Holt and Company.

Little, A., & McMillan, M. (2016). Invisibility and the Politics of Recognition in Australia: Keeping Conflict in View. *Ethnopolitics*. Online version in advance of print.

Luke, A. (1997). The material effects of the word: Apologies, 'stolen children' and public discourse. *Discourse (St Lucia, Qld), 18*(3), 343–368.

Mackey, E. (1998). Becoming indigenous: Land, belonging, and the appropriation of aboriginality in Canadian Nationalist Narratives. *Social Analysis: The International Journal of Social and Cultural Practice, 42*(2), 150–178.

Mackey, E. (1999). As good as it gets? Apology, colonialism and white innocence. *Bulletin (Olive Pink Society), 11*(1–2), 34.

Macklin, J. (2007). *Transcript of doorstop—Heidelberg, VICTORIA* 22 June 2007. http://parlinfo.aph.gov.au/parlInfo/download/media/pressrel/ZXFN6/upload_binary/zxfn62.pdf;fileType=application/pdf. Accessed 30 July 2007.

Macoun, A. (2011). Aboriginality and the Northern Territory intervention. *Australian Journal of Political Science, 46*(3), 519–534.

Macoun, A., & Strakosch, E. (2013). The ethical demands of settler colonial theory. *Settler Colonial Studies, 3*(3–4), 426–443.

Maddison, S. (2011). *Beyond White Guilt: The real challenge for black-white relations in Australia*. Crows Nest: Allen and Unwin.

Moreton-Robinson, A. (2000a). *Talkin'up to the white woman: Aboriginal women and feminism*. St Lucia: University of Queensland Press.

Moreton-Robinson, A. (2000b). Troubling business: difference and whiteness within feminism. *Australian Feminist Studies, 15*(33), 343–352.

Moreton-Robinson, A. M. (2003). *I still call Australia home: Indigenous belonging and place in a white postcolonising society* (pp. 23–40). Uprootings/Regroundings: Questions of Home and Migration.

Moreton-Robinson, A. M. (2004). Indigenous history wars and the virtue of the white nation. In D. Carter (Ed.), *The ideas market* (pp. 219–235). Melbourne: Melbourne University Press.

Moreton-Robinson, A. (2009). Imagining the good indigenous citizen: Race war and the pathology of patriarchal white sovereignty. *Cultural studies review, 15*(2), 61.

Moreton-Robinson, A. (2011). The white man's burden: Patriarchal white epistemic violence and Aboriginal women's knowledge's within the academy. *Australian Feminist Studies, 26*(70), 413–431.

Moreton-Robinson, A. (2013). Towards an Australian Indigenous women's standpoint theory: A methodological tool. *Australian Feminist Studies, 28*(78), 331–347.

Moreton-Robinson, A. (2015). *The white possessive: Property, power, and indigenous sovereignty*. Minnesota: University of Minnesota Press.

Muldoon, P. (2008). The sovereign exceptions: Colonization and the foundation of society. *Social & Legal Studies, 17*(1), 59–74.

Nicoll, F. (2000). Indigenous sovereignty and the violence of perspective: A white woman's coming out story. *Australian Feminist Studies, 15*(33), 369–386.

Paradies, Y., Harris, R., & Anderson, I. (2008). *The impact of racism on Indigenous health in Australia and Aotearoa: Towards a research agenda*. Darwin: Cooperative Research Centre for Aboriginal Health.

Pholi, K., Black, D., & Richards, C. (2009). Is 'Close the Gap' a useful approach to improving the health and wellbeing of Indigenous Australians? *Australian Review of Public Affairs, 9*(2), 1–14.

Razack, S. (2002). *Race, space, and the law: Unmapping a white settler society*. Toronto: Between the Lines.

Recognise. (2016). Why recognise? http://www.recognise.org.au/why/why-recognition/. Accessed 6 April 2016.

Ross, T. (1990). Rhetorical tapestry of race: White innocence and black abstraction. *The William & Mary Law Review, 32*, 1.

Singh, D. (2007). White subjectivity and racial terror: Towards an understanding of racial violence. *ACRAWSA e-Journal, 3*(1), 7.

Smith, L. T. (1999). *Decolonizing methodologies: Research and indigenous peoples*. London: Zed Books.

Snelgrove, C., Dhamoon, R., & Corntassel, J. (2014). Unsettling settler colonialism: The discourse and politics of settlers, and solidarity with Indigenous nations. *Decolonization: Indigeneity, Education & Society, 3*(2).

Strakosch, E. (2015). *Neoliberal indigenous policy: Settler colonialism and the 'Post-Welfare' State*. Basingstoke: Palgrave Macmillan.

Strakosch, E., & Macoun, A. (2012). The vanishing endpoint of settler colonialism. *Arena Journal, 37*(38), 40–60.

Stringer, R. (2007). A nightmare of the neocolonial kind: Politics of suffering in Howard's Northern Territory Intervention. *Borderlands, 6*(2), 13.

Tuck, E., & Yang, K. W. (2012). Decolonization is not a metaphor. *Decolonization: Indigeneity, Education & Society, 1*(1).

Veracini, L. (2008). Settler collective, founding violence and disavowal: The settler colonial situation. *Journal of Intercultural Studies, 29*(4), 363–379.

Veracini, L. (2010). *Settler colonialism*. Basingstoke: Palgrave Macmillan.

Veracini, L. (2011). District 9 and Avatar: Science fiction and settler colonialism. *Journal of Intercultural Studies, 32*(4), 355–367.

Watson, I. (2009). In the Northern Territory intervention: What is saved or rescued and at what cost? *Cultural Studies Review, 15*(2), 45–60.

Wolfe, P. (2001). Land, labor, and difference: Elementary structures of race. *The American Historical Review, 106*(3), 866–905.

Wolfe, P. (2006). Settler colonialism and the elimination of the native. *Journal of Genocide Research, 8*(4), 387–409.

Chapter 7
Attitudinal Barriers to Reconciliation in Australia

Yin Paradies

Abstract Despite a raft of studies focused on reconciliation in Australia, we still have relatively little quantitative information about reconciliation-related attitudes among Australians, the key factors associated with these attitudes, effective approaches to attitudinal change, or divergent patterns by socio-demographic factors. This paper begins to address this gap in the literature by utilising recent key datasets, principally, representative telephone surveys undertaken at the local, state and national levels. While those with overt racist and anti-reconciliationist attitudes were in the minority, findings indicate the continued presence of problematic attitudes among both Indigenous and non-Indigenous Australians as well as overseas and Australian-born respondents. Awareness of white privilege appears to be an important correlate of reconciliationist attitudes, along with age and level of education. Evidence from public social marketing campaigns demonstrates that some attitudes are amendable to change while others remain resistant to modification. I conclude with recommendations for future research and action that could support viable reconciliation pathways in Australia.

Keywords Reconciliation · Racism · Attitudes · Indigenous · Non-Indigenous · Privilege · Whiteness

Introduction

As a nation with well over two centuries of English colonisation, Australia is haunted by a fraught and racist history laden with massacres, displacement, segregation, neglect, forced labour, and assimilation of Indigenous peoples who had inhabited the continent for the past 40,000 years (Nagle et al. 2016). As noted by Maddison (2016), Australia is the only former British colony that lacks a treaty with Indigenous peoples. However, the past few decades have witnessed attempts to

Y. Paradies (✉)
Deakin University, Burwood, Australia
e-mail: yin.paradies@deakin.edu.au

S. Maddison et al. (eds.), *The limits of settler colonial reconciliation*,
DOI 10.1007/978-981-10-2654-6_7

foster self-determination for, and reconciliation with, Indigenous peoples in Australia. Most recently, this includes a popular movement to recognise Indigenous Australians in the national constitution (http://www.recognise.org.au/) and government receptiveness to a treaty in Victoria, Australia's second most populous state (Reconciliation Australia nd).

Nonetheless, racism continues to be a contemporary reality for Indigenous Australians,[1] with a range of studies highlighting its ongoing prevalence in the media, education, employment, public housing, and the criminal justice system (Paradies 2006). A third (34 %) of Indigenous respondents in the 2014–2015 National Aboriginal and Torres Strait Islander Social Survey reported experiences of racism in the previous year (Australian Bureau of Statistics 2016), while almost all (97 %) of Aboriginal respondents in a Victorian study reported at least one experience of racism in the previous year (Ferdinand et al. 2012).[2] In addition, this same Victorian study revealed that nearly three quarters of participants anticipated people saying or doing something racist sometimes, often or very often. Furthermore, nearly two thirds sometimes, often or very often tried to avoid specific situations because of racism, while almost 70 % of respondents reported sometimes, often or very often worrying about racism (Ferdinand et al. 2012).

Social psychological studies that continue to demonstrate the persistence of racist attitudes suggest that these fears are well founded. Australians continue to think of Indigenous people in stereotypical ways; for example, as more likely to drink alcohol and as recipients of 'government handouts' (Pedersen et al. 2006; Balvin and Kachima 2011). Recent evidence indicates that 20 % of Australians admit they would be racist towards Indigenous people in retail settings, 10 % would not hire an Indigenous Australian, and 31 % think that Indigenous Australians should behave more like 'other Australians' (*beyondblue* 2014). Only 'people who don't speak English' were nominated more often by more respondents as likely targets of discrimination (43 %) than Indigenous Australians (39 %) (*beyondblue* 2014). Although important in themselves, these racist attitudes are also, to some extent, responsible for maintaining material structures of racial inequality in society. Clearly then, racist attitudes represent a key barrier to reconciliation in both its symbolic and practical manifestations (see the next section for further explanation).

Within this context, it is worth noting that anti-racism in Australia has a history as long as racism itself (see for example Land 2015). This includes activism by individual Indigenous people from the earliest days of colonisation (e.g. Bennelong) through to the early 20th century (e.g. Anthony Fernando, William Cooper and David Unaipon) as well as mass strikes (e.g. Cummeragunja and Wavehill), petitions (e.g. by the Yolngu to the House of Representatives) and social protests (e.g. Freedom rides) around the middle of last century. From the 1980s to

[1]This term will be utilised throughout as inclusive of both Aboriginal and Torres Strait Islander peoples of Australia.

[2]Figures for the prevalence of self-reported racism vary considerably due to approaches to sampling, the specific populations in question and the diverse nature and number of questions about racism that respondents are presented with.

early 2000s, reconciliation became the prevailing rubric through which to grapple with Australia's colonial history in seeking equity, justice, decolonisation and improved race relations between Indigenous peoples, the descendants of early, predominately (but not exclusively (Pybus 2006)) white settler-invaders, and subsequent waves of both white and non-white migrants. Over this same period, reconciliation also enjoyed strong worldwide appeal, with one-third of all peace agreements utilising this concept to some degree (McIntosh 2014).

The Australian context has witnessed a considerable body of academic research focused on aspects of reconciliation, including apologies (Hartley et al. 2013; Philpot et al. 2012; Short 2012), conflict resolution (Maddison 2016), disadvantage (Gunstone 2008), emotions (Gooder 2011), interventions (Kearins 2012), literature (Savvas 2012), local government (Nieman 2014), monitoring (McIntosh 2014), methods (Clark et al. 2012), geography (Johnson and Walliss 2014), reparations (Rae 2015), sovereignty (Muldoon and Schaap 2012), stereotypes (Balvin and Kachima 2011) and youth (Bourke and Geldens 2007). However, despite the increasing availability of representative survey data pertaining to reconciliation, there has been scant quantitative analysis of trends, correlates and plasticity of reconciliationist attitudes. The importance of such evidence is highlighted by the waning of reconciliation as a framework. In the last decade or so, reconciliation has, for many, become 'associated with meaningless platitudes rather than transformation' and largely faded from public consciousness (Maddison 2016:16).

Nonetheless, the *raison d'être* of reconciliation persists through institutional roles such as the Indigenous social justice commissioner (Australia Human Rights Commission, nd) and predominately non-Indigenous social movements such as Australians for Native Title and Reconciliation (ANTaR), state-based reconciliation groups and Reconciliation Australia as the national peak-body (Reconciliation Australia nd). In light of this persistence, this chapter brings quantitative evidence of attitudinal barriers to bear on the problem of finding successful reconciliation pathways in Australia.

The Trope of Reconciliation

As a concept, reconciliation can be parsed into the specific 'Rs' of remembrance, recording, re-historicising, recompense, reparation and restitution (Dodds 2012), in conjunction with the broader Rs of representation, recognition and redistribution (Fraser 2004). As both term and concept, reconciliation has been subject to considerable critique, varying from the almost querulously semantic, for example, the oft-repeated suggestion that *re*-conciliation implies conciliation of a relationship that did not exist in the first place (Maddison 2016) to the foundational; contending that reconciliation is nothing more than deep colonialism[3] in disguise (Short 2003).

[3]Denoting colonialism disguised in avowedly progressive postcolonial discourses (Rose 1996).

Most definitions of reconciliation understand that it is a complex task. Maddison (2016) considers reconciliation at the constitutional, institutional and relation levels, while historical acceptance, race relations, institutional integrity, unity, equality and equity are detailed in the Reconciliation Australia barometer (Reconciliation Australia 2013). Hamber and Kelly (2009) define reconciliation as focused on grappling with the past and fostering positive relationships through attitudinal and cultural change as well as economic, political and social change. The Australian Declaration towards Reconciliation, included in the Council for Aboriginal Reconciliation's final report to the Australian Parliament, includes statements spanning commitment, courage, sorrow, healing, forgiveness, respect, hope, uniqueness, connection to land, a lack of a treaty, past injustice, equity, self-determination and unity (Commonwealth of Australia 2001).

The era of 'practical reconciliation', which coincided with the Declaration, has since morphed into 'Closing the Gap' as the key Indigenous affairs platform, including a range of initiatives intended to address disadvantage (for example in health, education, employment and so on) and promote healing (for example through the work of the Healing Foundation). In parallel, there has been a focus on the 'symbolic', including the apology to the Stolen Generations (Rudd 2008) and the 'Recognise' campaign, which seeks to include Indigenous Australians in the Constitution (Recognize). However, largely absent to date, is a third pillar focused on 'hearts and minds' (statement seven of the Declaration) or, put more simply, understanding and changing attitudes towards reconciliation. As a participant in Maddison's (2016) research contended, if engaging in reconciliation is not about 'the minds and actions of Australians' then she was not 'sure what the point' of it was.

As noted above, reconciliation is situated at the nexus of relationships between white settler-invaders, Indigenous people and non-white migrants, with the last most neglected in Australia to date (Perera 2005; Clark et al. 2012; Rolls 2014). While the importance of reconciliation for Indigenous peoples (as a historically disenfranchised minority who continue to suffer from racism) is clear, what animates the drive towards reconciliation for settler-invaders (native or migrant) in a national context where there is no 'widespread threat of violence' from Indigenous peoples (Maddison 2016) it is not immediately self-evident. Although settler-invaders gain much from constituting the 'mainstream majority' of the Australian nation, they can also experience anguish over colonialism which can lead to assertions of colonial beneficence, a desire to assimilate indigenes into 'settlerness' (Veracini 2011) and/or a yearning for their own 'happy hybrid' autochthony (Bell 2014).

In light of such settler unsettledness, we can ask a number of key questions in relation to reconciliation: (1) what is the current shape of (non-) Indigenous attitudinal barriers to reconciliation? (2) how do these attitudes vary by socio-demographic factors? and (3) to what extent can Australian reconciliation be fostered through settler-invader moral reflexivity (for example an awareness of white privilege)? In the remainder of this chapter, I attempt to shed light on such questions utilising, in the main, evidence from the Reconciliation Barometer; the Victorian Attitudes to Race and Cultural Diversity (VARCD) survey (VicHealth 2014); the

Localities Embracing and Accepting Diversity (LEAD) program (Ferdinand et al. 2013); and *beyondblue*'s Stop. Think. Respect. campaign (TNS 2015).

Inspired by the annual South African Reconciliation Barometer first conducted in 2003, the Australian Reconciliation Barometer has monitored both Indigenous and non-Indigenous attitudes every 2 years since 2008, with samples of 1,000–1,200 non-Indigenous and 500–700 Indigenous respondents in each survey. The content of the Barometer was revised considerably in 2014, with the Indigenous sample drawn, for the first time, from a representative panel rather than via Indigenous networks (Polity 2015).

In 2006, the Victorian Health Promotion Foundation (VicHealth) conducted the 'More than Tolerance' survey to assess attitudes to multiculturalism and cultural diversity among a representative sample of 4000 Victorian[4] adults (VicHealth 2007). The 2013 VARCD survey was a follow-up to this, with some overlapping content along with a range of new content, involving a representative sample of 1,250 Victorian adults (VicHealth 2014). This survey included a few items of relevance to Indigenous Australians and reconciliation.

The LEAD program, auspiced by VicHealth with funding from a range of other partners, was conducted from 2009 to 2013 in one metropolitan and one rural municipality in Victoria (Ferdinand et al. 2013). The program included a 2010 baseline survey of race-related attitudes, and in particular a module on reconciliation-related attitudes among 300 respondents in a rural municipality.[5]

In 2014, *beyondblue* undertook their second Stop. Think. Respect. campaign, this time, with a focus on the impact of subtle or casual racism on the social and emotional wellbeing of Indigenous Australians, entitled 'the invisible discriminator' (*beyondblue* 2014). The campaign involved short video clips of Indigenous Australians being subject to racist judgements in a range of settings including in a job interview, being watched in a shop, being avoided on public transport and in a shopping mall, and being the butt of a joke in a pub. The campaign reached several million people (mostly in Melbourne and Sydney as the largest Australian cities) through television, digital and 'out of home' platforms, targeting 25–44 year-old non-Indigenous Australians, in particular. The campaign evaluation included representative surveys of 1,000 respondents before and after the campaign, undertaken in July and September 2014 (TNS 2015). Although a handful of previous anti-racism social marketing campaigns focusing on Indigenous Australians have been undertaken in Australia (for example Reconciliation Australia's 2009 'See the person, not the stereotype' campaign), the very few that include published evaluations have been at a local, rather than, national level (Balvin and Kachima 2011).

---

[4]Victoria is a south-eastern state of Australia with a 2016 population of about 6 million people (31 % born overseas and 0.7 % Indigenous) (ABS, nd).

[5]This rural locality is a major regional centre located 200 km from Melbourne (capital of Victoria), with a 2011 estimated population of about 60,000 people.

Reconciliationist Attitudes

With Indigenous people constituting only 2.5 % of the Australian population, it is difficult to over-estimate the political importance of non-Indigenous attitudes as an impetus for reconciliation in its various forms. Of the range of attitudes, beliefs and perceptions that have been measured to date in Australia, I will focus here on relevant negative racist attitudes as a barrier to reconciliation, alongside positive reconciliationist attitudes that may foster reconciliation.

In relation to racist attitudes, the reconciliation barometer surveys indicate that, between 2008 and 2014, 8–13 % of non-Indigenous Australians agree that 'non-Aboriginal Australians are superior to Aboriginal Australians' (Polity 2015). Surprisingly, a considerable proportion of Indigenous Australians also agreed with this statement, dropping from 14 to 12 to 9 % in 2008, 2010 and 2012, but more than doubling to 19 % in 2014, compared to only 8 % in 2014 for non-Indigenous Australians (Polity 2015). At the same time, the proportion of Indigenous people who strongly agree that they are proud of Indigenous cultures dropped from 86 to 92 % from 2008 to 2012 to 51 % in 2014 (Polity 2015).

Among 5000 adults in the 2001 Challenging Racism survey, conducted in New South Wales and Queensland (Western Sydney University, nd), 28 % expressed concern about a close relative marrying an Aboriginal person, with this figure being 25 % in the 2006 'More than Tolerance' survey (VicHealth 2007). However, in the 2008, 2010 and 2012 Reconciliation Barometers, only 11 and 13 and 14 % (respectively) of non-Aboriginal Australians expressed concern about a close relative marrying an Indigenous Australia (Reconciliation Australia 2013).

Other negative feelings towards Indigenous people were surprisingly low. Only about 3 % of VARCD respondents reported cold or very cold feelings towards Aboriginal Australians. This is only slightly higher than the 2 % who felt cold/very cold towards Anglo-Australians and much lower than figures for those from Asian (6 %), African (11 %), refugee (11 %), Middle Eastern (14 %) or Muslim (22 %) backgrounds (VicHealth 2014). Similarly, Indigenous Australians were nominated as a group that does not fit into Australia society by only 1 % of respondents in 2014, down from 2 % in 2006 (VicHealth 2007, 2014).

In the VARCD survey, 28 % of respondents did not appreciate the barriers to success that Aboriginal people face, this figure was 21 % of those with a university degree and 30 % of those without a formal qualification; 41 % of 18–24 year-olds and 23 % of those aged 65 years or over, with no variation by gender. In addition, 30 % of respondents overall believe that current levels of government funding for Aboriginal people are too high; 20 % of those with a university degree and 39 % of those without a formal qualification, with no variation by age or gender. Similarly, 34 % of non-Indigenous and 25 % of Indigenous Australians in the 2014 Barometer agreed that Indigenous Australians 'are responsible for their own disadvantages today'.

Repeated cross-sectional data from the Stop. Think. Respect campaign highlights both the durability and malleability of these attitudes. Among all respondents,

42 % agreed that 'Indigenous Australians are given unfair advantages by the government' before the campaign, with 47 % agreeing after the campaign. Importantly, there was no difference between those exposed to the campaign and those who weren't. Exposure to the campaign did not attenuate the heightened agreement with the assimilationist sentiment that 'Indigenous Australians should behave more like other Australians' (32 % agreement at benchmark rising to 37 % among the exposed and 38 % among the unexposed).

There were, however, also improvements that could be attributed to the campaign. The item 'Indigenous Australians hold a special place as the first Australians' rose from 74 % agreement at benchmark to 78 % agreement among exposed, falling to 68 % agreement among unexposed. The view that 'Indigenous Australians benefit Australian society' increased from 62 % agreement at benchmark to 71 % agreement among exposed, falling to 57 % agreement among unexposed, while agreement that 'being an Indigenous Australian makes it harder to succeed in Australian society today' rose from 56 % agreement at benchmark to 62 % agreement among exposed, with no change among the unexposed. Finally, while the 56 % of respondents who, before the campaign, agreed that 'being an Indigenous Australian makes it harder to succeed in Australia today' was unchanged for who didn't see the campaign, agreement rose to 62 % among those who reported seeing the campaign (TNS 2015).

There are further encouraging findings. Other positive indicators include the 71 % of non-Indigenous and 87 % of Indigenous respondents in the 2014 Barometer survey who agreed that Indigenous people 'hold a unique place as the first Australians'. Similarly, 83 % of VARCD respondents agreed that Aboriginal Australians hold a special place as the first Australians, with this proportion not varying by age, gender or level of education.

The 2008–2012 Barometers asked people if they 'would like to help disadvantaged Indigenous people and if they knew how they could help. Among the non-Indigenous sample across the three different waves of the survey, 4–8 % strongly agreed that they would like to help. However, only 2–5 % strongly agreed that they knew how to do so. Although framed in terms of reconciliation rather than disadvantage, results were comparable in the 2014 Barometer (TNS 2015). Understandably, strong agreement with both questions was much higher among Indigenous respondents, between 62 and 65 % strongly willing to assist and 39–46 % strongly confident that they knew what to do. However, the group of strongly identified 'baffled willing helpers' (Rowse 2012) was still quite high among Indigenous Australians, at 11–40 %, compared to 20–50 % among non-Indigenous respondents (Reconciliation Australia 2013; TNS 2015).

In summary, the current evidence points to a small proportion of non-Indigenous Australians with strong anti-Indigenous attitudes (that is, overt racists), varying from 1 to 15 % across the indicators considered in this chapter. Although a strong majority (70–80 %) of non-Indigenous Australians acknowledge the status of Indigenous peoples as 'first Australians', a considerable proportion (about a quarter) fail to recognise the disadvantage experienced by Indigenous Australians, with such views attenuated through both formal and public education but, alarmingly, considerably higher among youth compared to older respondents. Moreover, strongly identified anti-racists (as measured by high willingness to help) are, at 4–8 % of the population, less common than overt racists, with up to a half of this select group lacking confidence in what action can be taken to advance reconciliation and reduce Indigenous disadvantage.

These findings also highlight problematic attitudes among Indigenous people themselves, specifically feelings of inferiority and lack of pride in their culture. Such findings suggest a need for Indigenous people to reconcile with themselves (see, for example, Kim 2014 in the Canadian context) whilst simultaneously pursuing reconciliation with non-Indigenous Australians. It may be possible to counteract internalised racism (Bennett 2014; Dudgeon et al. 2000; Gorringe et al. 2011) by rejecting pernicious fantasies of indigeneity (Paradies 2006) and refusing 'the offer of a future without an identity' Birch (2007: 112) wherein acknowledgement of Aboriginal descent is not accompanied by a collective imagined future as Aboriginal people (Les Malezer in Maddison 2016).

In the next section, I consider the role of race and nativity on attitudes to reconciliation, including a focus on the oft-neglected group of non-white non-Indigenous Australians, while also delving into non-Indigenous Australians' awareness of privilege as an influence on their reconciliationist attitudes.

Privilege, Race and Nativity

Although the intersection between white privilege and Indigenous affairs has been the focus of some Australian scholarship (Kowal 2011; Quayle and Sonn 2013; Walter and Butler 2013; Hollinsworth 2016), we know little about its quantitative relationship with reconciliation-related attitudes. The VARCD survey revealed that 49 % of respondents acknowledge that 'Australians from an Anglo background (of British descent) enjoy an advantaged position in our society'. Encouragingly, there was a 6 % increase in recognition of white privilege between 2006 and 2013, although this occurred amidst a worsening of other attitudes such as reduced support for multiculturalism (responding to the statement 'racial/ethnic minorities benefit Australia'), increased feelings of symbolic threat (responding to the statement 'retaining cultural beliefs and values threatens Australian way of life'), and attenuated awareness of racism (VicHealth 2014).

The VARCD findings display a clear pattern, with those who recognise white privilege espousing more support for reconciliation and more positive attitudes to Indigenous Australians generally. For example, in the VARCD, respondents believed that: being Aboriginal makes it harder to succeed in Australia today (72 % of those recognise white privilege vs. 47 % of non-recognisers), Aboriginal people get more government money than they should (26 % recognisers vs. 37 % non-recognisers), and Aboriginal people hold a special place as the first Australians (87 % recognisers vs. 79 % non-recognisers). A similar pattern was found among LEAD respondents, with those recognising that 'Australians from a White background have a privileged position in our society' exhibiting higher endorsement of reconciliation items including: Aboriginal heritage and culture makes life in the area better (58 % recognisers vs. 34 % non-recognisers); the council should permanently fly the Aboriginal flag beside the Australian flag (59 % recognisers vs. 43 % non-recognisers); you approve of the road signs acknowledging the traditional Aboriginal owners (66 % recognisers vs. 53 % non-recognisers); to assist educating the wider community about Aboriginal culture, places that have Aboriginal names should have the English translation on their signs (54 % recognisers vs. 48 % non-recognisers); it adds to the sporting and cultural life of the community to have Aboriginal-based sporting clubs (79 % recognisers vs. 62 % non-recognisers); and it is important that the government gives money for Aboriginal specific services to address disadvantage such as in health, education and employment (67 % recognisers vs. 53 % non-recognisers).

In relation to nativity, the difference in the proportion of Anglo-Celtic versus Culturally and Linguistically Diverse (CALD)[6] LEAD respondents who endorsed reconciliation-related items varied from 1.5 to 19 %, with support consistently higher among Anglo-Celtic, rather than CALD, respondents. This was also the case when comparing Australian- to overseas-born, although with only 10 % of LEAD respondents born overseas, there was limited statistical power, and only the two largest differences reached significance (6 and 13 %). Similarly, although data on ethnic/racial identity wasn't available in VARCD, while 63 % of Australian-born respondents recognised the barriers to success that Aboriginal people face, this was the case for only 53 % of overseas-born respondents. However, no significant differences by place of birth were found for the other two VARCD reconciliation items.

The higher level of support for reconciliation among both White Australians and the Australian-born was not explained by differential acknowledgement of white privilege. Among VARCD respondents, endorsement of white privilege did not vary by place of birth (i.e. Australia or overseas) and there was *higher* recognition of white privilege for CALD (36 %) versus Anglo-Celtic (33 %) and by place of birth (35 % recognition of white privilege for Australian-born vs. 41 % for overseas-born) among LEAD respondents.

There was, however, evidence that the impact of white privilege awareness on reconciliation-related attitudes was stronger for Anglo-Celtic, compared to CALD, respondents. This could be seen through a higher variation in response to reconciliationist items among Anglo-Celtic respondents who acknowledged or denied white privilege, compared to variation among CALD respondents. Among VARCD respondents, this variation was comparable for symbolic items (such as 'Aboriginal people hold a special place as the first Australians'), but was about 15 % less among CALD respondents for non-symbolic items (such as 'being Aboriginal makes it harder to succeed in Australia today' and 'Aboriginal people get more

---

[6]Anglo-Celtic respondents were defined as those who reported a racial/ethnic background as English, Scottish, Welsh or Irish, with all other respondents classified as CALD.

government money than they should'). However, there were no clear variations in endorsement of reconciliationist items by race/ethnicity among LEAD respondents.

White privilege was acknowledged by men (53 %) more often than women (46 %) among both VARCD respondents and in LEAD (39 % for men vs. 33 % for women), by almost twice the proportion of tertiary educated (62 %) than those with other levels of education (36–41 %) in VARCD but with much less variation in LEAD (44 % among the tertiary-educated vs. 37 % for those without formal qualifications). Similar to the VARCD findings above in relation to recognising Indigenous disadvantage, there was a disturbingly low recognition of white privilege among 18–24 year-olds (27 %) compared to 43 % among those aged 65 years or older in LEAD. Recognition was much higher among VARCD respondents, with little variation by age (43 % for 18–24 year-olds vs. 45 % among those aged 65 years or older).

To summarise, an awareness of white privilege appears to be an important driver of a positive attitudes to Indigenous Australians and reconciliation, in particular. Although there is evidence that such awareness is increasing in general and already higher among CALD than Anglo-Celtic respondents, its impact is, nonetheless, weaker for CALD than for Anglo-Celtic Australians.

Conclusion

Through an examination of attitudes assessed in large-scale representative surveys, this chapter has highlighted the potential of quantitative evidence to elucidate the complex terrain of reconciliation in Australia, identifying a range of key attitudinal barriers that must be overcome before reconciliation in Australia can advance. As with other research methods that focus on sensitive topics such as race and racism, responses to the survey questions examined here may have been affected by social desirability biases. However, at present there is mixed evidence as to whether respondents consider expression of racist norms, anti-racism norms or neither as most socially desirable (Ivarsflaten et al. 2010; Janus 2010), let alone how exactly this impacts on self-reported race-related attitudes (Holmes 2014).

In spite of this limitation, exploring existing Australian survey data reveals the importance of considering attitudes disaggregated by age, gender, education, Indigeneity, race/ethnicity, nativity. With scant research examining gender differentials in white privilege awareness, this finding of increased awareness among men compared to women is notable. Spanierman et al. (2012) have suggested that 'fear of losing power and privilege are critical aspects of White men's experiences, and may be less relevant for White women' (175) who suffer from sexism despite being white. Future qualitative and quantitative research should investigate this finding further along with exploring the apparent deterioration of positive reconciliationist attitudes among the youngest cohort of Australian adults.

While research has demonstrated the value of formal education in combating racist attitudes (Carvacho et al. 2013), it is also clear that the mere provision of information is not sufficient to change attitudes or behaviours (Pedersen et al. 2011); with this finding also applying to Indigenous reconciliation specifically (Maddison and Stastny, this volume). Instead, there is also a need to foster reflection on, and personal responsibility towards, these difficult issues by cultivating egalitarian values, seeking meaningful relationships with Indigenous people (where possible), and drawing parallels with experiences of oppression in their own lives (Krejci 2007; Smith and Redington 2010).

This chapter has also used survey research to demonstrate for the first time an association between white privilege and reconciliationist attitudes. As noted by Mbembe (2008: 12) in relation to reconciliation in South Africa, it is all too easy for white people to ignore both their white privilege and the 'accumulated atrocities' upon which it is founded. In a study of 86 young people in rural Victoria, Bourke and Geldens (2007) found a 'reluctance to reflect on their position of White privilege' and a need for improved understanding of 'their position of privilege' among non-Indigenous Australians 'if reconciliation is to develop' (618).

Although the causal direction of the association between white privilege awareness and support for reconciliation described above is unclear at present (i.e. whether reconciliation support leads to white privilege awareness, vice versa, or both are influenced other factors), an emerging body of scholarship demonstrates that increasing awareness of white privilege is achievable through training programs among students (Banales 2014; Case 2007; Crawford 2010; Kernahan and Davis 2007; Palmerio-Roberts and McDonough 2014; Paone et al. 2015; Soble et al. 2011) and professionals (Muszynski 2009), with one study even showing sustained improvements a year after attending training (Kernahan and Davis 2010). However, this same study was also the only to include non-white participants (without reporting on them separately). As such, we know little about how to foster awareness of white privilege amongst those who aren't white or why the impact of such awareness seems to be attenuated compared to whites.

The poorer attitudes of CALD Australians may be explained to some extent by the weaker role played by white privilege awareness in driving reconciliationist attitudes among this group, especially when it comes to acknowledging Indigenous disadvantage and the need for funding to address it. It is plausible that the guilt and shame consequent to privilege awareness among whites (see for example Soble et al. 2011) is not as salient for non-white non-Indigenous Australians. This suggests a need to explore the utility of alternative concepts such as settler privilege or settler complicity, which can highlight the need to take action without necessarily suggested that all non-white settlers are advantaged compared to Indigenous peoples (Dhamoon 2015).

Recent literature has critiqued the concept of 'white privilege', suggesting that it serves to elide institutional racism, leaving whites more complacent and 'restoring…[their] sense of moral rightness' (Margolin 2015), and should therefore be replaced with more appropriate concepts such as 'unearned white advantage' (Monahan 2014) or 'white supremacy' (Lensmire et al. 2013). Furthermore, given the existence of white stigma (Kowal 2011) and a dynamic of fear of abuse among white Australians if they offend Indigenous people (as identified by Mick Gooda, the Aboriginal Social Justice Commissioner in Maddison 2016), it may be possible to utilise white affinity groups (Michael et al. 2009; Blitz and Kohl 2012) to build pre-dialogue confidence among whites as a group (Maddison 2016) and, perhaps also to help disrupt 'silencing' styles of communication that serve to reinforce white privilege (Striley and Lawson 2014). Such affinity groups, modelled on existing forums for minority groups such as Black caucuses (DiAngelo 2011) may provide a safe space in which to explore cognitive and emotional reactions to race and difference and face the challenges of creating positive and engaged forms of white racial identity (Malott et al. 2015).

Evidence from the Stop. Think. Respect. campaign indicates considerable volatility in reconciliationist attitudes, shown in this case through a worsening across a 2-month timeframe. Further research should investigate longitudinal trends in such attitudes and whether these are linked to political trends or other key events (for example. de Rooij et al. 2015). Although not assessed in the Stop. Think. Respect. campaign, there is also potential for public education initiatives to foster awareness of white privilege amongst non-Indigenous Australians.[7] Given the findings above of a considerable group of 'baffled willing helpers' (Rowse 2012), such programs could also focus on strengthening knowledge and confidence of how best to further reconciliation in Australia among those most committed to doing so.

Finally, a recent example of the potential widespread impact of online campaigns was illustrated through the 'Google doodle'. This image, entitled 'Stolen Dreamtime', depicted an Aboriginal woman mourning her stolen children 'and a life that never was'. It was selected from among 26,000 school student entries to commemorate Australia day in 2016. With almost 30 million visits to www.google.com.au each day (Geoghegan 2015), through this choice, 'Google reminds non-Aboriginal Australians of the price that Indigenous people have paid for their privilege' (Paula Gerber, online comment in Bowden 2016). While the impact of this image was not evaluated, there are a number of emerging online methods for tracking changing patterns of racism over time, and for assessing the impact of racist and anti-racism events and interventions on such trends (Chae et al. 2015; Chaudry 2015; Gitari et al. 2015) that could be utilised in future research.

Acknowledgments Work on this paper was supported by the Australian Research Council (FT130101148). Thanks to Melody Velasquez-Tan for her assistance with data analysis.

References

ANTaR. (nd). Official website. https://antar.org.au. Accessed July 25, 2016.
Australian Bureau of statistics. (nd). Australia. Census of population and housing 2006 and 2011. http://profile.id.com.au/australia/population. Accessed July 25, 2016.

[7]In the U.S., see for example: http://unfaircampaign.org/.

Australian Bureau of Statistics. (2016). *National Aboriginal and Torres Strait Islander Social Survey, 2014–2015*. Canberra, ACT: Australian Bureau of Statistics.

Australia Human Rights Commission. (nd). Aboriginal and Torres Strait Islander Social Justice Commissioner. Mr Mick Gooda'. https://www.humanrights.gov.au/about/commissioners/aboriginal-and-torres-strait-islander-social-justice-commissioner. Accessed July 25, 2016.

Balvin, N., & Kachima, Y. (2011). Hidden Obstacles to Reconciliation in Australia: The Persistance of Stereotypes. In D. Bretherton & N. Balvin (Eds.), *Peace psychology in Australia* (pp. 197–219). New York: Springer.

Banales, J. (2014). The sustained impact of an engaging diversity program on college seniors' color-blind racial attitudes. *CrissCross, 2*(1), Article 1.

Bell, A. (2014). *Relating indigenous and settler identities: Beyond domination*. New York: Palgrave Macmillan.

Bennett, B. (2014). How do light skinned Aboriginal Australians experience racism? Implications for social work. *AlterNative: An International Journal of Indigenous Peoples, 10*(2), 180–192.

Beyondblue (2014). The invisible discriminator. https://www.beyondblue.org.au/for-me/stop-think-respect-home/the-invisible-discriminator. Accessed July 25, 2016.

Birch, T. (2007). 'The invisible fire': Indigenous sovereignty, history and responsibility. In A. Moreton-Robinson (Ed.), *Sovereign subjects: Indigenous sovereignty matters* (pp. 105–117). Crows Nest, NSW: Allen & Unwin.

Blitz, L. V., & Kohl, B. G. (2012). Addressing racism in the organization: The role of white racial affinity groups in creating change. *Administration in Social Work, 36*(5), 479–498.

Bourke, L., & Geldens, P. (2007). Perceptions of reconciliation and related indigenous issues among young residents of shepparton. *The Australian Journal of Social Issues, 42*(4), 603–621.

Bowden, E. (2016, January 26). Australia Day 2016 Google doodle 'shining a light' on Indigenous culture. *The Sydney Morning Herald*, p. 8.

Carvacho, H., Zick, A., Haye, A., González, R., Manzi, J., Kocik, C., et al. (2013). On the relation between social class and prejudice: The roles of education, income, and ideological attitudes. *European Journal of Social Psychology, 43*(4), 272–285.

Case, K. A. (2007). Raising white privilege awareness and reducing racial prejudice: Assessing diversity course effectiveness. *Teaching of Psychology, 34*(4), 231–235.

Chae, D. H., Clouston, S., Hatzenbuehler, M. L., Kramer, M. R., Cooper, H. L. F., Wilson, S. M., et al. (2015). Association between an internet-based measure of area racism and black mortality. *PLoS ONE, 10*(4), e0122963.

Chaudry, I. (2015). #Hashtagging hate: Using Twitter to track racism online. *First Monday*, 20(2).

Clark, T., Walsh, M., & de Costa, R. (2012). Resonating opinions and identities: Using poetics methods to explore non-aboriginal attitudes towards aboriginal reconciliation in Australia. *Asiatic: IIUM Journal of English Language & Literature, 6*(2), 110–127.

Crawford, E. K. (2010). *Qualitative and quantitative outcome analysis of a required human diversity course*. Psy.D. dissertation, Pacific University.

de Rooij, E. A., Goodwin, M. J., & Pickup, M. (2015). Threat, prejudice and the impact of the riots in England. *Social Science Research, 51*, 369–383.

Dhamoon, R. (2015). A feminist approach to decolonizing anti-racism: Rethinking transnationalism, intersectionality, and settler colonialism. *Feral Feminisms, 4*, 20–37.

DiAngelo, R. (2011). White fragility. *International Journal of Critical Pedagogy, 3*(3), 54–70.

Dodds, G. G. (2012). Government apologies and political reconciliation. In B. Charbonneau & G. Parent (Eds.), *Peace-building, memory and reconciliation: Bridging top-down and bottom-up approaches* (pp. 130–145). New York: Routledge.

Dudgeon, P., Garvey, D., & Pickett, H. (2000). *Working with Indigenous Australians: A handbook for psychologists*. Perth: Gunada Press.

Ferdinand, A., Paradies, Y., & Kelaher, M. (2012). *Mental health impacts of racial discrimination in Victorian Aboriginal communities*. Victorian Health Promotion Foundation (VicHealth): Carlton, Victoria.

Ferdinand, A., Paradies, Y., & Kelaher, M. (2013). The role of effective partnerships in an Australian place-based intervention to reduce race-based discrimination. *Public Health Reports, 128*(3), 54–60.

Fraser, N., Dahl, H.M., Stoltz, P., & Willig, R. (2004). Recognition, Redistribution and Representation in Capitalist Global Society: An Interview with Nancy Fraser. *Acta Sociologica, 47*(4), 374–382.

Geoghegan (2015, October 19). 'Australian internet statistics 2015'. *Payperclick*. http://www.payperclick.net.au/australian-internet-statistics-2015. Accessed July 25, 2016.

Gitari, N. D., Zuping, Z., Damien, H., & Long, J. (2015). A lexicon-based approach for hate speech detection. *International Journal of Multimedia and Ubiquitous Engineering, 10*(4), 215–230.

Gooder, H. (2011). *The sorry people: Non-indigenous Australians and emotional geographies of co-presence*. PhD thesis, The University of Melbourne.

Gorringe, S., Ross, J., & Fforde, C. (2011). *'Will the real Aborigine please stand up': Strategies for breaking the stereotypes and changing the conversation*. Canberra, ACT: Australian Institute of Aboriginal and Torres Strait Islander Studies.

Gunstone, A. (2008). Reconciliation and Australian Indigenous Health in the nds: A Failure of Public Policy. *Journal of Bioethical Inquiry, 5*(4), 251–263.

Hamber, B., & Kelly, G. (2009). Beyond coexistence: Towards a working definition of reconciliation. In J. R. Quinn (Ed.), *Reconciliation(s): Transitional justice in postconflict societies* (pp. 286–310). Montreal: McGill-Queen's University Press.

Hartley, L. K., McGarty, C., & Donaghue, N. (2013). Understanding disagreement within the majority about action to atone for past wrongs. *Journal of Applied Social Psychology, 43*(S2), E246–E261.

Hollinsworth, D. (2016). Unsettling Australian settler supremacy: Combating resistance in university Aboriginal studies. *Race, Ethnicity, and Education, 19*(2), 412–432.

Holmes, J. D. (2014). Impression management pressures on racial attitude surveys. *The Social Science Journal, 51*(2), 302–308.

Ivarsflaten, E., Blinder, S., & Ford, R. (2010). The anti-racism norm in Western European immigration politics: Why we need to consider it and how to measure it. *Journal of Elections, Public Opinion & Parties, 20*(4), 421–445.

Janus, A. L. (2010). The influence of social desirability pressures on expressed immigration attitudes. *Social Science Quarterly, 91*(4), 928–946.

Johnson, F., & Walliss, J. (2014). Reconciling history: Inserting an indigenous space into the University of Melbourne Campus. *Landscape Review, 15*(1), 47–63.

Kearins, H. (2012). History on a bus: Using sociodrama to address racism and reconciliation. *Australian and Aotearoa New Zealand Psychodrama Association Journal, 21*, 31–43.

Kernahan, C., & Davis, T. (2010). What are the long-term effects of learning about racism? *Teaching of Psychology, 37*(1), 41–45.

Kernahan, C., & Davis, T. (2007). Changing perspective: How learning about racism influences student awareness and emotion. *Teaching of Psychology, 34*(1), 49–52.

Kim, J. J. (2014). *They made us unrecognizable to each other: Human rights, truth, and reconciliation in Canada*. PhD dissertation, University of Tennessee.

Kowal, E. (2011). The stigma of White privilege: Australian anti-racists and indigenous improvement. *Cultural Studies, 25*(3), 313–333.

Krejci, J. M. (2007). *Allies, activists, and advocates: A dissertation on the analysis of the experiences and processes that led thirteen white men to anti-racist work*. PhD thesis, University of California.

Land, C. (2015). *Decolonizing solidarity: Dilemmas and directions for supporters of indigenous struggles*. London, U.K.: Zed Books.

Lensmire, T. J., McManimon, S. K., Dockter, T. J., Lee-Nichols, M. E., Casey, Z. A., Lensmire, A., et al. (2013). McIntosh as synecdoche: How teacher education's focus on white privilege undermines antiracism. *Harvard Educational Review, 83*(3), 410–431.

Maddison, S., & Stastny, A. (this volume). Silence or deafness? Education and the non-Indigenous responsibility to engage.
Maddison, S. (2016). *Conflict transformation and reconciliation: Multi-level challenges in deeply divided societies*. London and New York: Routledge.
Malott, K. M., Paone, T. R., Schaefle, S., Cates, J., & Haizlip, B. (2015). Expanding white racial identity theory: A qualitative investigation of whites engaged in antiracist action. *Journal of Counseling & Development, 93*(3), 333–343.
Margolin, L. (2015). Unpacking the invisible knapsack: The invention of white privilege pedagogy. *Cogent Social Sciences, 1*(1), 1053183.
Mbembe, A. (2008). Passages to freedom: The politics of racial reconciliation in South Africa. *Public Culture, 20*(1), 5–18.
McIntosh, I. S. (2014). Reconciliation, you've got to be dreaming: Exploring methodologies for monitoring and achieving aboriginal reconciliation in Australia by 2030. *Conflict Resolution Quarterly, 32*(1), 55–81.
Michael, A., Conger, M. C., Bickerstaff, S., Crawford-Garrett, K., & Fulmer, E. F. (2009). Becoming an anti-racist white ally: how a white affinity group can help. *Perspectives on Urban Education, 6*(1), 56–60.
Monahan, M. J. (2014). The concept of privilege: A critical appraisal. *South African Journal of Philosophy, 33*(1), 73–83.
Muldoon, P., & Schaap, A. (2012). Aboriginal sovereignty and the politics of reconciliation: The constituent power of the aboriginal embassy in Australia. *Environment & Planning D, 30*(3), 534–550.
Muszynski, M. N. (2009). *Influence of a multidimensional model of antiracism training on White clinicians' positive self-regard, White privilege attitudes and social identity development*. Master's dissertation. Smith College.
Nagle, et al. (2016). Antiquity and diversity of aboriginal Australian Y-chromosomes. *American Journal of Physical Anthropology, 159*(3), 367–381.
Nieman, G. L. (2014). *Aboriginal people and local government. A shepparton story*. PhD thesis. Deakin University.
Palmerio-Roberts, R., & McDonough, C. (2014). Changing attitudes: A classroom pedagogy to foster multicultural awareness and acceptance. *The AFCU Journal, 11*(1), 20–41.
Paone, T. R., Malott, K. M., & Barr, J. J. (2015). Assessing the impact of a race-based course on counseling students: A quantitative study. *Journal of Multicultural Counseling and Development, 43*(3), 206–220.
Paradies, Y. (2006). Beyond black and white: Essentialism, hybridity and indigeneity. *Journal of Sociology, 42*(4), 355–367.
Pedersen, A., Walker, I., Paradies, Y., & Guerin, B. (2011). How to cook rice: A review of ingredients for teaching anti-prejudice. *Australian Psychologist, 46*(1), 55–63.
Pedersen, A., Dudgeon, P., Watt, S., & Griffiths, B. (2006). Attitudes toward Indigenous Australians: The issue of "special treatment". *Australian Psychologist, 41*(2), 85–94.
Perera, S. (2005). Who will I become? The multiple formations of Australian Whiteness. *Australian Critical Race and Whiteness Studies Association Journal, 1*, 30–39.
Philpot, C., Balvin, N., Mellor, D., & Bretherton, D. (2012). Making meaning from collective apologies: Australia's apology to its indigenous peoples. *Peace and Conflict: Journal of Peace Psychology, 19*(1), 34–50.
Polity Research and Consulting. (2015). *Australian reconciliation barometer 2014*. Canberra: Reconciliation Australia.
Pybus, C. (2006). Black founders: The unknown story of Australia's first black settlers. Sydney: UNSW Press.
Quayle, A. F., & Sonn, C. C. (2013). Explicating race privilege: examining symbolic barriers to Aboriginal and non-Indigenous partnership. *Social Identities, 19*(5), 552–570.
Rae, M. (2015). When reconciliation means reparations: Tasmania's compensation to the stolen generations. *Griffith Law Review, 24*(4), 640–656.
Reconciliation Australia. (nd). http://www.reconciliation.org.au. Accessed July 25, 2016.

Reconciliation Australia. (nd). Treaties and agreement. http://www.reconciliationvic.org.au/pages/treaties.php. Accessed July 25, 2016.

Reconciliation Australia. (2013). *Australian reconciliation barometer 2012*. Canberra, ACT: Reconciliation Australia.

Recognize (nd). Official website. http://www.recognise.org.au. Accessed July 25, 2016.

Rolls, M. (2014). 'Are there any poor people here?' Immigrants, aborigines, and multicultural perceptions. *The Journal of the European Association for Studies of Australia, 5*(1), 36–44.

Rose, D. (1996). Land rights and deep colonising: The erasure of women. *Aboriginal Law Bulletin, 3*(5), 6–13.

Rowse, T. (2012). The Australian reconciliation barometer and the indigenous imaginary. In T. Rowse (Ed.), *Rethinking social justice: from 'peoples' to 'populations'* (pp. 201–216). Canberra, ACT: Aboriginal Studies Press.

Rudd, K. (2008, February 18). *Apology to Australia's indigenous peoples, hansard, house of representatives* (pp. 167–173). Canberra, ACT: Parliament of Australia.

Savvas, M. (2012). Storytelling reconciliation: The role of literature in reconciliation in Australia. *International Journal of Diversity in Organisations, Communities & Nations, 11*(5), 95–108.

Short, D. (2003). Australian 'Aboriginal' reconciliation: The latest phase in the colonial project. *Citizenship Studies, 7*(3), 291–312.

Short, D. (2012). When sorry isn't good enough: Official remembrance and reconciliation in Australia. *Memory Studies, 5*(3), 293–304.

Smith, L., & Redington, R. M. (2010). Lessons from the experiences of White antiracist activists. *Professional Psychology: Research and Practice, 41*(6), 541–549.

Soble, J. R., Spanierman, L. B., & Liao, H. Y. (2011). Effects of a brief video intervention on White university students' racial attitudes. *Journal of Counseling Psychology, 58*(1), 151–157.

Spanierman, L. B., Beard, J. C., & Todd, N. R. (2012). White men's fears, white women's tears: Examining gender differences in racial affect types. *Sex Roles, 67*, 174–186.

Striley, K. M., & Lawson, S. (2014). Theorizing communication orientations of privilege: How white discourses (De) construct. *Journal of International and Intercultural Communication, 7*(2), 170–191.

The Parliament of the Commonwealth of Australia. (2001). *The Australian declaration towards reconciliation*. Canberra, ACT: Commonwealth of Australia.

TNS Social Research. (2015). *Beyondblue stop. Think. Respect*: (Phase two) Communications Evaluation Final Report. Canberra, ACT: *beyondblue*.

Veracini, L. (2011). On settlerness. *Borderlands, 10*(1), 1–17.

Foundation, Victorian Health Promotion. (2007). *More than tolerance: Embracing diversity for health*. Victorian Health Promotion Foundation (VicHealth): Carlton, Victoria.

Victorian Health Promotion Foundation. (2014). *Findings from the 2013 survey of Victorians' attitudes to race and cultural diversity*. Victorian Health Promotion Foundation (VicHealth): Carlton, Victoria.

Walter, M., & Butler, K. (2013). Teaching race to teach Indigeneity. *Journal of Sociology, 49*(4), 397–410.

Western Sydney University, School of Social Sciences and Psychology. (nd). *Research methodology*. http://www.uws.edu.au/school-of-social-sciences-and-psychology/ssap/research/challenging_racism/surveys. Accessed July 25, 2016.

Chapter 8
Cultivating Sympathy and Reconciliation: The Importance of Sympathetic Response

Joanna R. Quinn

Abstract It is generally assumed that societies emerging from abuse will necessarily be receptive to programs of acknowledgement and reconciliation. Yet often they are not, and efforts to promote reconciliation fall on unreceptive audiences at the national level and below. This paper traces the factors that hamper the uptake of reconciliation and the acknowledgement of past events, and develops the following hypothesis: *thin sympathy must be developed or acknowledgement will not occur*. The paper considers the importance of building a critical level of understanding or "thin" sympathy in the population through exposure to the "other" and helping people see through new lenses about the other's experiences. It argues that reconciliation efforts fail when there is not even "thin" sympathy or basic understanding of the experiences of the other within civil society. Through the lens of Canada, a number of factors that obscure this kind of knowledge translation are explored: lack of national identity, and the strategy of self-preservation single-mindedly pursued by government.

Keywords Transitional justice · Acknowledgement · Sympathy · Canada

Introduction

Mass atrocity, including the atrocities of colonialism, leaves individuals and families shattered. More broadly, it devastates whole societies. When these impacts are not addressed in the short-term, their legacy is felt even many years on. As such,

---

This chapter was first presented at the Annual Convention of the International Studies Association, 17 March 2016, Atlanta. Research for this project was carried out with assistance from the Social Sciences and Humanities Research Council Standard Research Grant Residual Fund (The University of Western Ontario), and research assistance from Tammy Lambert.

J.R. Quinn (✉)
University of Western Ontario, London, Canada
e-mail: jquinn2@uwo.ca

S. Maddison et al. (eds.), *The limits of settler colonial reconciliation*,
DOI 10.1007/978-981-10-2654-6_8

even in cases of historical atrocity, much is required. To rebuild the social infrastructure, and to help people in the communities hit hard by violence—or by the residue of that violence—begin to grapple with the consequences of their lived experiences, those societies increasingly turn to the pursuit of accountability and redress for survivors and for inter-generational survivors.

Much of the transitional justice literature assumes that post-conflict, decolonising societies will embrace programs and processes that address social needs in a comprehensive and substantial way, and ultimately work toward rebuilding social trust, repairing a fractured justice system, and building a democratic system of governance, through the acknowledgement of past human rights abuses. But often this is not the case, and social rebuilding processes are met with indifference or outright hostility. Survivors are left to pursue social reconstruction alone, while the perpetrators of the violence disengage completely—ultimately 'let off the hook' by the disinterest of others in pursuing justice. Bystanders and outsiders, then, can easily ignore the situation in which survivors find themselves, and they commonly do. In contemporary settler colonial societies, this neglect, benign or otherwise, is manifested in deep inequalities that may have persisted for decades.

The Canadian case illustrates this point. It has been reported that about 150,000 aboriginal, Inuit and Métis children were removed from their families and communities and forced to attend one of the schools in the Indian Residential Schools system (CBC 2011), which ran from the early 1800s until the last school closed in 1996. Under that system, Aboriginal children were required to attend schools that would 'take the Indian out of the child (Churchill 2004), a form of 'aggressive assimilation' (CBC 2011) exacerbated by psychological, emotional, and sexual abuse. The impact of these policies has been extensive:

> It is generally accepted that the forced removal of children from their families was devastating for Aboriginal individuals, families, communities and cultures. This is regularly being confirmed by researchers today.
>
> [As a direct result,] First Nation communities experience higher rates of violence: physical, domestic abuse (3× higher than mainstream society); sexual abuse: rape, incest, etc. (4–6× higher); lack of family and community cohesion; suicide (6× higher); addictions: drugs, alcohol, food; health problems: diabetes (3× higher), heart disease, obesity; poverty; unemployment; illiteracy; high school dropout (63 % do not graduate); despair; hopelessness; and more (IRS Survivors' Society).

The residential schools were a part of a broader set of policies that have greatly affected Canadian Indigenous communities. These include continued near-universal regulation under the Indian Act, legislation that dates to 1876 and effectively sets Indigenous Canadians apart from the rest of Canada; the Indian Act has resulted in social inequalities including unequal access to health care, justice, and education, inadequate housing, and increased rates of poverty, unemployment, incarceration, child deaths and suicide. There are also a number of unresolved treaty claims—treaties that were signed between the British Crown and Indigenous nations at the time of colonisation—against the government that have given rise to illegal mining and other occupations. And Indigenous peoples continue to be left out of Canadian governance and decision-making.

In early 1998, in reporting on the Royal Commission on Aboriginal Peoples, then-Minister of Indian Affairs and Northern Development, Jane Stewart, offered 'a solemn offer of reconciliation,' which acknowledged the role of the Government of Canada in the Indian Residential Schools (Notes 1998). Although there was significant negotiation between Aboriginal groups and the churches that had, in many cases, run the schools, the Government did very little until it finally signed the *Indian Residential Schools Settlement Agreement* in 2006 (A Condensed Timeline 2008, 64–65). The Settlement Agreement is touted by the Government as 'the largest class action settlement in Canadian history… Implementation of the IRSSA began on September 19, 2007' (INAC). The Settlement Agreement included a common experience payment for Indian Residential Schools survivors, an independent assessment process to investigate claims of sexual and other abuse, a truth and reconciliation commission, and other commemorative activities.

And in 2008, then-Prime Minister Stephen Harper made a 'Statement of Apology' in which he recognised the negative consequences of the Indian Residential Schools policy and further recognised the impact that a lack of apology had had on conciliation processes. His lack-lustre apology was this: 'Therefore, on behalf of the Government of Canada and all Canadians, I stand before you, in this Chamber so central to our life as a country, to apologize to Aboriginal peoples for Canada's role in the Indian Residential Schools system' (Prime Minister 2008).

For the Harper government, these minimal efforts were seen as a final solution to the claims that had been swirling about, claims that Indigenous communities were unhappy and seeking a solution. Harper saw the settlement concluded between the government and claimants in the Indian Residential Schools Settlement Agreement as the furthest limit of what government was prepared to do, without recognising that the issues that the IRSSA represented were merely the tip of the proverbial iceberg. In response to a question about how an inquiry into missing and murdered Indigenous women would be handled by his government, for example, Harper said, 'It isn't really high on our radar, to be honest' (quoted in Maloney 2015). Harper's government, further, refused to sign the United Nations Declaration on the Rights of Indigenous Peoples.

Canada elected a new government in late 2015, under Prime Minister Justin Trudeau. Trudeau's government seems much more open to considering these issues, and it is possible that perceptions, too, are changing. Immediately upon being elected, Trudeau pledged to pursue 'nation-to-nation' relations with Indigenous communities, and to follow up on five election promises, including the launch of a public inquiry into missing and murdered Indigenous women; investment in education for First Nations; lifting funding caps for First Nations programs; implementing the recommendations of the Truth and Reconciliation Commission; and repealing all legislation unilaterally imposed on Indigenous people by the Harper government (Mas 2015).

In this chapter, I argue that such efforts are ultimately much less successful when they are convoked without at least the very basic engagement of bystanders and outsiders. It is critically important for post-conflict and/or decolonising societies to acknowledge the past, no matter how painful. But without a basic understanding of the needs of the 'other' (the survivor)—what I refer to, below, as *thin sympathy*—bystanders and outsiders, let alone perpetrators, simply do not engage in the healing process. The utility and influence of these kinds of processes is greatly diminished without the way having been paved first for bystanders and outsiders to cultivate thin sympathy.

Methodology

This chapter is a theoretical exploration of the role of sympathy, and in particular, of thin sympathy, in the process of acknowledgment. It seeks to clarify the process by which that thin sympathy develops—or not. And it focuses largely on what sympathy, acknowledgement, and reconciliation could mean for bystanders and outsiders, because of the critical role they could play. It is based in part upon the situation in which Canada currently finds itself: after the completion of the Truth and Reconciliation Commission, waiting for more to be done to address the inequities that make up the lives of Indigenous peoples.

Before getting to the argument, it is useful to define what I mean, here, by 'bystanders and outsiders': I define bystanders and outsiders as those people who were not directly involved in the violence. They are distinct from survivors and their families, and from perpetrators. In many cases, bystanders and outsiders were separated from the violence by time or by space. But at the same time, they are also members of the society that has been torn apart. Or they may be bystanders and outsiders to inequalities that stem from both broad, systemic and/or specially targeted violence—resulting in widespread structural discrimination—put in place as part of a program of historical violence. As such, bystanders and outsiders bear a responsibility to set things right.

I have been working in post-conflict contexts—notably, Uganda, Haiti, Fiji, and Solomon Islands—for almost 20 years. My work there has focused on truth commissions, and on traditional practices and customary justice, as mechanisms that could foster acknowledgement, and, ultimately, reconciliation. My interest in Canada, however, stems from my curiosity as to whether the lessons I have learned in post-conflict contexts could reasonably be applied not in a 'post-conflict' society, per se, but in a consolidated democracy that is struggling with what decolonisation looks like, and how to correct the centuries of inequity that have existed between non-Indigenous and Indigenous Canadians.

Traditionally, decolonising societies were not considered by the field of transitional justice. Transitional justice was concerned with post-conflict, democratising and transitional societies (Arthur 2009). Yet by now it is abundantly apparent that even in established, consolidated democracies, redress is needed—particularly with reference to violence committed by the state against Indigenous communities (see, for example, Winter 2014).

Acknowledgement and Reconciliation

Acknowledgement is the 'spelling out [of] facts, publicly stating facts… a kind of avowal or marking out of what we know' in the aftermath of gross violations of human rights and repression (Govier 2003, 70–71). This kind of admission of fact about the past must culminate in a public admitting to and accepting a knowledge of events that have taken place. As I define it, acknowledgement itself is the accretion of a number of personal and interpersonal processes that begin with an emotional response to the recognition of what has taken place, and subsequently coming to terms with the details, then a conscious remembering, followed by the commemoration of past events. It is my hypothesis that acknowledgement is the one stage through which any successful process of societal recovery must pass.

As I have argued elsewhere, this kind of acknowledgement is a necessary but not sufficient condition in the process of social rebuilding that must take place in communities that have suffered harms through gross violations of human rights, repression, and so on (Quinn 2010, 15–33). As I have previously pointed out, '[t] here is a strong and causal relationship between acknowledgement and forgiveness, social trust… and reconciliation' (Quinn 2009a, 178). That is, it seems that societies, and the individuals who make up those societies, must engage in a process of acknowledgement before any of the other acts of social rebuilding, like forgiveness and reconciliation, can take place (Govier 1999).

In many communities, however, the events of the past are simply never discussed. Rather, the history of the events themselves and the many consequences of those events are left to bubble beneath the surface—allowing perpetrators, bystanders, outsiders, and others in the broader community to move forward, seemingly oblivious to what has taken place, while survivors, and their descendants, often remember in excruciating detail. In Canada, this can be seen in the manner in which missing and murdered Indigenous women have been largely forgotten—by everyone, that is, except their families and friends and their *gemeinschaft* communities.[1] Until the 2016 federal election, it seemed doubtful that any public inquiry would be launched, or that the details would be brought to light. I argue that unless these atrocities are both privately and publicly acknowledged by individuals within a society, including survivors and perpetrators, bystanders, and outsiders, the society cannot move forward on the continuum of social rebuilding (Quinn 2010).

Individually, acknowledgement is accomplished through deep introspection and confronting the past. The growing awareness of details of abuse and harm often sets off an emotional response. This causes a person to begin to accept and deal with details that can be difficult or unpleasant to admit. Putting this information into context often causes it to come sharply into juxtaposition with what was previously

[1]Ferdinand Tonnies divided societies into two distinct groups: "*Gemeinschaft* society is one in which people live together in primary groups, tightly wound around the institutions of kin, community and church." See Howard (1995), 25–26.

assumed, and this can be difficult to face. But once the individual, through both personal development and interpersonal awareness, has admitted the past, he or she is compelled to remember it.

Publicly, acknowledgement may be carried out through the establishment of mechanisms of transitional justice: The testimony offered at a hearing held by a truth commission, for example, can assist in establishing a narrative account of what has taken place once it is disseminated, which can lead to the official recognition of what happened. Likewise, a public apology offered by a head of government to a group that was wronged can constitute an admission of these events and the suffering that occurred as a result. The literature is replete with descriptions and evaluations of all sorts of modalities that can result in the public acknowledgement of past events.

Sympathetic Response

Conventional theories have assumed that societies emerging from abuse and harm are necessarily receptive to programs of acknowledgement and reconciliation almost as soon as they are offered. Pablo De Greiff, for example, presupposes that individuals have an implicit understanding of the value of truth-telling and support it (De Greiff 2006, 199). More than thirty-five truth commissions have been established around the world since 1974, and millions of dollars have been spent on their operation. Yet the literature increasingly demonstrates that the mechanisms themselves are not trusted by the population, and that they often have very little impact because the population as a whole fails to engage in them (Chapman and van der Merwe 2008; Kiss 2006; Quinn 2009b; UN Secretary General 2011, 7). The same has been said for other kinds of social rebuilding processes the world over.

I want to argue here that this failure results when the foundational requirements for real success are not firmly in place when such processes are implemented. Horticulturalists, for example, amend soil that is not suitable for growing particular kinds of plants to make that soil more hospitable to those plants, and to increase their viability. In the same way, I think, the conditions for success need to be put in place for repairing and rebuilding strategies to thrive. Without any 'amendment' to the 'soil' of post-conflict or decolonising societies, the effective purchase of these processes is substantially weakened. The mechanisms simply cannot gain any traction, and so cannot flourish, and nor can they make any change. I posit that the needed amendment is *thin sympathy*.

Sympathetic response is the key intervening variable that stimulates the impulse to acknowledge. The use of the term *sympathy* here does not refer to the more popular, colloquial meaning, 'to feel sorry for'. Rather, I utilise the technical definition of sympathy as something approximating 'understanding, awareness, recognition, and appreciation'.

First defined by Smith (1759), sympathy entails 'acquiring detailed knowledge about the way [the 'other'] lives,' (Eisikovits 2010, 60) while its counterpart, the more dynamic *empathy*, is understood as a 'full-blown curiosity and emotional openness towards another' (Halpern and Weinstein 2004, 570). These terms are often used interchangeably in the literature, although incorrectly. Sympathy is considered to be 'an other-oriented, emotional response that is based on the… comprehension of another's emotional state or condition', whereas empathy is 'a state of emotional arousal… which is similar to, or congruent with, what the other person is feeling (or should be expected to feel)' (Losoya and Eisenberg 2001, 23, 22). Scholars including LaCapra (2004, 1994, 2000) and Gobodo-Madikizela (2013a: 217–226, 2013b) argue that empathy influences how a person comes to terms with another's experience (Gobodo-Madikizela 2013b), and is required to deal fully with past events (Daye 2004; LaCapra 2004; Regan 2010; Gobodo-Madikizela 2013a, b).

Before that can occur, however, the most basic step toward either sympathy *or* empathy is a kind of 'thin sympathy,' which involves a simple understanding of what has happened to the other, and reflects a rudimentary recognition of both his humanity and his needs (Quinn 2015). That is, a person needs to at least become aware of the situation that has befallen the survivor and/or his family and/or the wider community. Govier allows that this awareness may be 'implicit' (Govier 2003, fn. 11). This awareness, you will remember, is the first step in any process of acknowledgement. And while it might seem obvious that this kind of awareness is a prerequisite to dealing with the problems that exist, it is surprising just how often this basic comprehension just does not exist. For example, near the beginning of the mandate of the Truth and Reconciliation Commission of Canada, I had a conversation with a dear friend—a middle-class, middle-aged, non-Indigenous Canadian woman—about the Indian Residential Schools. We talked about how the work that I have done on truth commissions in other parts of the world, including Uganda and Haiti, could be at all relevant to what had taken place in Canada. As I described the abuse that took place in the schools, my friend responded by saying, 'I don't think so. I am a Canadian. If those things had happened here, I would know.' She then went on to lament that she had only been able to go to a public school in rural Manitoba, and had not been 'lucky' enough to go to a private school like the Indigenous kids. My friend clearly had no idea about what had taken place in the Residential Schools. And her misunderstanding not only obscured her understanding of events, it also created a sense of anger and resentment toward the people who had attended those schools, without any understanding of the abuse many suffered there, or of the sub-standard quality of education they received. Likewise, Canadian broadcaster Shelagh Rogers said of her own experience: 'Like many Canadians, I thought I knew our history. But many of us grew up on the "Milk of Amnesia" approach to the story of Canada. I don't recall ever learning about residential schools. Or the Sixties Scoop. Or the Indian Act' (Rogers 2014).

In Canada, as in Australia (see Sarah Maddison and Angelique Stastny's chapter in this volume) non-Indigenous Canadians have been prevented from engaging in any understanding of both what happened in the residential schools and beyond. As

Ry Moran notes in his chapter, not many non-Indigenous Canadians had even heard about what took place before the TRC. As the TRC Report made clear, 'The beliefs and attitudes that were used to justify the establishment of residential schools are not things of the past: they continue to animate much of what passes for Aboriginal policy today' (TRC 2015, 4).

'Thick sympathy' takes this a step further, and involves the development of a simple compassion toward others. Had my friend more deeply understood the nature, let alone the scope and scale, of abuse that happened in the residential schools, or understood the impact of that abuse on survivors and their families, she might have begun to feel an emotional response to their harm. That feeling, what I define as 'thick sympathy', is simply the 'the act or capacity of entering into or sharing the feelings or interests of another' (Merriam-Webster 2016). Simon postulates that this kind of learning happens 'within the disturbances and disruptions inherent in comprehending these events' (Simon et al. 2000, 3). In his chapter in this volume Peter Read speaks of something similar when he discusses the need to find a way to 'thicken' non-Indigenous feelings.

Empathy is the densest of the categories, and is only rarely achieved among post-conflict, decolonising populations in divided societies, except in a handful of instances. Brecht defines empathy as a 'feeling for another based on the assimilation of the other's experience to the self' (2005, 5). It has been described by Eisenberg as the 'retrieval of relevant information from memory that fosters an understanding of the other individual's feelings or situation' (Eisenberg et al. 1991). LaCapra argues that experiencing trauma can 'upset expectations and unsettle one's very understanding of existing contexts,' a shock to the system that can cause an individual to 'explore in a telling and unsettling way the affective or emotional dimensions of experience and understanding' (2004, 117–118, 132). For LaCapra, the experience of trauma may be primary, as in, experienced by the individual him- or herself, or secondary, through hearing another person's story, whether as testimony or even as a fictional account. The jarring experience of trauma—whether first- or second-hand—is enough to prompt what LaCapra calls 'empathetic unsettlement… [that is] affective involvement in, and response to, the other' (La Capra 2004, 135).

Thin sympathy, thick sympathy, and empathy can be seen as being on a continuum from the least engaged (thin sympathy) at one end, to the most engaged (empathy) at the other. I argue that unless there is at least basic understanding (thin sympathy) there can be no acknowledgement, and that reconciliation cannot be achieved without the more robust empathy (Quinn 2015). As such, thin sympathy is a fundamental building block of acknowledgement, and must be in place for both thick sympathy and empathy to occur. More to the point, while it is perhaps too optimistic to hope that everyone in any society could feel empathy toward people affected by harm and abuse, I argue that empathy makes individuals much more open to becoming involved in the healing process of the community.

To be clear, thin sympathy is not the least desirable. It is simply a pragmatic recognition that it might never be possible to achieve more than this. The thinner things are, the more brittle they often are, which is problematic. If a proper engagement, to paraphrase the now-famous idiom used by American and South Vietnamese governments during the war in Vietnam to win the support of the Vietnamese people in defeating the Viet Cong, is about 'hearts and minds' then thin sympathy is the engagement only of the mind. Thick sympathy engages both the mind and the heart. Empathetic response goes still further and engages the mind and the heart and the hands. That is, thin sympathy implicates only a superficial cognition of the past. Thick sympathy translates that basic awareness into a feeling of concern. Empathy, though, is the capacity to recognize or even share the emotions being felt by another.

Indeed, those individuals who become empathetically involved in the stories of the 'other' and begin to engage with them in the healing process often become *champions* for social reconstruction. That is, they take up the cause and seek to better the situation for survivors and their families. In referring to what he calls 'policy entrepreneurs,' Kingdon writes of 'people who are willing to invest their resources in pushing their pet proposals or problems, are responsible not only for prompting important people to pay attention, but also for coupling solutions to problems and for coupling both problems and solutions to politics' (Kingdon 1984, 21). Kingdon's policy entrepreneurs are, in fact, empathetic champions.

One example, in the Canadian context, is broadcaster Shelagh Rogers, who serves as an 'Honorary Witness' to the TRC. Rogers is among 44 exceptional Canadians who have agreed to take on the role of bearing witness to the truths revealed at the TRC, some of whom have also gone on to found an organization called 'Canadians for a New Partnership' (The Story 2016). Rogers has been an unrelenting champion for the TRC, and a voice for Indigenous Canadians. While Rogers herself was not a victim of the residential schools, she has very obviously been touched deeply by them. This squares with LaCapra's understanding of second-hand trauma. Rogers recounted her experience at the Northern TRC National Event, where she was inducted as an Honorary Witness:

> I was the first of a group to be inducted at a ceremony in front of 800 people, mostly residential school survivors. I got up and promised I would share the stories and statements I would witness at every opportunity. My induction was followed by that of a Holocaust survivor; then a person who had seen his village destroyed in Bosnia. He was followed by an Australian who had helped set up a group to support largely Aboriginal, people affected by past policies of "forcible removal"; then there was a man who had survived torture in Guatemala. I had a strong sense of 'one of these things is not like the other': What is the white middle-aged woman doing in their company? I came to understand that I could use my voice to speak to Canadians the length, breadth and height of this country…
>
> Those who accept the invitation to bear witness have a responsibility to remember and to take the story forward. It means opening yourself to the truth, allowing yourself to be changed by it. Everyone who attends these events is a witness. We share a collective responsibility to make things better. To act. Because if we do nothing, nothing will change (Rogers 2014).

Rebuilding initiatives are almost always impelled by exceptional advocates, empathetic champions, who push for things to happen. Often, those people are survivors. But sometimes they are bystanders to the violence, or outsiders who have no particular or direct history with that past, except through a second-hand encounter. These outsiders are particularly able to push for change, and to sway opinion and policy.

The literature provides some hypotheses about why these extraordinary people choose to act: Staub has written that 'to reduce their own distress, passive members of the perpetrator group tend to distance themselves from victims… This reduces empathy' (Staub 2006, 872). The same, I think, applies to bystanders and outsiders. Eisikovits argues that as bystanders and outsiders become geographically more removed from the perpetration of violence, their 'context becomes thinner' and there is less impetus to acknowledge survivors' circumstances (Eisikovits 2010, 63; Mencl and Ray 2009, 206). As is sometimes argued, 'We can care deeply, selflessly, about those we know, but that empathy rarely extends beyond our line of sight' (Interstellar 2014). Others, however, argue that bringing people closer together produces a kind of thin sympathy that will open the door for acknowledgement (Donnelly and Hughes 2009). Certainly, Nusso et al. contend that 'countries in which there is greater social proximity between survivors and perpetrators as well as weak group membership may reduce mutual distrust, facilitate an understanding of the other's perspective as well as greater willingness to engage in conciliatory activities, and produce shared frames of social reference' (2015, 353). Thin sympathy, then, is the basis for acknowledgement (Quinn 2015).

This hypothesis seems to be validated by parallel work taking place in the cognitive neurosciences. In particular, the role of mirror neurons in the building of empathy has fostered significant debate. Ramachandran (2000) found that a form of imitation of the behaviour of others can precipitate an empathetic response (see also Oberman et al. 2007). This happens in the medial temporal cortex of the brain, when neurons called 'mirror neurons' cause a person to mimic a particular behaviour. Iacoboni et al. have argued that "[u]nderstanding the intentions of others while watching their actions is a fundamental building block of social behavior' (2005, 1). Others contend that 'a dysfunctional "mirror neuron [network]" may underlie… social deficits' (Dapretto et al. 2006, 28–30). Canada's TRC attempted to harness this type of response by appointing Honorary Witnesses like Shelagh Rogers, whose own response gives an appropriate basis upon which to model subsequent bystander and outsider behaviour. The physiological response must not be discounted in understanding a person's capacity for thin sympathy.

Two lessons are important here: First, without people like Rogers, people whom I think of as 'empathetic champions', there would be no impetus to intervene on behalf of survivors and their families. Second, beyond those empathetic champions, the development of thin sympathy among a critical mass of the population—that is, the smallest number of people needed to make something happen—is essential. In its absence, empathetic champions will find no uptake of their ideas, and processes of social healing will ultimately break down, if they begin at all.

Social Reconstruction Blocked

Efforts at this kind of social reconstruction tend to be obscured or even blocked by two distinct factors. These factors demonstrate a decided lack of even thin sympathy, and in fact prevent the building blocks of thin sympathy from forming. Two factors that are of importance here are a lack of national identity and the failure of government to model thin sympathy. Each of these is discussed, in turn, below:

Lack of National Identity

One of the arguments to be made about how and why non-Indigenous Canadians are not paying more attention to the stark issues confronting Indigenous communities is the question of national identity. Without paying attention, the basic building blocks of thin sympathy cannot even form. While the 'two solitudes' analogy in Canada originally described the perceived lack of communication, and, frankly, a lack of will for communication between Anglophone and Francophone people in Canada, a demonstration of the failure of thin sympathy to form in another Canadian context—today it might more usefully apply to the relationship between non-Indigenous and Indigenous Canadians.[2] The two communities are separate in so many ways.

In fact, a substantive racism exists. The Final Report of the Chippewas of Nawash Unceded First Nation to the Ipperwash Inquiry includes a report entitled 'Encountering the Other: Racism Against Aboriginal People.' The report looks at the 'particular kinds of racism that First Nations' people face all the time—the kind that they must deal with because simply because they are Native and the kind they must deal with because they are members of a group (a Native Band) that is collectively asserting land claims and/or constitutionally recognised aboriginal and treaty rights' (Chippewas of Nawash 2005, 1). That bias is deeply felt: 'There is a very strong perception among urban Aboriginal peoples in Toronto [and also in other cities] that non-Aboriginal people hold a wide range of negative and distorting stereotypes of Aboriginal people' (Environics 2010, 36).

Keeping the groups separate, without any useful interchange between the two groups, does nothing to facilitate thin sympathy. The groups must begin to interact with one another—even through media reports or joint activities—that will help them to understand the history of what has happened.

---

[2]The term is credited to author MacLennan (1945).

Failure of Government to Model Thin Sympathy

While it appears that Canada sits on the precipice of change, it is clear that successive past governments have served to impede progress on the Indigenous relations file in Canada. Governments, including the Harper government, and also Liberal governments before it, stopped progressive changes that were being proposed, including the Kelowna Accord that would have improved education, employment, and living conditions for Indigenous peoples through governmental funding and other programs; the Kelowna Accord was never endorsed by Prime Minister Harper.[3] Even Jean Chrétien, former Prime Minister and, before that, Minister of Indian Affairs, recently stated that taking action on the Indigenous file will take time, meaning that the process of reconciliation will be stalled further (Chrétien 2016).

In many ways, governments are constrained by what they perceive to be mandates from their electorates. As such, in responding to the perceived opinions of the electorate, governments make decisions that are carefully designed to keep them in elected office. This was certainly the case when Prime Minister Harper, who responded to the claims made by Indian Residential Schools survivors with some reluctance. He was determined to do only as much as was absolutely necessary, and no more.

Appreciating these blockages is important because they help to explain the lack of uptake of ideas in post-conflict and decolonising societies. More significantly, however, they are important because they have blocked the development of thin sympathy throughout the country. This helps to explain the extent to which such strategies have failed to gain popularity or acceptance among the general population. The effectiveness and impact of any effort is significantly less without at least thin sympathy.

Fostering Thin Sympathy

If the hypothesis that I have laid out above, that thin sympathy—defined here as a basic understanding or general awareness—is essential to acknowledgement, and that acknowledgement is a necessary but not sufficient condition for social rebuilding, is true, then it is essential that thin sympathy be developed in post-conflict or decolonising societies. This is not a new concept. The Truth and

[3]The Kelowna Accord was a 2005 initiative to 'close the gap' on the standard of living between Indigenous and non-Indigenous Canadians. With a budget of $5 billion, the plan would have targeted health, education, housing, infrastructure, economic opportunity, accountability, and the relationship between Indigenous Canadians and the Government of Canada. A change in government in early 206 meant that the plan was never really implemented (The Canadian Encyclopedia).

Reconciliation Commission itself had a fairly specific mandate in this regard. In seeking to 'inform all Canadians about what happened in Indian Residential Schools' (TRC 'FAQs'), the TRC was 'to provide for wider dissemination of the report pursuant to the recommendations of the Commissioners' (TRC 'Our Mandate').

Efforts to bring about 'thin sympathy' within a population may be systematised in a progressive, three-step trajectory that includes the following: 1. The gathering and dissemination of information; 2. Sensitising the population to the information; and 3. Educating the population about how the pieces of the bigger picture fit together. Each of these is explored below.

First, factual information must be disseminated. That is, details about what has happened need to be made publicly known. Even with the 15 December 2015 release of the final report of the Truth and Reconciliation Commission, entitled 'Honouring the Truth, Reconciling for the Future,' a great number of Canadians continue to know little or nothing of the abuses that took place within the residential schools. It seems likely that few have even read any or all of the 94 recommendations of the Truth and Reconciliation Commission, let alone the whole report. Media outlets including the Canadian Broadcasting Corporation have taken up the call to begin to regularly report on matters dealing with the history of abuse. More needs to be done.

Second, the population must be sensitised to that information. Sensitisation causes a person to respond to certain stimuli, and makes them sensitive to the information they hear. Sensitising Canadians, for example, to the violence that has taken place in nearly every corner of the country, I am convinced, would spur a simple recognition of the humanity and the vulnerability of the survivors of the abuse and their families, and of people, generally, from whatever background. The value of sensitisation is discussed at length in the scholarly literature on genocide, with particular reference to the genocide in Rwanda, where President Kagame's National Unity and Reconciliation policy—for better or worse[4]—has focused on sensitisation as a social good. Properly utilised, a sensitisation campaign could begin to change hearts and minds by making them more sensitive to the experiences of people from elsewhere in the country.

The third step, then, would be to help people understand how the pieces fit together. That is, while people might be aware of factual details, and may even have developed a sensitivity to that information, they may not understand that the discrete events they understand are, in fact, part of a broader system or structure of abuse. This appears, at least on the surface, to be true in all post-abuse situations. The Haitian truth commission report was one of the first truth commission reports to develop a quantitative database that allowed for detailed analyses of patterns of abuses that happened in specific geographic areas or to certain types of people (Quinn 2010, 82). Understanding that the abuse was not merely confined to one

[4]Kagame's policy also includes *Ingando* solidarity camps that are little more than forced political re-education camps. See Thomson (2011).

small area, but is part of a broader pattern of abuse, can help to cement the development of thin sympathy, and open the process of acknowledging what has taken place.

Making information available to a population, whether through dissemination, sensitisation, or by drawing clear lines between abuses to establish patterns and systems, is important. People need not only to know what happened, but also to understand it clearly. This holds true for survivors, who might know only their own story. It is also true for perpetrators who might come to understand how the small role they played contributed to a bigger whole with more egregious consequences. But it is critically important that bystanders and outsiders are engaged in the building of thin sympathy. They make up the bulk of the population, and are often the deciding factor in whether or not a particular program or process will be implemented—particularly in democratic or nominally-democratic systems. Their understanding is critical to furthering social rebuilding processes.

For people like Shelagh Rogers, learning about what happened in the residential schools has not only stoked her awareness of the subject, it has caused her to want to do something in response. This has not necessarily been the case for others. An Angus Reid poll completed in June 2015, at the close of the TRC's final event, found that 70 % of Canadians recognise that what happened in the schools was cultural genocide (CBC 2016). Awareness of the residential schools has 'risen by 15 points since 2008 to 66 %,' and that awareness of the specific consequences of that system and of the connections between those abuses and the residential schools has grown to 73 % (Adams 2016). The President of Environics, the firm that conducted the latest polling, says 'these results suggest that Canadians would rather be moving along the path to progressive change, even if we stumble, than standing still or moving backward' (Adams 2016). As Maddison and Stastny's chapter in this volume points out, there may be no basis to assume that this will translate into practical change, and from the 'learning' frame into mobilisation. Perhaps, in the Canadian case, it is too soon to tell.

Conclusions

This paper has demonstrated the location of thin sympathy in the broader context of sympathetic engagement. Thin sympathy is a very basic step, and requires only a straightforward understanding of the events of the past, and the effect on the other. Further along on the continuum of sympathetic response is thick sympathy: that is, compassion. An even thicker engagement consists in 'full-blown curiosity and emotional openness towards another' (Halpern and Weinstein 2004, 570).

The hypothesis regarding thin sympathy is simple: *thin sympathy must be developed or acknowledgement will not occur*. In the Canadian case, thin sympathy was not developed and so acknowledgement did not occur. We know that acknowledgement is a necessary but not sufficient condition for effectively dealing with the past. As such, for bystanders and outsiders, particularly, the small act of learning what has happened to the other and recognising his suffering—without any further emotional attachment or action—is extremely important. The effectiveness and impact of social reconstruction efforts is significantly less without thin sympathy.

References

A Condensed Timeline of Events. (2008). In M. B. Castellano, L. Archibald, & M. DeGagné (Eds.), *From truth to reconciliation: Transforming the legacy of residential schools*. Aboriginal Healing Foundation: Ottawa.

Adams, M. (2016). The door to reconciliation is truly open. [Op-ed.] *The Globe and Mail* (8 June.)

Arthur, P. (2009). How 'transitions' reshaped human rights: A conceptual history of human rights. *Human Rights Quarterly, 31*(2), 321–367.

Brecht, B. (2005). Quoted in Jill Bennet. *Empathetic vision: Affect, trauma, and contemporary art*. Stanford: Stanford University Press.

CBC News. (2008). A history of residential schools in Canada. [FAQ on-line.] Available from http://www.cbc.ca/news/canada/story/2008/05/16/f-faqs-residential-schools.html. Accessed 21 April 2011.

Chapman, A. R., & van der Merwe, H. (2008). *Truth and reconciliation in South Africa: Did the TRC deliver?*. Philadelphia: University of Pennsylvania Press.

Chippewas of Nawash Unceded First Nation. (2005). Encountering the other: Racism against aboriginal people. In *The final report of the Chippewas of Nawash Unceded First Nation to the Ipperwash inquiry*.

Chrétien, J. (2016, January 23). Keynote address: Pursuing peace in an age of insecurity. In *Social Science Academic Conference*, Western University.

Churchill, W. (2004). *Kill the Indian, save the man*. San Francisco: City Lights Books.

Dapretto, M., Davies, M. S., & Pfeifer, J. H. (2006). Understanding emotions in others. *Nature Neuroscience, 9*, 28–30.

Daye, R. (2004). *Political forgiveness*. Maryknoll, NY: Orbis Books.

De Greiff, P. (2006). Truth telling and the rule of law. In T. A. Borer (Ed.), *Telling the truths: Truth telling and peace building in post-conflict societies*. Notre Dame: University of Notre Dame Press.

Donnelly, C., & Hughes, J. (2009). Contact and culture: Mechanisms of reconciliation in schools in Northern Ireland and Israel. In J. R. Quinn (Ed.), *Reconciliation(s): Transitional justice in postconflict societies*. Montreal: McGill-Queen's University Press.

Eisenberg, N., Shea, C. L., Carlo, G., & Knight, G. P. (1991). Empathy-related responding and cognition: A 'chicken and the egg' dilemma. In W. M. Kurtines, J. Gewirtz, & J. L. Lamb (Eds.), *Handbook of moral behavior and development, vol. 2: Research*. Hillsdale, NJ: Erlbaum.

Eisikovits, N. (2010). *Sympathizing with the enemy: Reconciliation, transitional justice, negotiation*. St. Louis, MO: Republic of Letters Publishing.

Environics, (2010). *Urban aboriginal peoples study: Toronto*. Toronto: Environics Institute.

Gobodo-Madikizela, P. (2013a). Acting out and working through traumatic memory: Confronting the Past in the South African context. In M. Linden & K. Rutkowski (Eds.), *Hurting memories and beneficial forgetting: Posttraumatic stress disorders*. London: Elsevier.

Gobodo-Madikizela, P. (2013b). Reconciliation and mutual recognition after mass trauma. In Keynote address presented at "*peace from the ground-up: Post conflict socialization, religion and reconciliation in Africa*." Monkey Valley Conference Centre, Cape Town, South Africa.

Govier, T. (1999). Acknowledgement and forced confession. [Typewritten Manuscript]. Calgary, AB: author's collection.

Govier, T. (2003). What is acknowledgement and why is it important? In C. A. L. Prager & T. Govier (Eds.), *Dilemmas of reconciliation: Cases and concepts*. Waterloo: Wilfrid Laurier University Press.

Halpern, J., & Weinstein, H. M. (2004). Rehumanizing the other: Empathy and reconciliation. *Human Rights Quarterly, 36*(3), 561–583.

Howard, R. E. (1995). *Human rights and the search for community*. Boulder: Westview.

Iacoboni, M., Molnar-Szakacs, I., Gallese, V., Buccino, G., Mazziotta, J. C., & Rizzolatti, G. (2005). Grasping the intentions of others with one's own mirror neuron system. *PLoS Biology, 3*.

Indian and Northern Affairs Canada. What is the Indian Residential Schools Settlement Agreement and how does it address the legacy of Indian Residential Schools. Available from http://www.ainc-inac.gc.ca/ai/rqpi/faq-eng.asp#IRSSA-1. Accessed 21 April 2011.

Indian Residential School Survivors' Society. History. [Article on-line. Available from http://www.irsss.ca/history/. Accessed 21 April 2011.

Kelowna Accord. *The Canadian Encyclopedia*. Available from https://en.wikipedia.org/wiki/Canadian_federal_election,_2006. Accessed 14 July 2016.

Kingdon, J. W. (1984). *Agendas, alternatives, and public policies*. London: Longman.

Kiss, C. (2006). The misuses of manipulation: The failure of transitional justice in post-communist Hungary. *Europe-Asia Studies, 58*(6), 925–940.

LaCapra, D. (1994). *Representing the holocaust: History, theory, trauma*. Ithaca: Cornell University Press.

LaCapra, D. (2000). *Writing history, writing trauma*. Baltimore: Johns Hopkins University Press.

LaCapra, D. (2004). *History in transit: Experience, identity, critical theory*. Ithaca: Cornell University Press.

Losoya, S. H., & Eisenberg, N. (2001). Chapter two: Affective empathy. In Judith A. Hall & Frank J. Bernieri (Eds.), *Interpersonal Sensitivity: The LEA series in personality and clinical psychology*. Mahwah, NJ: Lawrence Eribaum Associates Publishers.

MacLennan, H. (1945). *Two solitudes*. Montreal: Wm. Collins and Sons & Co.

Maloney, R. (2015, September 14). Harper reportedly denies saying MMIW inquiry wasn't high on 'radar'. *The huffington post Canada*. Available from http://www.huffingtonpost.ca/2015/09/14/harper-missing-murdered-indigenous-women_n_8136604.html. Accessed 15 Feb. 2016.

Mas, S. (2015, December 8). Trudeau lays out plan for new relationship with indigenous people: 5-point plan includes a national inquiry into missing and murdered indigenous women. CBC News. Available from http://www.cbc.ca/news/politics/justin-trudeau-afn-indigenous-aboriginal-people-1.3354747. Accessed 15 Feb. 2016.

Mencl, J., & Ray, D. R. (2009). The effects of proximity and empathy on ethical decision-making: An exploratory examination. *Journal of Business Ethics, 85*(2), 201–226.

Merriam-Webster On-Line Dictionary. Available from http://www.merriam-webster.com/dictionary/sympathy. Accessed 13 Feb. 2016.

Nolan, J., & Nolan, C. (2014). *Interstellar*. Los Angeles: Paramount Pictures.

Notes for an Address by the Honorable Jane Stewart, Minister of Indian Affairs and Northern Development, on the occasion of the unveiling of *Gathering Strength — Canada's Aboriginal Action Plan*. (1998, January 7). Ottawa, Ontario. Available from http://www.ainc-inac.gc.ca/ai/rqpi/apo/js_spea-eng.asp. Accessed 21 April 2011.

Nusso, E., Rettberg, A., & Ugarriza, J. E. (2015). Survivors, nonsurvivors and their opinions on transitional justice: Findings from the colombian case. *International Journal of Transitional Justice, 9*(2), 316–335.

Oberman, L. M., Pineda, J. A., & Ramachandran, V. S. (2007). The human mirror neuron system: A link between action observation and social skills. *Social Cognitive and Affective Neuroscience, 2*(1), 62–66.

Prime Minister Harper offers full apology on behalf of Canadians for the Indian Residential Schools system. (2008, June 11). Available from http://www.ainc-inac.gc.ca/ai/rqpi/apo/index-eng.asp. Accessed 21 April 2011.

Quinn, J. R. (2009a). What of reconciliation? Traditional mechanisms of acknowledgement in Uganda. In J. R. Quinn (Ed.), *Reconciliation(s)*. Montreal: McGill-Queen University Press.

Quinn, J. R. (2009b). Haiti's failed truth commission: Lessons in transitional justice. *Journal of Human Rights, 8*(3), 265–281.

Quinn, J. R. (2010). *The politics of acknowledgement: Truth commissions in uganda and haiti.* Vancouver: UBC Press.

Quinn, J. R. (2015). Failure to launch: The consequences of prematurely conceived transitional justice. In *A paper presented at the European Consortium for Political Research.* Montreal. 27 August.

Ramachandran, V. S. (2000). Mirror neurons and imitation learning as the driving force behind 'the great leap forward' in human evolution. Available from http://www.edge.org/documents/archive/edge69.html. Accessed Sep. 19, 2015.

Regan, P. (2010). *Unsettling the settler within: Indian residential schools, truth telling, and reconciliation in Canada.* Vancouver: University of British Columbia Press.

Rogers, S. (2014, March 29). Reflections on being an honorary witness for the TRC: CBC's Shelagh Rogers participates in the Truth and Reconciliation Commission. CBC News. Available from http://www.cbc.ca/news/aboriginal/reflections-on-being-an-honorary-witness-for-the-trc-1.2587064. Accessed 15 Feb. 2016.

Simon, R. I., Rosenberg, S., & Eppert, C. (2000). Introduction: Between hope and despair: The pedagogical encounter of historical remembrance. In Roger I. Simon, Sharon Rosenberg, & Claudia Eppert (Eds.), *Between hope and despair: Pedagogy and the remembrance of historical trauma.* Baltimore: Rowman and Littlefield Publishers.

Smith, A. (1759). *The theory of moral sentiments* (London: A. Millar, A. Kincaid, and J. Bell, 1759; reprint New York: Digireads, 2010).

Staub, E. (2006). Reconciliation after genocide, mass killing, or intractable conflict: Understanding the roots of violence, psychological recovery, and steps toward a general theory. *Political Psychology, 27*(6), 867–895.

The Story of Canadians for a New Partnership. Canadians for a New Partnership. Available from http://www.cfnp.ca/about-cfnp/the-story-of-cfnp/. Accessed 16 Feb. 2016.

Thomson, S. (2011). Reeducation for reconciliation: Participant observations on ingando. In Scott Straus & Lars Waldorf (Eds.), *Remaking Rwanda: State Building and human rights after mass violence.* Madison, WI: The University of Wisconsin Press.

Truth and Reconciliation Commission of Canada. (2015). *The final report of the truth and reconciliation commission of Canada, Vol. 5: The legacy.* Montreal: McGill-Queen's University Press.

Truth and Reconciliation Commission of Canada. "FAQs." [Website.] Available from http://www.trc.ca/websites/trcinstitution/index.php?p=10. Accessed 14 July 2016.

Truth and Reconciliation Commission of Canada. "Our Mandate." [Website.] Available from http://www.trc.ca/websites/trcinstitution/index.php?p=7. Accessed 14 July 2016.

Truth and Reconciliation: Canadians see value in report, skeptical government will act; 7 of 10 Canadians agree with TRC's characterization of residential schools as 'cultural genocide'. (2016, July 9). CBC News. Available from http://www.cbc.ca/news/aboriginal/truth-and-reconciliation-canadians-see-value-in-report-skeptical-government-will-act-1.3144271. Accessed 9 June 2016.

United Nations Secretary General. (2011, October 12). *The rule of law and transitional justice in conflict and post-conflict societies: Report of the secretary-general.* New York: United Nations.

Winter, S. P. (2014). *Transitional justice in established democracies.* New York: Palgrave MacMillan.

Chapter 9
'You Can't Have Reconciliation Without Justice': How Non-Indigenous Participants in Canada's Truth and Reconciliation Process Understand Their Roles and Goals

Jeffrey S. Denis and Kerry A. Bailey

Abstract A central objective of the Truth and Reconciliation Commission (TRC) of Canada was to foster healing and reconciliation between Indigenous and non-Indigenous peoples. After six years of national and community events, statement-gathering, and archival research, and the well-publicized release of the TRC's final report in 2015, nearly one in five settler-Canadians remains oblivious to the TRC and most have not participated in reconciliation initiatives. Nevertheless, thousands of settlers did attend TRC events and many are engaged in ongoing solidarity activities with Indigenous peoples. To understand how some settlers become engaged and how they understand their roles in the process, we interviewed forty non-Indigenous Canadians who attended TRC events. In this chapter, we examine what reconciliation means to them, what they are doing (and think they should be doing) to pursue it, and whether (and why or why not) they identify as allies. Since allyship is partly about accountability to Indigenous peoples and respecting their knowledges and voices, we also critically assess and reflect on participants' perspectives by comparing them to those of Indigenous scholars and activists and of the TRC itself. In doing so, we shed light on the possibilities and limits of reconciliation in settler colonial Canada.

Keywords Allies · Canada · Decolonization · Indigenous · Land · Racism · Reconciliation · Settler · Treaty

J.S. Denis (✉) · K.A. Bailey
McMaster University, Hamilton, Canada
e-mail: denisj@mcmaster.ca

K.A. Bailey
e-mail: baileka@mcmaster.ca

S. Maddison et al. (eds.), *The limits of settler colonial reconciliation*,
DOI 10.1007/978-981-10-2654-6_9

'Reconciliation is not an aboriginal problem—it is a Canadian problem. It involves all of us.'—Justice Murray Sinclair, Chair of the Truth and Reconciliation Commission of Canada (quoted in Fedio 2015*).*

*The real task of reconciliation, however, is not in Canada waiting around to be forgiven for colonialism so business can carry on as usual; it is for Canadians to end the ongoing colonial violence that still suffocates Indigenous lives.' – Erica Lee (*2016*), Nehiyaw youth activist.*

While documenting the history and impacts of the Indian Residential School system, a central objective of the Truth and Reconciliation Commission (TRC) off Canada was to foster healing and reconciliation between Indigenous and non-Indigenous peoples. After six years of national and community events, statement-gathering, and archival research, and the well-publicised release of the TRC's (2015: 5) final report, which described a system of 'cultural genocide' and issued ninety-four recommendations for change, nearly one in five settler-Canadians remains oblivious to the TRC and most have not participated in reconciliation initiatives (Angus Reid 2015).[1] Nevertheless, thousands of settlers did attend TRC events and many are engaged in ongoing solidarity activities with Indigenous peoples.

To understand how some settlers become engaged and how they understand their roles in the process, we interviewed forty non-Indigenous Canadians who attended TRC events, as public statement providers, volunteers, and observers. In this chapter, we examine what reconciliation means to them, what they are doing (and think they should be doing) to pursue it, and whether (and why or why not) they identify as allies. Since allyship is partly about accountability to Indigenous peoples and respecting their knowledges and voices (see, for example, Gehl 2012, 2014), we also critically assess and reflect on participants' perspectives by comparing them to those of Indigenous scholars and activists and of the TRC itself. In doing so, we shed light on the possibilities and limits of reconciliation in settler-colonial Canada.

Although participants' visions of reconciliation generally aligned with core aspects of the TRC's vision, including an emphasis on respectful relationships, historical awareness, cultural understanding, healing, and 'closing the gap' on socioeconomic and health outcomes, most were strikingly disconnected from wider movements for decolonisation and Indigenous land struggles.[2] Further, although most participants identified as allies, they attributed diverse meanings to the term, including listening to and learning from Indigenous peoples, educating fellow settlers, speaking out against racism, and lobbying for changes in government policies. While such roles are potentially useful and not mutually exclusive, these same 'allies' sometimes conceived of the ultimate goals in divergent ways, ranging from

[1]An Angus Reid poll in July 2015 found that eighteen per cent of Canadians knew nothing about the TRC, thirty-one per cent had scanned a few headlines, thirty-five per cent had seen some media coverage and had the odd conversation about it, and seventeen per cent were closely following it in the news and discussing it with family and friends (http://angusreid.org/aboriginal-truth-and-reconciliation/).

[2]The disconnect is striking insofar as decolonisation and land struggles have been a priority for most Indigenous activism in Canada (see, for example, Coulthard 2014). Moreover, claiming to reconcile or be in alliance, while ignoring or marginalizing Indigenous perspectives, may be seen as a colonial act in itself.

the integration of Indigenous peoples into multicultural Canada to the radical transformation of society, based on respect for Indigenous self-determination and nation-to-nation treaties. Although this wide range of settler perspectives creates challenges for reconciliation, it also may be necessary, given that Indigenous perspectives also vary by nation and region.

Indigenous Perspectives on Reconciliation

To provide a basis for comparison, we begin by outlining salient Indigenous perspectives on reconciliation and allyship in the Canadian Indigenous-settler relations context.

Reconciliation is a complex, multidimensional phenomenon whose nature and prerequisites have been debated. As noted in the introduction to this volume, there is no broadly agreed upon definition. However, dictionary definitions tend to focus on ideas of re-establishing friendship after a conflict. The TRC notes in its final report that such definitions are problematic because 'friendship' never existed between Indigenous and settler peoples in some regions. Yet, the notion of peaceful co-existence and 'healthy relationships…going forward' certainly resonates (TRC 2015: 113).

To this end, the TRC issued ninety-four Calls to Action, based on ten principles of reconciliation. The first principle is using the United Nations Declaration on the Rights of Indigenous Peoples (UNDRIP) as 'the framework for reconciliation at all levels and across all sectors of Canadian society' (TRC 2015: 3). Based on decades of negotiations, the UNDRIP outlines individual and collective rights of Indigenous peoples, prohibits discrimination, and 'promotes their full and effective participation in all matters that concern them, as well as their right to remain distinct and to pursue their own visions of economic and social development' (UN 2007: 2).

From the TRC's (2015: 3–4) perspective, implementing the UNDRIP and fostering meaningful reconciliation would entail, among other things:

- recognising and respecting the treaty, constitutional, and human rights of First Nations, Métis, and Inuit peoples;
- healing relationships through 'public truth sharing, apology, and commemoration';
- 'addressing the ongoing legacies of colonialism' and creating 'a more equitable and inclusive society by closing the gaps in social, health, and economic outcomes';
- respecting and learning from the 'perspectives and understandings of Aboriginal Elders and Traditional Knowledge Keepers';
- supporting cultural revitalisation, including 'integrating Indigenous knowledge systems, oral histories, laws, protocols, and connections to the land into the reconciliation process';
- joint leadership, trust building, accountability, and resource investments; and
- 'sustained public education and dialogue…about the history and legacy of residential schools, Treaties, and Aboriginal rights, as well as the historical and contemporary contributions of Aboriginal peoples to Canadian society'.

Ultimately, the TRC (2015: 121) concludes, reconciliation is 'an ongoing individual and collective process' that requires 'the commitment of multiple generations' of Indigenous and non-Indigenous people and will result in 'a better, stronger Canada.'

The TRC's report and vision were quickly applauded and endorsed by mainstream Indigenous organisations and leaders. The Assembly of First Nations National Chief Perry Bellegarde said the TRC provides an opportunity for Canadians 'to understand their role in our shared history and our shared future, and…to work with us as partners' towards 'closing the gap in the quality of life between First Nations and Canada' (AFN 2015: 1). First Nations child advocate Cindy Blackstock likewise argues that reconciliation requires eliminating inequalities between Indigenous and non-Indigenous children, including the systematic under-funding of First Nations child welfare services (Amnesty International 2015). Inuit leaders stressed the need for healing, including investment in mental health services to address historical trauma, and overhauling public education systems to promote 'cultural understanding' (Zerehi 2015). The Native Women's Association of Canada (2015: np) underscored the 'urgent need' for a national inquiry into missing and murdered Indigenous women, while echoing calls for friendship and mutual support.

Indeed, some Indigenous writers emphasise reconciliation at the interpersonal and family levels, not just the societal level. Anishinaabe journalist and musician Wab Kinew (2015: 211) writes:

> Reconciliation is not something realized on a grand level…when a prime minister and a national chief shake hands. It takes place at a much more individual level. Reconciliation is realized when two people come together and understand that what they share unites them and that what is different between them needs to be respected.

This emphasis on local-level healing and relationship-building, often grounded in traditional teachings, is echoed by Reconciliation Canada and some other Indigenous-led groups.

Thus, despite differences in emphasis, there appears to be a relative consensus among the TRC and most Indigenous leaders and organisations that reconciliation should be pursued through healing from historical trauma, closing socioeconomic and health gaps (through equitable distribution of resources), improving public education, implementing the UN Declaration, and building mutual understanding and respectful relationships.

Even before the TRC was appointed, however, some Indigenous scholars and activists—especially those affiliated with the Indigenous Governance Program at the University of Victoria (the 'Victoria school')—questioned the notion of reconciliation as 'an orienting goal.' Taiaiake Alfred and colleagues have described reconciliation—at least as reflected in public discourse—as 'weak-kneed,' 'emasculating,' and 'pacifying,' an acquiescence to settler-colonialism that distracts from and undermines 'deep decolonizing movements' (Alfred 2009: 181; Corntassel 2012: 91; Coulthard 2014).[3] Instead, these scholars advocate for restitution (especially the return of land), the

[3]To be clear, these critiques were not directed at the TRC, but were mostly articulated earlier, amidst the B.C. Treaty Process.

regeneration and resurgence of Indigenous nations, and the creation of sustainable alternatives to hetero-patriarchal colonial-capitalism. Far from 'walking together' in harmony, Alfred (2009: 183) says, justice 'can only be achieved through contention and...constructive conflict with the state and with the Canadian society'.

Similarly, Corntassel (2012: 91–92) depicts reconciliation initiatives as 're-inscribing the status quo'. Rather than legitimating the state and reconciling with settler-colonialism, he promotes a return to local, 'community-centered actions premised on reconnecting with land, culture and community' (Corntassel 2012: 91–92). More generally, a growing number of Indigenous scholars advocate turning away from the state and settler society, rejecting recognition politics, embracing the politics of refusal, and focusing on regenerating politically autonomous and culturally vibrant Indigenous nations (cf. Coulthard 2014; Simpson 2014; Tuck and Yang 2012; Waziyatawin 2009).

The Victoria school and others have also criticised the UNDRIP as a mechanism for substantive change, in part because it is legally non-binding and, as per Article 46, prohibits 'any action which would dismember or impair, totally or in part, the territorial integrity or political unity of sovereign and independent States' (UN 2007: 14–15). In other words, it recognises Indigenous rights only insofar as they do not disrupt the status quo or question the legitimacy of settler-colonial states.

Still other Indigenous scholars and activists straddle the boundaries between mainstream/TRC and radical/Victoria visions. Rather than dismissing reconciliation, they emphasise that it can and must be achieved *through* decolonisation, Indigenous resurgence, and honouring the spirit of the original peace and friendship treaties. Realising this in practice, however, would mean transforming settler society and respecting Indigenous self-determination. It also would mean revitalising Indigenous laws and institutions and the ability to 'enjoy their cultures, languages, territories and political systems free of state interference' (Lee 2012: np).

While noting the merits of the TRC report, Anishinabek writer Leanne Simpson (2016: np) highlights its relative lack of emphasis on the land,[4] even though 'residential schools were a strategy used by Canada to break the connection between Indigenous peoples and our lands, so the state could access the land for settlement and for natural resources'. Simpson (2016: np) continues:

> If reconciliation is to be meaningful, we need to be willing to dismantle settler colonialism as a system [and] tackle the root causes of Indigenous oppression in Canada... It means giving back land, so we can rebuild and recover from the losses of the last four centuries and truly enter into a new relationship with Canada and Canadians.

Through such processes, Simpson suggests, peaceful co-existence and respectful relationships—and hence reconciliation—may be forged between Indigenous peoples and settler-Canadians (cf. Lee 2016; McMahon 2016). However, it will not be 'cheap' or easy and it will require more than friendship.

---

[4]In fairness, the TRC's Calls to Action #43–47 call for the repudiation of the Doctrine of Discovery and *terra nullius*, the implementation of the UNDRIP, and the reaffirmation of nation-to-nation relationships, which would have substantial implications for land ownership, control, and stewardship.

Indigenous Perspectives on Allyship

Given these multiple visions of reconciliation, what roles can and should settler-Canadians play? More generally, what would it mean for settlers to be allies?

From a radical perspective, one might argue that it is impossible for settlers to be allies if they remain on occupied lands (however much they empathise with the colonised) (Memmi 1965). One important aspect of the Canadian context, however, is the existence of treaties (in some regions), which entail rights and responsibilities for both Indigenous and settler peoples.[5] The processual worldviews of many Indigenous peoples also encourage relationships of accountability rather than either/or thinking (see, for example, FitzMaurice 2010). Moreover, most Indigenous scholars and activists believe that settlers can make valuable contributions to Indigenous-led movements. Rather than demanding that they leave Turtle Island, for example, Alfred (2005: 153) says settlers must demonstrate 'respect for what we share—the land and its resources—and mak[e] things right by offering us the dignity and freedom we are due and returning enough of our power and land for us to be self-sufficient.'

The TRC also sees a vital role for non-Indigenous Canadians. As Justice Sinclair has said, reconciliation is 'a Canadian problem' that involves 'all of us' (Fedio 2015: np). Thus, he and fellow Commissioners encouraged all Canadians to follow the TRC process, listen to and learn from residential school survivors, and read and reflect on their reports.

Consistent with settler scholar Paulette Regan's (2010: 19) 'unsettling pedagogy,' TRC Commissioners emphasised the role of witnessing. It appointed prominent Indigenous and non-Indigenous individuals from various regions and sectors as 'honorary witnesses' responsible for listening to and remembering survivors' stories, being accountable to them, and sharing their significance with others.[6] The TRC also encouraged settlers—especially government and church officials, teachers, and others involved in operating or overseeing residential schools (and their descendants)—to give public statements or 'expressions of reconciliation,' which could potentially facilitate healing and serve as public commitments to behavioural change. Further, most of the ninety-four Calls to Action were directed at settler-Canadians and their governments and institutions. While the specific responsibilities depend on social position, there is indeed a role for everyone.[7]

---

[5]There are, of course, significant differences between the more recent colonial-imposed treaties and the original peace and friendship treaties.

[6]For Regan (2010: 189–192), witnessing requires deep listening—'engaging our whole being,' sitting with the discomfort, and learning from it. Ultimately, she says, 'settler identity can…be transformed from that of colonizer to ally' only if we question Canada's 'benevolent peacemaker myth,' respect Indigenous counter-narratives of diplomacy, law, and peacemaking, and engage in 'positive action to confront the settler problem head-on' (16).

[7]The TRC's (2015: 126) final report outlines distinct roles for governments, churches, schools, businesses, and 'Canadians from all walks of life,' as well as Indigenous people themselves.

Beyond the context of the TRC, many Indigenous (and non-Indigenous) writers have offered advice on how to be an ally or act in solidarity with Indigenous peoples. Algonquin scholar-activist Lynn Gehl (2012, 2014), for example, distinguishes colonised versus decolonised allies and proposes an 'Ally Bill of Responsibilities.' For her, a 'genuine ally' engages in ongoing (un)learning, listens and reflects, is aware of their privilege and complicity, acknowledges their mistakes and apologises for them, is willing to challenge oppressive power structures, values differences rather than seeking to erase them, respects boundaries, does not take up space or resources, acts with the consent of Indigenous communities, and does not make their support conditional on personal or ideological agendas (Gehl 2012).

During the Idle No More movement of 2012/13, Mi'kmaq scholar-activist Pam Palmater (2013: np) spoke positively of 'allies' and First Nations 'partnering for justice', adding that Canadians must realise—and many are realising—that they need Indigenous peoples' help in order to build a more just and sustainable society. Similarly, Métis-Cree lawyer and blogger Chelsea Vowel (2014: np) says the best way for would-be allies to 'help' is by recognising that 'Indigenous peoples have the power to find solutions for ourselves' and supporting Indigenous-led movements. Amadahy and Lawrence (2009) provide concrete examples of such allyship, including fundraising, providing food/supplies, working at camps during land struggles, and completing tasks as needed and requested. More generally, they call on settlers to reflect on their positions and 'shift their ideological frameworks, value systems and conceptual understandings of how humans relate to land and the resources within it' (Amadahy and Lawrence 2009: 129–130). Being an ally to Indigenous struggles means building respectful relationships with Indigenous people but also 'being an ally to the land' (Amadahy and Lawrence 2009: 129–130).[8] Ultimately, these authors agree that an ally is not self-defined; it is a term bestowed on the basis of ongoing action.[9]

Data and Methods

To better understand how settlers become engaged in reconciliation activities, how they think about their roles and goals (including possibilities and limits), and what they do to make good on their commitments, we conducted in-depth interviews with forty non-Indigenous Canadians of various ages, genders, socioeconomic statuses, and racial/ethnic backgrounds who had attended at least one TRC event (as a minimal indicator of engagement). Compared to the general Canadian public, participants were somewhat older, whiter, and more often affiliated with Christian churches that

[8]Similarly, the TRC (2015: 123) states, 'Reconciliation between Aboriginal and non-Aboriginal Canadians, from an Aboriginal perspective, also requires reconciliation with the natural world.'

[9]Similar ideas have been discussed by non-Indigenous scholar-activists, including Barker (2010), Bishop (2002), Davis (2010), Fortier (2015), and Walia (2012).

ran residential schools. Interviewees also varied in terms of their TRC event roles, affiliations, and knowledge of and experience with Indigenous issues.

Our analysis in this paper focuses primarily on participants' responses to three questions:

- The meaning of reconciliation, whether they are actively pursuing it, and how they understand their role (and that of Indigenous peoples) in the process;
- Whether they identify as an ally, and why or why not; and
- Their vision for the future of Indigenous-Canada relations.

Using the above literature as a starting point, we categorised interviewees' responses in terms of the degree of overlap with Indigenous perspectives on reconciliation and allyship. Specifically, we coded their understandings of reconciliation as negative (rejecting reconciliation as a goal) or positive (endorsing reconciliation as a goal), and analyzed variations within these understandings (for example, whether they focused on relationship-building, healing, or 'closing the gap'). We also noted themes such as whether reconciliation was framed as 'closing a sad chapter' or as an 'ongoing process' and whether it entails modest reform or radical decolonisation.

Similarly, we coded participants' understandings of allyship as negative (rejecting the term ally) or positive (identifying as or striving to be an ally), and analyzed variations within these understandings (for example, whether they focused on self-reflection, ongoing (un)learning, or taking political action). Various other themes also emerged. For instance, some participants placed limits or 'conditions' on their allyship and/or expressed views that could be considered racist, paternalistic, or otherwise contrary to the spirit of reconciliation.

What Reconciliation Means to 'Engaged' Settlers

Participants expressed a range of views on what reconciliation means, and some had more detailed and nuanced responses than others. However, most conveyed a somewhat less comprehensive version of the TRC's vision for reconciliation. They generally agreed on the importance of awareness, education, relationship-building, supporting Indigenous healing and cultural revitalisation, and, to a somewhat lesser extent, 'closing the gap' in living conditions and pursuing 'social justice.' Some also mentioned the need to honour treaties, implement the UN Declaration, and reform Canadian laws and policies. Yet, unlike radical Indigenous scholars and activists, only a few made explicit connections between reconciliation and decolonisation or Indigenous self-determination and land struggles. Non-Indigenous participants were far more likely to promote 'walking together' for a 'better, stronger Canada' than struggling against the settler-colonial system and creating new sustainable and equitable ways of relating to one another and the land.

Consistent with the TRC, more than two-thirds of interviewees framed reconciliation, at least in part, in terms of building respectful relationships and working with

Indigenous peoples. For instance, some said that reconciliation means 'getting to know one another as human beings,' 'moving forward in a good way and developing positive relationships,' and 'living like brothers or cousins.' Some participants discussed close personal friendships with Indigenous people. Others described larger-scale relationship-building through local church groups and anti-racism and solidarity groups that collaborate on projects of mutual concern (for example, environmental campaigns). In these relationships, ongoing communication and accountability are key.

In order to build and sustain respectful relationships, awareness, understanding, education, and self-reflection were also deemed critical. In the context of the TRC, many stressed the importance of listening to and learning from residential school survivors:

> ...part of reconciliation is sitting down and listening to what Indigenous people have to say...educating myself about what is going on and...letting other people do the talking.

Reconciliation also means acknowledging the harm that residential schools and other colonial policies have caused, and appreciating how past injustices affect present circumstances. According to another interviewee:

> [Non-Indigenous Canadians] have to get out there and listen and talk to Indigenous people and...respect them... People really need to understand and get to know the history of what was done to them because that is the only explanation for what non-Indigenous people see as malfunctioning First Nations people.

As these comments suggest, many participants believe that reconciliation requires better education about the history and impacts of colonisation. Some called for overhauling public school curricula to ensure comprehensive, accurate Indigenous-related content at every grade level. A few also mentioned innovative models such as Project of Heart, developed by (white) Ottawa schoolteacher, Sylvia Smith, where students learn about the residential school system, its objectives and impacts, decorate tiles to commemorate residential school students, interact in person with a residential school survivor or Elder, and work together on a social justice project.

Beyond learning about the historical and contemporary conditions affecting Indigenous peoples, nearly half of participants felt that reconciliation required settlers to look in the mirror and reflect on their own identities, histories, and assumptions. As one woman said, echoing Regan (2010):

> I think we need to step out of our protective bubble of denial. As uncomfortable as that is, we need to shed [the idea] that we are here because we have done well and we have worked hard and we deserve it, and we have to look at ourselves very differently and recognise what we have done...on the backs of Indigenous people.

Equally important for some participants was the cultural/symbolic dimension of reconciliation. More than half discussed the need to accept and celebrate cultural diversity. For instance, some said that reconciliation means 'building awareness and understanding of the different cultures and worldviews'; 'looking at differences…as being good differences' and 'coming to a better understanding of each other's culture and valuing it.' Some specifically noted that settlers have much to learn from Indigenous knowledge. According to one interviewee, reconciliation requires:

> …taking leadership from First Nations people who know exactly how to [live sustainably] because they did it forever before we showed up and destroyed everything.

Another referred to 'two-eyed seeing,' or using the best of both Indigenous and Western knowledges to analyse or solve a problem (Bartlett et al. 2012). Still others said that reconciliation requires commemorating residential schools and other colonial practices, but also recognising the substantial contributions of Indigenous people to Canada—from the country's name to military and sports heroes, writers, artists, inventors, etc.

For many settlers, the concept of reconciliation is closely linked to healing and the revitalisation of Indigenous languages and cultures. According to one, 'my dream would be that they would be able to be proud of their culture, proud to be Aboriginal, that the spirituality and the culture of the Aboriginal community would be strong.' In order for this to happen, Indigenous people have the burden of healing from historical trauma. According to another interviewee:

> Reconciliation is about personal healing from the heritage of pain [and] abuse… when five generations of people are taken out of family and raised in an institutional environment that is abusive, [many] skills are lost. It's a very long journey for those communities to heal [but] they're working at it.

Although settlers' role in healing was not always clearly stated, many said they 'support' the process, and some, including the individual quoted above, said the Canadian government should provide more resources for Indigenous-led health care, healing, and cultural initiatives.

Although some participants understood reconciliation and their role in it in relatively passive ways, more than half said that reconciliation entailed moving from awareness to action, from acknowledgment to change. While the specific actions and changes required were sometimes vague, more than forty per cent said that reconciliation could only happen with equitable funding and resource investments, or, as the AFN has emphasised, 'closing the gap.' According to one participant, reconciliation means eliminating 'the inequities between the groups…in terms of health care and education and housing, lack of employment on reserves.' Several interviewees criticised the Harper government's hypocrisy in apologising for residential schools while simultaneously cutting funding for the Aboriginal Healing Foundation, scrapping the Kelowna Accord,[10] and under-funding First Nations schools and other services. As one said:

[10]The Kelowna Accord was a 2005 agreement between the federal government, all provinces and territories, and five national Aboriginal organizations that would have significantly increased funding for Indigenous education, health care, housing, and economic development.

> There are so many basic conditions that haven't been improved on so many reserves: housing, education, health care. How can you…say 'we apologise, we recognise all that we've done and our responsibility for what's happened and the connections between past and present,' and yet, in the same breath, 'we are going to cut the budget'?

Numerous participants stressed that while the government should provide funding, First Nations should be empowered to run their own programs. More generally, one said:

> …you can't have reconciliation without justice… and it's really up to the government to provide the leadership in helping us get to that place where non-Aboriginal people and Aboriginal people can enjoy the same standard of living and maintain their different cultures…

When asked about his personal role in this process, the interviewee referred to taking political action—writing MPs, signing petitions, and voting based on candidates' commitment to Indigenous and treaty rights. Several participants shared this position, and approximately half used terms such as 'justice,' 'equity,' or 'fairness' in describing what reconciliation means to them.

In general, aspects of reconciliation that would require substantial behavioural change from settlers were less likely to be advocated. It is often easier for non-Indigenous people to 'delegate' responsibility than to 'embody' the changes we would like to see (de Costa and Clark 2016). However, many participants did say they were willing to share power and resources with Indigenous peoples in the name of justice. According to one woman:

> We, the non-Indigenous, need to be willing to give up a little something, in order to be more egalitarian… I, for instance, would be willing to pay more taxes…

Another participant said that for reconciliation to occur, settlers must pay their 'debt' to Indigenous nations, given that the earliest settlers only survived with Indigenous peoples' help and then proceeded to steal their land and resources. In concrete terms, she said, this would mean eliminating poverty and changing 'government policies, the Indian Act, all of the systemic things that mitigate against Aboriginal people.' In other words, reconciliation is not just about healing from residential school trauma, but also about more fundamental changes in Canadian laws, policies, and institutions.

At least eight participants said that implementing the UN Declaration would be a step in the right direction, and some had protested the Harper government's initial refusal to endorse it. Similar numbers noted the importance of honouring Indigenous and treaty rights and holding the government accountable. According to one:

> We could be doing Truth and Reconciliation stuff just by starting to honour the treaties. Why aren't we doing that? … But of course that problematises the whole capitalist system [whereby] Canada still makes all of this money on resource exploitation.

This participant, who cited Taiaiake Alfred's influence on her thinking, was one of few to make explicit connections between reconciliation and decolonisation or radical structural change. Some participants, especially during and after the Idle No

More movement, did associate reconciliation with a shared commitment to protecting the environment. According to one woman in B.C.:

> One of the Indigenous people at a protest I went to, right after the TRC, said, 'So, you people said that you want to reconcile, then how can you do this? Stand with us against the pipeline.' I was already standing against the pipeline, but that just gave me a new angle on it… that, yes, this is something I can do with these people who are probably our only hope in stopping it.

A minority of interviewees also had participated in campaigns to defend Indigenous lands from further encroachment by developers and mining and forestry companies. However, very few said anything about returning land to Indigenous peoples, respecting Indigenous laws and jurisdiction in their daily lives, or dismantling the settler state or the capitalist system.

Finally, although ninety per cent of participants said they were actively pursuing reconciliation, a few expressed misgivings or rejected the term. For instance, one interviewee said reconciliation was 'not the right word' because, as a recent immigrant, 'I do not really feel like I have done anything wrong to them.' Another said that the term reconciliation was ambiguous, and he left a TRC event feeling frustrated: 'if there wasn't a clear picture or a consensus that emerged from that [group], it kind of reinforces in my mind that there isn't a commonly shared vision, and without that, it's going to be really difficult for people to work together.' Yet another interviewee noted that reconciliation is contextually contingent, so it may *have* to look somewhat different depending on the region and the specific Indigenous and settler peoples involved.

Being an Ally

When asked if they identified as 'allies,' more than three-quarters of participants said that they did, or strived to be. However, some were hesitant or uncomfortable with the label. A few said it was not a 'badge' they would claim for themselves but they would be happy to receive the honour. Others preferred terms such as supporter, friend, advocate, or co-conspirator, and one rejected labels altogether.

Those who did identify as allies tended to define the term somewhat more narrowly than most Indigenous scholars and activists define it. Specifically, participants emphasised 'walking together,' listening to and learning from Indigenous people, educating fellow settlers, speaking out against racism, and lobbying for changes in government policies. Only a few discussed being an ally to the land and supporting Indigenous self-determination and land struggles.

Consistent with their understandings of reconciliation, the most common meanings attributed to being an ally included building relationships, working together, and standing beside and supporting Indigenous peoples. For some, 'support' was operationalised at the level of interpersonal friendship and (literally or metaphorically) 'being by their side in their healing journey.' For others, it extended to political action, such as joining Idle No More rallies and signing petitions to enhance funding for social programs.

Most would-be allies felt they had a responsibility to be aware of historical and contemporary issues facing Indigenous peoples, and to use their knowledge to educate fellow settlers. One young man who had attended his first TRC event with his Indigenous girlfriend, and previously had known little about the issues, said he was inspired to learn more and felt that his role was to 'spread the knowledge.' An older teacher who had been working in solidarity with Indigenous peoples for decades said 'our main responsibility is to come out of the ignorance' and give future generations a better education that builds empathy, understanding, and respect. Some participants also described instances of countering racist comments at work, school, sporting events, and family dinners, and the dilemmas they faced as a result (for example, strained relationships).

As one woman put it, being an ally 'starts with listening' and supporting the needs and causes articulated by Indigenous people. If a community, especially one with whom one has a relationship, needs funding, food, or supplies, an ally would provide whatever resources they could. In the context of the TRC, one interviewee's husband transported Elders to and from events. A few participants specified that allies should respect boundaries and avoid driving the agenda. One said, 'I am trying really hard not to overstep where I should be as an ally… settlers can play an active listening role and engaging with what comes up, but they shouldn't be controlling the…process.'

Some also emphasised that being an ally requires critical self-reflection: acknowledging one's privileges and responsibilities, 'unlearning' stereotypes, and being 'aware of the ways in which [settlers] themselves have benefited from these historical relationships…and their complicity to the extent that they are unwilling to pressure governments to address these things.' Another advocated:

> …peeling away the layers of what we call 'privilege,' and looking at our whole thinking of who we are, where we come from, and…the assumptions that our culture has made…and just facing up to the arrogance…

More generally, some emphasised that being an ally requires humility, a willingness to acknowledge and atone for mistakes and to try-try again. An older couple recalled once inviting a Haudenosaunee Elder to do a traditional opening for an event they were organising on Anishinaabe land. After realising their error, they apologised and worked hard to regain trust.

For the most part, these perspectives on allyship are consistent with those of Indigenous scholar-activists cited above. However, an important blind-spot is that while many participants said that allyship meant supporting 'Indigenous causes,' few linked it specifically to Indigenous self-determination and land struggles. This speaks again to the seeming disconnect between reconciliation and decolonisation movements in Canada, and may indicate a limitation on how far some would-be allies are willing to go to pursue reconciliation.

Moreover, some interviewees rejected the idea of being an ally. A white male lawyer insisted that he is 'not on either side,' but only for 'the truth,' and that the concept of being an ally is divisive because it means being *against* somebody or something. Others placed firm conditions on their allyship. A health care worker in B.C. stated:

> I am not unconditionally an ally… I think it is healthy for relationships to have conditions… if a person [or] group decide[s] to become violent… I am more likely to support First Nations people who are working really hard to…get out of poverty, [who] want to get into education [and] be a participating member of society…

This stereotype-filled view clearly conflicts with that of Indigenous scholar-activists who suggest that 'genuine allies' should engage on Indigenous peoples' terms.[11] Yet, many settlers who participate in reconciliation activities may have limits and withdraw their support if Indigenous people do not meet their 'conditions'—a position that reinforces rather than challenges settler-colonial power dynamics.

Tensions and Contradictions

More generally, when asked about reconciliation, allyship, and their hopes and dreams for the future of Indigenous-Canada relations, participants expressed a range of tensions, contradictions, and divergent understandings that could constitute barriers to reconciliation. As hinted above, some also voiced paternalistic and colour-blind views that, consciously or not, serve to perpetuate structural inequities.

'All in it Together' Versus Respecting the Right Not to Engage

According to the TRC, reconciliation is 'a multi-generational journey that involves all Canadians' and 'will require commitment from all those affected' (TRC 2015: 121). Indeed, most settler participants seemed to take for granted that 'we are all in it together' and reconciliation necessitates everyone's involvement. Although such comments are often targeted at disengaged settlers (such as the one in five Canadians who claim they have never heard of the TRC), some also expressed frustration at the alleged unwillingness of some Indigenous people to engage with or trust them. Some self-proclaimed allies said they wished Indigenous people would be more open to collaboration, patient, trusting, forgiving, and not so angry or afraid of non-Indigenous people. According to an older woman in B.C.:

[11] It is also at odds with the concept of 'the clearing' outlined in Barker and Battell Lowman's chapter in this volume.

> I would just like to see that they would accept invitations [to settler-organised events], look non-Indigenous people in the eye…and smile… really get involved in their own culture and be proud of it and showcase it…so that non-Indigenous people can enjoy that and be part of it.

Such paternalistic and presumptuous responses often seem like attempts to control Indigenous peoples' emotions as well as the process of reconciliation, thereby reproducing familiar colonial relations.

Moreover, as the TRC is aware, some residential school survivors and others affected by colonial trauma may not be ready—and some may never be ready—to engage. Some are focused on their own healing. Others consciously refuse to reconcile with those who are seen as perpetuating injustices. As Nehiyaw youth activist Erica Lee (2016: np) puts it:

> We are never 'all in this together' while Indigenous communities are stripped to the bone for the fat to maintain Canada… Just as we follow rules of consent with intimate partners, Indigenous people reserve the right to choose which settlers with whom we are willing to reconcile.

As much as reconciliation is about building respectful relationships, it is also about respecting the right *not* to engage. At least a few interviewees agreed. One said that asking Indigenous people to reconcile with the government was like asking someone to reconcile with a partner who continues to abuse them. According to another interviewee: 'I don't think it is incumbent on [Indigenous people] to trust us [or] to give us another chance. I think we have to prove ourselves worthy.'

'Helping' Versus Working with or Taking Leadership from Indigenous Peoples

Another tension concerns participants' understanding of their roles in reconciliation. While some settlers, such as the health care worker quoted above, saw themselves 'helping' disadvantaged Natives, others saw themselves 'working with' or 'taking leadership from' Indigenous peoples. Given the current imbalance of power and material resources, some forms of 'help' are certainly sometimes desired and requested. However, some would-be allies displayed a sort of paternalism reminiscent of the attitudes that inspired residential schools and other assimilation policies. When asked about her vision for the future, a white female teacher said:

> I believe…we need to start…helping [young Indigenous women] from the time before they're pregnant and change our education system so [that] those moms would know how to feed their kids and how to read with them.

A B.C.-based lawyer declared that Aboriginal cultures are collectivist, and collectivist cultures have 'big flaws,' such as stifling individual rights and freedoms. He felt that his role, in part, was helping Aboriginal people move beyond 'tribal' thinking. Thus, some would-be allies are more inclined to treat their work with

Indigenous people as charity rather than justice, a stance that reinforces settlers' sense of superior group position (Denis 2015) and fails to meaningfully challenge the structure of Canadian society.

One member of a church-based Right Relations group noted that 'people are at different stages of understanding in our group,' and although they usually have good intentions, they sometimes make the mistake—as he admittedly did in the past—of speaking for Indigenous peoples or trying to control decision-making, rather than 'tak[ing] a back seat and allow[ing] Aboriginal people…to drive the process.'

However, far more interviewees said their role was to work in 'partnership' with Indigenous people. Phrases such as 'walking together' and 'standing beside' were especially common. Consistent with the views of Gehl (2012, 2014) and other Indigenous scholar-activists, a significant minority also emphasised that, as allies, they should take leadership from Indigenous people. As one university student put it:

> [An ally's] role is one of support and providing assistance or help when requested… and not one of 'this is what we need to do… I'll show you how it's done.' An ally is someone who…recognises that they hold responsibility to Aboriginal people, but also that it requires a certain humbleness… You're the support, behind the scenes…

Some participants appeared to be working through this tension and in the process of shifting mindsets. According to one interviewee who had just attended a workshop on 'Decolonising the Church':

> Sometimes I still have to stop and shake my head and say 'No, it isn't a matter of me helping them; it's a matter of all of us changing. And I can learn things from them.'

As Palmater (2013) says, settler-Canadians increasingly recognise that they need Indigenous peoples' help in the form of local Indigenous knowledge and rights that may protect the environment and contribute to a more just and sustainable society.[12]

Expecting Indigenous People to Teach Settlers Versus Taking Responsibility for One's Own Learning

Still, there is another tension between the expectation/demand of some would-be allies that Indigenous people 'teach' them versus the notion that settlers are responsible for their own learning. When asked about the role of Indigenous and non-Indigenous people in reconciliation, one participant replied, 'They've got to help us understand what has to be done.' According to another, 'they need to be spending more time engaging non-Aboriginal people and helping to move the educational process along.'

---

[12]This is not to suggest that allies should have no voice. As Bishop (2002) notes, it is important to maintain a critical perspective and 'be yourself.' However, allies need to listen more than talk and it is not an ally's role to tell Indigenous people what to do.

Some interviewees suggested that asking Indigenous people to teach them can be a form of 'respect'; rather than presuming to know what Indigenous people need or want, or speaking for them, they said they would defer to Indigenous colleagues' ideas. While this may be appropriate in some contexts, the insistence that Indigenous people should teach settlers whatever they want to know is a heavy burden. As several scholars and activists have noted, racism and colonialism are stressful and exhausting enough, without having to worry about settlers' education or feelings.

Some would-be allies, especially those who have been working in solidarity for years, clearly understand this. As one said:

> I think it's a process of self-education, and it's our responsibility to educate ourselves… you have to be willing to experience, to read books, watch programming on television, listen to interviews, expose yourself as much as you can…

When settlers demonstrate such commitments to self-education, Indigenous people may be more likely to 'help' them learn (when time and resources allow). One man recalled hearing a young Indigenous woman speak at a conference. She said, 'everything they [colonisers] have done to us, they've done to themselves first. And I want to challenge the settler society to do your own healing.' That, to him, was a wake-up call. Realising his own complicity in colonisation and 'knowing that it wasn't right,' he then undertook his own further reading and self-reflection, and was fortunate to meet an Indigenous Elder who served as an informal mentor:

> …that was huge for me. [The Elder's] leadership, his friendship…his willingness to trust me and engage me and invite me into that world…we [settlers] can't be in a right relationship until we do some healing. And we can't do our healing until we recognise that we need it… And walking with Aboriginal people was an opportunity to find my own healing.

This participant reiterated, however, that Indigenous people should not be expected to teach settlers; (un)learning and healing is our responsibility. But he was forever grateful to his Indigenous friends for their support, which deepened his understanding of his roles and his commitment to solidarity work.

Equity Versus Equality

A fourth tension concerns how would-be allies conceptualise justice. Many participants suggested that reconciliation was contingent on social justice, but they sometimes had different ideas about what this meant. Some interviewees emphasised equality of opportunity and/or living conditions. As one said, 'I'd like to see…equal access to the same social services… health, housing, water.' Such views are consistent with the TRC and AFN's emphasis on increasing funding for Indigenous social programs and 'closing the gap' in socioeconomic and health outcomes.

In stating the case, however, a few participants insinuated that Indigenous people were seeking and should not be granted special privileges. According to one:

> …the non-Indigenous need to be supporting equal health care and equal housing and equal things for everybody… and maybe the Indigenous need to too. Let's try to get some of this stuff off a racial basis.

The underlying message, in a few cases, was that Indigenous and treaty rights were an impediment to reconciliation. The lawyer quoted above said the 'key' was 'making people equal Canadians.'

Some also expressed colour-blind ideals that are likely to reproduce structural inequalities (Bonilla-Silva 2010). A white teacher said, 'I don't tend to see people's skin colour.' On a recent trip to New Zealand, a Maori church minister told her 'it might be more important that I be more aware of [differences] and maybe I should, but… I don't know… with my students I'm there teaching them math as people [and] you don't want something to sort of stick out and be different.'

While treating people 'the same' is sometimes warranted, other participants—consistent with most Indigenous and critical theorists—asserted that it is sometimes necessary to treat people differently in order to achieve a deeper form of substantive equality. Another teacher noted that some Indigenous students have different learning styles and benefit from different pedagogical approaches but that they are equally capable of learning. A minority of participants also emphasised the importance of honouring Indigenous and treaty rights. The interviewee who advocated 'equal access to the same social services' later added that she would 'also like to see a real respectful nation-to-nation relationship… Equality not as in sameness, but as in recognition…of Indigenous rights [and] sovereignty.' However, only a few interviewees explicitly promoted Indigenous self-determination and respect for Indigenous laws and jurisdiction.

This tension between equality and equity, or different understandings of justice (reflected to some degree in the writings of Indigenous scholars as well), is perhaps one of the greatest barriers to reconciliation.

Conclusion: 'A Better, Stronger Canada' Versus 'Deep Decolonising Movements'?

Settler-Canadians, even those engaged with the TRC process, display a wide range of views on what reconciliation means and how they understand their roles in it. This diversity creates challenges for reconciliation in that some would-be allies may be working at cross-purposes or even doing more harm than good. However, as King (2013) and other Indigenous scholars note, Indigenous peoples also have diverse political and cultural traditions and visions for the future. To the extent that Indigenous understandings of reconciliation (and decolonisation, resurgence, etc.) also vary by nation and region, the variation that we observe among settlers may be necessary. To think that there is any single pathway or role for settlers may be a colonial idea in itself. Moreover, the capacity to debate the meaning of terms such as reconciliation could be a sign of a functioning democracy.

Nevertheless, conflicts may arise when different visions are articulated within and between Indigenous and non-Indigenous communities. Perhaps the greatest sticking point is the tension between visions of reconciliation that lead to a 'better, stronger Canada' versus those that imagine a more radical societal transformation, including, at the limits, dismantling the settler state and the capitalist system and revitalising multiple overlapping Indigenous (and perhaps non-Indigenous) political-economic orders. The former vision has been promoted by the TRC and by many mainstream Indigenous leaders and organisations. As we have seen, it is also endorsed (sometimes within limits) by a majority of 'engaged' settlers. This pragmatic/reformist vision entails greater inclusion of Indigenous people in mainstream society, greater equality of socioeconomic conditions, and greater respect and understanding of Indigenous histories and cultures. Although the TRC and some interviewees also support the UNDRIP and Indigenous and treaty rights (at least to the extent that they do not challenge Canada's Constitution), many other settlers—especially perhaps those who are not so engaged with the TRC, but even some who are—promote a more integrationist philosophy ('making people equal Canadians'). As summarised by one interviewee, being an ally means 'I allow them to be [as] involved as they would like in harmony with the goals of Canada… and be given equal opportunity to live a satisfying life.' For another, reconciliation 'means that we all have a say and…that Canada is moving together with its people, all its people, on board.' Yet another called for 'one society, rather than two solitudes.'

What is missing from this vision is what is most central for some Indigenous scholars: the return of enough land and power for Indigenous nations to be self-sufficient (Alfred 2009). Moreover, these scholars say, respectful relations or peaceful co-existence between Indigenous and settler peoples would require more dramatic transformation of settler society—its political and economic structures, its ideological frameworks, its ways of relating to other peoples and the earth (Amadahy 2008; Coulthard 2014; Simpson 2016).[13] Only a few interviewees seemed willing to contemplate such possibilities. According to one:

> [decolonisation] seems almost impossible because we would need [to recognise] sovereignty to the people that were originally here… it would mean completely changing our government structure, our economic structure… it would be a very difficult process.

Such a process undoubtedly would be resisted by powerful forces who are vested in the status quo and even by many who adhere to the more reformist vision of an inclusive and equal-opportunity Canada. For the foreseeable future, then, reconciliation processes will continue to be marked by conflict, as much as by 'walking together' in peace and harmony (King and Lee 2015). By mapping the spread of settler perspectives against Indigenous perspectives, this chapter has identified some

[13]Although the TRC report calls for comprehensive change, the more radical changes emphasized by the Victoria School were largely ignored by a majority of interviewees.

of the stumbling blocks, as well as ideas and actions for developing truly respectful relationships and just and sustainable ways of life. Perhaps one of the most important contributions settlers can make is to reflect on our histories and identities and what it would mean to honour not only the UNDRIP but the original peace and friendship treaties, which are the only legitimate basis for the country of Canada. Our collective challenge is to apply these principles not only in activist spaces but in the prosaic spaces of our everyday lives.

References

Alfred, T. (2005). *Wasáse: Indigenous pathways of action and freedom*. Toronto: University of Toronto Press.

Alfred, T. (2009). Restitution is the real pathway to justice for Indigenous peoples. In G. Younging, J. Dewar, & M. DeGagné (Eds.), *Response, responsibility, and renewal: Canada's truth and reconciliation journey* (pp. 179–190). Ottawa: Aboriginal Healing Foundation.

Amadahy, Z. (2008, June/July). Roundtable on relationship-building in Indigenous solidarity work. *Briarpatch*. http://collectiveliberation.org/wp-content/uploads/2015/02/Amadahy-Roundtable-on-Relationship-building.pdf.

Amadahy, Z., & Lawrence, B. (2009). Indigenous peoples and Black people in Canada: Settlers or allies? In A. Kempf (Ed.), *Breaching the colonial contract: Anti-colonialism in the US and Canada* (pp. 105–137). New York: Springer.

Amnesty International. (2015). Reconciliation means not having to say sorry a second time: Conversation with Cindy Blackstock. http://www.amnesty.ca/blog/reconciliation-means-not-having-to-say-sorry-a-second-time-conversation-with-cindy-blackstock-f.

Angus Reid. (2015). Truth and reconciliation: Canadians see value in process, skeptical about government action. http://angusreid.org/aboriginal-truth-and-reconciliation/.

Assembly of First Nations (AFN). (2015, June 2). AFN National Chief Perry Bellegarde calls for commitment from federal government to act on Truth and Reconciliation Commission's calls to action. Press Release. http://www.afn.ca/en/news-media/latest-news/assembly-of-first-nations-national-chief-perry-bellegarde-calls-for-co.

Barker, A. (2010). From adversaries to allies: Forging respectful alliances between Indigenous and settler peoples. In L. Davis (Ed.), *Alliances* (pp. 316–333). Toronto: University of Toronto Press.

Bartlett, C., Marshall, M., & Marshall, A. (2012). Two-eyed seeing and other lessons learned. *Journal of Environmental Studies and Science, 2*(4), 331–340.

Bishop, A. (2002). *Becoming an ally: Breaking the cycle of oppression in people* (2nd ed.). Halifax: Fernwood.

Bonilla-Silva, E. (2010). *Racism without Racists: Color-blind racism and racial inequality in contemporary America* (3rd ed.). New York: Rowman & Littlefield.

CBC Radio. (2016, March 27). We need decolonization before reconciliation, argues Ryan McMahon. *The 180 with Jim Brown*. http://www.cbc.ca/radio/the180/how-safe-cities-can-be-dangerous-the-problem-with-reconciliation-and-stop-saying-cuba-will-be-ruined-1.3507402/we-need-decolonization-before-reconciliation-argues-ryan-mcmahon-1.3507589

Corntassel, J. (2012). Re-envisioning resurgence: Indigenous pathways to decolonization and sustainable self-determination. *Decolonization: Indigeneity Education & Society, 1*(1), 86–101.

Coulthard, G. S. (2014). *Red skin, white masks: Rejecting the colonial politics of recognition*. Minneapolis: University of Minnesota Press.

Davis, L. (Ed.). (2010). *Alliances: Re/envisioning Indigenous–non-Indigenous relationships*. Toronto: University of Toronto Press.

De Costa, R., & Clark, T. (2016). On the responsibility to engage: Non-Indigenous peoples in settler states. *Settler Colonial Studies, 6*(3), 191–208.
Denis, J. S. (2015). Contact theory in a small-town settler-colonial context: The reproduction of laissez-faire racism in Indigenous-white Canadian relations. *American Sociological Review, 80* (1), 218–242.
Fedio, C. (2015, June 2). TRC report brings calls for action, not words. *CBC News*. http://www.cbc.ca/news/politics/truth-and-reconciliation-report-brings-calls-for-action-not-words-1.3096863.
FitzMaurice, K. (2010). Are white people obsolete? Indigenous knowledge and the colonizing ally in Canada. In L. Davis (Ed.), *Alliances* (pp. 351–367). Toronto: University of Toronto Press.
Fortier, C. (2015). *Unsettling movements: Decolonizing non-Indigenous radical movements in settler colonial states*. PhD Dissertation, Department of Sociology, York University.
Gehl, L. (2012). Ally bill of responsibilities. http://www.lynngehl.com/uploads/5/0/0/4/5004954/ally_bill_of_responsibilities_poster.pdf.
Gehl, L. (2014, February 24). A colonized ally meets a decolonized ally: This is what they learn. http://www.lynngehl.com/black-face-blogging/a-colonized-ally-meets-a-decolonized-ally-this-is-what-they-learn.
Kinew, W. (2015). *The reason you walk: A memoir*. New York: Viking.
King, H. (2013, January 9). We natives are deeply divided: There's nothing wrong with that. *The Globe and Mail*. http://www.theglobeandmail.com/globe-debate/we-natives-are-deeply-divided-theres-nothing-wrong-with-that/article7096987/.
King, H., & Lee, E. (2015, December 15). The truth is there, but reconciliation is deeply complicated. *The Globe and Mail*. http://www.theglobeandmail.com/opinion/the-truth-is-there-but-reconciliation-is-deeply-complicated/article27759105/.
Lee, D. (2012, January 1). Re-envisioning reconciliation. Book review: *Dancing on Our Turtle's Back. Briarpatch*. https://briarpatchmagazine.com/articles/view/re-envisioning-reconciliation.
Lee, E. (2016, March 1). Reconciling in the apocalypse. *Canadian Centre for Policy Alternatives*. https://www.policyalternatives.ca/publications/monitor/reconciling-apocalypse.
Memmi, A. (1965). *The colonizer and the colonized*. Boston: Beacon Press.
Native Women's Association of Canada. (2015, December 15). NWAC stands in solidarity with the #TRC. Press Release. http://www.nwac.ca/2015/12/nwac-stands-in-solidarity-with-truth-and-reconciliation-commission-upon-the-release-of-their-final-report-on-tragic-indian-residential-school-legacy-in-canada/.
Palmater, P. (2013, January 4). Idle no more: What do we want and where are we headed? *Rabble*. http://rabble.ca/blogs/bloggers/pamela-palmater/2013/01/what-idle-no-more-movement-really.
Regan, P. (2010). *Unsettling the settler within: Indian residential schools, truth telling, and reconciliation in Canada*. Vancouver: UBC Press.
Simpson, A. (2014). *Mohawk interruptus: Political life across the borders of settler states*. Durham, NC: Duke University Press.
Simpson, L. (2016, January 8). Land and reconciliation: Having the right conversations. *Electric City Magazine*. http://www.electriccitymagazine.ca/2016/01/land-reconciliation.
Truth and Reconciliation Commission (TRC) of Canada. (2015). *What we have learned: Principles of truth and reconciliation*. http://www.trc.ca.
Tuck, E., & Yang, K. W. (2012). Decolonization is not a metaphor. *Decolonization: Indigeneity, Education & Society, 1*(1), 1–40.
United Nations (2007). *United Nations declaration on the rights of Indigenous peoples*. http://www.un.org/esa/socdev/unpfii/documents/DRIPS_en.pdf.
Vowel, C. (2014, September). 'How can I help?' answered concretely. *âpihtawikosisân*. http://apihtawikosisan.com/2014/09/how-can-i-help-answered-concretely/.
Walia, H. (2012, January 1). Decolonizing together: Moving beyond a politics of solidarity toward a practice of decolonization. *Briarpatch*. https://briarpatchmagazine.com/articles/view/decolonizing-together.

Waziyatawin. (2009). You can't un-ring a bell: Demonstrating contrition through action. In G. Younging, J. Dewar, & M. DeGagné (Eds.), *Response, responsibility, and renewal* (pp. 191–202). Ottawa: Aboriginal Healing Foundation.

Zerehi, S. S. (2015, December 15). Inuit leaders call for healing and education in wake of TRC final report. *CBC News*. http://www.cbc.ca/news/canada/north/inuit-truth-reconciliation-final-report-1.3366487.

Chapter 10
The Poetics of Non-Indigenous Reflexive Self-awareness: Strategies of Embodiment and Delegation in Focus Group Discussions in Australia

Angélique Stastny, Sasha Henriss-Anderssen and Tom Clark

Abstract This chapter will explore how research into non-Indigenous attitudes and identities surfaces certain forms of reflexive self-awareness in the course of Australian conversations about Australia's history and about Aboriginal and Torres Strait Islander peoples and cultures. Emerging research from Canada and Australia highlights the ideational and connotative significance of non-Indigenous people's discourse styles for their self-understanding 'as non-Indigenous'. Recent focus group research in Canada (de Costa and Clark 2015) suggests that we may characterise variations in non-Indigenous attitudes to settler-colonial history and to Indigenous people and cultures in terms of 'delegation' and 'embodiment'. This chapter will examine in close detail eight recent focus groups conducted at locations around Australia to ask what stylistic and semantic paradigms of reflexive self-awareness may characterise non-Indigenous discourses in Australia.

Keywords Reconciliation · Non-Indigenous people · Australia · Poetics · Focus groups · Delegation · Embodiment · Personal pronouns

---

The original version of this chapter was revised: The keywords were incorrect. The corrected keywords are added. The erratum to this chapter is available at 10.1007/978-981-10-2654-6_17

A. Stastny (✉)
University of Melbourne, Parkville, Australia
e-mail: a.stastny@student.unimelb.edu.au

S. Henriss-Anderssen · T. Clark
Victoria University, Melbourne, Australia
e-mail: Sasha.Henriss-Andersse@vu.edu.au

T. Clark
e-mail: Tom.Clark@vu.edu.au

S. Maddison et al. (eds.), *The limits of settler colonial reconciliation*,
DOI 10.1007/978-981-10-2654-6_10

Introduction

In a recent paper on non-Indigenous people's perception of the responsibility to engage with Canada's colonial history, and Indigenous people and cultures, de Costa and Clark (2015, 16) conclude that:

> Locality matters. Among broad groups of people who indicate a concern about the injustices experienced by Indigenous peoples in the colonization of Canada and contemporary society, the location (both historic and spatial) of the community you live in has some influence over the ways you conceive of what taking responsibility is and who bears that responsibility.

The authors observe that a stronger sense of personal responsibility, coupled with a greater distrust of government action for reconciliation, exists in northern British Colombia than in the large metropolis of Toronto—where responsibility is more readily delegated to Indigenous people, the government, or 'Canada' more broadly. In Canada as in other settler colonial societies, this dialectic of delegation (handing over responsibility) and embodiment (taking responsibility), and the importance of locality as a variable in non-Indigenous tendencies towards either the former or the latter are crucial to understanding current attitudes and power relations within these societies.

This present chapter emerges from a joint Australian Research Council funded project in Australia, and sits as something of a counterpart to de Costa and Clark's contribution. It explores the ways non-Indigenous people in Australia understand their responsibility (or non-responsibility) to build and/or improve relationships with Aboriginal and Torres Strait Island people and to develop a greater understanding of Indigenous history and cultures. The argument developed here is based on focus-group methods that generated semi-structured conversations amongst non-Indigenous people in four different localities in Australia. This chapter specifically engages with the ways that a close analysis of these conversations helps us identify modes of *delegation* and *embodiment* when it comes to a sense of responsibility.

The key to that close analysis is a focus on moments when the participants display forms of *reflexive self-awareness*. By reflexive self-awareness this chapter specifically means a consideration among non-Indigenous people of their own situations in the context of questions about a non-Indigenous responsibility to engage: do participants see themselves as non-Indigenous to any meaningful extent? Do they work with an explicit relationship towards Aboriginal and Torres Strait Islander people? Do their understandings of their own situations influence their views about a responsibility to engage?

As the following discussion explains, we have grounded our analysis in illustrative examples of the discourse that participants have used in the focus group discussions, because such discourse contains the most direct evidence of reflexive self-awareness. The main body of this chapter begins with a discussion of the background to the research that has generated this chapter. It then draws on illustrative examples from the focus group discussions to set out our key Findings.

These are broadly gathered under two themes or aspects of reflexive self-awareness: (i) participants' individual and collective self-positioning, which we particularly observe through their use of plural personal pronouns; and (ii) their framing of relations towards our research project itself, typically by addressing statements and questions towards the facilitator.

Background

The concept of 'reconciliation' has been comparatively more central to public discourses in Australia than it has in Canada, and it therefore occupies a more central place in our analysis than it did in the Canadian article. Initially set out by the Council for Aboriginal Reconciliation, created in 1991, the meanings and goals of reconciliation have greatly varied across time, contexts, and people. One purpose of the research project in Australia has therefore also been to unpick participants' understanding of reconciliation and their positions on it. Rather than a sign of adherence to, or a normative claim regarding, reconciliation, the centrality of 'reconciliation' in our analysis stems from an understanding that the question of non-Indigenous responsibility to engage with Indigenous people and cultures is fundamentally 'a question situated at a particular moment in history' (de Costa and Clark 2015, 2).

A growing literature has explored attitudes between Indigenous and non-Indigenous people in Australia, with works focusing on both Indigenous and non-Indigenous attitudes to negotiating relationships across this colonial divide, and to reconciliation. While works such as Philpot et al. (2013) have analysed Australian Indigenous reactions to PM Kevin Rudd's apology, and the possibilities of reconciliation and 'forgiveness', a growing literature—concomitant to the growth of settler colonial studies[1]—has turned the gaze towards the non-Indigenous attitudes to these relationships. Such works have generally focused on the nature of attitudes (in both positive and negative terms) towards Indigenous people or reconciliation, and their underlying emotions (ranging from guilt and fear to indifference) or on the relationship between identity and attitudes (Bulbeck 2004; Pedersen et al. 2004; Halloran 2007). The work of Gomersall et al. (2000) analyses the causal factors between Australian identity and support for reconciliation. Halloran (2007), through a survey and questionnaire amongst university students and the general public, has investigated the relationship between the value of egalitarianism and reconciliation attitudes amongst Australians and between collective guilt and positive reconciliation attitudes amongst Australians. Some works have also been interested in the generational variations amongst non-Indigenous

---

[1]Settler colonial societies have become the focus of growing scholarly attention as the product of a distinct form of colonialism. Lorenzo Veracini (2010) and Patrick Wolfe (1999, 2006) have emerged as prominent figures within this literature and the *Settler Colonial Studies* journal, the main publication.

attitudes with a particular focus on the younger generation (Burridge 2006; Bourke and Geldens 2007; 'Yarn About Youth' 2013). Less explored has been what informs people's decisions to engage or not within these relationships and how these decisions relate to their identity and locality.

A limited amount of research has adopted locality as a starting point and engaged with the importance of locality (spatial-historical location) in shaping non-Indigenous attitudes and explaining attitudinal variations in Australia (Pedersen et al. 2000; McCallum 2003).[2] Pederson et al. (2000) compared residents of Perth and Kalgoorlie, and analysed the propensity of negative/positive attitudes depending on whether their judgement were based on observation and experience, or on values and indirect knowledge. Andrew Gunstone (2008) has conducted interviews in Gippsland, Victoria, on local attitudes and practices around reconciliation. McCallum (2003) has analysed localised experiences of reconciliation and how local social discussions as well as public and media discourses inform public opinion's understandings of reconciliation. She has done this through semi-structured individual and group interviews in Canberra, Dubbo and the NSW South Coast. Significant for our purposes is this observation (McCallum 2003, 128):

> The reflexive way participants understood reconciliation highlights the significance of studying locally situated knowledge of public-policy issues…While individuals and groups engage with media-specific frames in their talk, they do not merely mimic media frames, nor do they have underlying 'attitudes' that can be plucked out to explain a response to a framed question. Rather, they adapt and apply them to their local understanding and experiences.

Taking its cues from these studies, this chapter grounds its analysis in individually and locally lived experiences. It seeks to make sense of how non-Indigenous people relate to history, Indigenous people and cultures, as well as to reconciliation, sharing McCallum's emphasis on the 'reflexive' nature of that meaning-making. In doing so, our Findings and Conclusions sections explain what these individual and localised modes of engagement reveal about public opinion's understanding of relationships across colonial divides and reconciliation policies. Ultimately, this chapter suggests that 'responsibility', a less-analysed emotion in the field, is a crucial factor that informs relationships within settler colonial societies.

Findings

Our research approach to political discourse does not capture the full range of non-Indigenous attitudes towards a *responsibility to engage*, nor does it offer any measure of popularity for the attitudes that it canvasses. Such findings could be

---

[2]We note this has been a stronger theme of research into Indigenous attitudes and identities, both in Australia and internationally.

extremely valuable, if they were verifiable. Rather, our research offers insights into the ways that gatherings of non-Indigenous people make sense of, and respond to, prompts to reflect on their personal and collective responsibility to engage. It draws into view the discursive and interactive techniques that such people resort to in such circumstances. In other words, taking its cue from the Canadian research, our approach offers insights into how non-Indigenous communities in Australia are given to process debates and events that have a bearing on their identities as non-Indigenous and on their understandings of relationships with Aboriginal and Torres Strait Islander peoples.

This chapter distils that offer in two ways. One, fairly obvious, is to limit the focus to Australian focus groups—albeit discussed here in the context of Canadian comparator-research. That distinction does not feel at all arbitrary in practice: our professional facilitator did not prompt discussion of the Canadian context, and in turn only two of the focus group participants—both immigrants from North America—gave it even a passing mention. A second distillation, more fundamental, is that we focus closely on elements of the discourse that our participants used, which offer a particular insight into the scope for reformulating non-Indigenous identities in Australia, and for articulating a non-Indigenous responsibility to engage with Aboriginal and Torres Strait Islander peoples. That is, we are focusing here on the language techniques that people use in scoping their own options for identity and for engagement.

So-expressed, readers might reasonably infer that this chapter's interests are inherently grammatical at some level. It is concerned with relevant norm-bound properties of the discourses that our focus groups manifest, while at the same time it seeks to extrapolate how those properties create or reinforce norms for future such discourses. Because discourse is itself concrete evidence of ideation, that means we are looking for the ways that people's ideas are discursively prescribed and discursively prescribing. We might simplify the distillation as a dichotomy, then: on one hand, *our research project* uses understandings of the discursive norms that apply to these people discussing this topic in order to scope their preparedness to engage with Aboriginal and Torres Strait Islander peoples, and to accept personal or collective responsibility for Australia's relationship between Indigenous and non-Indigenous peoples; on the other hand, *this chapter* focuses on discursive evidence of the participants' reflexive self-awareness to ask how they see themselves positioned in relation to that potential for engagement.

Grammar is a specific element of ideology. This chapter shows how clearly we may apply that theorem, by using the discursive norms of focus group discussions to scope the ideological dispositions of their participants. That orientation towards ideological salience has pointed us towards elements of the focus group discussions that seem particularly significant for the participants' *framing* of their situations.[3]

[3]Framing is a concept that George Lakoff (2005) has popularised in studies of political discourse, especially political reception, heavily indebted to frame analysis theory as developed by Erving Goffman (1974). Goffman, in turn, acknowledged a strong debt to Voloshinov (Voloshinov 1929).

Thus we have zeroed in on interpersonal characteristics of the lexicogrammar as used in the discussions. These particularly include: (i) participants' individual and collective self-positioning, which we particularly observe through their use of plural personal pronouns; and (ii) their framing of relations towards our research project itself, typically by addressing statements and questions towards the facilitator.

'Interpersonal' and 'lexicogrammar' are categories of analysis that the functionalist approach to linguistics pioneered (e.g. Halliday 1976, 1978), and ours is a particularly affective take on those categories. Embodiment and delegation are concepts that draw us particularly towards participants' framing of their emotional dispositions towards matters under discussion—their assumptions of proximity or distance, their stances of acceptance or rejection, their willingness or unwillingness to explore and negotiate.

Us/Them, and the Limits to Who We Are

Several papers from our research program have noted the ideationally loaded terrain that non-Indigenous discussants navigate when they use plural personal pronouns to spell out a we-population and a they-population—in Canada (de Costa and Clark 2015) and Australia (Clark 2012) alike. Speaking generally, these terms are capable of great vagueness—often that is a leading reason for their use—but there were many occasions during the focus group discussions when it was literally or contextually clear exactly whom a participant meant to reference by using a given pronoun: *we*, *us*, *our*, *they*, *them*, and *their*. There was also an interesting dynamic around an impersonal second person *you*, *your*, which we discuss in detail below.

When participants divided their world into an 'us' camp and a 'them' camp, they clearly did it in response to discussion prompts—both those provided by the group setup and those that flowed from conversation between peers. Addressing all the topics that these focus groups covered, the most commonly assumed paradigm in all the focus groups was (i) *a we that comprises all non-Indigenous people in Australia* and (ii) *a they that comprises Aboriginal and Torres Strait Islander peoples*. This implies there are problems between these two camps, and they merit people of good will thinking seriously about how to work through those problems. This quote from an Australian-born participant in Perth is indicative of both the usage and the underlying attitude:

> (Patrick 2)[4]
>
> It's almost a degree of arrogance on our part to sort of put our, to sort of suggest that the Aborigines have got all these opportunities or they're better off or whatever now, it's an arrogance on our part because you know we're putting our values and things on what is good for them, and that might not line up with what they appreciate at all.

[4]In line with the ethics approval for our research, we use pseudonyms for all participants.

One variation often complicates this leading paradigm, while three others sometimes do. Often the complications are tacit, but sometimes they are clearly salient in the minds of participants. Interestingly, no participants ever intentionally take those complications so far as to refute the leading paradigm, even though there are plenty of occasions where this might be a natural result of the tension between frames of reference.

The most common complication is that participants quite often imagine a culturally more exclusive we-population, namely white people. This happens somewhat more often in the groups of Australian-born participants, and somewhat more often in the two regional centres (where the non-Indigenous population is itself predominantly of European descent), but in truth it happens in all groups and in all locations. For example, this highly reflexive contribution from an Australian-born participant in Perth:

(Trevor)

I think they're a real conundrum for, in so many ways, you know it's a problem, I use the word problem very carefully, you know it's a challenge, say it's a challenge for society to try and resolve, you know we bring a white man's approach to life, and then expect them to understand that, if they're a true Indigenous person, but then we say you know we provide these things for them and they're not respected, but then what's their basis of respect, is it the same as ours? So to me it is a real absolute conundrum that is very, very difficult to solve and you know I've had a lot of experience when I was at school here in Perth in trying to bring Indigenous boys down into the school, we would send them back, they would be boarding with us, we'd send them back with a complete suitcase full of clothes and they'd come back with nothing, they'd be sent back at the beginning of next term with no clothes because the clothes would have to be spread amongst the family, so we'd have to kit them out again completely. You know and stuff like that, it's very, I think it's very difficult to try and you know bring a balance to it

Very often, whiteness is referenced by racialised adjectives and nouns, rather than by personal pronouns, allowing several moments when the 'whiteness complication' occurs during remarks that are also affirming the more multicultural we-population, namely all non-Indigenous people in Australia. Mulling over Adam Goodes' depiction of Aboriginal people's mixed feelings about Australia Day, an overseas-born participant in Bega demonstrates how easily—how frictionlessly—the categories can merge and overlap:

(Gary)

Well white survival day, I mean you know or, and you know a different day than our day because we've come here, but I know a day that maybe reflects a little bit of how they're feeling, not how we're feeling, because we've come here and made Australia to what it is, in our eyes.

A somewhat less common complication is that participants occasionally replace reference to we/us/our with a generalised (impersonal) 'you.' This often carries a sense of common knowledge, as with this overseas-born participant in Gladstone:

(Steve)

I think up north it's a lot more segregated than down here and down in Brisbane, up in Townsville and Cairns there's bigger communities, but just as you were saying Rosie, about crossing the road, like up at Townsville people that do that, you stand a relative chance of getting spat on or be called a white cunt or something like that, if you choose not to cross the road. So it's not the case down here and it's certainly not the case in Brisbane where I've also lived, I don't know if anyone's been to Townsville or Cairns.

Substituting 'you' for 'we' can also indicate a posture of moral guidance. This Australian-born participant in Perth illustrates the trope while contemplating who should take a lead role in acknowledging the historical travails of Aboriginal and Torres Strait Islander peoples. His response seeks to bring a measure of moral clarity to a scene of historical complexity:

(Patrick 1)

Yeah I was going to say it's pretty hard to look at a huge group of people and say whether or not something's better or not for them without looking at each thing individually, because what's good for one person is going to be bad for someone else, so you can't really judge an entire demograph of people.

Less common still is when people reflect explicitly on the very idea of 'us and them' in a discussion of non-Indigenous identities and responsibility to engage. This example comes from an Australian-born participant in Bega:

(Jane)

And we need to address issues more apart from, not just say the them and us, you know, this group needs more help than that group and that's what we need to do.

When this reflexively self-aware trope occurs, it uniformly treats 'us and them' as a troubling paradigm—and yet there is never a moment when a participant goes on to replace that paradigm with an alternate system of reference that would collapse the distinction—a typical sequence is to note the disquiet and then return to normal usage, as in this exchange from the same group:

(Dennis)

You've got to "they" again, there are lots of different, like you said lots of different language groups, lots of different nations, if there is going to be leadership it has to come from a person who can be a leader for every single Aboriginal language group.

(Roy)

I don't think there needs to be a leader, I think that we need to look at them as a whole and appreciate them for the good things.

Least common of the complications is when people expressly try to build an all-inclusive we, one that references all Australians. This is always couched as a moral aspiration when it occurs, which is not to say that it comes without cynical overtones. On the occasions when this inclusive 'we' interpolates with the normal usage, there again seems to be remarkably little friction in the switching to or fro.

(Nadia)

That's a work in progress, but I think that's just the most obvious first reaction, it's like oh well this is Australia Day and that's the most widely recognised way that we can get a reaction from both sides, so we'll just do that, because it requires the least amount of effort to get some sort of reaction from people.

Boundaries and interrelations between us and them are intrinsically important concepts in situations of conflict or "postconflict" (Little 2014). As the above discussion indicates, those categories are quite regular—but not rigidly unvarying—when non-Indigenous people are asked to reflect on their responsibility to engage with Aboriginal and Torres Strait Islander peoples and cultures. At the same time, other categories than 'Indigenous' and 'non-Indigenous' are clearly in currency. The lack of difficulty participants have in switching between frames of reference suggests that other frames such as 'whiteness' may well emerge as the normal patterns as soon as the context changes. That hypothetically should include any alternative research project that altered our explicit terms of membership and topics of discussion for the focus groups. At least this much is clear: a stable non-Indigenous identity expresses itself richly enough in contexts that are conducive to it, but apparently less so in others. Nonetheless, without any noticeable exception, non-Indigenous people are willing to inhabit a non-Indigenous collective identity, much as their Canadian counterparts also are. The consistency of that willingness may offer promise to social actors who would mobilise such an identity in pursuit of political agendas for the improvement of the relationships between Indigenous and non-Indigenous people. The recognition of an interrelated 'us and them' is the necessary ground for any meaningful relationships of equals between the two camps.

Yet, although 'us' and 'them' seem to be consistent categories of identification, they are not systematically articulated as relationships of equals ('us and them') but as oppositional relationships (us-vs-them) or relationships of domination (us-over-them). This oppositional paradigm is fuelled by perceptions of Indigenous people as competition and a threat to non-Indigenous presence and interests. The interrelation between 'us' and 'them' is considered insomuch as it is confined within the existing settler colonial polity and denies Indigenous sovereignty. For instance, when asked about their opinion on changing the Constitution to include Indigenous people, participants seemed wary of the wider implications it might have, and subtly pointed out that it might threaten non-Indigenous land ownership (italics are our emphasis):

(Paul 1)

I think it'll depend a lot on exactly how it's worded and how exactly they're acknowledged because if it's acknowledge in the constitution then *that also would override a lot of any laws about land ownership and anything, that's been put in after that, so if it's, very much depends on how it's worded*

(Peter)

Exactly

(Paul 1)

If it's worded badly it could stir up a whole heap of extra stuff

Framing of Relations Towards the Research Project Itself

One especially salient reflection on the dynamics of relational proximity and distance is where participants pass comment on the research project itself. In the previous sections, we have analysed forms of embodiment/responsibility and delegation at the level of the individual participants. Uses of pronouns and their entailments have been effective clues for identifying attitudes of embodiment and delegation adopted by the research participants. In this section, we look at participants' conscious discursive interactions with the research project—that is, at those moments when participants put forward statements and questions for the research project, typically by addressing the group facilitator directly. Here we analyse such moments when participants "tap" the research as bivalent in purpose and often ambivalent in mood. On the issue of intent, we find these moments can express both delegation—when the responsibility to act is put on the researcher—and embodiment—when the responsibility to contribute intellectually to the debate is taken up by the participants.

There can be a number of explanations for why participants delegate. In the focus groups that we conducted, we could identify two typical forms of delegating responsibility to or through the research team. One form is based on the participants' sense of not being in an apt position to give an answer. Ron in the Parramatta focus group (Australian-born) says: "I've got no answers, but I think the answer lies with them [Indigenous people] not with us". It is a perspective that came back a few times in the focus groups. When asked about their perspectives on changing Australia Day, participants in the two Parramatta groups answered as follows (italics are our emphasis):

> (Charlie, Australia born)
>
> I feel like *we're the wrong people to ask*… I mean we can guess at what we think it might do, *but really you'd have to ask the Indigenous people*, and if it turns out to be a minority who think that it would make any difference, if the majority are like well it doesn't matter, then in that case it's probably not worth changing the day… I just wonder you'd have to ask them… for like our celebration of Australia Day… I don't know what the answer is necessarily.
>
> (Gemma, overseas born)
>
> I don't think we can speak for them, they'd have to all sit around a table

This form of delegation is based on participants' assumptions that they are not the most apt to be asked the questions—either because they do not consider themselves informed enough or because they do not see themselves concerned about the issue. Changing Australia Day, for instance, is seen by the participants as being primarily an issue for Indigenous people. This form of delegation is bivalent as it doesn't necessarily put the responsibility to think through the issue onto the research team, but prods the latter to redirect their research focus onto Indigenous people. Its ambivalence comes from the fact that it can be seen as a way to avoid engagement with the issue (delegation), while it can also be seen as the participant taking on an active role in engaging with, and advising on research methods. In this form of delegation, the delegate might be seen as better informed, or equipped with the adequate skills and networks. In a focus group conducted in Gladstone for instance, one participant delegated responsibility to answer a question to the facilitator, believing he was better informed on the topic:

(Facilitator)

What changes do you think it might mean for non-Indigenous, do you think most non-Indigenous people would worry, assuming it's a public holiday, or do you think they'd be upset if we changed the date. If the date was changed from January 26th?

(Stephanie)

You've done focus groups, you probably know more than us.

(Facilitator)

I'm interested in your views not mine.

(Stephanie)

Most Australians it's a day off, put it on another day as long as they get a day off I think they'll be fine.

Similarly, in a focus group in Bega (overseas born), a participant suggested that scholars may be in a better position than participants to engage with the history and with issues surrounding the relationships between Indigenous and non-Indigenous people.

(Nicole)

You need the academic, you need some of the history behind it, but academia totally doesn't relate to the real world, but you need to have some sort of history and the reasoning behind trying to find a better pathway.

While delegation to the facilitator (as intermediary) or to Indigenous people arose within both Australia-born and overseas born focus groups, a form of delegation to overseas-born people also emerged among one Australia-born focus group in Bega. To the facilitator's question on whether people in Australia have a responsibility to do something, to acknowledge Aboriginal and Torres Strait Islander peoples, to acknowledge their history and their culture, a participant evades the question by suggesting asking it to recent immigrants:

(Roy)

Have you had these groups, the same discussion in other areas, because this little bit of Australia is a remnant white area if you like, as you were saying you go up to Sydney… they don't have the generational history, albeit a short one, of people in this area can trace their ancestors back to pretty much very early white settlement times…It might be interesting to see what difference there was in attitudes to the so called problem we've talked about.

(Facilitator)

I can't answer because it's fairly early in the

–(Dennis)

Well I don't think we'd be able to answer these questions with people in Western Australia or anything like that, I think this is like regional kind of discussion

Again, this form of delegation is somewhat bivalent: it can also be interpreted as embodied—as participants actively making suggestions for the research.

Another form of delegation observed in the focus groups can be likened to blame-shifting (Bartling and Fischbacher 2012), in which a close connection between delegation and blame can be observed. In this form of delegation, participants not only delegate responsibility to *get the knowledge* and to *acknowledge*; they also evade responsibility for the current state of affairs and the consequences of potential future decisions. In the Parramatta focus group (Australia born), Nancy believed: "like with all of us, the only way we can, they can be helped is if they look inside themselves, and help themselves." Here the responsibility (which may really mean blame in this case) has been shifted onto Indigenous people. In Bega, a participant, Jack, evaded responsibility for past atrocities between Indigenous and non-Indigenous people, explaining his trope of delegation on the ground that responsibility is not carried over generations:

(Jack)

Yes, we, present generation we're not, have not been responsible for the atrocities of past generations, the early settlers, because we consider ourselves now to be more enlightened and more compassionate towards Aboriginal people. So I don't think we can be held responsible for what happened in the past directly, therefore it follows that really we've got nothing to apologise for in one sense, we're only apologising for the behaviour of our ancestors.

Delegation necessarily relies on a temporal distantiation, even a severing, between the past and the present. This temporal distantiation relies on a modern European conception of progress, where the past is understood as morally inferior and continually transcended by present efforts of moral readjustment. John says that "we consider ourselves now to be more enlightened and more compassionate towards Aboriginal people." Delegation therefore takes different forms, follows numerous directions, and serves various purposes. As we have briefly mentioned, some forms of delegation are complex and ambivalent. While they delegate responsibility, they also reflect the participants' self-positioning as active agent in the research project. These ambivalent forms of delegation tend to another end of the spectrum, where "tapping" the research team may also be an oblique form of embodiment.

Participants' engagement with the observer-researcher may also act as a form of embodiment—as a self-enactment by the participant, acting as a sort of co-researcher—where participants take an active role in developing the reflection further, and suggesting possible pathways for research. In his analysis of focus groups as research method, Smithson argues (2000, 105):

Focus groups… should not be analysed as if they are naturally occurring discussions, but as discussions occurring in a specific, controlled setting… From this perspective, language is viewed not as a neutral conveyor of information, but as functional and constructive, as a medium which people use to achieve a variety of actions.

In this particular context, participants' "tapping" the research team may function to give participants specific agency by interrogating, challenging, and suggesting research methods. For instance, a participant in Bega (overseas born) prodded the facilitator to redirect the research focus onto Indigenous people as a way to open up the conversation and allow for a dialogue to take place (italics indicate our emphasis):

(Facilitator)

Okay, so it sounds like no one in this particular group is wedded to January 26th or John you think it should stay January 26th.

(Jack)

Not necessarily no, *I keep saying, I keep saying to you ask the Aboriginal people what they want.*

(Facilitator)

But they're only part of the total Australian picture so.

(Jack)

I know but we're dealing with an issue about Aboriginal people and European settlers aren't we, it's all very well for us to sit around tables and in parliament making decisions about these things, *but let's ask the Aboriginal people what they want, I mean you might get some clues.*

Several participants in different focus groups show similar concern to engage both Indigenous and non-Indigenous in the discussion, and show wariness about speaking *for* Indigenous people instead of *with* them. Maria in Parramatta (overseas born) suggests that "perhaps we should ask them, you know, that'd be the generous thing to do." In Gladstone, Stephanie (Australia born) holds similar views:

(Stephanie)

I also don't think we can speak for Indigenous people, I guess as a university study with focus groups, do you have focus groups of Indigenous people?

(Facilitator)

I believe that's a separate part of the project yes.[5]

(Stephanie)

So there is, yeah because I think, you said that I know more, I still will not give opinion at work for example because I work for learning and teaching services and we have indigenisation as a curriculum and I tell people if you want help with that you go to our Indigenous engagement section, because I don't believe it's my place to comment on that, even though I do have experience. That's just my opinion, but I think we can speak for one side, but as you said do the Indigenous people feel the same way, I think they need to be asked that.

[5]The facilitator has conflated our project with others in his answer here (and below), but that is a rather typical miscommunication arising from the decision to contract out facilitation to a third party. In any case, it does not materially affect our analysis on any of the points discussed here.

Very significant is the way these moments can be read as forms of embodiment, where the participants identify their position in the debate but call for an engagement and expertise which would be shared between Indigenous and non-Indigenous people. In the overseas-born focus group in Gladstone, a participant questioned the facilitator on the research process:

(Eva)

Do you ever have these discussions with an Aboriginal crowd of people like you've got here?

(Facilitator)

I'm not having that conversation but I believe the conversation is taking place as well.[6]

(Eva)

Yeah, that needs to happen.

Here, we see the participant calling on the research team's responsibility to ensure that Indigenous people contribute intellectually to the debate too. This embodiment takes the form of an invitation for a shared (by Indigenous and non-Indigenous people) responsibility to engage in the debate. Yet, suggestions of a shared responsibility do not necessarily engage a shared conversation. Participants' suggestions unanimously position the research team as intermediary between two projected parallel discussions (one among non-Indigenous participants, the other among Indigenous participants). On no occasion is the possibility of a focus group gathering both Indigenous and non-Indigenous participants suggested. So when one overseas born participant identified herself as an Indigenous person from a country other than Australia, this self-identification affected the conversation quite radically.

This highly revealing vignette occurred a few minutes into the overseas-born focus group in Gladstone. Speaking in response to some participants' comments about alcohol and drug abuse and social disadvantage among Aboriginal communities, one participant identified herself as Maori. She related her experience in New Zealand with the bad reputation that Indigenous people get in Australia—unfairly, in her view:

(Sharon)

I've been here nearly a year now in Australia, I come from New Zealand, there's some interesting points by everybody, but being part Maori myself I can understand when they talk about being the native of the land and how they are treated differently, you know, if they talk about them being high and drinking and substance abuse and everything else, but that goes right across the board, not just them so yeah.

(Facilitator)

Did you know much before you came here?

(Sharon)

[6]See previous note.

> About Aboriginals, I did a little bit of research do you know what I mean, I knew they were the natives and what they went through, but yeah I've had a few comments from people here to keep away from them, and I'm pretty open minded, and I have come across a few and I've had no problems with them so, and the same I have no problems with them.

At this moment in the conversation, our on-site observer noticed a distinct shift in the group dynamic and in the mood of the participants, flagged by changes in behaviour and a conspicuous tensing in participants' body language. After the revelation of the Maori participant, the group discussion shifted away from comments on Indigenous people's deficiencies and disadvantages (i.e. lack of respect for government, drug and alcohol abuse, holding grudges, unable to move ahead despite government help) to participants acknowledging and mentioning the wrongs committed against Aboriginal people:

> (Irene)
>
> My husband he's 65 and he remembers when Aboriginal people were given the vote in I think it was '66 or '67, so it was legal for Aboriginal people to vote, but it was illegal to encourage them to vote, and the other thing that I've learned is that the Aboriginal people were only taken off the flora and fauna list in 1982.
>
> (Molly)
>
> In some legislation they're still considered.
>
> (Irene)
>
> They're still considered fauna, yeah.
>
> (Molly)
>
> It is terrible.
>
> (Irene)
>
> It is terrible, and if that didn't give you a complex I don't know what would.

Other participants also acknowledged that their understanding of Indigenous people and cultures has mostly been formed by indirect knowledge. An illustrative example is when Declan states:

> (Declan)
>
> Indigenous people, they get a lot of bad publicity, but yeah not really had too much interaction to be able to give a personal viewpoint on it.

After Sharon's contribution and self-identification as Maori, it became harder for the facilitator to draw information out of the participants voluntarily and self-unconsciously. There was a lull in the discussion and the facilitator resorted to calling out specific people more often than usual. This revelation disrupted the general assumption that they were therefore in company of non-Indigenous people exclusively. The unexpected presence of an Indigenous—albeit neither Aboriginal nor Torres Strait Islander—person in their midst was manifestly troubling. It presented a challenge to the us-and-them framework of reference, according to which participants largely understood and articulated relationships between Indigenous and non-Indigenous people in Australia, and so the discussion became appreciably more complex. As mentioned above, the idea of discussing issues pertaining to Australia's history, Indigenous people and cultures with Indigenous people had not been a present possibility for the participants to that point, and so the unforeseen realisation of an Indigenous presence rapidly emerged as a challenge to the participants' self-identity formation. As we see, one participant remarked about the wrongs done to Indigenous people "if that didn't give you a complex I don't know what would"—we cannot help noticing the complex that emerged in a conversation whose setup took this suddenly complicating turn.

It was only when one of the participants turned back to New Zealand and applied an oppositional us-and-them framework to that country's history that the discussion retrieved its original flow:

> (Eva) You [New Zealanders] seem to be, not have the problems that we've got and whichever has been going on for years and years, you must've found some way of being able to integrate with them in New Zealand.

Eva applied the us-and-them dichotomy to New Zealanders, where the "us" ("you") represents non-Indigenous New Zealanders and "them" represents Maoris. She also used a "we" that possibly encompasses all Australians, or possibly refers to non-Indigenous Australians and casts Aboriginal Australians as "the problems." Extrapolating from Eva's other comments, the latter seems more likely. In any case, this comment pulls the conversation back into a familiar framework of phrasing and reference. Eva articulates New Zealand's social relations as ahead of Australia's and enables the group to be equipped again with familiar and comfortable frames of reference (us/them, "behind"/"ahead") while attending to the Maori participant's sensibility. Australia's unexplained incapacity to resolve issues in social and political relations becomes another strategy for delegation. Thus, the impact of Sharon's intervention and self-identification supports the argument that forms of embodiment and delegation are intrinsically linked to self-identity formation.

Conclusion

The analysis developed in this chapter shows that non-Indigenous responsibility to engage is embedded in the discourse around this topic—often inconspicuously—vested in various reflexive tropes of self-awareness that non-Indigenous people routinely use in their conversations. As our previous research had led us to expect, this is clearly manifest in an oppositional us-vs-them paradigm across all locations. Unlike the Canadian context, and contrary to what we expected, in Australia a non-Indigenous understanding of the responsibility to engage does not seem to vary significantly according to locality. Substantially differing paradigms of discourse could not be identified between urban and regional areas for instance. Similarly, the oppositional us-vs-them paradigm was taken up by both Australian-born groups as well as the more culturally diverse overseas-born groups. In the case of Australian-born groups, the "we" population was however culturally more exclusive, and quite often equalled whiteness. The fact that the oppositional us-vs-them paradigm also had a strong presence amongst overseas-born people—among whom some were very recent immigrants—shows the adaptability and tenacity of such frameworks of reference.

Findings from these focus groups suggest that the tenacity of the oppositional paradigm—partly sustained by non-Indigenous perceptions of Indigenous people both as a threat and as competition—may greatly constrain non-Indigenous engagement with Indigenous people and cultures. At the same time, we need to reflect on whether alternative paradigms which would not engage with the Indigenous/non-Indigenous dualism might allow any more promising scope for enabling the discussion of engagement—our research has not clearly turned up any. What is more, being so ubiquitous in the grammar of these conversations, the dualistic us-and-them paradigm—instead of the oppositional us-vs-them or us-over-them paradigm for instance—has a clearly assumed plausibility for carriage of this topic. To the extent that it may mobilise non-Indigenous people to engage with their structural and collective relationship towards Aboriginal and Torres Strait Islander peoples and their history, this paradigm seems more likely than any other to address reconciliation's limitations and contested purposes.

Meanwhile, our analysis of the focus group discussions through a lens of embodiment and delegation here strongly indicates a lack or paucity of embodiment. In all focus groups the responsibility to engage was overwhelmingly delegated—to the various levels of government, to the education system, to Indigenous people themselves, to recent immigrants, even to the facilitator and the research team. These delegations often took the ambiguous forms of 'shared responsibility.' Interestingly, while participants made suggestions to the research team about carrying out focus groups or interviews with Indigenous people, on no occasion did the participants suggest research methods that would engage both Indigenous and non-Indigenous people simultaneously. In the terms the participants adopted, shared responsibility did not clearly translate into a shared conversation or into any suggestion of the need for a collective and wider structural change to happen.

In summary, it seems the dualistic us-and-them paradigm must be entrusted with a pivotal role in shaping non-Indigenous people's sense of responsibility to engage with Indigenous people and cultures. Engagement across this social and political divide may require, as a precondition, even closer critical attention to non-Indigenous people's self-awareness and strategies of identity-formation—especially those that allow evading responsibility in relationships between Indigenous and non-Indigenous people in Australia.

References

Bartling, B., & Fischbacher, U. (2012). Shifting the blame: On delegation and responsibility. *Review of Economic Studies, 79*(1), 67–87.

Bourke, L., & Geldens, P. M. (2007). Perceptions of reconciliation and related Indigenous issues among young residents of Shepparton. *Australian Journal of Social Issues, 4*, 603.

Bulbeck, C. (2004). The "white worrier" in South Australia: Attitudes to multiculturalism, immigration and reconciliation. *Journal of Sociology, 4*, 341.

Burridge, N. (2006). Meanings of reconciliation in the school context. *Australian Journal of Indigenous Education, 35*, 68–77.

Clark, T., Walsh, M., & de Costa, R. (2012). Resonating opinions and identities: Using poetics methods to explore non-Aboriginal attitudes towards Aboriginal reconciliation in Australia. *Asiatic—IIUM Journal of English Language and Literature, 6*(2), 110–127.

de Costa, R., & Clark, T. (2015). On the responsibility to engage: Non-Indigenous peoples in settler states. *Settler Colonial Studies* Online version.

Goffman, E. (1974). *Frame analysis—An analysis on the organisation of experience*. New York: Harper & Row.

Gomersall, A. M., Davidson, G., & Ho, R. (2000). Factors affecting acceptance of Aboriginal reconciliation amongst non-Indigenous Australians. *Australian Psychologist, 35*(2), 118–127.

Gunstone, A. (2008). *History, politics & knowledge: Essays in Australian Indigenous studies*. Melbourne: Australian Scholarly Publishing.

Halliday, M. A. K. (1976). *System and function in language: Selected essays*. London: Oxford University Press.

Halliday, M. A. K. (1978). *Language as social semiotic: The social interpretation of language and meaning*. London: Edward Arnold.

Halloran, M. J. (2007). Indigenous reconciliation in Australia: Do values, identity and collective guilt matter? *Journal of Community & Applied Social Psychology, 17*(1), 1–18.

Lakoff, G. (2005). *Don't think of an elephant! Know your values and frame the debate*. Australia: Scribe.

Little, A. (2014). *Enduring conflict: Challenging the signature of peace and democracy*. London: Bloomsbury Publishing.

McCallum, K. (2003). Walking and talking reconciliation. *Australian Journal of Communication, 30*(2), 115.

Pedersen, A., Beven, J., Walker, I., & Griffiths, B. (2004). Attitudes toward Indigenous-Australians: The role of empathy and guilt. *Journal of Community and Applied Social Psychology, 14*, 233–249.

Pedersen, A., Contos, N., Griffiths, B., Bishop, B., & Walker, I. (2000). Attitudes toward Aboriginal Australians in city and country settings. *Australian Psychologist, 35*, 109–117.

Philpot, C., Balvin, N., Mellor, D., & Bretherton, D. (2013). Making meaning from collective apologies: Australia's apology to its Indigenous peoples. *Peace & Conflict, 19*(1), 34–50.

Smithson, J. (2000). Using and analysing focus groups: Limitations and possibilities. *International Journal of Social Research Methodology, 3*(2), 103–119.

Voloshinov, V. N. (1929). *Marxism and the philosophy of language*. London: Seminar Press.

Yarn About Youth. (2013). *Youth Studies Australia 1*, 5.

Chapter 11
Truth, Sharing and Hearing: The Canadian Truth and Reconciliation Commission and the Challenge of Civic Engagement

Ry Moran

Abstract In 2009, three Commissioners were appointed to lead Canada's Truth and Reconciliation Commission (TRC). These Commissioners were tasked with helping the country come to an understanding of the harm and damage created by Canada's residential schools, with their mandate given to them by the Indian Residential Schools Settlement Agreement. Seven years, thousands of statements, documents, and pages of reports later, where are we as a country? What have we learned? How much change has resulted from the work of the Commission? This paper examines a select number of moments of engagement with non-indigenous peoples through the TRC's public events. Through these examples, the paper suggests that reconciliation needs to be felt before it can be understood; the Commission was most successful when it created events where people could understand what reconciliation was 'in the moment.' The paper continues to discuss the newly formed National Centre for Truth, and Reconciliation at the University of Manitoba. Explored are the opportunities for ongoing engagement through the powerful collection of oral history, government documents, and church records contained within the centre's archives.

Keywords Truth and reconciliation · Canada · Indigenous peoples · National Centre for Truth and Reconciliation · Oral history · Witnessing

Introduction

On the banks of the Red River in Winnipeg, Manitoba, sits a low brick building on the campus of the University of Manitoba. This building, formerly a house and home for the chancellor and later the president of the university, is now head office of the National Centre for Truth and Reconciliation (NCTR). But this building represents

R. Moran (✉)
Canadian National Centre for Truth and Reconciliation,
University of Manitoba, Winnipeg, Canada
e-mail: Ry.Moran@umanitoba.ca

S. Maddison et al. (eds.), *The limits of settler colonial reconciliation*,
DOI 10.1007/978-981-10-2654-6_11

far more than just a set of administrative offices. It is also the home for the statements and other documents collected by the Truth and Reconciliation Commission of Canada (TRC)—close to 7000 audio and video interviews with Survivors and others affected by the residential schools and over five million digitized documents—all collected in an effort to record a truth that was largely ignored by the Canadian public and one intentionally omitted from the history books.

In front of the building sits a large Turtle sculpture. The Turtle is one of the sacred clan animals of the Anishinaabeg and the carrier of the truth in that tradition. The Turtle is there as a reminder, as a symbol, and as a teacher. Long ago, when this land was covered entirely in water, Turtle volunteered to carry the world on its back. As mud was spread across it, land emerged, giving the creator a place to sit, and also giving us a home called Turtle Island. It is from this place that the province and the University of Manitoba derive their name—Manitou Ahbae: the place where the creator sits.

As the Red River slowly winds towards Lake Winnipeg, it is joined by the Assiniboine River at the Forks. Where these two great rivers join represents one of the oldest meeting places in all of Turtle Island—where indigenous peoples came together to celebrate, trade, share information, and now where cultures from all over the world join together for visits, events and celebrations.

The work of the Truth and Reconciliation Commission, and now the National Centre for Truth and Reconciliation, in many ways traces the path of these rivers. The TRC was tasked with recording and documenting the history and ongoing effect of the residential schools in Canada. These schools, which operated for the greater part of Canada's history as a nation, heaped colonial violence, theft, dispossession and hurt on indigenous communities across the country. The policies of aggressive assimilation implemented by the Canadian state saw children forcibly removed from their families, parents prevented from visiting or resisting the removal of their children, and indigenous languages, cultures and ways of being forcibly and intentionally suppressed by the Canadian state through the churches.[1]

But just as the Red River itself does not readily stay within its banks, neither have indigenous peoples stood by and readily accepted the path forced upon them by the Canadian government. Starting in the late 1980s, Survivors of the residential schools began to demand justice for the trauma and abuse they endured in the schools. Through court case after court case, Survivors were ultimately able to bring their case to the Supreme Court. Ongoing litigation was eventually settled in the largest class-action lawsuit in Canadian history.

Now, just as two great rivers join together in Winnipeg, it is there that national efforts have been undertaken in an effort to bring two histories together in Canada. One history is of indigenous peoples who have suffered greatly under the control and domination of an openly hostile Canadian state. The other is of non-indigenous peoples in Canadian society who have been largely unaware of the past and present realities faced by indigenous peoples. These two histories came together at the first

[1]For further information on the history of residential schools, please see Truth and Reconciliation of Canada (2015a, b).

National Event of the Truth and Reconciliation Commission at the Forks in 2010, and established the processes of truth sharing and engagement that would take place across the country over the next six years.

The demand for acknowledgement and justice by Survivors has driven the process of reconciliation in Canada. The mandate of the TRC was carefully crafted to ensure Survivor voices could and would be heard (TRC 2009). Edmund Metatawabin, a Survivor of the St. Anne's Residential School in Fort Albany, Ontario—one of Canada's most notorious schools, in which a crudely made electric chair was used for punishment of the students—writes about this need for justice. He states in his memoir *Up Ghost River* (2014: 285):

> There is no concept of Justice in Cree culture. The nearest word is *kintohpatatin*, which loosely translates to 'you've been listened to.' But *kintohpatatin* is richer than justice—really it means you've been listen to by someone compassionate and fair, and your needs will be taken seriously.

Going back as early as 1905, prominent people such as Dr. Peter Bryce sounded the alarm decrying the terrible conditions in the residential schools. Hundreds of other government and academic reports on child welfare, lands, justice, water, and suicide have been issued in this country. In 1996, the report of the Royal Commission on Aboriginal Peoples presented thousands of pages of analysis on the relationship between indigenous peoples and the Canadian state, and over 400 recommendations in addition to teaching materials and background reports, all of which were largely ignored by both governments and the Canadian public.[2]

Yet, despite this long-standing history of denial and ignorance in the country, something seems to be happening *now* in Canada—there is a momentum generated through the work of the Truth and Reconciliation Commission. Across the country, new conversations about old history are occurring. In nearly every sector—from business to health to education and beyond—individuals, organizations and the nation are sitting down with the Calls to Action of the TRC in honest and sincere attempts to better understand what the Calls to Action and the TRC Commissioners are asking of society. *Kintohpatatin* seems to be taking place.

This chapter outlines some critical moments in the journey of reconciliation and the engagement of non-indigenous peoples in the process of reconciliation. It will suggest that to bring about the deep structural and societal change envisioned by Survivors and indigenous peoples, shining light on past histories must go beyond words on a page and into the realm of experience, feeling and understanding of injustice on a visceral level. It is not enough to simply speak to a person's *mind* to

[2]The Royal Commission on Aboriginal Peoples created a special database of materials intended for distribution across the country. The database contained teaching materials, background research papers and the report. Sadly, while circulated, the contents never found their way into the hands of many, and the database became largely forgotten. Changes in technology eventually rendered the database completely inaccessible. Recent efforts between the NCTR, Library and Archives Canada and the original RCAP research team are proving successful in bringing these materials back to life. At the time of writing, it is hoped that this database will be once again be made available in late 2016 in honour of the 20th anniversary of RCAP (Dussault and Eramus 1996).

stimulate a process of reconciliation: a conversation with a person's *heart* must occur.

I will present examples of where reconciliation shifted from being an abstract concept, laden with questions around the definition, meaning, and an ultimate end state of what it *might be,* to a feeling, a moment, or an experience of understanding what it *is.* I will conclude by providing some thoughts and reflections on the prospects for reconciliation and the long path that still lies ahead of Canada as a nation.

These examples are drawn from my own personal experience with the TRC and now the National Centre for Truth and Reconciliation. As such, they are based largely on observation of moments that occurred and events that transpired. That said, the work of the TRC was complex, dynamic and constantly evolving. This chapter cannot, and does not attempt to, present a full history of events, and many important elements of the work are omitted by necessity. The examples presented are moments that stood out in my own experience and marked a turning point in the TRC's work.

Wild Rice and the Blood Reserve

On the evening of the final night of the Truth and Reconciliation Commission, a group of about 200 Survivors, supporters, friends, Honorary Witnesses and staff of the TRC gathered for a final dinner at the Wabano Centre in Ottawa. The event, intended to be a final thank-you dinner for all of those who had worked hard to realize the vision of the TRC, followed the release of the TRC's final report earlier that day.

As the group feasted on traditional foods prepared by Wabano staff, a series of speakers took to the microphone to offer words of appreciation or insight into the journey of the last six years. One of these speakers was former Supreme Court Justice Frank Iacobucci, who, adding to an already long and distinguished career, was instrumental in the creation of the Indian Residential Schools Settlement Agreement as Canada's lead negotiator. As people washed down bites of wild rice with iced wild mint tea, Justice Iacobucci spoke of what he felt was the most important and critical of all the mandated obligations of the TRC—the gathering and sharing of Survivor statements.

Iacobucci stated that in his view, the statements were *the* instrument that would bring people into the conversation of reconciliation. The horror, pain and anguish of parents, the interminable suffering of the children removed from their families and placed in the residential schools, combined with the stark reality that many children never returned home to their families, would, he felt, speak to the human soul and spirit in a way no other legal or compulsory process could. A truth-sharing process that revealed the sheer inhumanity of the Canadian state's actions towards indigenous peoples would be the most effective manner to move the public to action.

More recently, in a gymnasium on the Blood Reserve in southern Alberta, similar sentiments were framed in a different light. There, during a community engagement session of the NCTR, Elder Jerry Saddleback shared some powerful insights on the power of sharing truth. Saddleback stated that there are two ways to create action: you can *tell* people what to do and *force* action, or you can paint the need for change through narrative in an effort to *inspire* action. He went on to state that the best way to inspire action was to speak to a person's heart, and not to their mind. Just as the sun shines light from the east each morning and brings light to darkness, so too can thoughts and truth drive shadow into light.

The opening preamble of the Truth and Reconciliation Commission's mandate states that "the truth of our common experiences can set our spirits free and pave the way for reconciliation" (Truth and Reconciliation Commission of Canada 2009). The role of the many statement gatherers who worked for the TRC, and indeed of the Commissioners, was to operationalize this vision through *listening*. By giving Survivors voice to *finally* be listened to by someone "compassionate and fair," Survivors were given the opportunity to be heard. The pain, suffering and experiences of Survivors were not questioned, but were accepted as the truth. Through listening came validation—a mutual exchange that would leave the statement provider with the strong sense that they had been heard by someone who cared, and that their voice mattered.

By giving space to Survivors to share their statements in public, the TRC created opportunities for people from diverse walks of life to come together to understand and share in a spirit of open dialogue, healing, mutual support and humility. The TRC (2015c: 8) summarizes this approach, stating:

> [S]haming and pointing out wrongdoing were not the purpose of the Commission's mandate. Ultimately, the Commission's focus on truth determination was intended to lay the foundation for the important question of reconciliation. Now that we know about residential schools and their legacy, what do we do about it?

This open and accepting mode of hearing is a necessary condition for reconciliation to occur. Just as the Red River does not force the Assiniboine River to join it, a process of transformative engagement needed to occur organically, as waters from different rivers join and mix. Histories must be shared, must be heard and must be accepted in order for reconciliation to take place. Breaking down the barriers to sharing and hearing truth is akin to breaking down the dam that prevented the river from flowing.

The Experience of the TRC

The Canadian TRC was given an enormous task: to collect documents and statements, hold national and community events, issue a report, create a national research centre, and administer a significant commemoration fund. Upon commencement, despite the work of the Royal Commission on Aboriginal Peoples in the 1990s, the cries of thousands of residential school Survivors, and the national apology for residential schools in 2008, by 2010, many Canadians were still not aware of the residential schools or of the TRC itself. The flow of information to the Canadian public remained but a trickle.

Moreover, the country had not come to terms with what a truth commission was and why it was in existence. This was a commission that had an active mandate to change the entire trajectory of the national narrative *away* from the Western, colonial framework that had shaped history for so long, *towards* a new narrative inclusive of indigenous histories, cultures, perspectives and realities.

Questions weighed heavily on the TRC. How could the Commission show reconciliation? How could the Commission create public events that reflected compassionate and fair listening? How could the Commission provide opportunities for non-indigenous peoples to demonstrate their commitment to take the needs of Survivors seriously?

June 2010 marked a significant step in the Commission's activities, with the launch of the Winnipeg National Event. Hopes were high and the Commission was very much in the spotlight. The Canadian Broadcast Corporation sent its top anchor, Peter Mansbridge, to the ceremonies to provide live coverage. Survivors and indigenous peoples from across Canada arrived via bus, train, plane and personal vehicles. Church members from a wide variety of denominations also attended. All eyes were on the Commission as it began to take the lead on shaping what would be another five years of national engagement across the country.

But it was perhaps in the opening 'sharing circle' of the event that the TRC experienced one of its first insights into the power of truth sharing.[3] Together in an outdoor tent at the Forks, the Commissioners, along with a number of dignitaries, Survivors and others involved in the schools, assembled around the bentwood box of the TRC. A buffalo robe shielded it from the stage below. Chairs were placed around this circle and media crammed around the outside of the tent to record proceedings. Health supports, including Elders, professional therapists and trained resolution health support workers, distributed tissues and bottles of water to the members of the audience sitting in the circle. The event took on a sense of reverence, ceremony and solemn reflection of the past. As the microphone was passed around the circle, participants shared their own experiences of abuse, of hope, of longing, and their reflections on the history that had led to this moment.

When the microphone was passed to Charlene Belleau, she stated her hope to:

> give voice … to those women and children that went to residential school, that had babies from the residential school and lost those babies. The priests made them give them up for adoption. I need you to find those babies and reconcile those families. We brought one

[3]Survivors and others affected by the residential school system were invited to participate in sharing circles where they could share their experiences with a public audience. Those wishing to share a statement in a more private setting could give their statement in a one-on-one session in one of 25 statement-gathering rooms set up on-site. Survivors seeking apology directly from one of the churches involved with the schools could sit in a 'churches listening area' and seek apology directly from a member of the church.

> home to Alkali Lake, it was a beautiful ceremony, but a lot of those babies are lost somewhere across the country or in the United States. I need you to find them, and I need the government, I need the churches to open their records so that they will know where our people are. (quoted in Truth and Reconciliation Commission of Canada 2010)

Charlene continued by stating:

> I don't want to apologise for being emotional because we have been at this for 30 years, we have been asking to be heard for 30 years, and we now have a voice.

She passed the microphone to then Minister of Aboriginal and Northern Affairs Canada Chuck Strahl. There, with voice wavering and choking back tears, the minister vowed the federal government would "turn over every stone" to ensure the history was fully collected and preserved. As the minister began to choke up, Charlene's hand went to his shoulder to give him strength to pull through and finish his statement. Quietly—barely audible on the recording—you can hear her whisper, "It's okay."

In that moment, on national television, the realization of Justice Iacobucci's vision and Elder Saddleback's teachings converged. The country was shown that Survivors' voices, when shared in an open manner, free of doubt and with the suspension of hostility, could move people to a new understanding. The minister was given the opportunity to *hear,* and, in so doing, was moved to tears. His heart had been spoken to in a way no report or briefing note on the effects of residential schools ever could. The power of truth moved him on a personal level—light penetrated the shadows and change occurred in the moment. He vowed his government would take action.[4]

It would be another 12 months before the next National Event, one slated to take place in a remote area of Canada's Far North. At about 5:00 pm on the final day of the Northern National Event, Survivors were joined by members of their families, church officials, indigenous leaders, media, staff of the TRC and a large number of locals in a dimly lit room in the Midnight Sun Complex in Inuvik. Volunteers and staff distributed cupcakes to each person in the room and lit candles on each cupcake. The room was transformed from a dark annex in a northern conference centre to a sea of shining lights. The crowd joined in unison to sing "Happy Birthday" to all the Survivors in the room, led first in English, and then followed by indigenous languages of the North.

The birthday celebration was an opportunity to fuse the coldness and isolation experienced by the Survivors with a collective moment that went beyond speeches and words but articulated all of the pain, loneliness and corresponding resilience

---

[4]The TRC in fact encountered serious difficulties collecting documents from the Government of Canada. Actions speak louder than words, and what seemed to happen was that the words spoken at the National Event were not followed up with concrete and transparent action. Despite this, I have chosen to leave this in as an example. It is difficult to paint a full picture of the effect that moment had on the event—but without a doubt there was an "it" moment—one of those times at the Commission where we knew that if we could do more of "that," we would be on the right track.

and resistance of indigenous peoples through song, celebration and reflection. It was a celebration that acknowledged painful realities experienced by children—of never being able to celebrate a birthday while in school—while providing a form of symbolic redress for the past through giving Survivors back their many birthdays never celebrated. And as the song was sung in the indigenous languages of the North, and later across other regions of the country at all national events, it became a powerful affirmation of the importance of indigenous languages and a celebration of reclaiming these languages. Later in the Commission's mandate, the birthday celebrations took on an additional role—a call to action for everyone in the audience to go home and tell each person around them how much they loved them and to give their children a hug, because being unable to do so was one of the most lonesome and damaging parts of the entire residential school experience.

Following the Northern National Event, the Commission turned its attention to the Atlantic. Preceded by hearings and with solid coverage of the events, the Commission had built significant momentum going into the Atlantic event. Through this event, the Commission developed one final, major addition to the National Events—the incorporation of a youth-focused education day. Until this point, direct outreach to indigenous and non-indigenous youth had occurred on a largely ad hoc basis in response to calls from communities or via participation in preplanned events by agencies external to the TRC. The Atlantic National Event represented the first time the Commission actively created an opportunity for significant youth participation in a National Event by providing a special day dedicated fully to youth programming. More than a simple sharing of information with students, these education days would become critical opportunities for building both a present and a future state of respectful dialogue based upon engagement, truth sharing and the empowerment of youth.

In the view of the TRC, reconciliation is not possible without "an ongoing process of establishing and maintaining respectful relationships" (Truth and Reconciliation Commission of Canada 2015c: 16). As further articulated in the TRC's final report:

> Survivors have also said that knowing about these things is not enough. Our public education system also needs to influence behavior by undertaking to teach our children—Aboriginal and non-Aboriginal—how to speak respectfully to, and about, each other in the future. Reconciliation is all about respect. (Truth and Reconciliation Commission of Canada 2015d: 119)

As such, a future state of reconciliation is not possible without the establishment first of mechanisms through which respectful dialogue and discussion can occur.

Education days provided opportunities for students to learn directly from Survivors, from the Commissioners and from each other. Plenary sessions led by indigenous and non-indigenous youth provided opportunities for communication across perspectives and lived realities—all with the intent of creating opportunities to critically discuss the creation of a better future for everyone. By modelling respect, and by bringing this history to the students in a manner that sought not to burden them with the weight of history but to empower them to have hope for a better and brighter future, while also equipping them with some tools to engage in respectful dialogue, the Commission created another inclusive setting in which compassion, kindness and sincere reflection on the need for change were the primary drivers of the engagement.

Three years later, with the official closing ceremonies of the TRC taking place in June of 2015, it seemed that engagement in the TRC's processes had never been higher. After six years, over 900 community engagement sessions, close to 7000 statements and the collection of millions of documents, thousands of attendees crammed into a ballroom at the Delta Hotel in downtown Ottawa to listen to the Commissioners issue their findings and make 94 Calls to Action. It was at this event that the Commissioners declared the residential schools to have been an attempted cultural genocide of indigenous peoples, a statement echoed earlier in the week by Supreme Court Chief Justice Beverly McLaughlin. It was also at this event that the Commission experienced the highest recorded number of viewers on its webcast, with close to 100,000 hits over the two-day period. For those in attendance, it seemed that light was penetrating the shadows and an awakening to a new Canadian reality was occurring.

But, with the subsequent release of the final reports some six months later (in December 2015), marking the official closure of the TRC's offices, the country is now faced with a number of important questions. Critical amongst these questions are: Can reconciliation be achieved? What is the path of reconciliation that lies before us? Will the 94 Calls to Action be implemented? Was the work of the Commission sufficient to propel the country onto a new trajectory? Was the Commission successful in kick-starting a process to establish and maintain respectful relationships? As Senator Murray Sinclair stated at the closing event, "We have shown you the mountain. It is now your task to climb it" (Sinclair 2015).

As these and other questions circulate across the country, the National Centre for Truth and Reconciliation opened its doors in November of 2015. As the organization entrusted to carry the statements, documents and other materials forward, the NCTR is mandated to ensure the archives of the NCTR are preserved and made accessible in a respectful and dignified manner; that Survivors, their families and indigenous peoples are fully engaged in the work of the centre; that educators have access to the collection and that public education activities remain ongoing; and that new research is conducted to shed light on the past and path moving forward. As such, the NCTR is given the responsibility to be much more than a passive repository of information: it is also asked to carry forward the public education and engagement work of the TRC. The centre inherited the promises made throughout the TRC, wherein hundreds of TRC statement gatherers, staff and the Commissioners themselves promised Survivors that their experiences and truth would be brought to the public and would be shared with educators across the country. Put simply, the promise was that the words and experiences that the Survivors had shared with the centre would never be forgotten and would always be honoured.

In the words of Survivor Esther Lachinette-Diabo:

> I'm doing this interview in hope that we could use this as an educational tool to educate our youth about what happened.... Maybe one day the Ministry of Education can work with the TRC and develop some kind of curriculum for Native Studies, Indigenous learning. So that not only Aboriginal people can understand, you know, what we had to go through—the experiences of all the Anishinaabe people that attended—but for the Canadian people as well to understand that the residential schools did happen. And through this sharing, they can understand and hear stories from Survivors like me. (Truth and Reconciliation Commission of Canada 2015d: 124)

To guide the centre on its path, the teachings of the Turtle that sits in front of the centre are an important guide. Scholar Leanne Simpson (2011: 69), in recounting Waynabozhoo and the Great Flood in her piece *Dancing on Our Turtle's Back*, writes of the muskrat that dove deep under the waters that covered all of the lands of the earth following the great flood. The muskrat retrieved a handful of mud, of which the Turtle volunteered to "bear the weight of the earth on her back and Waynabozhoo placed the mud there." But in a detailed analysis of the story, Simpson goes on to state:

> we each have to dive down to the bottom of the vast expanse of water and search for our own handful of earth.... We each need to bring that earth to the surface, to our community, with the intent of transformation.... Once we have brought our paw full of dirt to the surface, it is then our responsibility to ensure that our action is collectivized. We need to ensure that the other members of the community act on our actions and carry the vision forward.

The examples from the Commission related in this chapter can be seen to be the handful of mud brought to the surface by the Truth and Reconciliation Commission—the Commission's offering to the country—and the centre holds an important responsibility to ensure that this work continues. But individuals, organizations and the nation as a whole also need to fully realize the need to bring their own offering to the surface as well.

To facilitate the ongoing need for truth and engagement, the NCTR officially launched the centre's public database in a room full of 1700 students, 350 school educators and hundreds of others. As part of the launch, TRC Survivor Committee and NCTR Governing Circle member Eugene Arcand recounted his own stories of suffering in the schools he attended, but also left the young people present with a powerful message of hope for the future. When Eugene shared his experiences with the room, it would have been possible to hear a pin drop.

The launch of this database marked the first time in Canadian history that Survivors, students, researchers, media and others had access in a single location to information on every residential school in the country. The locations of the residential schools are mapped with an interactive timeline that shows the locations of the schools, when they were built and when they were later decommissioned. This information is presented alongside school narratives produced by the Government of Canada, which document important events in the administration of each school. The data were specifically released to young people in order to acknowledge the critical role this information can play in classrooms and in shaping the future of the country.

But perhaps it is the bringing together of the two dominant rivers of information held by the databases of the NCTR that may contribute most to the ongoing understanding of the residential schools. By assembling these materials together in one place, those exploring the records will be able to delve into both streams of narrative in an effort to understand not only what was said by Survivors, but also was what being stated by the church and government officials responsible for the creation, maintenance and operations of the school. The database represents the first time that records detailing both the experience of being forcibly colonized and the act of colonization itself are together in one place in such an accessible manner.

While the Survivor statements detail loneliness, isolation, fear, abuse and longing for home, the government and church records are remarkably devoid of any mention of parents. Student home visits are described as 'privileges' that can be revoked or eliminated. Indigenous families often fail to appear in the records. It is as if the records are photographic prints and negatives of one another. The Survivor statements shed light and provide insight into how to read and understand the church and government records, just as the Survivor statements shed light on how to understand Canada's history and national narrative. The ongoing sharing of these Survivor perspectives on Canada's history is essential for reconciliation. As stated by Phil Fontaine (2015: 242), "the true legacy of the Survivors … will be the transformation of Canada."

The database of the centre also represents the distance between the two histories that exist in Canada—those of the indigenous peoples who were the subject of the schools' assimilative policies, and those of the state, church and non-indigenous society—have remained far apart and isolated from one another for most of the history of this country. Non-indigenous society dominated the national narrative and created the history present in this country today. Activities that transpired in the schools often occurred in remote areas of the country, hidden away from public view, relegated to activities at "indian schools" that were not discussed or explored. Non-indigenous peoples were given false information on indigenous cultures, histories and traditions in their schools, and all the while policy after policy was formed by the state without meaningful consultation or engagement with indigenous peoples.

The collective voicing of the experiences of Survivors and the sharing of these statements with the broader Canadian public have been a light that is now starting to penetrate the deepest shadows of Canada's national crime.[5] Highlighting this,

[5]The term "national crime" refers to a report written by Dr. Peter Bryce in 1922 that appealed to Canada to address health conditions in the residential schools. The residential schools continued to operate for close to another 90 years after original publication.

intergenerational Survivor and scholar Lorena Fontaine (quoted in Truth and Reconciliation Commission of Canada 2015c: 242) states:

> Without even thinking of the term reconciliation, I'm reminded about the power of story.... [People who watched the videos] said that when they saw the faces of Aboriginal women and heard their voices in the videos they understood assimilation in a different way. They felt the impact of assimilation.... It's far more powerful to have Aboriginal peoples talk about the impact of assimilation and hope for reconciliation than having words written down in a report.

The Path Forward

The Canadian Museum of Human Rights now sits at the Forks, at this historic place of coming together. In the opening gallery, a bronze footprint is set into the floor—the transport of a moccasin-clad footstep taken some 800 years ago into the present day. Where was this person walking? What were they thinking when they took that step? What did those rivers represent as they walked across the clay soil of the Red River valley?

Today, the galleries upstairs at the museum explore genocides and other mass atrocities committed by humans against other humans. Residential schools, forced relocation of indigenous peoples and other crimes committed against indigenous ways of knowing and being feature prominently throughout the museum. Past actions of aggression, violence and disrespect are framed against contemporary actions of renewal, justice and the codification of universal human rights for all people. Visitors are encouraged to reflect upon these histories and be active agents of change.

Rivers meet, ideas mix and the waters continue to flow.

The path of reconciliation that lies before Canada will not be a straight line. While much has been achieved with regard to the engagement of the Canadian public in a conversation, real change—systematic and transformative change—will take many years. Serious questions regarding land, title, reparation and the acknowledgement of a host of other injustices heaped upon indigenous peoples in the creation and maintenance of the Canadian state remain open and unanswered.

However, the actions of the TRC have shown us one thing in Canada: despite the time it will take to achieve full reconciliation, the open sharing of truth, met by open and listening audiences willing to really hear that truth, can have a powerful and transformative effect on a society. From the public apologies offered by church and government officials to the meaningful and ongoing reflections and truth-sharing roles played by the Honorary Witnesses, those in attendance at the TRC events were given the opportunity to see reconciliation in action.

So too were Survivors given the opportunity to turn to their family members and offer public apologies for their actions as adults suffering through the journey to learn what it means to be a parent after having been raised by an institution. This point was illustrated by Bob Watts (2014) from the Aboriginal Healing Foundation, who stated:

> I think about my friend Ken, who was in his sixties when he told his daughter for the first time that he loved her. He didn't know that was part of the deal being a parent, because he never got that himself as a kid. To me that's reconciliation. I think there's going to be hundreds and thousands and maybe tens of thousands of little wee tiny reconciliations. But all those have a force.

These "wee tiny reconciliations" are extremely powerful. They are the change that can and does occur in the moment—those small steps in the proverbial journey of a thousand miles. These reconciliations took shape through the creation of space for respect, love and understanding to emerge. They were facilitated through creating spaces in which *kintohpatatin* was served—where audiences took the needs of Survivors and others affected by the schools in with open hearts and open minds in a spirit of respect and kindness. Statement gatherers and Commissioners honoured Survivors through finally listening, giving Survivors an opportunity to shine their light on the darkest shadows of the nation.

These processes sit in contrast to the typical ways in which problems are addressed by governments. As stated by then Minister of Aboriginal and Northern Affairs Canada Chuck Strahl in the opening sharing circle of the Commission's work:

> Sometimes it is frustrating, you know, you wish it could move quicker and things could happen better and faster.… But mostly you have to wrestle with a bunch of things that government people are very poor at wrestling with because of relationship issues. Governments like to write policy, and they like to write legislation, and they like to codify things and so on. And Aboriginal people want to talk about restoration, reconciliation, forgiveness, about healing, about covenants, about truth. And those are all things of the heart and of relationship, and not of government policy (Strahl, quoted in Truth and Reconciliation Commission of Canada 2010).

Reconciliation is much more than just words on a page. But it cannot simply be conversation without action. A significant challenge that lies ahead for Canada is how to continue to share the voices of indigenous people with mainstream society. While the Commission welcomed hundreds of thousands of people to the national conversation about reconciliation, there are millions more who have yet to hear a Survivor share their experiences.

Recent public polling conducted by the Environics Institute (2016), in collaboration with the NCTR and a number of other organizations, reveals that across the country, close to 30 % of Canadians have not even heard of a residential school, while close to 60 % of Canadians are not even aware of the existence of the TRC. The poll also revealed that of those who claimed awareness of the TRC, few could name any of the Calls to Action in definitive terms. These findings demonstrate that despite the light now shining on our past, there is a significant amount of work still to do to bring Canadians to even a basic understanding of our collective history.

Moreover, the relatively weak understanding among Canadians of either complex indigenous rights frameworks or the effect past actions still have on the present-day realities faced by indigenous peoples is another significant barrier to reconciliation. This is the work that lies ahead for the National Centre for Truth and Reconciliation: the continued sharing of history so that someday, every person in this country will have the opportunity to better understand what has transpired. Critical in this is the voicing of indigenous realities and perspectives.

In the sharing of this information, it will be necessary to ensure the same care and attention are paid to those hearing it for the first time as to those who heard it through the TRC's formal processes. Intergenerational Survivors will be an especially important part of this sharing as they come to terms with the ongoing effect of the schools on their own lives. Non-indigenous Canadians must also realize that they too share in the responsibility given to them by virtue of dancing on the Turtle's back—that they too "have to dive down to the bottom of the vast expanse of water and search for [their] own handful of earth" (Simpson 2011: 69).

The recent endorsement of the United Nations Declaration on the Rights of Indigenous People by the Canadian government, the apology issued by the province of Ontario, the passage of the *Pathways to Reconciliation Act* in the province of Manitoba, and the Alberta Joint Commitment to Action on education are all positive developments. Many more such initiatives have been passed or announced in the last year, giving hope for a better future.

But action is key and words alone will not get us there. Former National Chief Phil Fontaine, himself a Survivor of the residential schools and a lead figure in the creation of the Indian Residential Schools Settlement Agreement, states:

> If this partnership between all founding peoples of the federation is to be meaningful, mutual responsibility and accountability must also define the relationship.… Reconciliation then, implies a solemn duty to act, a responsibility to engage, and an obligation to fulfill the promises inherent in an advanced democratic and ethical citizenship. (quoted in Truth and Reconciliation Commission of Canada 2015c: 217)

The sharing of truth is a powerful agent of change, one that has brought us to a new moment in Canadian history. But we know that, despite the collective best efforts of many, there is still much work to be done.

As I look out the window from my office at the National Centre for Truth and Reconciliation, the Red River has once again shed its icy coat and runs free, heading north towards the elders and the Assiniboine River. Will we, as a nation, be able to create one bigger river—a sum greater, wider, deeper, richer than our individual histories—or will the rivers stay separate, distant and apart? Can these same rivers meet and mix in a manner that does not constitute the dominance of one over the other?

These are complicated questions that strike at the heart of the journey of reconciliation. One thing for certain is that an in-depth understanding of the path each river has taken is essential to charting a future course.

References

Dussault, R. & Eramus, G. (1996). *Report of the royal commission on aboriginal peoples*. Ottawa: The Commission. http://hdl.handle.net/1974/6874. Accessed July 28, 2016.

Environics Institute for Survey Research. (2016). *Canadian public opinion on aboriginal peoples: Final report*. http://www.environicsinstitute.org/uploads/institute-projects/canadian%20public%20opinion%20on%20aboriginal%20peoples%202016%20-%20final%20report.pdf. Accessed July 28, 2016.

Fontaine, P. (2015). Foreword. In P. Fontaine, A. Craft, & the Truth and Reconciliation Commission (Eds.), *A knock on the door: The essential history on residential schools from the Truth and Reconciliation Commission of Canada*. Winnipeg: University of Manitoba Press.

Metatawabin, E., & Shimo, A. (2014). *Up Ghost River: A chief's journey through the turbulent waters of native history*. Toronto: Alfred A. Knopf Canada.

Simpson, L. (2011). *Dancing on our turtle's back: Stories of nishnaabeg re-creation, resurgence, and a new emergence* (p. 285). Winnipeg: Arbeiter Publishing.

Sinclair, M. (2015). *TRC closing event*. NCTR.ca. http://nctr.ca/map.php. Accessed July 28, 2016.

Truth and Reconciliation Commission of Canada. (2009). 'Schedule N,' *Indian residential school settlement agreement*. http://trc.ca/websites/trcinstitution/File/pdfs/SCHEDULE_N_EN.pdf. Accessed July 28, 2016.

Truth and Reconciliation Commission of Canada. (2010). *Opening sharing circle*. Winnipeg: Statement from the TRC's Winnipeg National Event.

Truth and Reconciliation Commission of Canada. (2015a). *Honouring the truth, reconciling for the future: Summary of the final report of the Truth and Reconciliation Commission of Canada*. Montreal: McGill-Queen's University Press.

Truth and Reconciliation Commission of Canada. (2015b). *Canada's residential schools: Reconciliation. The final report of the Truth and Reconciliation Commission of Canada* (Vol. 6). Montreal: McGill-Queen's University Press.

Truth and Reconciliation of Canada. (2015c). *Canada's residential schools: The history, part 1, origins to 1939. The final report of the Truth and Reconciliation of Canada* (Vol. 1). Montreal: McGill-Queen's University Press.

Truth and Reconciliation of Canada. (2015d). *Canada's residential schools: The history, part 2, 1939 to 2000. The final report of the Truth and Reconciliation of Canada* (Vol. 1). Montreal: McGill-Queen's University Press.

Watts, B. (2014). *Full circle: The aboriginal healing foundation and the unfinished work of hope, healing and reconciliation*. http://www.ahf.ca/downloads/full-circle-2.pdf. Accessed July 28, 2016.

Part III
The Politics and Policy of Settler Colonial Reconciliation

Chapter 12
The Spaces of Dangerous Freedom: Disrupting Settler Colonialism

Adam J. Barker and Emma Battell Lowman

Abstract This chapter expands on two related concepts developed by Mohawk scholar Alfred (2005): that of 'the clearing' and the 'space of dangerous freedom.' We examine how the embodied encounters in the clearing can model a powerful practice for transforming relationships in place through ritualised relational protocols. The clearing is rooted in Haudenosaunee practices and customs but can be applied to a wide variety of meetings between Indigenous peoples and Settler communities, supporting struggles for Indigenous resurgence. We follow on work by Hunt and Holmes (2015) on the complexities of pursuing decolonisation through (inter-)relational encounters in 'everyday' domestic spaces, and Haiven and Khasnabish (2014) on effective spaces generated in support of social justice movements.

Keywords Decolonisation · Space · Relationship · Sovereignty · Resurgence

Beginnings

Early one morning in the summer of 2006, we set off from Adam's longtime family home in Stoney Creek, Ontario, to make the hour long drive to 'Six'—that is, the Six Nations of the Grand River Reserve.[1] The Mohawk Nation Conference was beginning that day, and we had been invited by our friend, Bonnie, to attend.[2]

---

[1]The Haudenosaunee Confederacy, often called the Iroquois or Six Nations, are the dominant Indigenous polity in the territories where we were born and raised, specifically centred on the Six Nations of the Grand River reserve. For an excellent history of the Haudenosaunee settlement on the Grand River, see *We Share Our Matters* (Monture 2014). For a publically accessible recounting of the Confederacy, its history, and political traditions, see: www.digitalwampum.org.
[2]We are extremely grateful to Bonnie Whitlow for her friendship and teaching.

A.J. Barker (✉)
University of Leicester, Leicester, UK
e-mail: ajb154@le.ac.uk

E. Battell Lowman
University of Hertfordshire, Hatfield, UK

S. Maddison et al. (eds.), *The limits of settler colonial reconciliation*,
DOI 10.1007/978-981-10-2654-6_12

This conference did not start in a seminar room or lecture theatre. It started in a field, on the edge of the reserve territory. There, we gathered in three small clusters of people, worked out in friendly but quiet conversations. We were then met by several local Mohawks who explained that we needed to start with a ceremony to ask permission to enter the home of the Six Nations community. They turned our attention to a small group of people standing to one side of a small fire pit where some kindling was laid out. They, our hosts explained, were kin who had also come from abroad: they had travelled from the Mohawk communities of Akwesasne and Kanesetake, to the east. They too needed to ask permission to enter, but would lead the ceremony. We were directed to stand off to one side of their group, and as the sun rose slowly higher in the sky, we were joined by several more visitors—one more white Settler Canadian like ourselves, and people from different nations, including some Cree and Anishinaabe folks.

Without fanfare, the visiting Mohawk contingent set to work on the fire. They dragged evergreen boughs, just trimmed and still damp, and raised and lowered them above the fire, setting the needles smouldering. Big billows of dark smoke rose slowly above the trees surrounding the clearing on each rise of the boughs. We watched, quietly, and we waited.

After some time, we heard drums coming closer. On foot, about two dozen women and men, from children to elders, entered the clearing from the road, playing water drums[3] and singing. Soon, an elder stepped forward to explain. Traditionally, Haudenosaunee villages were built inside a palisade, and around this high picket fence was a clearing—all trees and brush removed for some distance. When visitors wished to enter a village, they stepped into the clearing and lit a fire to show themselves, then waited for the village to respond. They had to be visible, present, and patient. This is what we were doing.

We couldn't understand the exchanges that followed in Mohawk, but at the conclusion of the ceremony, we were welcomed to the territory. Then the children and youth ran together leading the way and we followed by car to Six Nations Polytechnic to continue the conference.

In the years since, we have returned to this story many times, thinking and feeling our way through the experience of participating in this ceremony. We re-turn through what it meant for us—and to us—as Settler Canadians to follow Mohawk protocol for respectfully requesting permission to enter their territory. Now, in our efforts to create strategies and processes for meaningful Settler decolonisation in relationship with Indigenous resurgence, we come back to this story and to the clearing.

[3]Traditional Haudenosaunee hand-held drums.

Introduction

In this paper, we propose expanding on the utility of two related concepts developed by Mohawk scholar Taiaiake Alfred (2005): that of 'the clearing' and the 'space of dangerous freedom.' We examine the relationship between these concepts, which we believe can serve a powerful and practical metaphor for working through the complexities and challenges of transforming relationships between Indigenous and Settler people, and between Indigenous and Settler *peoples*. We do this with the intention of supporting Indigenous resurgence, which is fundamentally varied and variable (Simpson 2011), and which demands accountability and responsibility from would-be Settler supporters.

Alfred's reference is to the traditional practice that occurred when 'outsiders' approached a Mohawk village, which was re-enacted in our opening narrative. We are, of course, wary of over-generalising this practice. However, as Settler people born and raised in Haudenosaunee territories and educated in large part by Haudenosaunee scholars and teachers, this particular practice has specific resonance. We then develop the relevance of Alfred's concept of the space of dangerous freedom for Settler people like ourselves. From this, we draw out understandings of how, when, and where Settler people can engage with Indigenous people and communities, and assert that this process holds wider value and relevance beyond Haudenosaunee territories for confronting settler colonialism more generally.

Settler Colonial Ways of Knowing

Settler colonisation is collective, meaning that undoing settler colonialism is also necessarily a collective effort. In our theory of Canadian settler colonialism, settlement is expanded and normalised through an interlocking set of *structures* (such as the triangular set of subjectivities that create racial and class hierarchies around settler selves, and Indigenous and exogenous Others), *systems* (of governance, economics, legalism, and socio-political organisation), and *stories* (such as the peacemaker myth or *terra nullius*). In this, we emphasise that it is possible to live on Indigenous lands in ways that are not colonial, but that at present, the structures, systems, and stories of settler colonialism are so pervasive as to make participation in settler colonialism almost inescapable. The point here, however, is that Settler people can exercise agency and struggle against settler colonialism in their own lives and socio-political contexts and that this has importance and potential for change even though it may not exempt them from complicity with settler colonisation writ large (Battell Lowman and Barker 2015).

Settler colonialism colours how we view our pasts—consider the contrast between the peacemaker myth (Regan 2010) and the violence and mass murder necessitated by Canadian settlement (Daschuck 2013)—and it also shapes how settler futurity is shaped and produced. Our settler colonial stories gravitate towards the 'vanishing end point' (Strakosch and Macoun 2012) of settler indigenisation and Indigenous disappearance. We can see this process at work even in progressive social movements, such as in the triumphal narratives of the Occupy movements that clearly articulated an individualist, rights-based, egalitarian future that foreclosed indigeneity (Grande 2013; Barker 2012). The structures, systems, and stories of settler colonialism, then, guide what future settler societies can look like, not just in their institutional continuity but in how they prefigure even radical breaks from or resistances to those institutions and systems.

Consistent with Derek Gregory's construction of the geographical imagination in the context of colonialism (1994), and Veracini's re-articulation of this concept with respect to the specificities of settler colonialism (2010), settlers attempt to transform the world around them to match their expectations of colonial space. This also indicates, however, that settler colonialism limits the horizons of the possible, both conceptually and materially, by foreclosing the 'radical imagination' of Settler people.[4] In order to decolonise, we must imagine, dream and feel beyond the boundaries that settler colonialism polices with force *and* comfort. We have to challenge ourselves to imagine relationships in and through places differently (Barker and Pickerill 2012) and then conceptualise, experiment, enact, and embody these relationships.

Decolonisation is a fraught and difficult process related to colonisation, and the very idea of settler peoples—colonisers who cannot escape their coloniality, cannot 'refuse' the gifts of colonialism (Memmi 1965)—having a role in decolonisation is not uncontroversial. For us, the point of scholarly engagement with settler colonialism is to learn how it can be challenged, dismantled, and ultimately defeated. However, for decolonisation to occur, the far more necessary element is the resurgence of Indigenous nationhood. Resurgence, as a concept, has been taken up by Indigenous scholars on Turtle Island (Alfred 2005; Alfred and Corntassel 2005; Corntassel and Bryce 2012; Coulthard 2014; Simpson 2011, 2014) to describe the process of reasserting and rebuilding relationships between Indigenous peoples and between Indigenous peoples and the land. Resurgence necessitates the defeat of settler colonialism, but the reverse is not necessarily true. However, dismantling settler colonial structures is a political project that Settler people hoping to work in solidarity with resurgent Indigenous communities can pursue. It is work that we can do that does not fall into the traps of deferring responsibility or moves to innocence or comfort by relying exclusively on Indigenous direction and effort, but maintains focus on the need for Indigenous leadership and the ultimate prioritisation of resurgence within a broader movement.

In order to assist Indigenous resurgence movements, Settler people have to encourage the failure of their own sovereign regimes. And it is here, in failure, that there is some inspiration to be found in how Settler people can make a positive contribution. Judith Halberstam (2011) explores the idea of 'failure'—to meet

[4]This is in reference to Haiven and Khasnabish discussion of neoliberal austerity as limiting the ability of radical movements to envision futures beyond struggles against these systems (2014).

dominant norms and expectations, to experiment with different ways of seeing and being in the world even if they are not sustainable—as a necessary corrective to the unattainable 'success' of neoliberal inclusion. Likewise, as Settler people who do not want the settler colonial project to succeed, we must practice 'failing' as Settler people in order to disrupt settler colonial spaces. As Halberstam notes, this ideology of failure 'turns on the impossible, the improbable, the unlikely, and the unremarkable. It quietly loses, and in losing it imagines other goals for life, for love... and for being' (2011: 88). This is what we hope to do: to fail to uphold settler colonial relationships, to fail to properly inhabit and embody settler colonial structures, systems, and stories, and by necessity find ways to build relationships differently. We cannot change who we are as Settler people alone, so we must work to create a broad base, to build communities that undertake these efforts together. This experimentation runs counter to everything on which settler colonial Canadian society is premised, which means it is and will be opposed. So, if we want to be other than settler colonisers, we have to collectively struggle to change, in order to 'fail' to conform to settler colonial norms. And in so doing, we open up the possibility of worlds beyond those norms, of something beyond the hope of Settler success.

Reconfiguring Relationships: People and Places

Our call to centralise the principle 'Always in Relationship' in Settler decolonisation struggles (Battell Lowman and Barker 2015: 116–120) recognises that Settler people and Indigenous people are always already in relationship. However, at present these relationships are heavily influenced by colonial power, resulting in colonial spaces being built around and through the act of relating. Indigeneity is often equated with a kind of tribalism that threatens the belonging of recently arrived settlers (Coleman 2016), and also runs against deep seated settler colonial fears of frontier violence (Morgensen 2011). These existential fears and structural diversions mean that Indigenous-Settler relationships are enacted at large, macro scales and rarely reach the more intimate scales of personal interaction in a meaningful or self-critical way.[5] A direct result of this structural dependency is a social deferral of responsibility for relating to Indigenous peoples and nations to an institutional scale, seen as more appropriate to treat the social 'sickness' of indigeneity. This creates a double-bind: Settler individuals and groups see Indigenous people as a 'national' responsibility and thus something that should not impact on their lives, even as the federal government works to divest itself of responsibility for Indigenous communities.

Settler colonial relationships between Indigenous and Settler peoples—and by extension, between Settler peoples and the land—have proven incredibly resilient to

[5]See also Clark et al. in this volume.

educational intervention, media critique, or political recognition and rights-based protections (Coulthard 2014). Likewise, as a variety of scholars have critically described, even (radical) activists with robust analyses and critiques of colonial hierarchy (Barker and Pickerill 2012; Lagalisse 2011), and respect for spiritual and cultural connections that exist outside the Western paradigm (Watts 2013), have repeatedly failed to relate to Indigenous peoples and lands in respectful ways. Knowing that settler colonialism exists, that it is entangled with state violence and capitalist dehumanisation and oppression, and even that settler societies like Canada remain actively engaged in erasure and dispossession of Indigenous peoples does not necessarily correlate to the creation of anticolonial and decolonising relationships of solidarity. Decolonisation, by contrast, has to be about changing relationships and making them healthy, supportive, and safe, not just in spite of colonial power, but actively against it (Hunt and Holmes 2015).

Decolonising relationships to both people and places must be approached in an affective rather than a mechanistic manner (Barker 2013). As such, Settler people cannot necessarily 'think' their way out of settler colonialism: the attachments to institutions of power and privilege and narratives of superior culture and knowledge are almost unavoidable pitfalls to this approach (Tuck and Yang 2012: 19–22; Mihesuah and Wilson 2004; Smith 1999). Settler research and knowledge production can be anticolonial (Battell Lowman 2014; Lewis 2012), but instances of this are usually the result of prior relationship-building. Instead of pursuing another intellectualised pathway to decolonisation, wherein Settler people attempt to rationalise their way through settler colonialism, complicity, anti-colonialism and decolonisation, we believe that reconfiguring relationships must be premised on the creation of spaces that encourage pre-cognitive, emotional engagements with personal and collective settler colonial complicity. We cannot expect to simply 'act differently together' in any successful or sustainable manner without recognising that, even when we are physically together, we are not occupying the same spatialities. Settler and Indigenous peoples are, in effect, always on 'uncommon ground,' but as Paul Chatterton has argued, understanding that we literally occupy different conceptual spaces does not the prevent forging of different kinds of relationships between those spaces (Chatterton 2006).

Decolonisation and the Space of Dangerous Freedom

How do we create the conditions for this sort of affective rupture and 'unsettle' in a way that sustains the embodied change of state associated with affective responses that precede decolonising solidarity work? Decolonisation, as a social project, must simultaneously denormalise this settler colonial ontology and disrupt the material functioning of settler colonial extraction, appropriation and erasure of Indigenous peoples. The only way to generate a persistent, affective state is to continually confound material privilege and perceived benefits of being Settler (Battell Lowman and Barker 2015), such that Settler people are forced to consider what

Memmi has called the inconceivable (1965): their own end, the world that does not need them, places without 'us'. What this means in practice is somewhat hard to say: it is tempting to forecast or imagine alternative post-settler futures, but doing so is inherently problematic. In some places, there are clear relational frameworks, such as in Haudenosaunee territory where the tradition of the Guswenta (Two Row wampum treaty) and the Silver Covenant Chain have generated clear political and legal orders that account for newcomers living in Haudenosaunee territories (see: Turner 2006: 48; Wallace 1994). However, in many other places, traditions are less clear: for example, in British Columbia where there are very few treaties, or across the prairies which are covered by the Numbered Treaties but where Indigenous and Settler governments have rarely agreed on the meaning of these agreements. There are some few historical examples of non-colonial newcomer settlement, and unexpectedly, several of the most prominent are situated in what is now the United States. Anthony Hall makes the case that the British in what is now New York State during the early 1700s fit this bill (Hall 2003). However we would argue that this is an imperfect example as the British in New England were an imperial power engaging in classical or metropole colonialism, often directly contrary to the interests of settler colonies. The settlement of New Sweden is a more intriguing example, as John Mack Faragher as pointed out (2014: 186–188). Swedish (and Finnish, and a few Dutch and British) settlers generally lived harmoniously alongside Lenape communities in the mid-1600s, trading and mediating or negotiating most disputes. Scandinavian settlers did not see the Lenape as 'inferior' or primitive, in part because they perceived their hunting and building techniques to be similar. While the New Sweden colony did not displace Indigenous communities, this is a somewhat problematic observation as Lenape communities had already been disrupted by the incursions of Dutch, English, and French colonial forces. Yet there was a great deal of peaceful interchange and interaction between the Lenape and the newcomers of New Sweden until the colony was conquered by the Dutch in 1655.

We learn from Johnson Hall and New Sweden that the potential exists for relationships beyond the commonly repeated settler colonial formations. Beyond this, however, even in the presence of treaty orders, we must be careful not to commit to any particular vision of the future for contemporary Settler people on Indigenous lands because Indigenous societies must first re-articulate and re-build their own practices on the land, including methods for dealing with newcomers and outsiders. In the absence of regenerated Indigenous nationhood, settler futurity becomes a trap, a distraction, and a move to innocence. Indigenous futures need to be secured first before Settler futures can be discussed (Tuck and Yang 2012). At best, we can probably agree that there will be an enormous variety of different ways that Indigenous people will deal with 'post-settlers,' and our most reasonable course of action is to consider carefully how our actions in the present impact on Indigenous sovereignty and nationhood. Settler people must develop a critical consciousness that simultaneously deconstructs settler colonial hegemony, while opening space for greater and more varied experiments with relationships on the land: through revitalising existing treaties, through making entirely new ones, through regimes we cannot yet imagine or that have yet to be articulated fully. We must assert different ways of being on the land, both against the broad 'structures of invasion' and also against individual phenomenological experiences of 'being settled'.

This is where we believe that Alfred's concepts of the clearing and spaces of dangerous freedom can be of great use because they force Settler people to think about place and space differently. We must revisit these concepts and understand how they function differently for Indigenous actors, which is who Alfred addresses in his original work, and Settler people like ourselves as we try to adapt these concepts across colonial difference (Barker 2013: 180). Alfred describes Indigenous resurgence as emanating outwards from decolonising spaces generated by Indigenous communities reasserting connections with lands and territories while creatively contending with the settler state and capitalist exploitation. Thus, the village stands in as a generative space of 'authentic' indigeneity, surrounded by 'the clearing' and, beyond, the forest—the space of dangerous freedom. This 'dangerous freedom' refers to the possibility that, through expanding struggles for resurgence and to paraphrase Albert Memmi, 'everything may change,'[6] meaning in this context that the structures of settler colonial invasion could be dismantled and relationships between Indigenous peoples, newcomers, and lands and territories completely reconfigured.

For Settler people, this geography must be inverted. The forest represents the pervasive, encompassing settler colonial social reality—it surrounds pockets of resurgent indigeneity, and for Settler people, our own struggles to move through and find spaces in this 'forest' can be read as shorthand for the common cultural narrative of rugged individualism and frontier survival. Likewise, the space of dangerous freedom is the indigenised space (the Mohawk village at the centre of the clearing) where Settler people can become something other than settler but only by leaving behind much of what they know and value as vital parts of national, cultural, regional, religious and other identities. So while in Alfred's original concept, Indigenous people pass through the clearing on their way outwards, into the space of dangerous freedom that is the world in need of transformation, Settler people dwell in the clearing as they seek ways to transform themselves and their own society.

The clearing, as a concept, is not easily incorporated into existing spatial theories or methods of understanding spatial relationships.[7] The clearing is very much part of living, Indigenous space, and the manner in which Settlers (or, as in the example that starts this paper, other Indigenous visitors) approach this space is about

[6]Albert Memmi theorised that colonisers who explicitly refuse the colonial project are limited in their ability to support decolonisation struggles because 'everything may change' and 'it is too much to ask one's imagination to visualize one's own end, even if it be in order to be reborn another' (Memmi 1965: 40–41). Given this cognitive barrier, one of our goals here is to envision affective ways of resolving this impasse.

[7]Our thanks to geographer Ben Coles for conversations that helped clarify the state of geography in relationship to this concept.

transitioning *between* spaces in a way that is visible and legible to those in the village beyond the clearing. As a space of resurgent indigeneity, defined by Haudenosaunee traditions of relationship, family, diplomacy, peace making, autonomy, and diversity, the clearing is not a space that can be easily appropriated by 'dominant hegemonies' (Hunt 2014). Nor does entry to the clearing imply a 'moving forward' that is often associated with liminal spaces, as it is instead a place of dwelling, of waiting, and of allowing time to pass without direction or influence. The clearing represents a space of political encounter, but not just that. It is a place where Settler people must attempt to pursue multiple relational configurations—with each other, with the land, with a present but not fully accessible indigeneity. Nor should the clearing be collapsed into concepts like autonomous zones (Day 2005), as while the village beyond the clearing is autonomous, the clearing is in fact open: anyone may enter, and the manner in which they enter may or may not prompt different responses. The clearing is an Indigenous space, but not necessarily a space asserted as 'autonomous' against the backdrop of a wider hegemonic landscape; its meaning is not dialectical, dependent on the opposition of settler colonialism, but rooted in much longer, deeper traditions of relational politics. And while the clearing is a contingent space, it is not a temporary space that may represent a fleeting line of flight away from the domination of state and capital, because the clearing is created and recreated wherever Haudenosaunee assert their relationships to the land amidst outsiders, newcomers, and Settler Others.

The clearing can be read into many different contexts, but there are some concrete examples that are of use here. Indigenous protest camps, for example, often evidence clear interior spaces, exterior spaces, and meeting or convergence points that function in a similar manner to the Haudenosaunee clearing in a variety of different cultural contexts and traditions. For example, consider both the long-standing 'gateway' or 'soft camp' erected in the path of proposed oil and gas pipelines by Unist'ot'en Clan of the Wet'suwet'en nation in the interior of British Columbia, and the longest-running protest camp in Canadian history, the Anishnaabe protest against clear cutting and mercury contamination at Grassy Narrows, Ontario. Protest camps come in a wide variety (Frenzel et al. 2013), and Indigenous protest camps are no less diverse. However, they do evidence some broad characteristics across those differences that help us to understand how clearing spaces can and do function in the present.[8]

The Unist'ot'en camp has become a place where many anti-pipeline, anti-fracking, pro-environmentalist, and pro-Indigenous rights activists have coalesced. But the Unist'ot'en camp is far from an open space, where anyone is free to enter. Rather, the features of the land itself have become part of a definitive clearing space. Consider, for example, the barricaded bridge over the Widzin Kwa (Morris River), which has become the iconic image of the camp. As the only land route into

[8]For more on Indigenous protest camps, and both the Unist'ot'en soft camp and Grassy Narrows blockade, see Barker and Ross (2017). On the Unist'ot'en camp specifically, see their website unistoten.camp; on Grassy Narrows, see the work of Willow (2010, 2011, 2012).

and out of the camp, the bridge has become a meeting point where anyone seeking entry must wait for the occupants of the camp to come and meet them. Solidarity activists are required to answer a series of questions—called the Free, Prior and Informed Consent Protocol—before being admitted to the camp, including their motivations for supporting the Unist'ot'en and detailed descriptions of how they can contribute to life in the camp. Of course, simply following these protocols does not abrogate the Indigenous sovereignty being exercised through the creation of these clearing spaces. For example, also in 2015, representatives of Chevron, one of the major pipeline construction companies currently seeking access to Unist'ot'en territory, came to the bridge with water and tobacco to ask for permission to enter the territory. They were summarily denied and their gifts rejected (Al Jazeera Plus 2015): as discussed, 'successful' decolonisation does not only happen if settlers enter the space of the clearing—the space of dangerous freedom remains beyond, and may be temporarily or permanently inaccessible.[9] The risk of rejection—of failure—must be present or there is simply nothing dangerous or free about this space of 'dangerous freedom.'

The Anishnaabe community around Grassy Narrows, meanwhile, has many years of experience of how to deal with well-intentioned if often-blundering newcomers. As Wallace (2010) described, there have been various times and places where usually-southern, usually-white Settler activists have impinged on Anishnaabe self-determination, imposing particular strategies and tactics which they prefer or have experienced previously. In these instances, rather than being pulled into a hegemonic order of settler protest practices, the Grassy Narrows community has often turned to traditional governance and decision making structures. In these spaces, Anishnaabe leadership has frequently decided to exclude problematic Settler activists from particular actions, to exclude them from particular spaces, or to ask them to leave the territory all together (Wallace 2010: 50–56). The clearing, therefore, need not be as clearly identifiable as it is rendered by the palisade of a traditional Mohawk village: it can also exist in spaces where solidarity is being produced and contested, so long as everyone working in or moving through these spaces recognises the contingency of Settler belonging and the primacy of Indigenous community decisions.

However, we should remember that at the core of the clearing is the domestic space—the hearth and home of Haudenosaunee communities. In Alfred's construction, this is the source of an outwardly-moving decolonization movement; in ours, it represents a re-centring or re-orienting of spatial perceptions as Settler people try to build complementary spaces. As such, when we think about the spaces of dangerous freedom, we should think about them in many spatial variants, including how they might relate to contemporary spaces of domesticity, and the way that affective relationships between Indigenous and Settler people, necessary

[9]Of course, it should be noted that the Chevron employees were not approaching the clearing with decolonising intent. However, the point stands: even decolonising commitments do not earn or guarantee admittance to Indigenous spaces.

for decolonisation, are often built in intimate, domestic spaces. Hunt and Holmes (2015: 156) examine the ways that their experiences of daily life on the West Coast, while in some ways similar (as queer-identifying women), also sharply diverge as Indigenous (Hunt) and Settler (Holmes) people. This divergence, however, does not imply that the authors (or any Indigenous and Settler people) are ever truly disconnected. Rather, they seek to foreground 'the intimate and everyday practices of allyship and decolonisation that are often made invisible when we focus solely on social action strategies taking place in more 'public' spaces such as community coalitions.' Like our construction of the clearing and the Mohawk village beyond which we assert and assume the normality and centrality of indigeneity, Hunt and Holmes seek to 'queer White settler colonialism… to render it abnormal, to name it and make it visible in order to challenge it' (2011: 156).

Drawing from African–American feminist Bernice Johnson Reagon, Hunt and Holmes (2015: 160–162) make a distinction between home spaces (at ease and comfortable) and coalition spaces (active political struggle and the uncomfortable) and troubled attempts to build movements. They argue that the relationships built in these home spaces are necessary to effective coalition building and movement organizing, serving as spaces for 'developing trust and communication across differences, challenging one another, and creating solidarity with one another' as well as leading to confrontations as intimate interactions necessarily raise the spectre of settler colonialism, white supremacy, gender violence and so on. As such, friendships cannot simply be entered into—they are relationships that must be approached carefully and with respect, taking time to build and grow naturally so that they are secure enough to withstand the potential (or perhaps inevitable) buffeting of affective anticolonial engagements.

We are also moved by the work of Haiven and Khasnabish (2014) on the creation of spaces of social movements and mobilisation in an era of overwhelming disempowerment for the political Left. Given the pervasiveness of neo-liberal capitalism, Khasnabish and Haiven describe a similar situation to the one that Indigenous and Settler activists working on decolonisation are grappling with: a variety of actors (in their case, social movement activists), already inherently in relationship, trying to find ways to support each other and achieve their own ends non-hegemonically, while under constant pressure and attack from the forces of state-driven austerity. One of Haiven and Khasnabish's most important interventions is the idea that scholars have a role to play in generating solidarity and affinity-based relationships through the creation of shared spaces for critical self-reflection and collective accountability. They describe their attempt through the concept of "convocation" which is at the core of their community research project in Halifax, Canada. Convocation results from an attempt to escape academic practices of description (writing about social movements as if the academics are not actually related to them) or representation (academics claiming a particularly vocal position in which they speak for a movement), which they addressed through the creation of a project that brought a variety of activists into sustained, reflective, and often intimate communication with each other, without agenda beyond the belief that such communication is important and often lacking.

As noted above, the structures, systems, and stories of settler colonialism are collectively produced, occupied, and consumed. Every settler subject plays a role in generating settler colonial dominance (and therefore has the power to challenge it), but none is individually responsible. Further, settler colonial society disciplines those who seek to escape the hegemony of settler space, coercing the complicity of otherwise rebellious subjects through the selective granting or withholding of privilege and benefit (Battell Lowman and Barker 2015). In effect, settler colonialism can tolerate the recognition that Settler people have a responsibility to Indigenous peoples—after all, a paternalistic relationship of care is still a relationship founded on a notion of 'responsibility'—but sets limits to the extent to which Settler people can practice 'accountability'. This has prompted us to think about the pursuit of relationships of accountability, and how resonances between Khasnabish and Haiven's spaces of convocation, and Alfred's concept of the clearing as a space of dangerous freedom lead to particular insights that can help us to understand how we can generate accountability while pursuing decolonisation.

Clearings and Convergences

The clearing can be thought of as a sort of 'convergence space,' where 'activists from participant movements embody their particular places of political, cultural, economic and ecological experience with common concerns, which lead to expanded spatiotemporal horizons of action' (Routledge 2003). However, the clearing represents *a very particular kind of convergence*: a space where indigeneity is not only vital and visibly active on the land, but also where the space is in fact created through the mutual acknowledgement of the power and authority of indigeneity in and with that place. The clearing is more than just a temporary space that reveals process of relationships converging within it. It is definitively an assertive and productive space, a space that settler colonialism cannot claim for itself in part because of the obvious assertion of indigeneity at the core of the space and also because of the willful 'failure' of Settlers to claim the space in any way. By being 'bad settler colonisers' and recognising the autonomy and sovereignty of Indigenous peoples, Settler people can help to stall the trajectory of settler colonial indigenisation and (temporarily) help to hold back the invasive power of settler colonial society.

Consideration of Settlers failing as settler colonisers re-emphasises that the clearing does not simply represent a space in which there is an absence of settler colonial power. An absence of the markers of settler colonialism, such as capitalist hierarchy, rational social ordering, and so on, could also be noted in the imagined *res nullius* of movements like Occupy (Barker 2012). Rather, the clearing is a space where Indigenous spatial power is dominant in specific reference to Settler people. Contrasted with how Settler societies often define themselves in the negative with respect to perceived-Other populations (non-Aboriginal/non-Indigenous, for example; see: Veracini 2015), these spaces 'Other' settler colonisers, forcing them to present themselves as who and what they are: outsiders who must configure their relationship to a new place through existing systems of local Indigenous nationhood. In effect, Settlers in the clearing must be confronted with their own foreignness, and with a resurgent Indigenous sovereignty with the power to recognise, admit, deny, or erase the Settler belonging in that space.

Passing through clearings lead Settler people into forms of dangerous freedom as passing through them implies an undoing of the unequal relationship at the root of settler colonialism. By centring indigeneity—the Mohawk village as the Settler's space of dangerous freedom—we face the ultimate fear of settler societies: that Indigenous societies will never 'go away,' and that the settler project has failed to provide the levels of peace, prosperity, and equality promised to Settler people, a fact that Veracini points out (2015), which can lead us to question the authority of settler colonial sovereignty, and by extension the world that it shapes and structures. Settler colonialism shapes both Settler and Indigenous belonging. Freedom from this, however, is not freedom from risk for Settler people, but rather the acceptance of it. Some risk may be perceived in relationships with Indigenous peoples—with fear of 'violent natives' underpinning much of the Settler identity (Battell Lowman and Barker 2015: 92–95; Morgensen 2011)—but the real risk is often from the disciplinary powers of the settler state.

As Coulthard (2014: 116) notes, blockades and other actions that simultaneously assert Indigenous sovereignty in situ, while also disrupting the material and especially the economic functioning of settler colonialism, are both the most effective forms of Indigenous protest historically, and also almost guaranteed to generate a state response. As Alfred argues, there is a fine line in which Indigenous peoples can engage in non-violent direct action to effectively disrupt the settler colonial state, but also expose any violent state responses as illegitimate and inhumane (2005). This is part of what has made the Unist'ot'en and Grassy Narrows occupations so effective: they have primarily targeted pipelines and logging trucks, and while there are occasional rumblings of mass police incursions, there is nothing in the actions of the protestors (Indigenous or Settler) that would justify such an attack in the minds of even most Settler people. This was demonstrated during the Oka standoff in 1990, where the Canadian government did, in fact, send the army into the Mohawk community of Kanesatake, leading one journalist to darkly quip that 'We are about to become a nation that when asked to choose between a massacre and a long drive to work, chose the massacre.'[10] Since then, while police violence against Indigenous peoples continues, there has been much greater reluctance to actively intervene in clearly established areas of Indigenous sovereign authority. Yet the threat remains.

When settler states turn their disciplinary apparatus on areas of Indigenous sovereignty, the presence of settler solidarity activists can be a help or a hindrance. For many Settler people, facing the potential violent power of the state—from which they are often insulated by a combination of privileges—can be a terrifying

[10]This quote is given anonymously in Macleod (1992).

experience which, combined with the unsettling effect of dwelling in Indigenous spaces like the clearing, can be a deterrent to sustained solidarity work. However, it would be a mistake to think that violent state responses are the norm: as stated, direct action disruptions have proven an incredibly potent form of exerting Indigenous sovereignty, and post-Oka, Canadian governments have become increasingly wary of trying to challenge these spaces directly. For example, both Grassy Narrows and the Unist'ot'en camp have been called 'illegal' occupations for years, and yet while both have experienced various levels of police harassment, direct assaults have not been forthcoming and the campaigns of harassment have not sapped the resolve of the Indigenous communities at the heart of the protests. Further, it would be a mistake to equate spaces of dangerous freedom simply with spaces of dangerous protest. In addition to the domestic spaces, described above, spaces of dangerous freedom can also be found in a variety of temporary assertions of Indigenous sovereignty. During the winter of 2012–2013, Idle No More staged a series of flash-mob style protests that entailed mass round dances in public spaces like shopping malls and urban intersections (see: Kino-nda-niimi Collective 2014). These round dances temporarily transformed spaces of concentrated settler colonial power into spaces filled with indigeneity (Barker 2015), and they were explicitly intended to allow for the participation of Settler solidarity activists and community supporters. To be sure, there were protocols to be followed (different depending on the territory) but there were ways that relationships could be formed between Indigenous and Settler peoples, in support of Indigenous self-determination. Indigenous peoples crossed their own clearings and, fully visible to Settler society, refused to act like 'Indians' are supposed to act, a radical and subversive assertion.[11] Simultaneously, these acts temporarily created indigenised spaces and Settler supporters were invited to cross their own clearings, participating in the dances, meeting folks directly, filming and broadcasting, and otherwise pursuing a very different form of dangerous freedom simultaneously. Then, the dance was over: flashmobs dispersed and with some exceptions, state violence was not an issue. This underscores that the clearing, as a metaphor, does not ossify our ideas about how and where Indigenous and Settler people can relate, but rather opens up possibilities for finding clearing spaces even in the midst of contention and violence. In short, while challenging the state may be a fearful experience for Settler people, the affective relationship building that occurs through the spaces of dangerous freedom may prove powerful enough to overcome these fears and generate lasting bonds of solidarity across the colonial difference.

Finally, it is important to consider how some social movements have explicitly sought out engagement with Indigenous sovereignties, explicitly in contrast to the ways that settler colonialism tends to set people in opposition to each other. For example, settler colonial societies tend to encourage migrants, racialised communities, and other marginalised groups to seek acceptance and privilege in part by demonstrating overt antipathy to indigeneity (Byrd 2011). For these groups, the

[11]Our thanks to Ravi de Costa for this articulation.

spaces of dangerous freedom could be seen as doubly-dangerous: even as they may be rejected or discouraged by the Indigenous communities whom they might approach, they may also face discipline and reprisal from the white supremacist settler state when they leave those spaces. Yet, in practice, there has been enormous potential revealed through the respectful approach to Indigenous sovereignty adopted by some marginalised communities. Perhaps the best example of this is No One Is Illegal (NOII), the migrant justice and anti-borders movement that has risen to prominence over the past decade around the globe, but particularly in places like Vancouver and Montreal. NOII is not an Indigenous peoples' movement, and as it advocates for the free movement of peoples across international borders, it might be seen as antithetical to Indigenous nationhood, which rests at least partially on the ability to control mobility across traditional territorial bases. However, NOII has explicitly placed Indigenous resurgence and decolonisation at the core of how they interpret migrant justice: seeking to confront the imperial-colonial-capitalist nexus that renders migrants in settler colonies 'stolen labour on stolen lands,' NOII has sought to build alliances between migrant agriculture workers, other undocumented migrants, and Indigenous communities like the Unist'ot'en (Walia 2013: 248–276). The Unist'ot'en, for their part, have reciprocated, offering sanctuary and friendship to migrants, and welcoming them onto the land and creating powerful alliances that challenge the very basis of the settler state. While the state undoubtedly is mobilised against this alliance, it has thus far been very successful at generating affective social change among groups of people who, in different spaces, might see themselves at odds.

There are many other possible considerations that are raised by thinking through the clearing as a spatial metaphor, including the idea of leaving and returning, perhaps positioning Settler rituals of returning as a parallel to Indigenous rituals of renewal (Little Bear 2004)—an active rather than passive waiting that happens not once, but again and again and again without end, for as long as the practice is useful. This repetition without end, which inherently denies preoccupation with settler futurity while establishing opportunities for personal accountability, may be what makes this a space of dangerous freedom: our actions and decisions in one instance will play out in the response of Indigenous community members to our return. In this space absent Settler sovereignty, we will have to truly grapple with what it means to be accountable to Indigenous resurgence.

References

Alfred, T. (2005). *Wasase: Indigenous pathways to action and freedom*. Peterborough, ON: Broadview Press.

Alfred, T. (2009). Colonialism and state dependency. *Journal of Aboriginal Health, 5*, 42–60.

Alfred, T., & Corntassel, J. (2005). Being indigenous: Resurgences against contemporary colonialism. *Government and Opposition, 40*(4), 597–614.

Al Jazeera Plus. (2015). Unist'ot'en camp: Holding their ground against oil & gas pipelines [documentary video]. http://www.youtube.com/watch?v=5qUw3bqIHks

Barker, A. J. (2012). Already occupied: Indigenous peoples, settler colonialism and the Occupy movements in North America. *Social Movements Studies, 11*(3–4), 327–334.
Barker, A. J. (2013). (Re-)Ordering the new world: Settler colonialism, space and identity. PhD dissertation: University of Leicester, United Kingdom.
Barker, A. J. (2015). 'A direct act of resurgence, a direct act of sovereignty': Reflections on idle no more, indigenous activism, and canadian settler colonialism. *Globalizations, 17*(1), 43–65.
Barker, A. J. (2017). *Settling: Invasion, space making, and the transformation of North America.* Vancouver: UBC Press. (forthcoming).
Barker, A. J., & Pickerill, J. (2012). Radicalizing relationships to and through shared geographies: Why anarchists need to understand indigenous connections to land and place. *Antipode, 44*(5), 1705–1725.
Barker, A.J. & Ross, R. (2017). Reoccupation and resurgence: Indigenous protest camps in Canada. In: G. Brown, A. Feigenbaum, F. Frenzel, & P. McCurdy (Eds.), *Protest Camps in International Context: Spaces, Infrastructures, and Media of Resistance.* Bristol: Policy Press.
Battell Lowman, E. (2014). Indigenous methodologies, missionary lives. PhD thesis, University of Warwick, United Kingdom.
Battell Lowman, E., & Barker, A. J. (2015). *Settler: Colonialism and identity in 21st century Canada.* Winnipeg: Fernwood Press.
Bobel, C. (2007). 'I'm not an activist, though I've done a lot of it': Doing activism, being activist and the 'perfect standard' in a contemporary movement. *Social Movement Studies, 6* (6), 147–159.
Byrd, J. (2011). *The transit of empire: Indigenous critiques of colonialism.* Minneapolis: University of Minnesota Press.
Chatterton, P. (2006). 'Give up activism' and change the world in unknown ways: Or, learning to walk with others on uncommon ground. *Antipode, 38*(2), 259–281.
Coleman, D. (2016). Indigenous place and diaspora space: of literalism and abstraction. *Settler Colonial Studies, 6*(1), 61–76.
Corntassel, J., & Bryce, C. (2012). Practicing sustainable self-determination: Indigenous approaches to cultural restoration and revitalization. *Brown Journal of World Affairs, XVIII* (II), 151–162.
Coulthard, G. (2014). *Red skin, white masks.* Vancouver: UBC Press.
Daschuck, J. (2013). *Clearing the plains: Disease, politics of starvation, and the loss of aboriginal life.* Regina: University of Regina Press.
Day, R. J. F. (2005). *Gramsci is dead: Anarchist currents in the newest social movements.* Toronto: Between the Lines.
Faragher, J. M. (2014). Commentary: Settler colonial studies and the North American frontier. *Settler Colonial Studies, 4*(2), 181–191.
Frenzel, F., Feigenbaum, A., & McCurdy, P. (2013). Protest camps: An emerging field of social research. *The Sociological Review,* 1–18.
Grande, S. (2013). Accumulation of the primitive: the limits of liberalism and the politics of Occupy Wall Street. *Settler Colonial Studies, 3*(3–4), 369–380.
Greensmith, C. (2012). Pathologizing Indigeneity in the Caledonia 'Crisis'. *Canadian Journal of Disability Studies, 1*(2), 19–42.
Gregory, D. (1994). *Geographical imaginations.* Cambridge, MA: Blackwell.
Haiven, M., & Khasnabish, A. (2014). *The radical imagination.* London: Zed Books.
Halberstam, J. (2011). *The queer art of failure.* Durham: Duke University Press.
Hall, A. J. (2003). *The American empire and the fourth world: The bowl with one spoon.* Montreal: McGill-Queen's University Press.
Hunt, S. (2014). Ontologies of indigeneity: the politics of embodying a concept. *Cultural Geographies, 21*(1), 27–32.
Hunt, S., & Holmes, C. (2015). Everyday decolonization: Living a decolonizing queer politics. *Journal of Lesbian Studies, 19*(2), 154–172.
Kino-nda-niimi Collective (Ed.). (2014). *The winter we danced: Voices from the past, the future, and the Idle No More movement.* Winnipeg: ARP Books.

Klein, H. (2015). The Zapatista movement: Blending indigenous traditions with revolutionary praxis. In D. G. Maxwell & S. Craibs (Eds.), *No gods, no masters, no peripheries: Global anarchisms* (pp. 22–43). Oakland: PM Press.

Lagalisse, E. M. (2011). 'Marginalizing Magdalena': Intersections of gender and the secular in anarchoindigenist solidarity activism. *Signs: Journal of Women in Culture and Society, 36*(3), 653–678.

Lewis, A. G. (2012). Ethics, activism and the anti-colonial: Social movement research as resistance. *Social Movement Studies, 11*(2), 227–240.

Little Bear, L. (2004). *Land: The blackfoot source of identity*. Presented at 'Beyond Race and Citizenship: Indigeneity in the 21st Century' Conference. Berkeley, USA: University of California.

Macleod, A. (1992). *Acts of defiance [documentary film]*. Ottawa: National Film Board of Canada.

Memmi, A. (1965). *The colonizer and the colonized*. Boston: Beacon Press.

Mihesuah, D. A., & Wilson, A. C. (Eds.). (2004). *Indigenizing the academy: Transforming scholarship and empowering communities*. Lincoln: University of Nebraska Press.

Monture, R. (2014). *We share our matters: Two centuries of writing and resistance at six nations of the Grand River*. Winnipeg: University of Manitoba Press.

Morgensen, S. L. (2011). The Biopolitics of Settler Colonialism: Right Here, Right Now. *Settler Colonial Studies, 1*, 52–76.

Regan, P. (2010). *Unsettling the settler within: Indian residential schools, truth telling and reconciliation in Canada*. Vancouver: UBC Press.

Routledge, P. (2003). Convergence space: Process geographies of grassroots globalization networks. *Transactions of the Institute of British Geographers, 28*(3), 333–349.

Simpson, L. B. (2011). *Dancing on our turtle's back*. Winnipeg: Arbeiter Ring Press.

Simpson, A. (2014). *Mohawk interruptus: Political life across the borders of settler states*. Durham: Duke University Press.

Smith, L. T. (1999). *Decolonizing methodologies*. London: Zed Books.

Stevenson, L. (2012). The psychic life of biopolitics: Survival, cooperation, and Inuit community. *American Ethnologist, 39*(3), 592–613.

Strakosch, E., & Macoun, A. (2012). The vanishing endpoint of settler colonialism. *Arena Journal, 37*(38), 40–62.

Swamp, J. (2010). Kanikonriio: Power of a good mind. In L. Davis (Ed.), *Alliances: Re/envisioning indigenous-non-indigenous relationships* (pp. 15–24). Toronto: University of Toronto Press.

Tuck, E., & Yang, K. W. (2012). Decolonization is not a metaphor. *Decolonization: Indigeneity Education and Society, 1*(1), 1–40.

Turner, D. (2006). *This Is not a peace pipe: Towards a critical indigenous philosophy*. Toronto: University of Toronto Press.

UnistotenCamp. (2015). 'Batman vs Pipelines @ Unist'ot'en' [Youtube video]. http://www.youtube.com/watch?v=bBv1tbj58Ag.

Veracini, L. (2010). The imagined geographies of settler colonialism. In T. Banivanua Mar & B. Edmonds (Eds.), *Making settler colonial space: Perspectives on race place and identity* (pp. 179–197). London: Palgrave Macmillan.

Veracini, L. (2015). *The Settler Colonial Present*. S.L.: Springer.

Walia, H. (2013). *Undoing border imperialism*. Oakland: AK Press.

Wallace, P. (1994). *White roots of peace: The iroquois book of life*. Santa Fe, NM: Clear Light Books.

Wallace, R. (2010). Grassy narrows blockade: Reworking relationships between anishinabe and non-indigenous activists at the grassroots. *International Journal of Canadian Studies, 41*, 37–68.

Watts, V. (2013). Indigenous place-thought and agency amongst humans and non-humans (first woman and sky woman go on a European World Tour!). *Decolonization: Indigeneity Education and Society, 2*(1), 20–34.

White, R. (2011). *The middle ground: Indians, empires, and Republics in the Great Lakes Region, 165061815*. Cambridge: Cambridge University Press.

Wilkes, R., & Ricard, D. (2007). How does newspaper coverage of collective action vary? Protests by Indigenous people in Canada. *The Social Science Journal, 44*(2), 231–251.

Willow, A. J. (2010). Cultivating common ground: Cultural revitalization in anishinaabe and anthropological discourse. *American Indian Quarterly, 34*(1), 33–60.

Willow, A. J. (2011). Conceiving Kakipitatapitmok: The political landscape of anishinaabe anticlearcutting activism. *American Anthropologist, 113*(2), 262–276.

Willow, A. J. (2012). *Strong hearts, native lands: Anti-clearcutting activism at grassy narrows first nation*. Winnipeg: University of Manitoba Press.

Chapter 13
Reconciliation and the Quest for Economic Sameness

Jon Altman

Abstract Deploying the lenses of economics, this chapter considers why the Australian government has proven so incapable of progressing the process of reconciliation after setting up the statutory and institutional mechanisms to do so in 1991. My argument is that in policy thinking there is a perceived logical correlation between reconciliation and the quest for economic sameness. For decades now the nation's Indigenous policy framework has been framed as a project for 'Closing the Gap'. Such framing makes prospects for reconciliation difficult. This is because the very logic of reconciliation as progressively codified and emptied of substantive meaning presumes the eradication of difference—settler society looks to move from the elimination of the different to the elimination of difference. This elimination of difference is founded on an evolutionary moral sentiment of socioeconomic salvation discursively couched as neoliberal reason. As long as reconciliation is predicated on such a state-imposed project of economic sameness it will fail. Successful reconciliation will require a broader acceptance of the plurality of Indigenous aspirations and the diversity of Indigenous circumstances. Such national embrace of 'post-colonial' economic plurality that focuses on livelihood (not just statistical) improvements is a necessary first step to improved relations between Indigenous and other Australians. Optimistically, if the reconciliation process can embrace the notion of economic plurality or hybridity inclusive of 'difference recognition', prospects for reconciliation, whether defined as a process or as an end point, will be enhanced.

Keywords Economic sameness · Closing the Gap · Economic hybridity · Economic plurality · Native title · Land rights · Neoliberal policy · Neoliberal governmentality · Assimilation · Recognition of difference

---

J. Altman (✉)
Alfred Deakin Institute for Citizenship and Globalisation, Deakin University, Melbourne, Australia
e-mail: jon.altman@deakin.edu.au

S. Maddison et al. (eds.), *The limits of settler colonial reconciliation*,
DOI 10.1007/978-981-10-2654-6_13

Introduction

In this Chapter, I consider why the Australian government has proven so incapable of progressing the process of reconciliation after setting up the statutory and institutional mechanisms to do so in 1991. The perspective that I take is that of economics; I focus on the material wellbeing of Indigenous Australians both absolutely and relative to other settler Australians. My brand of economics is inclusive of cultural analysis and presumes the need to interrogate power relations, as well as (economic) history.

'Closing the Gap' in socioeconomic outcomes is the dominant mantra of national Indigenous policy that to date appears 'destined to fail'.[1] Similarly the quest to close the 'reconciliation gap' between Indigenous and other Australians is destined to fail if not radically reconceived. My argument is that in policy there is a perceived logical correlation between reconciliation and the quest for economic sameness. If the assessment of a successful reconciliation outcome is predicated on the pursuit of economic sameness, according to some statistical picturing of Indigenous Australians, it will fail. Conversely, if the reconciliation process can embrace the notion of economic plurality or hybridity inclusive of 'difference recognition', prospects for reconciliation, whether defined as a process or as an end point, will be enhanced.

In my analysis I could uncritically adopt the late Patrick Wolfe's theoretical perspective that the logic of settler colonial societies is the elimination of native societies (Wolfe 1999, 2006, 2015). As will become apparent, I am broadly sympathetic to the possibility that the state project of integration will result in disappearance, 'the elimination of the native'. Without doubt this is a goal that some powerful Indigenous and non-Indigenous political actors and people of influence (including media shock jocks) would welcome—the disappearance of any notion of a fundamentally different Indigenous society and economy, to be replaced by a late capitalist economy discursively and ideologically envisioned as individualistic and free market.

But in reality the Indigenous population is not disappearing, it is in fact growing. Nor is there evidence of widespread acquiescence to the state project of elimination —what might be referred to as the contemporary practice of 'state violence' (Butler 2012: 69–71). I am reminded too of Vine Deloria's (1969: 179) warning that equality must not be conflated or confused with sameness, 'civil rights is a function of man's desire for self-respect not for equality'.

Wolfe's (2015) contention is that the primary motive for elimination is access to territory—territoriality is settler colonialism's specific, irreducible element, expropriation of land and resources continue as a foundational characteristic of the settler society. Henry Reynolds (2013) describes the colonial land grab in Australia from

[1]It would be remiss of me not to acknowledge that Sanders (1991) presciently used this terminology with reference to the Aboriginal Employment Development Policy's goal articulated in 1987 to deliver statistical equality in employment between Indigenous and other Australians by the year 2000.

1788 as one of the greatest illegal appropriations of land in world history. And yet over the past 40 years this has been partially countered by a significant transfer of remote territory back to traditional owners, perhaps the greatest restitution of land without warfare in recent times (Altman and Markham 2015). This restitution has occurred for social justice and legal reasons responding in part to prolonged Aboriginal activism in this area. Today a third of the Australian continent is under some form of Indigenous title (see later maps), although property rights on much of this land remain weak despite the use of inaccurate terms like 'exclusive possession' that actually confer no right to exclude; and Indigenous political jurisdiction to self-govern is absent.

I raise the issue of territoriality in part to problematise Wolfe, but mainly to allude to one of the current paradoxes of linking reconciliation to economic sameness: the more Indigenous title, the less likely are the prospects for economic sameness as measured by standard statistical indicators based on Western metrics.

I also want to temper my deference to Wolfe with deference to many Indigenous Australians whom I regard highly, and who have committed to the reconciliation process over the past quarter century. I do not want to just dismiss their efforts and aspirations as ill-considered and the likely outcomes of the reconciliation process as futile. Sometimes in pessimistic moments I am attracted to the blunt view of Gary Foley that until Indigenous Australians get genuine self-determination, '"WE ARE FUCKED": economic independence is the key to political independence. We [Indigenous Australians] need to decide what we do, who we are, what our future is' (quoted in Watson 2016).

While I have not undertaken research directly on the reconciliation question for a decade, this has not always been the case. In 1991 I was greatly heartened by the passage of the Council for Aboriginal Reconciliation law by the Australian Parliament. Subsequently I collaborated with the Council for Aboriginal Reconciliation and participated in a number of key events including the Reconciliation Convention in June 1997, Corrobboree in May 2000 that included the Bridge Walk, the Deliberative Poll 'Australia Deliberates Reconciliation—Where to from Here?' in February 2001, and the National Reconciliation Workshop at Old Parliament House in May 2005.

In September 2003 at a Cranlana Symposium 'Articulating a Reconciled Australia' I delivered a paper 'Monitoring practical reconciliation: Evidence from the reconciliation decade 1991–2001' (Altman and Hunter 2003).

This research was of great personal significance in my relationship as a scholar and activist with the Howard government and its compliant officials.[2] Straightforward analysis of five-yearly census data showed quite clearly that the 'practical' reconciliation of John Howard's governments had fared no better than the Hawke and Keating governments' commitment to mixing the practical with the symbolic. This was not a popular interpretation although it was later replicated by

[2]It was also one element in the Commonwealth's short-lived action to defund the Centre for Aboriginal Economic Policy Research that I had established at the Australian National University.

the Commonwealth Grants Commission and highlighted in the Human Rights and Equal Opportunity Commission *Social Justice Report 2003* (Altman 2004).

A year later in 2004 I became an outspoken critic of the abolition by the Howard government of the Aboriginal and Torres Strait Islander Commission (ATSIC); and of its new mainstreaming approach (Altman 2004). By 2007 I could see no prospect for successful reconciliation in the aftermath of the Northern Territory Emergency Response intervention that constituted a futile project of 'Coercive Reconciliation' (Altman and Hinkson 2007).

Since then the nation's Indigenous policy and practice framework has been framed as a project for 'Closing the Gap' (Council of Australian Governments 2009). Such framing makes prospects for reconciliation difficult. This is because the very logic of reconciliation as progressively codified and emptied of substantive meaning presumes the eradication of difference—settler society looks to move from the elimination of the different to the elimination of difference. This elimination of difference is founded on an evolutionary moral sentiment of socioeconomic salvation couched as neoliberal reason (Altman 2014; Strakosch 2015). As long as reconciliation is predicated on such a state-imposed project of economic sameness it will fail. Successful reconciliation, in my view, will require a broader acceptance of the plurality of Indigenous aspirations and the diversity of their circumstances. Such national embrace of 'post-colonial' economic plurality that focuses on livelihood (not just statistical) improvements is a necessary first step to better relations between Indigenous and other Australians and the possibility of reconciliation.

Reconciliation as Policy

> The object of the establishment of the Council is to promote a process of reconciliation between Aborigines and Torres Strait Islanders and the wider Australian community, based on an appreciation by the Australian community as a whole of Aboriginal and Torres Strait Islander cultures and achievements and of the unique position of Aborigines and Torres Strait Islanders as the indigenous peoples of Australia, and by means that include the fostering of an ongoing national commitment to co-operate to address Aboriginal and Torres Strait Islander disadvantage. (Australian Government 1991)

It is difficult to take issue with such progressive policy sentiments expressed in 1991. Wearing economic lenses, it is discernible that the aim of this law was to make a national commitment to addressing disadvantage while simultaneously appreciating cultural diversity. As policy, the *Council for Aboriginal Reconciliation Act 1991* did not stipulate economic sameness; but it is often overlooked today that it was framed and passed at a typically complex moment towards the end of the Hawke administration 1983–1991.

As background to that framing, it is noteworthy that the Hawke government committed to, and then abandoned, national land rights by 1984; it had sponsored the comprehensive Miller Inquiry into Aboriginal Employment and Training Programs in 1985 (and responded with the Aboriginal Employment Development

Policy (AEDP)); it had initiated the Royal Commission into Aboriginal Deaths in Custody in 1987; had established the nationally-representative ATSIC in 1989; and had respectfully received the 1988 Barunga Statement calling for a treaty and committed to respond by 1991.

The Reconciliation process itself was arguably a second-best response to the political unwillingness to engage properly with the strong demands in the Barunga Statement, which called for mechanisms for achieving Indigenous economic independence and political empowerment, including a treaty.

It is frequently overlooked today that when the reconciliation legislation was passed, the AEDP—with its key goals to achieve employment, income and educational equity by the year 2000 (Australian Government 1987)—was official policy. Even as the new law was passed, Altman and Sanders (1991) were already suggesting that the pursuit of statistical equality was unrealistic and likely to fail.

While the broad thrust of policy during the Hawke years adhered to a diluted notion of self-determination left over from the Whitlam era, government aims for economic convergence had their genesis in the era of assimilation, officially defined in 1961 as:

> All aborigines and part-aborigines [sic] are expected to attain the same manner of living as other Australians and to live as members of a single Australian community enjoying the same rights and privileges, accepting the same responsibilities, observing the same customs and influenced by the same beliefs, hopes and loyalties as other Australians (Commonwealth of Australia 1961).

This definition fitted well with the modernisation paradigm in economic development dominant in 1961; there was no conceivable alternative to joining the mainstream economy and society.

This notion of assimilation accords with Wolfe's (2006) theorisation. While settler colonialism's negative dimension is the goal to dissolve native societies, an option emerges from the logic of elimination—the possibility of integration of Indigenous peoples as Australian citizens as the assimilation policy statement implies.

In *The Lucky Country* Horne (1964) commented that all governments were committed to assimilation, but lamented that the possibility that Aboriginal people would preserve their civilization was small; he was confident though that legally they were on the road to full citizenship.

An important crossing on this road was the overwhelming 'yes' vote in the 1967 Referendum. This resulted in the deletion of section 127 of the Constitution and meant that Indigenous people could be included for the first time in 'reckoning the number of people of the Commonwealth'. By rendering Indigenous people statistically visible census counts since 1971 have statistically verified that any project of physical elimination was failing. The Indigenous population count since 1971 has increased by 500 per cent reflecting both a growing willingness and pride to identify, as well as rapid natural increase—these are not disappearing peoples.

The availability of social indicator data from the census has made it possible to look at socio-economic outcomes for the Indigenous population—in areas such as employment, education, housing and life expectancy—and to compare these outcomes with the general population. There is a long subsequent and escalating history of such analyses in academia and the associated adoption of the notion of statistical convergence of outcomes for Indigenous and non-Indigenous Australians as a national policy priority, at least at the level of rhetoric.

Reconciliation legislation was followed in June 1992 by the Mabo High Court judgment recognising a form of native title land tenure existed pre-colonially. This judgment, and the passage of the bitterly contested Native Title Act 1993, as well as the report of the National Inquiry into the Separation of Aboriginal and Torres Strait Islander Children from Their Families established by the Keating government in 1995, marked the end of political bipartisanship over reconciliation and Indigenous policy more generally. In 2004 such bipartisan re-emerged as what I have termed a 'Canberra Consensus' on Indigenous policy (Altman 2014).[3]

The Political Strangulation of Reconciliation

Five years after the passage of reconciliation legislation the conservative Howard government was elected with no substantive Indigenous affairs policy beyond stated commitments to demonise and dilute three already iconic institutions of Indigenous Australia: ATSIC, the reconciliation process, and native title.

Under Howard's opposition leadership the Liberal party had been purged of its more liberal elements and social conservatives came to dominate: the 1996 winning election platform was 'For All of Us', code for prioritising mainstream over marginal interests. Immediately ATSIC's budget was slashed after a concocted special audit that found no impropriety; a process was put in place looking to dilute native title rights; and the Prime Minister himself singularly attacked reconciliation with an oppositional and angry speech at the Reconciliation Convention in Melbourne in May 1997 that saw delegates respond by turning their backs to him.

The Howard government quietly condoned the vitriolic 'history wars' and 'culture wars' in the name of open liberal democratic debate. And the government promoted itself as proudly socially conservative and fundamentally different to progressives: the conservatives favoured economic integration, progressives emphasised such integration alongside the right to live differently. A distinction was made by the government between the progressive period from 1972 to 1996 (when the so-called 'black armband view of Australian colonial history dominated) and the halcyon days of assimilation in the two decades before. At the heart of this debate were disputes about the right mix between the practical, economic

[3]This chapter was drafted during the 2016 federal election campaign when some differences in Indigenous policy between the Coalition Government and Labor Opposition emerged, while the Australian Greens took a far more progressive position around issues of reconciliation, constitutional recognition and treaty making.

integration; and what was termed the 'symbolic'—an Indigenous rights approach focused on social justice and the right to live differently.[4]

The two metrics of socio-economic progress according to statistics and the spatial coverage afforded by land rights and native title laws were increasingly deployed to discredit the performance of previous more progressive governments.

Howard and his colleagues argued that socioeconomic progress (as measured by statistics) had been too slow, overlooking the fact that statistical exclusion prior to 1971 meant that comparative information on the earlier assimilation era was unavailable. Statistical picturing that was effectively used by the Hawke government to demonstrate the extent of Indigenous need and to track anticipated progress to socioeconomic equality/economic sameness was now co-opted as a means of demonstrate that symbolic reconciliation was failing.

From 1998 the Howard government's stated aim was to focus only on 'practical reconciliation', a framework intended to reduce material disadvantage in the areas of health, housing, education and employment. While Howard committed to practical reconciliation and 'closing the gaps' in outcomes between Indigenous and non-Indigenous people, ever the wily politician he did not specify the rate or mode for improvement beyond the need to join the mainstream. So, unlike Hawke, Howard's government did not set statistical targets or time frames and there was no monitoring framework for assessing progress. The level of Indigenous disadvantage was deemed unacceptable, but was explained as a product of recent bad policy rather than a deeper history of colonial invasion and subsequent neglect.

Howard ran a dishonest and divisive campaign intended to terrify voters that native title claims and determinations in the wake of the Wik High Court decision of 1996 (which found that pastoral leasehold did not extinguish native title rights) would threaten their land holdings and national prosperity. He stated on national television:

> I think the Australian public will understand one very simple thing. What has happened with native title is that the pendulum has swung too far in one direction, particularly after the Wik decision. And what I have done with this legislation is to bring it back to the middle. Let me just show you a view of it. This shows 78 per cent of the land mass of Australia coloured brown on this map. Now, the Labor Party and the Democrats are effectively saying that the Aboriginal people of Australia should have the potential right of veto over further development of 78 per cent of the land mass of Australia. Now, that is a very simple message. I think the Australian people will understand that message'. (Howard 1997)

This is a classic example of what de Blij (2012: 65–66) terms a 'map of Bad Intentions' as a right to veto development was not an option on native title land. This was a shameless appeal for support from those Australian voters who might be aggrieved that the so-called 'judicial activism' of the High Court in Mabo and the subsequent native title laws passed by an 'over-progressive' Paul Keating were steps that would jeopardise their economic interests.

---

[4]Tim Rowse (2012) has demonstrated how the statistical production of Aboriginal populations and peoples has been variably deployed in two competing notions of social justice, the first favouring sameness the second difference.

Yet despite the best efforts of the Howard government to redefine and subvert the reconciliation process there was still considerable goodwill evident at the final major public events of the Council for Aboriginal Reconciliation Corroboree 2000 'Sharing our Future' and a series of national bridge walks in which the Prime Minister refused to participate.

The Neoliberalisation of Indigenous Policy

After the reconciliation decade a more corporatised model of reconciliation was established with the newly-created organisation Reconciliation Australia funded by the Australian government. As noted already, despite the rhetoric of three Howard-led governments, there was no clear statistical evidence that their approach was delivering better outcomes for Indigenous Australians than those of their predecessors.

Frustrated by this, and by the expansion of Indigenous territoriality, a different approach was promoted that has remained dominant for the past decade. The new approach was based on unabashed adherence to 'neoliberalism', a much used term conceived here, following Brown (2015: 30) and her reading of Foucault, as: an order of normative reason that takes shape as a governing rationality extending a specific formulation of economic values, practices and metrics to every dimension of human life. This shift in approach to transforming Indigenous subjectivity, especially in remote Australia, to that of an imagined *homo economicus*, took the form of what I have referred to as 'a neoliberal project of improvement' (Altman 2014). Again to quote Brown (2015: 31) '… neoliberal rationality disseminates the model of the market to all domains and all activities—even where money is not an issue—and configures human beings exhaustively as market actors, always, only and everywhere as *homo oeconomicus'*.

This shift that I date (with some plasticity) from 2004 has earlier origins in the long-standing conservative ambivalence to Indigenous difference already outlined. Arguably, the goal of convergence has always dominated Indigenous policy but the neoliberal turn associated with an attempted erasure of history that overlooked the failure of the assimilation era and the damage it wrought on many Indigenous people including the Stolen Generations.

In 2004, ATSIC was abolished, with a renewed political bipartisanship paradoxically not seen since the formation of the Council for Aboriginal Reconciliation in 1991. A new mainstreaming was created that saw ATSIC's Indigenous-specific programs dispersed to mainline government agencies; and its political apparatus—which had championed difference and diversity nationally and internationally—dismantled in favour of an appointed National Indigenous Council that operated as a rubber stamp for the government's agenda between 2004 and 2008 until disbanded by the Rudd government.

I cannot recount the recent history of policy change here in any great detail; this has been done elsewhere by Strakosch (2015). My synoptic analysis instead looks to briefly summarise some features of relevance to the process of reconciliation and the representation of the Aboriginal 'problem' in public discourse, something that has been analysed in detail by Macoun (2011) and Anthony (2013).

At the broadest level, as in other rich western countries like the United States and Britain, Australia has embarked on project of welfare reform. This reform looks to unilaterally redefine citizenship (including Indigenous citizenship) not just in terms of rights but also in terms of 'balancing' responsibilities—including the responsibility of individuals to use welfare in a manner that enhances engagement with mainstream education and the labour market (Kowal 2013). This reform agenda has been given strong moral authority by the writings of Noel Pearson (2000, 2009). At the same time there has been a shift in policy in accord with neoliberal thinking that interprets marginalisation first and foremost as a product of individual failing (Standing 2014) rather than of politico-structural factors including racism and discrimination.

As a result we have witnessed the promotion of a utopian myth that market capitalism is 'the' solution to Indigenous disadvantage, including in remote Indigenous Australia. Indeed more and more policy attention has focused on remote regions despite the fact that only 25 per cent of the Indigenous population lives there—all the is required is the promotion of the free market ideas of Friedrich Hayek and Milton Friedman and all economic and social problems would dissolve. This was a position promoted in Australia by the neo-conservative economist Helen Hughes (2007) in *Lands of Shame*.

Following Wiegratz (2010, writing on Uganda), this can be interpreted as the promotion of 'fake capitalism'. Or following Cahill (2014) one might view this emerging state project, in close alliance with the capitalist plutocracy, as seeking to embed neoliberalism throughout Indigenous Australia in class, ideological and institutional forms. However, this is not an approach that is based on the free market, but rather one that is ideologically conflicted and dependent on more state intervention in order to morally restructure Indigenous subjects using behavioural carrots and sticks. The problem with such an approach is that it is based on blind faith and continues to ignore the inconvenient evidence that it does not work for most.

Of special relevance has been the broad discursive shift from viewing remote Indigenous communities as *disadvantaged* (which they have been primarily because their residents have been treated inequitably as denizens rather than equitably and on a needs basis as citizens) to viewing them as *dysfunctional*. Non-Indigenous Australians are constantly bombarded with images of Indigenous Australians not just as dysfunctional, but also as welfare dependent and inactive, expensive to maintain and dangerous, constituting a risk to late modern Australian affluence (Altman and Hinkson 2010); while at the same time lauded for some achievements, mainly in the domains of the arts and sports.

This discursive shift has been most clearly seen in the Northern Territory with the 'Emergency' Intervention from June 2007 that refers to failed states, laments disorder and seeks to recolonise remote Indigenous communities and spaces so as to connect Indigenous citizens to the mainstream. This project was implemented unilaterally, punitively and paternalistically by the Australian government, aided and abetted by right wing think tanks and opportunistic bureaucrats and influential Indigenous opinion leaders (Altman and Hinkson 2010).

This approach has continued to gather pace, despite frequent changes in national governments and leaders. The unilateral establishment of the COAG Closing the Gap framework by the Rudd Government in 2008 (ironically as a part of the National Apology that Howard would not make) was foundational: a set of concrete statistical targets with timelines that resemble a domestic version of the millennium development goals was created. Then a series of National Partnership Agreements allocated significant resources to close statistical gaps in life expectancy, child mortality, educational achievements and employment outcomes, and most recently school attendance, but not of incarceration rates (Council of Australian Governments 2009).

Most of the emphasis has been on remote Australia where Western indicators indicate the greatest disparities (Productivity Commission 2015) but where there is also the most Indigenous land and a small proportion of the Indigenous population. Here too are the most visible vestiges of the colonial era, evident in what are statistically-defined as 'discrete Indigenous communities'. In Map 1 these 1200 communities, with a total population of just 100,000, are distributed over a map showing Indigenous lands of various titles. In Map 2 by contrast, the distribution of the estimated Indigenous population of 660,000 is shown over the same tenure map. The significance of these two maps side-by-side is that reconciliation applies to Map 2, the entire Indigenous (and non-Indigenous) population, whereas the focus of policy is disproportionately on the communities in Map 1 where people are arguably most different to mainstream Australians (Figs. 1 and 2).

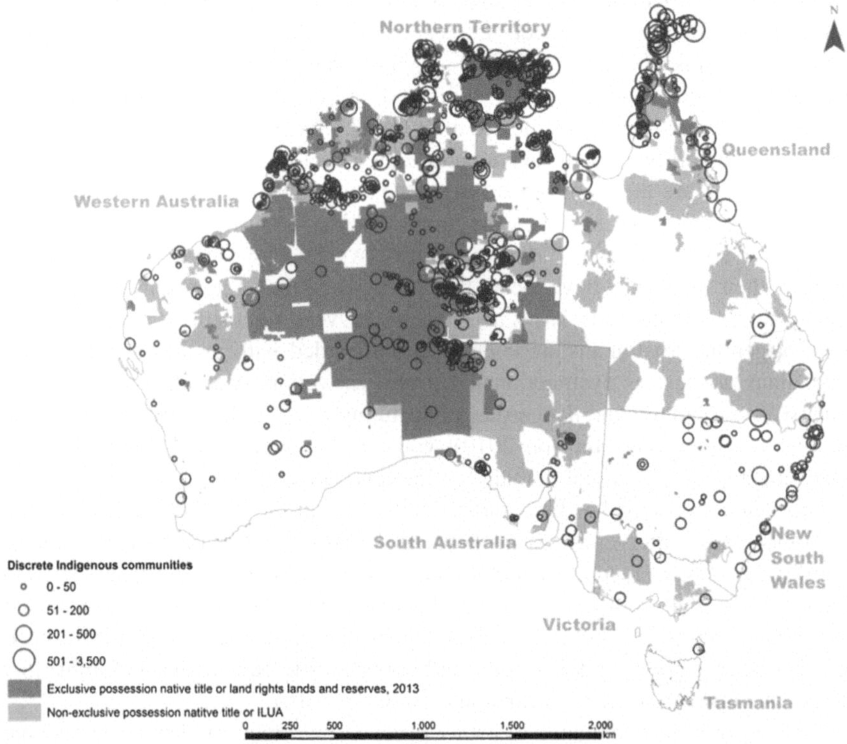

Fig. 1 Indigenous land title and 'discrete' communities. *Source* Based on Altman and Markham (2015)

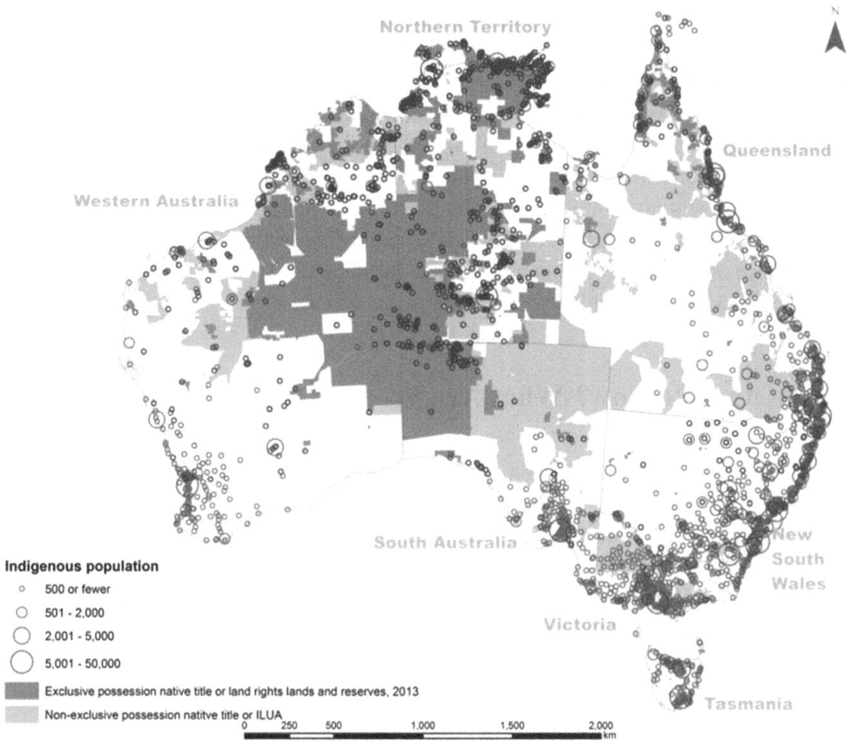

Fig. 2 Indigenous land title and Indigenous population distribution. *Source* Based on Altman and Markham (2015)

As an element of this approach of neoliberal governmentality (admixed with new public sector management as described by Sullivan 2011) there has been an extraordinary escalation in the collection of statistics about all aspects of Indigenous life that is regularly reported in the media, invariably showing that gaps are not closing as intended despite multi-billion dollar expenditures. These statistical collections constitute a form of industry in themselves, with the three most prolific statistical institutions being regular reports by the government's advisory body the Productivity Commission on *Overcoming Indigenous Disadvantage* (in 2003, 2005, 2007, 2009, 2011 and 2014, with just the last numbering 3252 pages); the biennial *Indigenous Expenditure Review* (2010, 2012 and 2014); and the Prime Minister's Annual Report to Parliament on Closing the Gap tabled on eight occasions since 2009. Recently, the Productivity Commission (2015: i), which has itself expended millions of dollars classified as Indigenous expenditures in monitoring, has called for a rationalising of the current expensive and overlapping reporting on Indigenous disadvantage.

Certainly all this reporting has had little impact on policy reframing instead inflaming non-Indigenous misconceptions about waste. I have increasingly critiqued such data collection. For example, it is unclear what we learn from information about the Indigenous share of expenditure on national defence on a population basis; or from information on the cost to government categorised as a part of the Indigenous spend of opposing native title claims. These reports tell us nothing about the extent of need, the effectiveness of expenditure, whether it accords with Indigenous priorities or what portion goes to deliverers of services rather than supposed beneficiaries. Paraphrasing historian Timothy Schneider (2010: 408) authoritarian regimes turn people into numbers … but these numbers need to be put into perspective … and it is for us humanists to turn these numbers back into people. The Productivity Commission (2015: i) suggests that there is a need for far greater emphasis on policy evaluation—what works and why —to achieve outcomes for Indigenous people as defined, I would add emphatically, by Indigenous people themselves not politicians and officials.

Where Are We Now? What Are We Pursuing as a Nation?

This volume comes at a time when Indigenous policy is at an unproductive dead end. Gaps are not closing and may in fact be widening; the discourse of sameness has become so naturalised that Indigenous difference is constantly discursively demeaned; and destructive history and culture wars are being reignited by the political party One Nation and ultra-conservative allies, potentially alienating many Indigenous and non-Indigenous Australians. The prospect for reconciliation, whether defined as symbolic, practical or both, is highly unlikely in the immediate future.

I want to briefly expand on these observations with references to recent reporting in the public domain.

The Productivity Commission's (2015) latest assessment makes it quite clear that the key Closing the Gap economic indicator to reduce employment disparity between Indigenous and other Australians is widening. In other words, things are getting worse (according to this indicator) rather than better. The Productivity Commission has come as close as an advisory body funded by government would to suggest that this is an impossible goal, especially in remote Australia.

Every year since 2009, with the opening of parliament, the Prime Minister tables the latest Closing the Gap: Prime Minister's Report. This annual ritual of parliamentary confession tells the nation how policy is failing, despite much effort, expenditure and good intention. It is interesting that such acknowledgment of failure by the powerful is acceptable, in marked contrast to the similar observations that Hunter and I made a decade ago, which were considered as heretical.

The tabling of the Report is accompanied by speeches to parliament by the Prime Minister and the Leader of the Opposition. In 2016 the Prime Minister's speech began with a surprise opening symbolically delivered in the Ngunawal language, recognising that Canberra is on Ngunawal country (although without acknowledging that Canberra's traditional ownership is highly contested). The speech ended as follows:

> Now, we are the most successful multicultural society in the world. The glue that holds us together is mutual respect—a deep recognition that each of us is entitled to the same respect, the same dignity, the same opportunities.
>
> Closing the Gap is more than another government indigenous policy.

> It speaks to all of us and it speaks about all of us—it is our best selves, our deep, just, fair values given practical form.
>
> When we close the gap we make ourselves more whole, more complete—more Australian (Turnbull 2016).

These are fine sentiments, but they were delivered just after the government had been informed that some gaps may never close, meaning that the promised national pathway to a more whole, complete Australia looked uncertain to say the least. One assumes that parliamentary speeches are made principally for the benefit of non-Indigenous Australians, who constitute 97 per cent of the nation's 24 million people. One wonders what intended or unintended messages accompanies such statements. One is reminded of Murray Edelman's (1977) observations about political language and words that succeed and policies that fail—except that in this case both the words and the policies appear to be failing.

How deeply conflicted Indigenous policy making and practice has become can be demonstrated from the published report. In the Prime Minister's Introduction it is noted:

> Indigenous economic development is at the heart of the national agenda, recognising that economic participation underpinned by cultural participation leads to vastly improved social outcomes. This requires a cooperative effort with Indigenous leaders and a greater emphasis on place-based solutions while creating the right conditions for people to feel they can participate (Australian Government 2016: 3).

Economic participation underpinned by cultural participation sounds as if it should accommodate economic plurality, as does reference to place-based solutions in all their diversity. As does the prime ministerial observation that … 'we too often talk about percentages and not enough about people' (Turnbull 2016).

And yet over and over again statements are made valorising the role of formal employment as the pathway to wellbeing, and demeaning the unemployed as undeserving and responsible for their own dire circumstances. Statements such as the following are commonplace:

> Being employed improves the health, living standards and the social and economic well being of individuals, families and communities. Employment not only brings financial independence and choice, it also contributes to self esteem. Growing up in a household where one or both parents are employed gives children strong role models to shape their own aspirations (Australian Government 2016: 26).

One wonders what messages such statements send to those who live where there are no employment opportunities and who nonetheless care about the life chances and wellbeing of their children? That you should move for employment? That you do not care? That aspirations for children are to be framed by employed people only?

It is a short and not entirely unpredictable journey from such policy contradictions to the inflammatory statements by radio shock jocks like Alan Jones, such as his statement in March 2016:

> … At the end of the day when Cook discovered as he did Australia what that means in the strict sense of the term is that he discovered ways in which to turn this continent in a way that would be beneficial and profitable to everybody and we would hope that in an Australia

> of tomorrow as in an Australia of yesterday the discovery of Australia brought very significant wealth. It opened up the country and everybody including Indigenous Australians have been beneficiaries of that. When there is disadvantage then I think it is fair and we need to be honest and say that government have worked very very hard to overcome it and that is the story of Australia that should be told (Sunrise nd).

Both above statements purport in different ways to tell a story of economic salvation afforded Indigenous Australians by the benign white 'settlement' of the continent and the benefits for them of the evolutionary shift from the hunter-gatherer (Jones refers to hunters, fishers and shooters) to the late capitalist mode of production.

The unrelenting focus on convergence in socioeconomic outcomes is a form of assimilation, or what was termed in the United States 'the termination era' (Bruyneel 2007: 16; see also Deloria 1969: 54–77). As Wolfe (2006: 388) notes, a positive outcome of the logic of elimination can include 'native citizenship' and … 'a whole range of cognate biocultural assimilations'. The measurement industry focuses on the socioeconomic characteristics of the Other that inevitably turn out to be deficits, unless measuring something like the ability to speak an Aboriginal language. One ponders, like the Productivity Commission does, the benefit of such statistical 'profiling' especially for any process of reconciliation. Following Simpson (2014) who writes about ethnographic refusal, it seems we might have reached a point in Australia where 'statistical refusal' is more productive than the constant deployment of statistics with dubious political intent, a little like John Howard's Mabo Map.

Strategic Options

Over the past decade, Indigenous peoples have become entangled in wider national welfare and Indigenous reform processes and global economic uncertainty that clearly demonstrate their vulnerability to, and inability to influence, state power and policy unilateralism. This powerlessness has seen the rapid erosion of some transformative gains of earlier decades such that today many are caught up in a broader reconceptualisation of 'the Aboriginal problem' that has gained considerable traction among the political, bureaucratic and corporate elites and increasingly in public perception in Australia.

The current state solution is to revisit a new version of the old solution of assimilation to eventual termination, deploying new policies informed by neoliberalism. Documented history suggests that such an approach is likely to fail. In the meantime, as a partial response to the rise of the global Indigenous rights movement, the Australia state has reluctantly delivered land and native title rights as a group territorial right that has allowed some groups to develop semblances of different ways of living, remaining physically connected to their ancestral lands and locationally distant from the mainstream.

Since 1976, as I have researched Indigenous development, I have advocated for forms of economic plurality; in the last decade and a half I have theorised this in terms of economic hybridity (Altman 2016). What I have looked to emphasise is that in many situations the Aboriginal economy includes the customary, especially when people enjoy native title rights in land and resources for domestic, if not commercial, use. Much of my research has been empirical and based in remote Arnhem Land and has shown transformations in forms of economy. I have also utilised secondary data from official sources like the National Aboriginal and Torres Strait Islander Social Survey (NATSISS) to show that forms of hybrid economy are prevalent nation-wide (Altman et al. 2012).

My research emphasis has been neither normative nor prescriptive; it is based on the observation that in many situations Indigenous people do not have opportunities, capabilities or aspirations for engagements with market capitalism. Indeed many hold clear aspirations to pursue forms of economy that are fundamentally different, irrespective of where they live. The challenge this raises is that in many situations such preferences will not result in the elimination of the statistical gaps that have become the ubiquitous metric of public discourse and governance. But empirical observation also shows that people's wellbeing can be enhanced through engagement in productive activity, often at the intersection of market, state and customary sectors. The hybrid economy is everywhere, as argued by Erik Olin Wright (2010), it is just that the absolute and relative size of the sectors and their articulations vary from place to place.

It is not unlikely that as more and more people get back their lands they will want to live in a reasonable manner on or near those lands. During the current 'neoliberal' ascendancy such possibility is anathema to political and bureaucratic elites and so creative possibilities for improved livelihood are not supported. In the contest between the highly individualistic values required for competitive success in late capitalist Australia and the distinctive relational values of many Indigenous people, especially those connected to ancestral places and living in communities of kin—it is the powerful who dictate the terms of engagements.

In her research on Indigenous people and crime, Anthony (2013: 27) describes the ruse of recognition: 'The Janus-face of sentencers shows a face of leniency that basks in its humanity and morality in recognising a wronged group and its cultural peculiarities *and* a face of penality that glares at difference with condemnation to rationalise its exclusion of a risk group'.

From 2004 this Janus-face has been very evident in what I consider a 'ruse of tolerance', a pretence that policy is sympathetic to cultural difference even as it shifts to eliminate the right to be different, with disastrous consequences for many groups.

One such group that I am very familiar with is the Kuninjku of western Arnhem Land with whom I have worked since 1979. In recent years they have seen their own transformative project rapidly shift away from their control as the paternalistic state has taken over in the name of imagined improvement that has in reality further impoverished people living in poverty (Altman 2016).

Such reform for sameness can be assessed against some principles proposed by Standing (2014: 123–124) to test if they are socially just that I summarise as follows:

1 Security Difference Principle: a policy or institutional change is only socially just if it improves the security of the most insecure groups in society (among whom I count the Kuninjku)
2 Paternalism Test Principle: a policy or institutional change is socially just if it does not impose controls on vulnerable groups that are not imposed on the most free groups in society; and
3 Dignified Work Principle: a policy or institutional change is only socially just if it promotes capacity to pursue work that is dignified and rewarding. (Altman 2016: 292).

Clearly, for Indigenous Australians, already among the most insecure groups in Australian society, policy changes that paternalistically emphasise economic sameness only are transgressing these principles. Underpinning this reform, now formalised as the Indigenous Advancement Strategy, is an absence of social empathy that fails to ask: How might *you* perform in similar locational, cultural, economic and historical circumstances?

The dominant approach to Indigenous economic development is framed with a strong emphasis on 'Closing the Gap' statistical equality. This has privileged a hegemonic and monolithic vision increasingly intolerant of pluralistic forms of economy and associated values. Unconventional and inconvenient alternatives may not eliminate disparity, but might accord better with the aspirations of Indigenous peoples and might, if accepted by the settler majority, enhance prospects for reconciliation.

How might Indigenous peoples garner the political means to create such post-colonial development possibilities? Certainly at present appealing to domestic and international publics unknown for such a different approach appears an almost insurmountable challenge of power and representation. But if reconciliation as a substantive process is to have a future, an important first step must be the reconstitution of a national Indigenous representation organisation like ATSIC—be it an expanded and properly resourced National Congress of Australia's First Peoples or some other entity—that is empowered to negotiate with the Australian settler state. Given the failure of successive Australian governments to advance the project of reconciliation, it might be time to empower Indigenous Australians and their institutions to take over. If all Australians can be persuaded to be more tolerant of difference, particularly at a time of deep global economic uncertainty, we might see positive movements: on reconciliation; on Closing the Gap in situations where such metrics have relevance; and in promoting better livelihoods and wellbeing in situations where people choose to live differently.

Acknowledgments I would like to thank participants at the workshop 'The Non-Indigenous Responsibility to Engage: Scoping Reconciliation and its Alternatives' held in April 2016 in Melbourne for input, Angelique Stastny for some generous research assistance, Alissa Macoun for insightful commentary as discussant, and Melinda Hinkson and the editors for constructive feedback.

References

Altman, J. C. (2004). Practical reconciliation and the new mainstreaming: Will it make a difference to Indigenous Australians? *Dialogue, 23*, 35–46.

Altman, J. C. (2014). Indigenous policy: Canberra consensus on a neoliberal project of improvement. In C. Miller & L. Orchard (Eds.), *Australian public policy: Progressive ideas in the neoliberal ascendancy* (pp. 115–132). Bristol: Policy Press.

Altman, J. C. (2016). Self-reflections: 1977–2014. In W. Sanders (Ed.), *Engaging indigenous economy: Debating diverse approaches* (pp. 289–303). Canberra: ANU Press.

Altman, J. C., Biddle, N., & Buchanan, G. (2012). The Indigenous hybrid economy: Can the NATSISS adequately recognise difference? In B. Hunter & N. Biddle (Eds.), *Survey analysis for indigenous policy in Australia: Social science perspectives* (pp. 163–191). Canberra: ANU Press.

Altman, J.C., & Hinkson, M. (Eds) (2007). *Coercive Reconciliation: Stabilise, Normalise, Exit Aboriginal Australia*. Melbourne: Arena Publications.

Altman, J. C., & Hinkson, M. (2010). Very risky business: The quest to normalise remote living Aboriginal people. In G. Marston, J. Moss, & J. Quiggin (Eds.), *Risk, welfare and work* (pp. 185–211). Melbourne: Melbourne University Press.

Altman, J. C., & Hunter, B. (2003). *Monitoring 'practical' reconciliation: Evidence from the reconciliation decade, 1991–2001*. Centre for Aboriginal Economic Policy Research. The Australian National University. http://caepr.anu.edu.au/sites/default/files/Publications/topical/Monitoring%20Practical%20Reconciliation.pdf. Accessed 6 June 2016.

Altman, J. C., & Markham, F. (2015). Burgeoning Indigenous land ownership: Diverse values and strategic potentialities. In S. Brennan, M. Davis, B. Edgeworth, & L. Terrell (Eds.), *Native title from Mabo to Akiba: A vehicle for change and empowerment?* (pp. 126–142). Sydney: The Federation Press.

Altman, J. C., & Sanders, W. (1991). Government initiatives for Aboriginal employment: equity, equality and policy realism. In J. C. Altman (Ed.), *Aboriginal Employment Equity by the Year 2000* (pp. 1–18). Canberra: Centre for Aboriginal Economic Policy Research, Australian National University.

Anthony, T. (2013). *Indigenous people, crime and punishment*. Milton Park, Abingdon: Routledge.

Australian Government. (1987). *The aboriginal employment development policy statement: Policy paper no. 1*. Canberra: Australian Government Publishing Service.

Australian Government. (1991). *Council for aboriginal reconciliation act no. 127*. https://www.legislation.gov.au/Details/C2004A04202. Accessed 6 June 2016.

Australian Government. (2016). *Closing the Gap Prime Minister' report 2016*. http://closingthegap.dpmc.gov.au/assets/pdfs/closing_the_gap_report_2016.pdf. Access 7 June 2016.

Brown, W. (2015). *Undoing the demos: Neoliberalism's stealth revolution*. New York: Zone Books.

Bruyneel, K. (2007). *The third space of sovereignty: The postcolonial politics of U.S.-indigenous relations*. Minneapolis: University of Minnesota Press.

Butler, J. (2012). *Parting ways: Jewishness and the critique of zionism*. New York: Columbia University Press.

Cahill, D. (2014). *The end of laissez-faire? On the durability of embedded neoliberalism*. Cheltenham: Edward Elgar.

Commonwealth of Australia. (1961, April 20). *Parliamentary debates [Hansard]*. House of Representatives, 1051.

Council of Australian Governments. (2009). *National indigenous reform agreement*. http://www.federalfinancialrelations.gov.au/content/npa/health_indigenous/indigenous-reform/national-agreement_sept_12.pdf. Access 7 June 2016.

De Blij, H. (2012). *Why geography matters more than ever*. Oxford: Oxford University Press.

Deloria, V., Jr. (1969). *Custer died for our sins: An Indian manifesto*. New York: Macmillan.

Edelman, M. (1977). *Political language: Words that succeed and policies that fail*. New York: Academic Press.
Horne, D. (1964). *The lucky country*. Sydney: Penguin.
Howard, J. (1997, September 4). *Television interview with Kerry O'Brien. The 7.30 report. ABC*. https://pmtranscripts.dpmc.gov.au/release/transcript-10469. Accessed 6 June 2016.
Hughes, H. (2007). *Land of shame: Aboriginal and Torres Strait Islander 'homelands in transition*. Sydney: Centre for Independent Studies Limited.
Kowal, E. (2013). Responsibility, Noel Pearson and Indigenous disadvantage in Australia. In G. Hage & R. Eckersley (Eds.), *Responsibility* (pp. 43–56). Melbourne: Melbourne University Press.
Macoun, A. (2011). Aboriginality and the Northern Territory Intervention. *Australian Journal of Political Science, 46*, 519–534.
Pearson, N. (2000). *Our right to take responsibility*. Cairns: Noel Pearson and Associates.
Pearson, N. (2009). *Up from the mission: Selected writings*. Melbourne: Black Inc.
Productivity Commission. (2015). *National reform agreement performance assessment 2013–14*. http://www.pc.gov.au/research/supporting/indigenous-reform-assessment. Access 7 June 2016.
Reynolds, H. (2013). *The forgotten war*. Sydney: NewSouth Publishing.
Rowse, T. (2012). *Rethinking social justice: From 'peoples' to 'populations'*. Canberra: Aboriginal Studies Press.
Sanders, W. (1991). Destined to fail: the Hawke Government's Pursuit of Statistical Equality in Employment and Income Status between Aborigines and Other Australians by the year 2000 (or, a Cautionary Tale Involving the New Managerialism and Social Justice Strategies). *Australian Aboriginal Studies, 1991*(2), 13–18.
Schneider, T. (2010). *Bloodlands: Europe between Hitler and Stalin*. New York: Basic Books.
Simpson, A. (2014). *Mohawk interruptus: Political life across the borders of settler states*. Durham: Duke University Press.
Standing, G. (2014). *A precariat charter: From denizens to citizens*. London: Bloomsbury Academic.
Strakosch, E. (2015). *Neoliberal indigenous policy: Settler colonialism and the post-welfare state*. New York: Palgrave Macmillan.
Sullivan, P. (2011). *Belonging together: Dealing with the politics of disenchantment in Australian indigenous policy*. Canberra: Aboriginal Studies Press.
Sunrise (nd). *Uni students told Captain Cook invaded Australia. Sunrise*. https://au.tv.yahoo.com/sunrise/video/watch/31211487/uni-students-told-captain-cook-invaded-australia/#page1 [my transcription]. Accessed 7 April 2016.
Turnbull, M. (2016, February 10). *Speech to Parliament on the 2016 closing the gap report*. http://www.malcolmturnbull.com.au/media/speech-to-parliament-on-the-2016-closing-the-gap-report. Accessed 6 June 2016.
Watson, M. (2016). *Aboriginal Activist Gary Foley Made Things Awkward for Mike Baird's Government at the Sydney Biennale*. http://junkee.com/aboriginal-activist-gary-foley-made-things-awkward-mike-bairds-government-sydney-biennale/74958#y6lAHETQhBpRI7iY.99. Access 7 June 2016.
Wiegratz, J. (2010). Fake capitalism? The dynamics of neoliberal moral restructuring and pseudo-development: the case of Uganda. *Review of African Political Economy, 37*(124), 123–137.
Wolfe, P. (1999). *Settler colonialism and the transformation of anthropology: The politics and poetics of an ethnographic event*. New York: Cassell.
Wolfe, P. (2006). Settler colonialism and the elimination of the native. *Journal of Genocidal Research, 8*(4), 387–409.
Wolfe, P. (2015). *Traces of history: Elementary structures of race*. London: Verso.
Wright, E. O. (2010). *Envisioning real utopia*. London: Verso.

Chapter 14
Silence or Deafness? Education and the Non-Indigenous Responsibility to Engage

Sarah Maddison and Angélique Stastny

Abstract Schools are understood as an important site for the circulation of discourses pertaining to colonisation and reconciliation. Wider community educational practices have also engaged with these concerns, including initiatives such as the Reconciliation Study Circle Kits that were developed by the Council for Aboriginal Reconciliation in Australia in the 1990s. This paper considers the role of school and community education in developing non-Indigenous Australians' understanding of, and engagement with, Australia's post-invasion history and reconciliation with Aboriginal and Torres Strait Islander peoples. Drawing on original focus group and interview research the paper highlights some of the key areas where education appears to have transformed non-Indigenous perspectives in recent decades, while also highlighting areas for further policy and curriculum development.

Keywords Education · Reconciliation · Australia · Schools · Responsibility · Council for aboriginal reconciliation

Introduction

Paulo Freire has famously suggested that, while education 'is not the ultimate lever for social transformation… without it transformation cannot occur' (Freire 1998: 37). Such a statement may apply to a range of social and political contexts, and certainly to contemporary settler colonial societies in which the legacies and continuities of colonialism continue to shape social relations. In contemporary settler colonial societies, education remains a contentious domain. Historically, colonial education was used to deliberately marginalise and subjugate Indigenous population groups, either by structuring inequalities into the education system, or by

S. Maddison (✉) · A. Stastny
University of Melbourne, Parkville, Australia
e-mail: Sarah.maddison@unimelb.edu.au

A. Stastny
e-mail: a.stastny@student.unimelb.edu.au

S. Maddison et al. (eds.), *The limits of settler colonial reconciliation*,
DOI 10.1007/978-981-10-2654-6_14

denying access to education altogether. Linguistic exclusion was (and remains) common, with Indigenous peoples often forced to learn in the languages of their oppressors. These legacies of colonial education systems are profound, and require long-term commitment to reform and redress. Further—and to the heart of what follows in this chapter—both formal and informal education is seen as an important site for engaging the wider population in a process of social transformation centred on debates about colonial history and the structural injustices that it perpetuates in the present. The effectiveness of such efforts, however, remains far from clear.

A non-Indigenous responsibility to engage is not articulated here as a neo-colonial, paternalistic form of intervention. It is not responsibility *for* or *over* Indigenous people, but a responsibility *to* Indigenous people. Non-Indigenous engagement is understood here as the process of taking political responsibility in regards to the legacy of settler colonialism. The first step consists in non-Indigenous people recognising colonial privilege, and their social and 'structural connections' to settler colonialism (Noxolo et al. 2012: 418). In other words, it requires non-Indigenous people to recognise themselves as 'implicated in the social forces that create the climate of obstacles the other must confront' (Bowler 1999: 189), through what Alfred (2005: 153) calls a 'ritual of disclosure and confession'. A further step is about learning to relate differently, not through exploitation or domination, but with humility—yielding space, voice, and power to Indigenous peoples. With such disposition, non-Indigenous people, as individuals, acknowledge and take responsibility and obligation to transform their attitudes to Indigenous people, the history and the land. Likewise, they accept and respect Indigenous people's decision as to whether, how, and when they may wish to engage in these relationships in the present.

In the 1990s the desire for transformation was pursued through an official policy of 'reconciliation', formalised through the passing of the *Council for Aboriginal Reconciliation Act* (1991) (Commonwealth of Australia 1991). The Act both created the Council for Aboriginal Reconciliation (CAR) and set out the timeline for the formal process, to conclude in 2001. The Minister for Aboriginal Affairs at this time, Robert Tickner, who drove the creation of the Act and championed the merits of the formal process, has since described the need to educate non-Indigenous Australians about Aboriginal and Torres Strait Islander culture and the extent of disadvantage still experienced by Indigenous people as one of the central aims of Australian reconciliation (Tickner 2001). Changing Australian hearts and minds in relation to the nation's history and its impact on Indigenous peoples was seen as crucial if any further structural or institutional change were to be possible. The newly created Council for Aboriginal Reconciliation was to publicly lead this education strategy, actively encouraging attitudinal changes through the development of learning materials such as the *Australians for Reconciliation Study Circle Kit* released in 1993.

A significant obstacle to such educative initiatives, both then and now, has been the confusion about what the concept of reconciliation actually means. Since the advent of reconciliation policies, the concept has been debated and contested. For some, reconciliation means acknowledging and addressing past injustices as a means of 'healing' those who have been harmed. Others are more concerned with the need to overcome the continuing disparities in today's society that are thought to have resulted from past actions (what became known as 'practical reconciliation'). Still others have talked about the need for unity, and have defined reconciliation as a nation-building paradigm. Each view has also been criticised, whether for denying Indigenous people's sovereignty and placing a colonial 'ceiling' on assimilationist reconciliation efforts (Short 2003: 291), or for failing to address the structural flaws that allow socioeconomic disparities to persist.

It is in the context of this conceptual confusion that this article seeks to engage with public understandings of reconciliation, within the broader focus on the notion of a non-Indigenous 'responsibility to engage' that animates this volume. A growing literature has sought to look back on these reconciliation decades and gauge popular response to these policies. Far less scholarship has focused on people's understanding of reconciliation or where and how their understanding was formed. Drawing on focus group and interview research, this chapter explores non-Indigenous attitudes to reconciliation, Indigenous people and cultures, and the various sites through which the general public learn about these aspects of Australian society.

To do so, it addresses the following two key questions: where, how, and what do non-Indigenous people learn about Australia's history, Indigenous peoples and cultures? Does this education lead to greater understanding and engagement between Indigenous and non-Indigenous people (namely, reconciliatory practices)? In what follows, the chapter first provides an overview of the place of education in Australia's reconciliation efforts and the scholarship that has attempted to document its efficacy. It then explores the various educational sites engaged with by non-Indigenous participants in this study,[1] and considers the extent to which these sites promote engagement with Indigenous people. Finally, we consider whether the educational sites used by the participants motivate a responsibility to engage with Indigenous people, and therefore encourage reconciliatory practices. We conclude that there is little evidence to suggest that education is a deeply transformative site with regard to non-Indigenous attitudes to Aboriginal and Torres Strait Islander people and/or reconciliation.

Reconciliation and the Great Australian Silence

Education is thought to have an important role to play in addressing silences and biases about historical violence and injustice, supporting the revision of national narratives in order to reflect critical truths (Cole 2007: 20). In his 1968 Boyer lectures, the anthropologist W.E.H Stanner spoke of the 'great Australian silence' about the injustices perpetrated against Aboriginal and Torres Strait Islander people. Stanner argued that this silence could not be explained by mere 'absent-mindedness' but had been structured into the Australian identity, creating 'a view from a window which

[1]The argument developed in this chapter is based on an analysis of the focus group research outlined in the appendix to this volume.

has been carefully placed to exclude a whole quadrant of the landscape' (Stanner 2009 [1968]: 188–189). Stanner called for 'a less shallow, less ethnocentric social history' (Stanner 1991 [1968]: 26). Over time, this ethnocentric history began to be addressed, and over the last 30 or so years of the twentieth century Aboriginal and Torres Strait Islander people increasingly demanded that history also be told from their perspectives. Public reports such as the Royal Commission into Aboriginal Deaths in Custody (RCIADIC 1991, discussed further below), *Bringing them home*[2] (HREOC 1997) and other efforts to foreground Aboriginal and Torres Strait Islander experiences contributed to new and contested accounts of Australia's colonial history. These accounts eventually made their way into school curricula to some limited extent, although these changes were themselves contested through what became known as the 'history wars.' A more critical historical view was also the focus of the *Study Circle kits* produced by the CAR, which were intended to enable small, self-managing groups to undertake an 8-week programme exploring reconciliation and a range of Aboriginal and Torres Strait Islander issues (Gunstone 2009: 96).

In light of these developments, a growing literature has sought to analyse non-Indigenous attitudes towards, and engagement with, reconciliation and Indigenous people. Such works have generally focused on the nature of attitudes (positive and negative, supporting or rejecting) towards Indigenous people or reconciliation, the underlying emotions that drive non-Indigenous attitudes and behaviours (ranging from guilt and fear to ignorance and indifference), and on the relationship between identity and attitudes (Sweeney et al. 1996; Gomersall et al. 2000; Bulbeck 2004; Pedersen et al. 2004; Singh 2005; Halloran 2007; Maddison 2011). These have included foci on specific populations groups, such as Michael Singh's (2005) research into attitudes to reconciliation among Australian citizens who identify as Asian–Australian and the political gap that seems to exist between Indigenous Australians and Asian Australians, and Michael Halloran's (2007), exploration of the relationship between the value of egalitarianism and reconciliation attitudes, and between collective guilt and positive reconciliation attitudes, amongst university students and the general public. Others have focused on specific age groups, with the younger generation being a prominent focus of attention (Saxton 2004; Green and Sonn 2005; Burridge 2006; Bourke and Geldens 2007; Halloran 2007; Yarn About Youth 2013).

A more limited scholarship has focused on people's understanding of reconciliation and on where and how this understanding was formed (Gunstone 2012; Pederson et al. 2000; McCallum 2003). Schools and community education have been understood as important sites for the circulation of discourses pertaining to historical memory and reconciliation. Gunstone (2012) has specifically focused on the connections between 'Reconciliation and the "Great Australian Silence"' through an analysis of Council for Aboriginal Reconciliation publications that were

[2]This inquiry produced the seminal report *Bringing them home: Report of the national inquiry into the separation of Aboriginal and Torres Strait Islander children from their families*. The inquiry had been instigated by the Keating Government in 1995 in response to Indigenous demands for greater recognition of the impact of child removal policies.

developed to educate the wider community, concluding that the scope and impact of these publications was limited by the nation-building orientation of the Australian reconciliation project. Indeed, the period of the formal Australian reconciliation process (1991–2000) has been widely criticised for its focus on the education of the non-Indigenous population rather than on justice for Aboriginal and Torres Strait Islander peoples, suggesting what Damian Short has described as an 'intense resistance' to any more structural or decolonising approach to reconciliation (Short 2008: 7, 36). Those who have defended the educational approach of the Australian reconciliation process, including Tickner (2001), suggest that without education about both Australia's history of injustice towards Indigenous peoples, and the contemporary impacts of these injustices in Aboriginal and Torres Strait Islander people's lives, no other transformative change would be possible. As a result, considerable effort and expenditure on reconciliation in Australia was directed towards strategies designed to educate and engage non-Indigenous people.

After 10 years of such effort, however, it was difficult to observe much positive impact from the efforts to 'engage' non-Indigenous people. Focus groups undertaken at the end of 1999 and the start of 2000 found universal agreement that the position of Aboriginal people in Australia was a 'tragedy', and widespread agreement that Aboriginal people had been 'badly treated by the early white settlers.' At the same time, however, many people found it 'hard to face up to this,' with the more defensive participants in the research arguing that 'there was bad behavior on both sides.' There were 'few' who were 'inclined to see one side as the invader and the other as the invaded', or who were willing to accept responsibility for what they saw as historical wrongs (Newspoll et al. 2000: 37). Many Australians also felt 'perplexed and confused' about how to make progress in this area, becoming 'caught between calling for inspired leadership and compassion and the comforts of racism and cynicism' (Green and Sonn 2005: 483, 2006: 380). These findings are reflected in our more recent research, suggesting that the ambition to use education to foster a non-Indigenous responsibility to engage has largely failed.

Educational Sites and Sources for Non-Indigenous Learning

Focus groups and interview responses show that non-Indigenous people tend to learn about Australian history, Indigenous people and cultures, and reconciliation from four main educational sites: school; media (including television, films, radio, books, and newspapers); work; and family and friends. The analysis that follows will focus on the two primary educational sites—schools and the media.

School, it seems, is the main site of learning, followed by the media, the workplace, and the participants' community. Yet although school emerges from the focus group discussion as the main educational site for participants, it is also seen as an educational site that has only recently engaged in teaching about Australia's history, Indigenous people and cultures—a point frequently made by older participants across the focus groups. Participants quite unanimously comment that teaching about Indigenous peoples and cultures at schools used to be very minimal if not completely non-existent. Participants in Bega for instance recall the following:

> Basil (Australian born): When I went to school nothing was taught about Aborigines …You didn't even hear the word.

> Jack (Overseas born): When it comes to knowing, I came here a long time ago and went to high school—absolutely nothing about Aboriginals. In fact the only history we did was English history, nothing else.

Participants in Perth also suggested that they did not learn much about Indigenous peoples or culture at school. While some cultural traditions were taught, colonial encounters and conflicts between Indigenous and non-Indigenous people were left out:

> Jordan (Australian born): Not a whole lot. What I learnt in school basically […] just the basics that everyone knows, the dreamtime stories and the connection with the land and their elders.

> Patrick (Australian born): But then there was the massacres, […] These sort of things that are not taught in the schools—they certainly weren't taught when I was teaching.

Several participants note that this has started to change quite recently, with a greater emphasis on Australia's history, the introduction of protocols such as Welcome to Country and Acknowledgement of Country at school events, and teacher-training programmes intended to develop historical and cultural awareness. Other advances have been even more dramatic, for example, a participant in Bega suggests that,

> Schools have made enormous progression from, say, when most of us were at school in Australia. I don't think I went to school with an Aboriginal student, and the Department of Education had things in the teacher's handbook up until 1974 where if a parent complained about an Aboriginal student in their class, they [teachers] were supposed to remove them. That's 1974 when that was taken off the books—it's not that long ago! And [now] in this part of the world there's a programme called 'No Gap, No Excuse', which specifically targets […] teachers to learn about the cultural heritage of the area that they live in, and to talk with the community […] It's the community that delivers that programme—the community makes contact with the schools. It's community members that present it to the teachers. And it really brings about a shift in people's attitude, which is important, and then that gets translated into further modules about incorporating these aspects when you're teaching. So I think it's improving dramatically from what it was before. (David, Bega, Aust. born)

But although there is now greater emphasis on the teaching of Australian history, several participants argue that the focus continues to be on the history of 'European settlement', which marginalises Indigenous perspectives and cultures:

> Charlie (Australian born): I think there's probably good coverage in terms of history in terms of like history of European settlement […]. In terms of actual cultural understanding I think there's still work to be done there.

History, participants argue, continues to be largely nationalistic and taught from a non-Indigenous perspective:

> Stephanie (Australian born): I think we hear more about World War One and World War Two when we're at school, and very little about the history of Australia.
>
> Carol (Australian born): That's changing though with the Australian curriculum […] But then that's probably more a white man's view of the history, because we've got some Islander kids in the class and they sort of think, 'Well that's not how we tell that story', and so it's really interesting to ask them 'Well you tell us that story as you know that history', and sometimes the two don't align very well.
>
> Dina (Overseas born): A lot of the Aboriginal history that our students get in class is textbook from an Anglo Saxon point of view, not from an Indigenous person's point of view.

Participants articulate four other main critiques of school education in this domain. First, some participants contend that despite recent changes, the curriculum remains limited, and dissuades students from learning any Indigenous content in more depth.

> Roy (Australian born): They're not encouraged as much to learn that [Indigenous cultures], they sort of touch on it at school a little bit now, but not in any great depth.

Second, measures to promote multiculturalism are seen as marginalising Indigenous cultures further. A participant in Parramatta for instance recounts how school events and symbolism privilege non-Australian cultures over Australian Indigenous cultures:

> Diedre (Australian born): I think because we have been accused of being racist so much now, that the kids next door to the school they learn all Arabic dancing and Indian dancing. While I'm not saying they shouldn't do it, [I think] they should [also] learn some Aboriginal dancing, but they hone in on specifically those two groups because it's the majority of the group that attends this school. They have flags on every building, different flags and they learn about that country—and I know the Aboriginal flag doesn't represent like a country per se, but there's not one Aboriginal flag flying and they have 15 flagpoles.

Third, students' discriminatory attitudes learnt at home are mentioned as an obstacle to learning in schools and as a barrier to attitudinal changes. In a conversation between two participants in Perth, one speaks from her own experience as a teacher:

> Pamela (Australian born): I think a lot of the negative things that are said about Aboriginals are said by the parents of children, and then they go to school and they say those things to the children that they're meeting at school, so…
>
> Heather: I have to agree with that, yes, I do. I mean I'm a teacher and we do have to teach Aboriginal studies […] but we do hear comments coming from children
>
> Pamela: Yes, negative…
>
> Heather: Yes, negative comments from the children even at 5 and 6, and it's quite appalling.

Fourth, participants suggested that the level of engagement of non-Indigenous students in learning about Indigenous people and cultures is impaired by the fact that the benefit of learning from Indigenous people and cultures is not made explicit to students, who bring a very instrumental understanding about education to the classroom:

> Paul (Overseas born): My two oldest kids have just finished high school and they did do Aboriginal studies, but all I ever got was that 'It's boring Dad', and [the sense that] what they were learning were things that they couldn't use. Education is about something that you can use, and if you don't find that subject interesting, and *the way that Aboriginal culture is presented to the white people is not interesting…* (our emphasis)

In addition to suggesting areas for potential improvement, these criticisms show that education about the country's history, Indigenous people and cultures is also the subject of personal reflection for many non-Indigenous Australians, despite the marginal place still assigned to this politics in the classroom and in the wider society.

The media was the second most frequently mentioned site of learning for participants, although many of them recognised the biases and limitations inherent to media-based learning:

> Gladstone (Aust. born): We only hear what's in the media […] and, as I said, it's the trouble-makers that make that sort of media. You don't hear of those that are living in suburbia, that are doing their own thing, that are members of society sending their children to school…

> Bega (Aust. born): We're sort of saturated with the negative stories in our media, and the journos will ignore 15 good stories about Aboriginal people and pick up on the one negative one […]. And unfortunately I think we sort of get programmed a little bit into identifying with problems rather than positive things.

These criticisms of Australian media reporting of Indigenous affairs are shared with many Aboriginal and Torres Strait Islander people in Australia (see Maddison 2009), although participants in this research seemed unaware of this commonality. Nevertheless, it is evident from such comments that the popularity of educational media does not necessarily equal an absence of criticism. Further, it is clear from the discussion of both school- and media-based education that the sites most discussed by participants are also the sites they are most likely to challenge.

These sites also consist almost entirely of indirect learning. Analysis of participants' engagement with the four educational sites mentioned in the research reveals that the experiences that shape participants' understanding most strongly were largely informed by indirect learning. In both school- and media-based learning, participants make sense of Australia's history, Indigenous people, and cultures through mediated interaction with textbooks, books, newspapers and television, rather than through direct interactions with Indigenous people (Fig. 14.1).

When engaging with the school and the media, participants seem more likely to position themselves as passive agents of learning who do not control the content of the learning they receive. This is evident in participants' comments (such as those above) in which they express a ready critique of the school and the media. By contrast, the two other educational sites identified in this research—the community (individual, family, neighbours) and the workplace—and the learning that participants attain in these spaces, are not challenged in the way that the school and the media are. On the contrary, interactions with Indigenous people that sometimes result in an attitudinal change are often described as a positive self-awareness. For

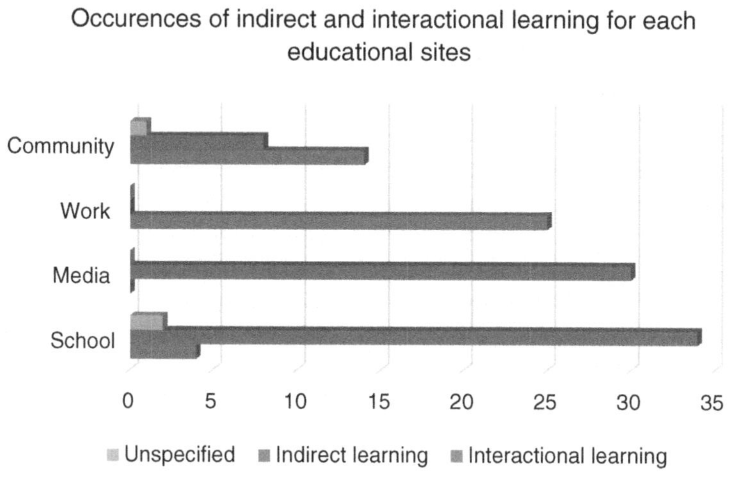

Fig. 14.1 Occurences of indirect and interactional learning for each educational sites

example, some participants mention specific events that changed their perceptions and attitudes, particularly in the workplace. For example, a participant in Bega suggests that working alongside an Indigenous coordinator at a school-based community event was 'a powerful experience' that made him realise that 'there's been a lot of history and a lot of things that have happened to Aboriginal people that have been pretty harsh and very difficult to deal with, and we sometimes forget that when we're looking at a range of things.' (David, Australian born) Similarly, a participant in Gladstone spoke of working in Alice Springs for 3 weeks as 'an eye-opener' that was far from the romantic view of Indigenous cultures she held. (Angelica, Australian born)

In community and work-based educational sites participants position themselves more readily as active agents of learning, making sense of Australia's history, Indigenous people and cultures through first-hand experience. The connection between these experiences and attitudinal changes however may be more complex to identify and gauge. Indeed, it is possible that in many cases, participants adapt these experiences to their own framework of understanding without considering it a form of 'education'. Yet the degree of passive versus active engagement in learning does not seem to produce vastly different outcomes. It seems that the ways in which non-Indigenous people make sense of Australia's history, Indigenous people and cultures, is consistent and recurrent across all educational sites, regardless of whether the participants position themselves as passive or active agent of the learning process, as we will now turn to see.

Non-Indigenous People's Understanding of Settler Colonial History, Indigenous Peoples and Cultures, and Reconciliation

Our focus group data suggests that participants learn about Australia's history, Indigenous people and culture in fairly consistent ways across the four educational sites that they discussed. Participants mention learning about the European aspect of Australian history, but also about injustices and racism, massacres, reconciliation and, to a far lesser extent, pre-colonial history. Unfortunately, the largely stereotypical understanding of Indigenous peoples and cultures that they draw from these four educational sites were also consistent, whether participants form their understanding from indirect or interactional forms of learning (Fig. 14.2).

It is apparent that all four educational sites have contributed to participants' views of Indigenous people as disproportionately deviant, although the media is clearly the strongest influence in this domain, and school education does emphasise learning about Aboriginal and Torres Strait Islander traditional culture. Throughout the data, however, references are made to Indigenous people's supposed violence, their consumption of alcohol and other drugs, vandalism, and other anti-social behaviour. An awareness of the bias and limitations inherent to various sites of education, discussed above, did not deter participants from repeating stereotypical and negative representations. For instance, a participant in Bega acknowledges that despite being aware of media bias he is still influenced by them:

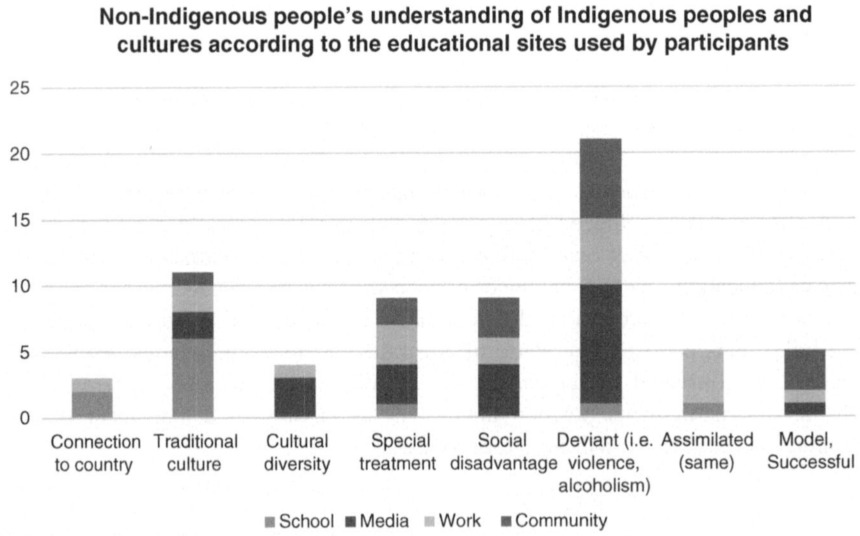

Fig. 14.2 Non-Indigenous people's understanding of Indigeous peoples and cultures according to the educations sites used by participants

Isaac (Overseas born): I know that I get influenced by what I see and you know I don't end up seeing the best side of the culture, […] On the news where there was a huge riot only a year ago or something where the Aboriginals wouldn't leave, and you know you just don't see a pretty side of the culture. You see the alcoholism and the, you know, just the rubbish and everything else.

While Indigenous people were generally understood as socially disadvantaged, they were also thought to be in receipt of 'special treatment' from government. For example, a participant in Parramatta conceded that 'they seem to live in absolutely terrible conditions out there', but asked 'Where's all the money going? [They] seem to be getting heaps and heaps of money' (Kim, Australian born). Counterbalancing such views, at various points Aboriginal and Torres Strait Islander people were also understood as part of rich and diverse cultures, as successful in society, and strongly connected to country. Many participants therefore sustain a Manichean view of Indigenous people, often describing them as having good/positive and bad/negative sides. A participant in Perth says '[he's] seen both sides of it, the extremities' (Trevor, Australian born).

Non-Indigenous participants' historical and inter-cultural understanding also shaped the meanings that they gave to ideas about reconciliation. Across the focus groups and in-depth interviews, reconciliation remained a concept that was both debated and diversely understood. Several participants considered reconciliation to be a kind of tabula rasa that would provide the opportunity for 'starting from scratch and working out a new relationship' (Amber, Australian born) or 'wiping the slate clean' (Oscar and Diana, Overseas born). Other participants, however, contested the possibility—or desirability—of a 'clean slate' approach to reconciliation, instead speaking of the need to acknowledge colonial history, for example in this exchange from Bega:

(Bill, Australian born): Reconciliation to me means—if it's at all possible—for the Aboriginals and the white people in Australia to come together and try and start off again with as clean a slate as possible, so that there are no preconceived ideas on either side. Now it would be much more difficult for the Aboriginal people to do that, I believe, than the Australians, because they've got all these…hang ups isn't the word… but the things that have happened to their nation haven't happened to the white people, and so therefore they've got a lot more ground to make up to achieve this clean slate and start again. But if they're able to do that then I think reconciliation would be a possibility.

(Mandy) I kind of disagree conceptually with that […] To me that's not what reconciliation is, because we can't come together with a clean slate. *It's actually more an acceptance and that acknowledgement of the past*, and then being able to come together […] To be at peace with what's happened, to accept it, to be at peace with it, and from then can you only move on in a meaningful way together.

(Bill) No, well, perhaps clean slate wasn't a very good analogy. What you said then was inherent in my thinking. Obviously you'd have to have that before you were able to achieve anything together (our emphasis).

Most participants in all focus groups shared the view that reconciliation should involve an apology, 'to make amends' and to compensate for the past. However, for many this type of exchange required a degree of reciprocity, defining reconciliation as:

> (Jack, Overseas born) … the coming together of two cultures or two people to reach an agreed outcome.

> (Percy, Overseas born) To achieve forgiveness between two people, to reconcile is to literally reach an understanding with another person.

> (Bill, Overseas born) …being able to coexist in a society or community that values each other's cultures.

For some, reconciliation was focused squarely on the idea of 'closing the gap':

> (Patrick, Australian born) I think in education there's a lot of talk about closing the gap in what's achieved by the Aboriginal people versus non-Aboriginal people, so I think maybe it's about basically you're getting them so that they're socially, economically, academically what have you, on the same level as pretty much the average Australian person.

While for others, the role of cultural understanding and connection was more significant:

> (Amber, Australian born) So maybe if we teach the children that, you know, 'This is part of our culture', instead of looking at it and going 'These are the Aboriginals and these are the Aussies', […] so they have that sense of 'Oh cool, in Australia this is the Aboriginals. They came from here and this is how they lived and this is the clothes they wore and these are the dances they did.'

> (Jane, Australian born) But I also think we need to understand and embrace more Aboriginal culture, I think it needs to be more entwined into our own culture.

Several participants understood reconciliation as involving 'a recognition of differences' and the need to engage across these differences to 'build a bridge' between cultures:

> (Dale) I think it's a recognition of our differences and establishing a bridge between them basically.

> (Jacob) I think it means understanding on both sides, that you build a bridge between them. But it's got to start with the understanding and that's why I say reconciliation is….it's not going that well in my view, because there is not the understanding, I don't think on either side, and it's not going to work unless you have that understanding first.

Not everyone shared these views of reconciliation as an essentially benign and desirable social goal. Some participants criticised reconciliation for its alleged Eurocentrism and assimilationist underpinnings, with the potential for 'skirting around' the more grievous wrongs of Australian history. Others advanced a more assimilationist view of reconciliation as requiring greater socioeconomic equality along with the 'blending' of cultures.

Yet despite the range of views about reconciliation evident among the research participants, there was also wide acknowledgement that they did not know enough about the idea, and that there should be more education and understanding about Australia's history, Indigenous people and cultures in both schools and society more generally. In light of the efforts that have gone into improving education in this domain, including the creation of both school- and community-based curricula, as well as into the training and development of journalists, this is a disappointing finding.

Reconciliation in Practice: The Question of Non-Indigenous Engagement

The idea of a non-Indigenous 'responsibility to engage'—both in the work of reconciliation and, more generally, with Aboriginal and Torres Strait Islander people—has been central to this research and was the subject of explicit discussion in the focus groups. Many participants understood that this kind of responsibility was implicit and necessary in efforts to create attitudinal change at community level, which could in turn lead to more significant structural change. For example, a participant in Parramatta argued that,

> …it's impossible to separate the two because I think that there's like large scale structural change and […] I don't know if it necessarily can be done better without like a grassroots change in a way that the majority of Australians see and think of Aboriginal people and Aboriginal issues. (Charlie, interview)

Charlie seems to be suggesting that change is needed in terms of wider Australian views about 'Aboriginal issues' being a problem to be fixed. Aboriginal and Torres Strait Islander people in Australia have rarely been seen as anything other than a 'problem to be solved', and racialised views of Indigenous competence have allowed for often-draconian policy to be justified as being 'for their own good.' This attitude is intrinsic to the logic of settler colonialism, wherein, as Dodson (2000: 13) has argued, at all stages in Australia's post-invasion history, policy has been about 'their [settlers] solutions to us as the problem':

> The problem of our being here.
>
> The problem of our disposal!
>
> The problem of our assimilation!
>
> And the problem of having us appreciative of all that governments have done 'for our own good'.

A central barrier to the sense of personal responsibility that would be required for such views to change appears to be the way in which the timescale of Australian settler colonialism is understood, which provided many participants with a reason to excuse themselves from responsibility (which they distinguished from 'acknowledgement'):

> (Charlie, Australian born) It's just acceptance and acknowledgement that yes this happened and no you personally weren't responsible.
>
> (Angelica, Australian born) That's what I tend to think, I know it isn't a good history, I know it's not nice what we did, but *we* didn't do it.Roy (Bega interview): Hum, my immediate thought is that it's something that's happened in the past. That's not really the responsibility of the current generation. I'm 51 and I don't feel responsible for anything that happened in the past. I guess it's a bit like comparing, you know, European countries to invasions that happened over the millennia and feeling any sort of responsibility for them and […] And I'd compare that to saying 'Well, how about you compensate me for the Stuarts losing the Crown?' You know, I find that about as relevant as trying to compensate

> the current generation of Australian Aboriginals for their losses, all those generations ago, you know?

Thus, while participants acknowledge that recognition of Australian colonial history is important, this recognition does not necessarily translate into a sense of responsibility to further engage on questions of reconciliation or justice in the present. This evasion of responsibility may be understood as either a reason or an excuse for many participants' non-engagement. Others seemed aware that such engagement was important, but were conscious that they did not make it a priority in their own lives:

> Charlie (interview): … I'm definitely not making the efforts I could be making to educate myself. I mean, you know, is it purely a function of like white privilege essentially? There's no pressing need for me to educate myself after other things, studying at uni that kind of thing, so I don't necessarily make that effort. Perhaps I should.

In his chapter in this volume, Yin Paradies analyses data suggesting that an awareness of white privilege is strongly correlated with what he terms 'reconciliationist attitudes.' It is not clear from the qualitative data presented here that an awareness of white privilege necessarily translates into a sense of responsibility to engage in a way that might bring about change.

It may be argued that educational sites can influence participants' sense of responsibility to engage, as some of the quotes above may suggest. It is also clear, however, that other educational sites seem to in fact solidify separateness between Aboriginal and Torres Strait Islander peoples and other people living in Australia. This was particularly true for the media, where participants consumed so many stereotypical and denigrating images of Indigenous people and cultures. As a participant in Bega noted, 'they're worlds apart to be honest in many areas, worlds apart. We see it on the news all the time' (Jack, Bega OS born).

In general terms, where participants did reflect on the responsibility to engage, they tended to understand such responsibility in purely individual terms:

> David, (Australian born): I'd like to see more *domestic leadership* […] So when for example someone hears a news story and it refers to an Aboriginal person committing some act, none of us should in our language extrapolate that to the whole of the Aboriginal community, because when a white person commits an act of vandalism nobody goes 'Oh bloody white people', you know? […] W*e are all leaders in our families and our work places and our communities and we need to get our heads around these issues*, because you know it is fundamental. Society works because of what individuals do, and if we sit around waiting for some person on a white horse, black horse, we're going to be waiting a long time. (our emphasis)

> …every individual has to look inside their own heart and work out what they've got. We can't sit in this room and say 'Right! None of us are going to be racist, that's it!' You can't! People have their own beliefs, people have their own opinions, and it just comes down to your own spiritual wellbeing, not what the government decides we are doing and we're all going to do it together.' (Amber, Australian born)

Even those who display a very strong sense of responsibility to engage, see it as an individual responsibility. As this participant in Bega put it, what is needed is:

> *An attitude transplant.* Look, it's something that I've looked at for a long time. It's something that's disturbed me for a long time. And I really don't know what the answer is. If I did, I'd be doing something more active about it. *All I do is try and set an example.* (Emily, interview)

Conclusion

Henry Reynolds has written specifically on the question of education about colonial history in his book *Why weren't we told?* (Reynolds 1999), in which he attempts to respond to this precise question, asked of him innumerable times by people who have listened to him speak. Reynolds (1999: 2) reflects that what he has heard in these questions is a sense of frustration, that 'They believed their education should have provided the knowledge, the information, and hadn't done so. They felt let down, cheated, sold short.' But as the research discussed in this chapter suggests, knowledge about colonial harms, whether learned in school, via the media, or through more personal interactions, does not fundamentally change attitudes, and nor does it provoke a sense of responsibility to engage. Even when non-Indigenous participants are aware of the history of dispossession, of continuing injustices and white privilege, and even when they recognise themselves as structurally implicated in these political forces of domination and oppression, they do not necessarily take the next step to transform these power relations and learn to relate differently. Reynolds has also noted that there is now a vast quantity of 'books, articles, films, novels, songs and paintings' that have 'filled out the space once claimed by Stanner's 'Great Australian Silence' (Reynolds 1999: 257). If our research participants are a reflection of the wider Australian population, as we think they are, it would seem that merely filling the silence with cultural and educational 'noise' is not sufficient for changing attitudes.

Thus, despite all the efforts to reform Australian school curricula, and the considerable expenditure on public education campaigns during the decade of formal reconciliation, it seems that the impact of these changes has been limited. The non-Indigenous resistance to engaging with Aboriginal and Torres Strait Islander peoples, let alone taking responsibility for past wrongs or contemporary settler colonial injustice, remains entrenched. It seems that the logic of settler colonialism also fosters a kind of 'deafness' to learning about Australia's history, Indigenous people and cultures, and an unwillingness to engage. The question of what to do next therefore remains a puzzle. Certainly no one would suggest that colonial history should not be taught in our schools. Nor would anyone suggest that biased or racist reporting should go uncriticised. What is clear, however, is that reforming these educational sites will not be enough. Even in the very best classrooms, the responsibility to engage may remain elusive.

References

Alfred, T. (2005). *Wasáse: Indigenous pathways of action and freedom*. Peterborough, ON: Broadview Press.

Bourke, L., & Geldens, P. M. (2007). Perceptions of reconciliation and related indigenous issues among young residents of Shepparton. *The Australian Journal of Social Issues, 42*(4), 603–621.

Bulbeck, C. (2004). The "white worrier" in South Australia: Attitudes to multiculturalism, immigration and reconciliation. *Journal of Sociology, 40*(4), 341.

Burridge, N. (2006). Meanings of reconciliation in the school context. *Australian Journal of Indigenous Education, 35*, 68–77.

Cole, E.A. (2007). Introduction: Reconciliation and history. In E.A. Cole. *Teaching the violent past: History education and reconciliation* (pp. 1–28). Lanham: Rowman & Littlefield.

Commonwealth of Australia. (1991). *Council for aboriginal reconciliation act*. Canberra: The Commonwealth of Australia.

Dodson, P. (2000). Beyond the mourning gate: Dealing with unfinished business, The Wentworth lecture. Canberra: Australian Institute of Aboriginal and Torres Strait Islander Studies.

Freire, P. (1998). *Teachers as cultural workers: Letters to those who dare teach*. Boulder: Westview Press.

Gomersall, A., Davidson, G., & Ho, R. (2000). Factors affecting acceptance of aboriginal reconciliation amongst non-indigenous Australians. *Australian Psychologist, 35*(2), 118–127.

Green, M. J., & Sonn, C. C. (2005). Examining discourses of whiteness and the potential for reconciliation. *Journal of Community & Applied Social Psychology, 15*(6), 478–492.

Green, M. J., & Sonn, C. C. (2006). Problematising the discourses of the dominant: Whiteness and reconciliation. *Journal of Community and Applied Social Psychology, 16*, 379–395.

Gunstone, A. (2009). *Unfinished business: The Australian formal reconciliation process* (2nd ed.). Melbourne: Australian Scholarly Publishing.

Gunstone, A. (2012). *Reconciliation and the "Great Australian Silence"*. Paper presented at the Australian Political Studies Association Conference, Hobart, September 24–26.

Halloran, M. J. (2007). Indigenous reconciliation in Australia: Do values, identity and collective guilt matter? *Journal of Community & Applied Social Psychology, 17*(1), 1–18.

Human Rights and Equal Opportunity Commission (HREOC). (1997). *Bringing them Home. National Inquiry into the Separation of Aboriginal and Torres Strait Islander children from their families*. Canberra: Commonwealth of Australia.

Maddison, S. (2009). *Black politics: Inside the complexity of Aboriginal political culture*. Crows Nest, NSW: Allen & Unwin.

Maddison, S. (2011). *Beyond white guilt: The real challenge for black-white relations in Australia*. Sydney: Allen and Unwin.

McCallum, K. (2003). Walking and talking reconciliation. *Australian Journal of Communication, 30*(2), 115.

Megan, B. (1999). *Feeling power: Emotions and education*. New York: Routledge.

Newspoll, S. I., Muller, D., & Mackay, H. (2000). Public opinion on reconciliation: Snap shot, close focus, long lens. In M. Grattan (Ed.), *Reconciliation: Essays on Australian reconciliation* (pp. 33–52). Melbourne: Black Inc.

Noxolo, P., Raghuram, P., & Madge, C. (2012). Unsettling responsibility: Postcolonial interventions. *Transactions of the Institute of British Geographers, 37*, 418–429.

Pedersen, A., Contos, N., Griffiths, B., Bishop, B., & Walker, I. (2000). Attitudes toward Aboriginal Australians in city and country settings. *Australian Psychologist, 35*, 109–17.

Pedersen, A., Beven, J., Walker, I., & Griffiths, B. (2004). Attitudes toward Indigenous-Australians: The role of empathy and guilt. *Journal of Community and Applied Social Psychology, 14*, 233–249.

Reynolds, H. (1999). *Why weren't we told?: A personal search for the truth about our history*. Ringwood, VIC: Viking.

Royal Commission into Aboriginal Deaths in Custody. (1991). *National reports* (Vols. 1–5). Canberra: The Government of Australia.

Saxton, A. (2004). Whiteness and reconciliation: A discursive analysis. *Australian Psychologist, 39*(1), 14–23.

Short, D. (2003). Reconciliation, assimilation, and the indigenous peoples of Australia. *International Political Science Review/Revue internationale de science politique, 24*(4), 491–513.

Short, D. (2008). *Reconciliation and colonial power: Indigenous rights in Australia*. Aldershot: Ashgate.

Singh, M. (2005). Identity conversion, citizenship, and social studies: Asian-Australian perspectives on indigenous reconciliation and human rights. In Y. Nozaki, R. Openshaw, & A. Luke (Eds.), *Struggles over difference*. Albany, NY: State University of New York Press.

Stanner, W. E. H. (1991 [1968]). *After the dreaming*. Crows Nest, NSW: ABC Enterprises for the Australian Broadcasting Corporation.

Stanner, W. E. H. (2009 [1968]). *The dreaming and other essays*. Melbourne: Black Inc.

Sweeney, S., Johnson, J., & Trimble, K. (1996). *Unfinished business: Australians and reconciliation*. Canberra: AGPS.

Tickner, R. (2001). *Taking a stand: Land rights to reconciliation*. Sydney: Allen & Unwin.

'Yarn About Youth'. (2013). *Youth Studies Australia, 1*: 5.

Chapter 15
The Limits of Reconciliation in Criminal Sentencing

Thalia Anthony

Abstract Indigenous people in Australia are vastly over-represented in police custody and prisons. This paper argues that there is a judicial responsibility to take notice of systemic and prejudicial post-colonial circumstances affecting Indigenous people to reduce imprisonment. This may represent a step on the path to reconciliation in the legal system. By eschewing this reconciliatory gesture, Australian courts are complicit in the over-representation of Indigenous people in prisons. By contrast, Canadian judiciaries and legislatures have taken notice of the systemic disadvantage imposed by the legal system and broader colonial society on First Nations people and have sought to promote non-prison sentences for Aboriginal people. But is it enough for Australian courts to adopt the Canadian approach? This chapter draws on the ideas of Alfred (Response, responsibility and renewal: Canada's truth and reconciliation journey. Aboriginal Healing Foundation, Ottawa: 179–187, 2009) that *reconciliation* absolves and entrenches colonial injustice by maintaining the dominance of postcolonial jurisdictions, processes and criminogenic assumptions. *Resurgence*, *restitution* and *regeneration* concepts that Alfred introduces as counterpoints to reconciliation, are essential for breaking down the postcolonial structures that subordinate Indigenous people. In the legal system, measures to privilege Indigenous perspectives and knowledges through Indigenous sentencing courts and Indigenous community pre-sentence reports challenge the whiteness of legal discourse and process. However, they are not a substitute for the resurgence of Indigenous governance and ongoing jurisdictional claims that push the limits of reconciliatory gestures in criminal sentencing.

Keywords Indigenous nations · Criminal justice · Colonial relations · Usurpation · Resurgence · Decolonisation · Indigenous justice strategies

Thalia would like to thank Alison Whittaker for her editing and thoughtful comments.

T. Anthony (✉)
University of Technology, Sydney, Australia
e-mail: Thalia.Anthony@uts.edu.au

S. Maddison et al. (eds.), *The limits of settler colonial reconciliation*,
DOI 10.1007/978-981-10-2654-6_15

Introduction: From Reconciliation to Resurgence

If one were to look for reconciliation in criminal sentencing courts, they would point to judicial attempts to recognise Indigenous people as having different backgrounds to non-Indigenous people. In sentencing courts, this has provided as much benefit to Indigenous people as in has provided detriment (see Coulthard 2014). Courts may acknowledge an Indigenous person's lesser culpability, due to their background of socio-economic deprivation, but equally they regard membership of an Indigenous community as a criminogenic factor that increases their risk to the wider community (Cunneen et al. 2013: 104; Anthony 2013: 83). In Australia, while recognising Indigenous difference of deprivation, the High Court has refused to consider systemic colonial injustices to Indigenous people in sentencing (*Bugmy* 2013) or to reconsider the legitimacy of its own authority over Indigenous nations (*Walker* 1994). Therefore, if reconciliation exists in criminal courts, it involves, as Alfred (2009: 181–182) explains, reconciling with colonization in a way that 'absolves colonial injustices and is itself a further injustice'. After all, how does a postcolonial system that exists by virtue of denying authority to the legal systems of Indigenous nations have capacity to reconcile with Indigenous nations without atoning for past injustice?

The starting point for reconciliation in the criminal law system requires that the system holds a mirror up to its own criminogenic role rather than pointing the mirror at Indigenous people. Courts need to recognise that the state's criminal law apparatus contributes to the problem of Indigenous people being criminalised. The first section of this chapter identifies the punitive colonial complex that has governed Indigenous Australians for almost 230 years. This chapter then identifies the High Court of Australia's recent decision in *Bugmy* that fails to consider systemic injustices to Indigenous Australians, and contrasts this with the Canadian approach. The third section considers more radical attempts to engage Indigenous community views in sentencing and thus displace the normality of white officialdom in the criminal justice system. This can provide openings for challenging the limits of reconciliatory gestures that are dependent on the white gaze of the courts. The final part reintroduces the ideas of Alfred (2009: 181) and his colleagues that suggest that Indigenous justice requires resurgence, regeneration and restitution, which involves Indigenous nations pushing back on colonial authority to force the state to return what has been stolen and accept coexisting Indigenous nations. This does not mean 'irredentism' but rather settlers giving back 'enough' power to Indigenous nations to demonstrate 'respect for what we share' and make 'things right by offering us the dignity and freedom we are due' (2009: 182). In the Australian justice space, this opens up questions about the legitimacy of the state's universal criminal law jurisdiction and the capacity for Indigenous nations to have a play a greater role in the justice, safety and wellbeing of their communities.

The Punitive Prism of Settler Colonial Relations

Settler colonial society forms its character through excluding Indigenous people and displacing Indigenous societies. In Australia, the British Crown invoked the notion that land belonged to no-one at the time of colonisation—legally termed as *terra nullius*—to give legal credence to its exclusive authority. This enabled the British Crown to reign supremely in the political and legal system, acquire title in all land and impose its economic system. The colonial legislatures and courts made Indigenous people subjects of their legal system. Indigenous people were under the authority of colonial police who could exercise brutal power without being held to account. For over 100 years after colonisation, colonial legislation provided separate punitive provisions for Indigenous people. The *Capital Punishment Amendment Act 1871* (WA) set down public execution solely for Aboriginal peoples. Corporal punishments were solely inflicted on Aboriginal offenders under the *Summary Trial and Punishment of Native Offenders Ordinance 1849* (WA) and the *Aboriginal Offenders Amendment Act 1892* (WA). Further, the South Australian Government enacted the *Breach of Contract Act 1842* with the *Aboriginal Native Offenders Act 1849* to regulate Indigenous employment, including by allowing 'whipping of up to two dozen lashes in lieu of or in addition to imprisonment' where an Indigenous worker objected to employment conditions or absconded (Thorpe 1992: 90–91).

Similar to the colonial policies in Canada, New Zealand and the United States, and consistent with the proposals of the British Select Committee on Aborigines (1837), Australian policies of segregation excluded Indigenous people from residing in the same places as non-Indigenous people. From the mid to late nineteenth century, exclusion was ensured under the Aboriginal Protection Acts. These Acts prohibited Indigenous people from exercising choices over their movement, culture, marriage and children, employment and money.[1] Instead, a myriad of non-Aboriginal Protectors made decisions in relation to all aspects of Indigenous peoples' lives, including their residence on missions, government settlements and place of employment. Under the *Northern Territory Aboriginals Ordinance* (1918) s6(1), the Chief Aboriginal Protector was entitled 'at any time to undertake the care, custody, or control of any aboriginal or half-caste'. Punishment for resisting the authority of the Aboriginal Protector included indefinite incarceration. In Queensland a number of islands, such as Fraser Island and Palm Island, were designated for such punishment. Palm Island in particular was known for holding Indigenous people who disobeyed white authority and spoke out against Queensland's *Aboriginals Protection and Restriction of the Sale of Opium Act 1897* (Watson 1995: 151).

[1]For example, *Aboriginal Protection Act 1869* (Vic); *Aborigines Protection Act 1886* (WA); *Aboriginals Protection and Restriction of the Sale of Opium Act 1897* (Qld); *Aborigines Protection Act 1909* (NSW); *Aborigines Act 1911* (SA); Aboriginals Ordinance 1911 (Cth); and Aboriginals Ordinance 1918 (Cth).

By the 1950s, the Aboriginal Protection Acts were repealed in favour of an official policy of assimilation (see Hasluck 1953, 1988). However, exclusive powers to police and punish Indigenous people persist under contemporary legislation in the Northern Territory. Originating in 2007, special laws in Indigenous communities, particularly in remote areas governed by Aboriginal land rights legislation, provide police with greater search and seize powers. In its current legislative form, the *Stronger Futures in the Northern Territory Act 2012* (Cth) makes it an offence to consume alcohol in designated 'alcohol protected areas' that cover Indigenous communities (ss 8, 27). This consumption offence goes further than the prohibitions under the Aboriginal Protection Acts that were directed to prohibiting the supply of alcohol to Aboriginal persons.[2] The *Stronger Futures in the Northern Territory Act 2012* in conjunction with the *Liquor Act 1978* (NT) s95, gives police powers to seize any vehicle carrying liquor in designated Aboriginal areas, and, in conjunction with the *Police Administration Act 1978* (NT) s119, to search an Aboriginal person's body or to enter a house to conduct alcohol searches without a warrant or permission. Aboriginal people have widely described this law as intrusive and punitive (see Pilkington 2009: 11, 52, 174).

With the removal of Aboriginal people from white-administered Aboriginal reserves, missions and settlements by the 1970s, police and welfare authorities alike increased their surveillance of Indigenous people. This led to a shift in practice from segregation of Aboriginal people in administrative enclaves to segregation through penal detention (Hogg 2001). Prejudicial policing of minor street offences led to a steep escalation of Aboriginal people in police custody and prisons (Eggleston 1976). Along with this increase came soaring numbers of Indigenous deaths in police custody and prisons (Royal Commission into Aboriginal Deaths in Custody 1991).

Today, Indigenous people are 28 times more likely than non-Indigenous people to be in prison (Australian Bureau of Statistics 2015).[3] Indigenous people are especially over-criminalised for crimes relating to public disorder. In the Northern Territory, special laws known as 'paperless arrests' were designed to take disorderly people off the streets, irrespective of whether they have committed a crime; the great majority of these people—over 70 %—are Indigenous (Hunyor 2015: 3). Indigenous women, youth and those with disability experience even greater rates of over-representation in prisons and juvenile detention (Australian Bureau of Statistics 2015). Most Indigenous people in prison have been victims of abuse or trauma and have not been able to access Aboriginal support or services (Sherwood 2013). To use the term of Pugliese (2007), imprisonment and other interactions with

---

[2]For example, *Aboriginal Protection Act 1869* (Vic) s6; *Aborigines Protection Act 1909* (NSW) s9; *Aboriginals Protection and Restriction of the Sale of Opium Act 1897* (Qld) s19.

[3]In addition to prison, criminal net widening has meant Indigenous people are more likely to also receive other forms of punishment, including fines and community corrections (such as intensive corrections and supervision orders, and parole). In 2011–2012, Indigenous prisoners were 13 times more likely to be serving time in community corrections than non-Indigenous prisoners (Australian Institute of Criminology 2014).

the criminal justice system are but one part of a series of ‘event traumas’ for many Indigenous people, which also include forced removal of Aboriginal children from families; undiagnosed and untreated disabilities; involuntary admissions to psychiatric institutions; and the experience of racist attitudes.

However, the criminal justice system does not seek to account for postcolonial circumstances facing Indigenous people. Rather, it drives and is driven by ‘constructions of Indigenous peoples, as the sole cause of their poor status’ and as responsible for their criminogenic profile (Sherwood 2013). The government's prevailing law and order agenda lacks compassion and empathy for Indigenous circumstances (Cuneen 2016; also see Quinn 2016). It does not address foundational issues relating to healing and justice for Australian Indigenous people on the one hand, or over-policing and over-criminalisation of Indigenous people on the other hand. As Sutherland (2002) explains in the Canadian context, the state and the legal system need to recognise their role in colonial policies and practices and endeavor to address the ‘root cause of crime: alienation and separation from indigenous heritage’. The following section addresses the long road that the Australian legal system has to embark on in order to come nearer to this vision of justice, particularly given the new injustices it has recently created. It goes on to discuss the Canadian judiciary's acceptance of its responsibility for postcolonial wrongs, but argues that restitution and decolonisation is an ongoing aspiration.

Refraining from Responsibility for Over-Imprisonment: The High Court of Australia in *Bugmy*

Since the high tide of assimilation policies in the 1950s, there have been several watersheds in Indigenous rights, especially in relation to land, Aboriginal organisational and community self-governance and national representation. However, the tendency in more recent years has been towards mainstreaming the state's governance of Indigenous people and nations. So-called culturally neutral approaches in Australian politics can be juxtaposed with Canadian governance patterns that have, to a greater extent, recognised the role of Indigenous nations in forming policy. The Canadian government's attitude, in response to decades of Indigenous activism, led to the establishment of Canada's Truth and Reconciliation Commission that examined the state's systematic forced removal of Aboriginal children for over 150 years. The position of the Canadian government and the ensuing gains for Canada's First Nations should not be overstated (see Regan 2010), but it may nonetheless help elucidate the divergence between the Canadian and Australian judicial position on sentencing Indigenous people. The Australian stance could be characterized as one of denial: denial of a colonial past; denial of the postcolonial present and enduring Indigenous trauma, and denial of the resilience of Indigenous nations. The Canadian stance is one of recognition and remorse for this colonial paradigm, although not, as Alfred (2009) proffers, one of restitution.

The culturally neutral approach to sentencing Indigenous Australians originates in the legislative framework. In general, sentencing is structured in legislation according to stipulated principles and purposes (e.g. proportionality, deterrence, protection of the community, rehabilitation and denunciation of the offender), a range of objective and subjective mitigating and aggravating factors (e.g. harm of offence, remorse and intoxication) and maximum or occasionally mandatory penalties. With very minor exceptions,[4] these laws do not make reference to Indigenous input or considerations in criminal sentencing. This contrasts with Canadian legislation that seeks to account for Aboriginal background circumstances (including relevant systemic colonial factors) and promote non-prison sentences for Aboriginal peoples. Within the confines of the legislation, Australian higher courts have considered the relevance of individual Indigenous factors, which indicate attempts at reconciling the legal system to Indigenous difference. Courts have identified the Indigenous defendant's impoverished upbringing, experience of intergenerational trauma created by systemic Aboriginal child removal, subjection to Aboriginal community punishment and alienation from imprisonment.[5] However, such reconciliation has brought to the fore stereotypes regarding widespread alcoholism and violence in Indigenous communities.[6] This reveals the malign side of reconciliation when it is predicated on white perceptions.

More recently the High Court of Australia, in its decision of *Bugmy v The Queen* (2013), rejected the relevance of Indigenous collective experiences in sentencing. In that case, the High Court was given an opportunity to recognise the responsibility of the criminal justice system in the over-incarceration of Indigenous people in the sentencing process, and to account for it as one systemic disadvantage facing Indigenous offenders. In its decision, the High Court did not put a mirror to its judicial face and consider how sentencing courts may be responsible for this over-representation. This is despite research over a number of decades that has found that Indigenous people are not sentenced as fairly as non-Indigenous people (Eggleston 1976: 176; Luke and Cunneen 1998: 80; Royal Commission into Aboriginal Deaths in Custody 1991: 217; Fitzgerald 2009: 4–5; Lockwood et al.

---

[4]In the Australian Capital Territory, Queensland and the Northern Territory, legislation refers specifically to the offender's cultural background. Sentencing legislation in the Australian Capital Territory specifies that the court must consider whether the cultural background of the offender is relevant. Courts in Queensland, when sentencing an Aboriginal or Torres Strait Islander person, must have regard to submissions made by a representative of the community justice group in the offender's community, including 'any cultural considerations' (*Penalties and Sentences Act 1992* (Qld) s9(2)(p)). In the Northern Territory, a sentencing court may receive information about an aspect of Indigenous customary law, or the views of members of an Indigenous community (*Sentencing Act 1995* (NT) s104A). However, there are major restrictions that limit the receipt of this information, including the fulfilment of certain procedural requirements (s104A), and excluding any information relating to cultural background or customary law to mitigate or aggravate a sentence (*Crimes Act 1914* (Cth) ss16A–AA). The latter provision originally required the suspension of the *Racial Discrimination Act 1975* (Cth) to allow its passage.

[5]Eg, *Fernando* (1992); *R v Minor* (1992); *Fuller-Cust* (2002).

[6]Eg *Fernando* (1992); *Munda* (2013).

2015: 769), which has contributed to their over-imprisonment.[7] Jeffries and Bond (2009: 55) claim that there are strong grounds for Indigenous contexts leading to a reduced sentence, stating that Indigenous identity sheds light on 'the causes or reasons for offending, and broader social and policy expectations' that make a 'theoretically strong' case for reducing sentence severity. However, the High Court ruled out consideration of systemic issues and accordingly absolved its own responsibility.

The defence in *Bugmy* (2013) unsuccessfully submitted to the High Court that it should adopt the Canadian approach. This approach seeks to reduce prison sentences for Indigenous offenders in an effort to redress the judiciary's contribution to their over-imprisonment. In 1996, in recognition of Aboriginal over-representation in prisons, the Canadian government introduced a new provision into the *Criminal Code*, RSC 1985, c C-46 ('*Canadian Criminal Code*'). Section 718.2(*e*) provides that 'all available sanctions other than imprisonment that are reasonable in the circumstances should be considered for all offenders, with particular attention to the circumstances of aboriginal offenders'. By explicitly directing attention to the 'circumstances of aboriginal offenders', the Canadian legislature has acknowledged the unique position of Aboriginal Canadians. This includes as a result of systemic disadvantage, discrimination and over-representation in prisons. Indeed, Canadian rates of Aboriginal imprisonment are comparable to those in Australia (Wahlquist 2016). By accounting for these factors in sentencing, Canadian courts can attribute a collective identity to the Indigenous person to ensure that they are sentenced according to their Indigenous experience rather than according to non-Indigenous experiences. This legislative amendment represents an act of reconciliation and an acknowledgement that the criminal justice system is part of the 'problem' for Aboriginal Canadians.

The Canadian courts, contrary to the High Court of Australia, accept judicial responsibility in over-incarcerating and discriminating against First Nations people. In the leading case of *Gladue* (1999: 734) on Aboriginal sentencing, the Supreme Court of Canada pointed to Indigenous disadvantage flowing 'from the staggering injustice currently experienced by aboriginal peoples with the criminal justice system'. In its subsequent seminal decision on sentencing, *Ipeelee* (2012: 479), the Supreme Court acknowledged that 'Canadian courts have failed to take into account the unique circumstances of Aboriginal offenders that bear on the sentencing process'. In line with the *Criminal Code*, Canadian courts now seek to remedy the systemic failure of courts to take proper account of the unique circumstances of Aboriginal offenders coming before their courts. The Supreme Court of Canada held in *Ipeelee* (2012: 474) that the *Canadian Criminal Code* s718.2 aimed to curb the 'discriminatory manner' in which sanctions operated. To do this required 'a specific direction' to judges that they properly 'undertook their duties' by paying

---

[7]Some studies indicate that courts send Indigenous people to prison at a higher rate because of their criminal history and the seriousness of their offending (Snowball and Weatherburn 2006: 5, 2007), although do not compare individual circumstances affecting culpability.

'particular attention to the circumstances of Aboriginal offenders' (2012: 474). The Supreme Court seeks to promote sentences that are 'remedial' and 'restorative' in nature, rather than penal (*Gladue* 1999: 737). It has identified the important role of sentencing judges in affecting outcomes for Indigenous people:

> Sentencing judges are among those decision-makers who have the power to influence the treatment of aboriginal offenders in the justice system. They determine most directly whether an aboriginal offender will go to jail, or whether other sentencing options may be employed which will play perhaps a stronger role in restoring a sense of balance to the offender, victim, and community, and in preventing future crime. (*Gladue* 1999: 723)

The Supreme Court of Canada was unequivocal that the judicial notion of individualised justice in sentencing required consideration of the unique and systemic factors bearing on Aboriginal offenders vis-à-vis non-Aboriginal offenders (*Gladue* 1999: 706, 708). It regarded the Indigenous offender as existing within the context of the collective experience of Aboriginal Canadians, which may explain the individual's offending behaviour (1999: 725, 728–729). These experiences include colonial and post-colonial dislocation, discrimination, child removal, socioeconomic disadvantage, lower educational attainment, community fragmentation, higher rates of substance abuse and suicide, and 'of course higher levels of incarceration for Aboriginal peoples' (*Ipeelee* 2012: 469, 484–486). The Court acknowledged that the same collective experience offers the potential for innovation in sentencing processes and unique Aboriginal pathways for punishment, healing and reform (*Gladue* 1999: 725–728).

To facilitate the reconciliation process in sentencing, courts accept *Gladue* Reports, generally written by First Nations people and organisations, about the Aboriginal offender's personal and community circumstances.[8] They provide information on issues relating to institutional racism, poverty, forced child removals by the state, over-incarceration in his/her community, high suicide rates in his/her community, lower education attainment, abuse (including in non-Aboriginal institutional settings) and health issues. Their reports explain offending behaviour within the collective history of Aboriginal Canadians, highlighting the link between the individual and collective experience, including the negative impact of prior government policies such as assimilation and segregation (April and Orsi 2013: 11; Jeffries and Stenning 2014: 256). The report writers also provide information on culturally-relevant sentencing options (such as healing programs and support groups) available in the Indigenous person's community (Hannah-Moffat and Maurutto 2010: 266). The Aboriginal organisations, such as the Aboriginal Legal Services in Toronto, that administer the report-writing process also provide support after the sentencing. The reports provide information by First Nations people rather than simply *about* First Nations people.

[8]*Gladue* Reports are not available for all Aboriginal offenders or across all provinces, preventing a significant proportion of Aboriginal offenders from having relevant information on their Nation's circumstances and background presented to sentencing courts.

The High Court of Australia in *Bugmy* did not recognise judicial responsibility in Indigenous over-incarceration in line with the Canadian approach, or that Indigenous collective experiences are relevant sentencing considerations. The case of Bugmy involved an appeal to the High Court on the grounds *inter alia* that his sentence was manifestly excessive and sentencing practices for Indigenous offenders should consider systemic postcolonial Indigenous circumstances. The case concerned William Bugmy, a 29-year-old Indigenous man from the remote town of Wilcannia in New South Wales, who assaulted a prison guard while he was on remand, due to a dispute over visiting hours. Bugmy threw a pool ball at a correctional officer, which caused him to lose sight in one eye. Bugmy's personal circumstances were of extreme disadvantage. His childhood involved exposure to violence and alcohol, including witnessing his father stab his mother 15 times. Bugmy started drinking and using illegal drugs at the age of 13 and was described as an alcoholic. He was unable to read or write and also had a history of head injuries and suffered from auditory hallucinations. He had made repeated suicide attempts and was receiving antipsychotic medication in custody. He had a lengthy criminal history from the age of 12, including violent offences. He had served numerous terms of imprisonment for these offences and had spent much of his adult life in prison. He had never attended a detoxification or rehabilitation facility, despite asking for help with managing his alcohol abuse on numerous occasions. He had a negative attitude towards authority figures, particularly the police, which were attributed to family 'cultural issues'.

Although the High Court allowed Bugmy's appeal, on the ground that the Court of Criminal Appeal had failed to determine whether Bugmy's sentence was manifestly inadequate, it maintained that 'tak[ing] judicial notice[9] of the systemic background of deprivation of Aboriginal offenders cannot be accepted' (*Bugmy* 2013: 594). It regarded such notice as 'antithetical to individualised justice' and potentially racially discriminatory (2013: 594). It failed to appreciate, in line with the Canadian approach, that accounting for systemic injustice to Indigenous people was a means of remedying judicial discrimination in the sentencing process, rather than a means of promoting discrimination (see Anthony et al. 2015: 67).

The consequence of the *Bugmy* decision is that Australian sentencing courts are not required to account for the relevance of the over-incarceration of Indigenous Australians. They are absolved from recognising the contribution of the criminal justice system to over-imprisonment and the need for it to provide some redress through reducing penal sentences and ordering more appropriate community-based sentences. Judicial responsibility for over-incarceration is a minimal step towards reconciliation in the criminal justice system. However, it is not a panacea in a system in which greater numbers of Indigenous people are being criminalised. In Canada, the judicial stance has not reduced rates of Indigenous over-incarceration, revealing reconciliation as a form of 'recognising' without 'restituting'. As discussed above, if postcolonial societies are to move away from their original penal

[9]An accepted fact that does not require additional information because of its reliability.

approaches to Indigenous people, decarceration is a signifier of this shift. However, it needs to also involve shifting the power balance towards Indigenous governance models. The following section identifies how Indigenous people have been empowered in criminal sentencing matters, but goes on to question what more needs to be done for restitution and Indigenous resurgence.

Moves from Reconciliation to Resurgence or More of the Same Settler Traditions?

In a powerful piece by Gaymarani (2011: 299), a Yolŋu Elder from Arnham Land (northern Australia), he asserts that justice in Indigenous communities requires vesting authority in the local (*Ngarra*) law and its governance practices. These practices have long traditions in law making and adjudicating matters in highly structured settings. He states that his community feels that criminal matters would be better resolved if the state's Court of Summary Jurisdiction was replaced by a Yolŋu community court that primarily applies *Ngarra* law. Gaymarani suggests that this model would more effectively enhance safety and the well-being of the Yolŋu, because it has the mechanisms to address the problems in the community and build on its strengths, but also because it has meaning for local people, which does not apply to Yolŋu people's engagement with the state criminal justice system. Gaykamangu (2012: 248) stresses that *Ngarra* law sentencing options need to be available to Indigenous courts, such as exile from family, community work orders, discipline by responsible Elders or compensating the victim of the crime. This is a plea for resurgence of Indigenous justice models. Alfred and Corntassel (2005: 610, also see Corntassel 2012; Alfred 2005) describe resurgence of Indigenous nationhood as requiring peaceful confrontation with colonisation to revitalise Indigenous traditions.

This section addresses Australian initiatives in relation to Indigenous sentencing courts and Indigenous law and justice groups. These initiatives promote Indigenous voices in the criminal sentencing process in order to empower Indigenous people and provide a fuller picture of circumstances facing Indigenous offenders, including systemic issues relating to their community's experience of colonisation, as well as seek to enable Indigenous justice practices to coexist with non-Indigenous justice practices. This section considers how these initiatives unsettle white voices in sentencing. It concludes that these initiatives can only displace the white criminalisation processes, and promote a subaltern vision of justice evocative of that proposed by Gaymarani and Gaykamangu, with ongoing contestations to colonising structures and attitudes.

Indigenous Sentencing Courts

In a small number of courts, typically local courts dealing with minor matters,[10] Indigenous offenders can have their sentencing heard by Indigenous Elders and/or other Indigenous respected persons. These Indigenous persons speak to the offender about their circumstances (e.g. lack of access to stable housing or health services), family relationships, the offence and its consequences for people in the community, and provide advice to the judicial officer on sentencing options that reflect the effect on the Indigenous community and pathways for the offender's reform.[11] The courts may reconcile the offender, victim and community and/or send the offender a message about the impact of his/her offence on the community. These 'Indigenous sentencing courts' transform the court process, space and outcomes in ways that are more compatible with Indigenous justice concepts (see Marchetti 2010: 271). Marchetti and Daly's (2012: 436) research shows how Indigenous sentencing courts provide 'innovative justice' by incorporating Indigenous knowledge, values, design and modes of social control into the sentencing process. In this way, Indigenous courts 'bend and change the dominant perspective of "white law"' (Marchetti and Daly 2007: 429). Such courts do not operate in Western Australia and the Northern Territory—the Australian jurisdictions with the highest rates of Indigenous incarceration and possessing strong Indigenous justice structures—after both jurisdictions recently outlawed or defunded their operations (Anthony and Crawford 2014; Banks 2015).

Initiatives around Indigenous sentencing courts emerged over 15 years ago due to Indigenous peoples' experience of the criminal justice system failing to incorporate Indigenous practices and perspectives.[12] Indigenous sentencing courts were first established in Port Adelaide, South Australia in 1999 and in Nowra, New South Wales in 2002 (Dick 2006: 6). Indigenous communities worked with judicial officers and court administrators to establish Indigenous sentencing courts, and to push for legislation to accommodate these courts.[13] The processes have evolved

[10]In South Australia and Victoria, the Indigenous court processes are also used in higher court levels for serious offences. Some limit the types of offenses that can come before the courts (e.g., breaches of family violence protection orders are excluded in Victoria but associated charges of assault can be brought before the Victorian courts; sexual offenses are excluded in all of the jurisdictions apart from Queensland and South Australia; and certain drug offenses and offenders who are addicted to illicit drugs are excluded in New South Wales and the Australian Capital Territory).

[11]Indigenous sentencing courts currently operate in some locations in New South Wales (circle sentencing), Queensland (Murri Courts), Victoria (Koori Courts) and South Australia (Nunga Courts).

[12]This issue was raised in the Australian Royal Commission into Aboriginal Deaths in Custody (1991) and was identified in its Recommendation 104 that Aboriginal communities and organisations be consulted in sentencing.

[13]Legislation supporting Indigenous sentencing courts include the *Magistrates' Court Act 1989* (Vic) s4D, the *Criminal Procedure Act 1986* (NSW) s348, and the *Penalties and Sentences Act 1992* (Qld) s9(2)(p).

organically based on the jurisdiction, judicial officer and the expectations and needs of Indigenous participants. They commonly involve Indigenous people, court actors, including the judicial officer, prosecutor and defence lawyer, support people and occasionally the victim siting in a circle; either in a court room, a room culturally significant to the Elders, or outdoors.

The judicial officer has significant discretion as to how the court runs, where it is held, where the Elders are seated and the sentencing outcome. Ultimately the judicial officer is the final arbiter on who constitutes the Community Court and whether the court operates for a particular hearing or altogether. Where judicial officers are reluctant to engage the authority of Indigenous Elders, the Elders will be required to physically sit underneath the judicial officer who retains his/her seating position above the court. They will also limit the participation of Elders in the court and the impact of Elders' advice on the sentencing outcome. Although most judicial officers who preside over Indigenous sentencing courts have a strong commitment to their operation and defer significant power to the Indigenous Elders, this remains dependent on the judicial officer's and other court participants' commitment to transformative practices (Marchetti and Ransley 2015: 15). Without this commitment, the courts fall short of their reconciliatory endeavours and are a far cry from opening up spaces for Indigenous resurgence. Alfred (1999: 27) warns that where 'unjust power relationships and colonized attitudes remain untouched', '"reform" becomes nothing more than a politically correct smokescreen obscuring the fact that no real progress is being made towards traditionalist goals'.

The sentencing advice provided by Indigenous Elders and Respected Persons to a magistrate or judge must fall within the confines of the state's criminal and sentencing laws, although these options *may* be interpreted broadly to include Indigenous punishments such as sending young boys who have offended to camp on country as part of their rehabilitation (see Anthony and Crawford 2014).[14] The Indigenous sentencing courts do not have capacity to determine sentences or processes that are purely consistent with Indigenous practices and punishments. However, they can have a positive impact on strengthening Indigenous community social controls and community relationships according to a number of studies (Beranger et al. 2010; Borowski 2010, 2011; Fitzgerald 2008; Morgan and Louis 2010; Blokland 2007: 10–11). Moreover, an evaluation by the Cultural and Indigenous Research Centre Australia (2008) found that Circle Sentencing has a 'dramatic influence on offenders beyond reoffending', such as in relation to substance abuse, employment and family relations. Overall, evaluations of sentencing courts show significant benefits derived for Indigenous participants where the judicial officer has been committed to engaging Indigenous perspectives and worldviews and transforming the nature of the court. In these situations, Indigenous

[14]In the Northern Territory, Indigenous people have the potential to be involved in a range of sentencing outcomes that conform with the legislation, including supervising community-styled orders such as exile and participation in a ceremony or a work camp. See Gosford; *R v Yakayaka and Djambuy* (Unreported, Supreme Court of Northern Territory, Riley CJ, 17 December 2012).

sentencing courts have empowered Indigenous Elders in justice outcomes and challenged the Anglo-centric nature of the justice system.

Indigenous Community Justice Groups: Examples from the Northern Territory

In the Northern Territory since the late 1990s, four remote Australian Indigenous communities have initiated Law and Justice Groups in order to enhance their input in the justice system. These groups formulated plans in conjunction with the Northern Territory Government and police to provide a range of strategies for two-way justice. Although there have been a number of breaches of the plans by the police that have caused significant concern to communities (see Anthony and Chapman 2008), Law and Justice Groups continue to both advocate the resurgence of Indigenous justice models and have input into sentencing decisions. This resilience prevails in spite of the government and judiciary's abolition of Indigenous community sentencing courts in 2011 (Hannam 2013). Law and Justice Groups (LJGs) provide written pre-sentencing advice to the magistrate based on an evaluation of the offence (in terms of its significance to the community) and the offender (including his or her risk to the community and capacity to rehabilitate and reintegrate into the community). There are currently four Law and Justice-styled Groups involved in pre-sentencing in the Northern Territory: Lajamanu's 'Kurdiji' Law and Justice Group (established in 1998 and reconstituted in 2009) and the Yuendumu Mediation and Justice Group (established in 2006) in Warlpiri communities in Central Australia, Wurrumiyanga's Ponki Mediators in the Tiwi Islands (established in 2009) and Maningrida's Bunawarra Dispute Resolution Elders in the Top End (established in 2012). The Kurdiji Group has a meeting area building and the group meets approximately every 8 weeks to discuss community safety, crime prevention, community governance, inter-agency collaboration and provide pre-sentence reports to the court on particular defendants (Central Land Council 2013; Kurdiji 2014).

In relation to sentencing, the process of report writing in Lajamanu, Wurrumiyanga and Maningrida involves the North Australian Aboriginal Justice Agency's community legal educator informing the LJG of the court list, offenders' charges, the summary of agreed facts and prior offending. The LJG then decides the cases for which they are prepared to write a letter of support, and writes references outlining the group's knowledge of the offender's background and community circumstances, information on the offender's role in the community, views about the offending, the offender's character, and ideas for the offender's rehabilitation and punishment, including as administered by community members such as participation in community work or ceremony or compensating the community.[15] The

[15]In addition, Indigenous community pre-sentencing reports also exists in Queensland. Unlike in the Northern Territory where the Indigenous community directed the process, in Queensland the

letters are provided to the defendant's lawyer before being submitted to the magistrate during sentencing submissions. The group members make themselves available for cross-examination if requested. In addition to this function, the group is involved in dispute resolution to resolve conflicts before they escalate and can play an important role in individual's rehabilitation (see Anthony and Crawford 2014). The LJGs play a broader role in community justice and law and justice planning, enabling defendants and victims to have appropriate support. The LJG is also strengthened through its involvement in sentence reports.

Pre-sentence reports, like Indigenous sentencing courts, are effective where they can advise on a broad range of sentencing orders that are relevant to the community, such as participation in local programs and activities.[16] They can promote appropriate, holistic and workable solutions and sentencing orders. They also ensure collective responsibility in implementing sentencing outcomes (Thomas 1999). Through promoting community-based solutions, the reports can have a dual benefit in the reconciliation process by, first, diminishing the tendency of the criminal justice system to incarcerate Indigenous people and, second, by strengthening the role of Indigenous laws and protocols in the lives of the defendant and thus strengthening the Indigenous community. In their most effective manifestations, Indigenous sentencing courts, report writing processes and justice plans can shift the power balance towards Indigenous systems of authority, elucidate the colonising nature of the criminal justice system that is otherwise blind to Indigenous perspectives, and reveal a pathway to resurgence.

Reconciliation with Colonisation?

While Indigenous sentencing courts and pre-sentence reports point to avenues for strengthening justice for Indigenous people in the criminal justice system, they do not challenge the jurisdiction of criminal courts, which many Indigenous people continue to question their legitimacy. Given that Australian sovereignty and land was never ceded; never the subject of a treaty or lost in battle, Indigenous nations still have legitimate claims to governance. These claims are facially strengthened in law by the High Court's recognition that British occupation relied on a false notion of *terra nullius* (*Mabo v Queensland (No. 2)* 1992), and the Federal Court's acceptance that

(Footnote 15 continued)

Department of Justice instigated the program. Community Justice Groups prepare 'cultural reports' with the assistance of an Indigenous coordinator from the Department of Justice to inform the court of the background of the offender and the availability of support services. This is a wide-spread program that seeks to be available to all Indigenous people in Queensland facing a sentence of imprisonment.

[16]The Royal Commission into Aboriginal Deaths in Custody noted the efficacy of having Aboriginal communities involved in determining, planning and implementing local community service orders: recommendations 109–115.

Yolŋu people in north-east Arnhem Land possessed an elaborate body of Indigenous laws prior to colonization (*Milirrpum v Nabalco Pty Ltd* 1971: 267).[17] In parts of Australia, especially more remote northern areas, Indigenous Elders are endeavouring to reset the justice arrangements between the state laws and their laws on the grounds that they have a lawful claim to live according to their justice systems (see Loy 2010; Gaykamangu 2012; Gaymarani 2011; Gondarra 2006, 2011).

From the early colonial period, the Supreme Court of New South Wales renounced the legitimacy of Indigenous punishment on the grounds that 'Indigenous tribes' were not constituted as 'sovereign states governed by laws of their own'. Rather, the British state had taken into 'actual possession' half of the Australian continent and could exercise 'the rights of Domain and Empire' (*R. v. Murrell & Bummaree* 1836: 211). The High Court of Australia has more recently ruled that Indigenous people cannot be subjected to their own criminal laws, procedures and punishment processes. This is based on a circular rationale that the state's criminal law is universal and unable to coexist with other law systems. High Court Chief Justice Mason stated in *Walker v State of New South Wales* (1994: 50) that 'English criminal law did not, and Australian criminal law does not, accommodate an alternative body of law operating alongside it'. The High Court does not address what gave the British Crown and the postcolonial Australian state its exclusive university authority, given that Indigenous nations exercised jurisdiction over its people for thousands of years before colonisation in 1788. Indeed, in the Northern Territory, courts recognise the ongoing operation of Indigenous punishment practices, but nonetheless outlaw them because they offend non-Indigenous values (see *Re. Anthony* 2004; *R v Sims & Walker* 2012).

The judicial (and political) unwillingness to consider shared jurisdiction highlights the precarious nature of Indigenous inclusion in sentencing processes. This precarity is brought into sharp relief when Indigenous justice initiatives and community courts lose state funding and support (see Anthony and Crawford 2014; Banks 2015; Karp 2016). It is otherwise apparent through Indigenous sentencing courts continuing to operate on the margins and their inability to challenge the foundation and content of western law. Aside from the small enclaves of Indigenous sentencing courts, most Indigenous people are subjected to a white legal system with white participants—judicial officers, lawyers, community corrections officers and juries—and a white law steeped in a western worldview.[18]

Indigenous resurgence requires more than the inclusion of Indigenous voices in sentencing, but a regeneration of Indigenous governance structures, such as those referred to by Gaykamangu and Gaymarani in relation to Arnhem Land, that continue to have capacity to strengthen Indigenous nations. This requires engaging

---

[17]However, in *Mabo v Queensland* (No.2) (1992: 44–45), Brennan J noted that Indigenous traditions will be observed in so far as they do not fracture the 'skeleton' of the common law, and as an 'act of state', the High Court could not challenge state sovereignty because it would threaten the courts of the state. See a critique of this position in Anthony (2009).

[18]Sutherland (2002) states that Canadian Aboriginal justice programs also do not threaten a western worldview, instead they have the effect of replicating it based on their limited jurisdiction.

with Indigenous communities, Elders and lawmakers in a way that decentres postcolonial power. The idea of resurgence, according to Alfred (2009: 182), is not irredentism, but power sharing that enables Indigenous expressions of power over their affairs. The Aboriginal Provisional Government (1990) articulated a vision of power sharing in terms of Indigenous nations having control of their political and legal system on Aboriginal land acquired through land rights legislation, and the retention of non-Indigenous governance on non-Indigenous land, with agreements between the two jurisdictions governing their coexistence. Although the intricacies of Indigenous nation building need to be determined by local Indigenous nations, this type of proposal promotes resurgence that challenges the complacent foundations of colonialism (see Alfred 2005: 130). It advocates 'enough' power for Indigenous nationhood to be sustainable alongside non-Indigenous jurisdictions (Alfred 2009: 182).

Conclusion: Decolonising the Criminal Justice System

If we are to transcend the limits of reconciliation and seek something more—such as resurgence and decolonisation—there needs to be a deconstruction of the authority of the criminal justice system as it applies to Indigenous and non-Indigenous people. This is because criminal justice in Australia is based on excluding Indigenous societies and people. This chapter traces that story of exclusion in Australia to point to the limits of attempts at reconciliation within criminal justice institutions that deny Indigenous authority. In Australia, racism persists through exclusion of Indigenous laws and practices and failure to accommodate Indigenous difference in the legal system leading to unfair sentences. The 'norm of colorblindness', according to critical race theorist Harris (1993: 1768), upholds 'whiteness' by denying the 'historical context of white domination and Black subordination'. The current High Court of Australia position accords responsibility to Indigenous people for their over-incarceration, which nullifies the responsibility of the white system. It also overlooks the strengths that Indigenous communities offer Indigenous people, such as strong family and kinship relationships, healing programs and support services, to promote restorative outcomes. Accordingly, it is unable to look beyond the penal system—both in its prison and diversion forms (Steele et al. 2016)—and towards solutions in community and on country.[19] So long as the criminal justice system fails to see its role in contributing to the imprisonment problem for Indigenous people, it perpetuates the over-imprisonment.

However, reconciliation involving recognition of Indigenous difference in sentencing is also problematic. It lets the Australian judiciary and legislature off the hook. This strategy short circuits a more confronting inquiry into the legitimacy of

[19]Numerous studies have pointed to the benefits of being on Country for Indigenous people in terms of their mental wellbeing (Hinton et al. 2015; Burgess et al. 2005).

the colonial legacy that displaced Indigenous justice processes and laws. According to Moreton-Robinson (2003: 23), whiteness is based on 'an invisible regime of power that secures hegemony' through the 'epistemological a priori' of the righteousness of white claims to law and governance. This sense of righteousness paralyses the High Court's ability to reexamine the basis of the criminal justice system in the same way that it has reexamined the land tenure system and provided for coexisting native title rights, *al beit* with limited gains for Indigenous land rights.

The responsibility of the non-Indigenous criminal justice system is *not* tantamount to making postcolonial courts better; it is about the transformation of postcolonial authority. This involves reconstituting jurisdictions to shift power from non-Indigenous appointed judicial officers and legal precedent, towards Indigenous community justice strategies, laws and knowledge systems. Adopting this responsibility would bring into sharp relief the otherwise white ontology of judicial officers and the white epistemology of the legal system and provide a channel for undoing the injustice towards Indigenous people that the postcolonial state's criminalizing system has created.

Given that sovereignty was never ceded by Indigenous nations, or lawfully acquired by colonisers, there are grounds for challenging the authority of the criminal courts. Indeed, a number of nations have already put demands challenging the authority and prejudicial functioning of the non-Indigenous criminal justice system (e.g. Warlpiri people, see Loy 2010; Yolŋu people, see Gaymarani 2011; Gondarra 2006). Other nations have developed hybrid systems of justice where state and Indigenous laws, dispute resolution practices and justice values coexist. These have been successful where they are owned by Indigenous communities and integrated with Indigenous law and governance instruments (see Blagg 2008: 140). There are Australian models of local community justice frameworks and law and justice plans and agreements between Indigenous nations and governments. Essential to these tasks is that colonial modes of justice and power are decentred and Indigenous modes are elevated in Indigenous lives and beyond. Indigenous resurgence can take many forms in the criminal justice space, but mere recognition of Indigenous difference is not one of them.

References

Cases

Bugmy v The Queen (2013) 249 CLR 571.
Bugmy [No 2] [2014] NSWCCA 322.
Elias v The Queen; Issa v The Queen [2013] HCA 31.
Fernando (1992) 76 A Crim R 58.
R v Fuller-Cust [2002] VSCA 168,
Ipeelee [2012] 1 SCR 433.
Mabo v State of Queensland (No. 2) (1992) 175 CLR 1.

Milirrpum v Nabalco Pty Ltd (1971) 17 FLR 141.
Munda v Western Australia (2013) 302 ALR 207.
R v Gladue [1999] 1 SCR 688.
R v Minor (1992) 105 FLR 180.
R v Murrell & Bummaree [1836] NSWSC 35 (5 February 1836).
Re. Anthony (2004) 142 A Crim R 440.
The Queen v Sims & Walker [2012] NTSC (Unreported, 27 February).
Walker v State of New South Wales (1994) 182 CLR 45.
Wong v The Queen (2001) 207 CLR 584.

Secondary materials

Aboriginal Provisional Government. (1990). Towards Aboriginal Sovereignty. Online article. Aboriginal Provisional Government. http://nationalunitygovernment.org/sites/default/files/sites/default/files/pdf-doc/towards%5B1%5D.pdf.

Alfred, T. (1999). *Peace, power, righteousness: An indigenous manifesto*. Ton Mills, ON: Oxford University Press.

Alfred, T. (2005). *Wasáse: Indigenous pathways of action and freedom*. Peterborough, ON: Broadway Press.

Alfred, T. (2009). Restitution is the real pathway to justice for indigenous peoples. In G. Younging, J. Dewar, & M. DeGagné (Eds.), *Response, responsibility and renewal: Canada's truth and reconciliation journey* (pp. 179–187). Ottawa: Aboriginal Healing Foundation.

Alfred, T., & Corntassel, J. (2005). Being indigenous: Resurgences against contemporary colonialism. *Government and Opposition, 40*(4), 597–614.

Anthony, T. (2009). *Indigenous people, crime and punishment*. Oxford: Routledge.

Anthony, T. (2013). Commentaries on colonialism: Australian judicial interpretation. In W. Prest (Ed.), *Blackstone and his commentaries biography, law, history* (pp. 129–150). Oxford: Hart Publishing.

Anthony, T., & Blagg, H. (2013). STOP in the name of who's law? Driving and the regulation of contested space in central Australia. *Social & Legal Studies, 22*(1), 43–66.

Anthony, T., & Chapman, R. (2008). Unresolved tensions: Warlpiri law, police powers and land rights. *Indigenous Law Bulletin, 7*(5), 9–18.

Anthony, T., & Crawford, W. (2014). Northern Territory Indigenous community sentencing mechanisms: An order for substantive equality. *Australian Indigenous Law Review, 17*(2), 79–99.

Anthony, T., Bartels, L., & Hopkins, A. (2015). Lessons lost in sentencing: Welding individualised justice to Indigenous justice. *Melbourne University Law Review, 39*(1), 47–76.

April, S., & Orsi, M. (2013). *Gladue practices in the provinces and territories*. Ottawa: Department of Justice.

Ashworth, A. (2002). Sentencing. In M. Maguire, R. Morgan, & R. Reiner (Eds.), *Oxford handbook of criminology* (3rd ed.). Oxford: Oxford University Press.

Australian Bureau of Statistics. (2015). *Prisoners in Australia (No. 4517.0)*. Canberra, ACT: Author.

Australian Institute of Criminology. (2014). *Australian crime: Facts and figures*. Canberra: Author.

Banks, A. (2015, August 14) Aboriginal court gets the chop. *Western Australian*.

Behrendt, L. (2002). Aboriginal women and the criminal justice system. *Judicial Officers' Bulletin, 16*(6), 41–44.

Beranger, B., Weatherburn, D., & Moffatt, S. (2010). Reducing indigenous contact with the court system. *Crime and Justice Statistics Bureau Brief, 54*, 1–4.

Blagg, H. (2008). Colonial critique and critical criminology: Issues in aboriginal law and aboriginal violence. In T. Anthony & C. Cunneen (Eds.), *The critical criminology companion* (pp. 129–146). Sydney: Hawkins Press.

Blokland, J. (2007, September 7). *The Northern Territory experience.* Paper presented at Australian Institute of Judicial Administration Indigenous Courts Conference at Mildura. Melbourne: Australian Institute of Judicial Administration.

Borowski, A. (2011). In Courtroom 7—The children's Koori Court at work: Findings from an evaluation. *International Journal of Offender Therapy and Comparative Criminology, 55*(7), 1110–1134.

Borowski, A. (2010). Indigenous participation in sentencing young offenders: Findings from an evaluation of the children's Koori Court of Victoria. *Australian and New Zealand Journal of Criminology, 43*(3), 465–484.

British House of Commons. (1837). *Report of the Select Committee on Aborigines.* British Parliamentary Papers No 15.

Burgess, C., Johnston, F., Bowman, D., & Whitehead, P. (2005). Healthy country: Healthy people? Exploring the health benefits of Indigenous natural resource management. *Australian and New Zealand Journal of Public Health, 29*(2), 117–122.

Central Land Council. (2013). *Kurdiji building opening day.* Online report. Central Land Council. http://www.clc.org.au/files/pdf/130625_kurdiji_opening_feedback_final_compressed_version.pdf.

Corntassel, T. (2012). Re-envisioning resurgence: Indigenous pathways to decolonization and sustainable self-determination. *Decolonization: Indigeneity Education & Society, 1*(1), 86–101.

Coulthard, G. (2014). *Red Skin, White Masks: Rejecting the politics of recognition.* Minneapolis: University of Minnesota Press.

Cultural and Indigenous Research Centre Australia. (2008). *Evaluation of circle sentencing program.* Sydney: NSW Attorney General's Department.

Cuneen, C. (2016). How 'tough on crime' politics flouts death-in-custody recommendations. Online article. *The Conversation.* https://theconversation.com/how-tough-on-crime-politics-flouts-death-in-custody-recommendations-57491.

Cunneen, C. (2001). *Conflict, politics and crime: Aboriginal communities and the police.* Sydney: Allen & Unwin.

Cunneen, C., Baldry, E., Brown, D., Schwartz, M., Steel, A., & Brown, M. (2013). *Penal culture and hyperincarceration: The revival of the prison.* Oxon: Routledge.

Dick, D. (2006, February 10–12). *Circle sentencing of aboriginal offenders.* Paper presented at the Conference on Sentencing: Principles, Perspectives and Possibilities, Canberra. Sydney: Indigenous Justice Clearinghouse.

Edney, R. (2005). Imprisonment as a last resort for indigenous offenders: Some lessons from Canada? *Indigenous Law Bulletin, 6*(12), 23–26.

Eggleston, E. (1976). *Fear, favour or affection: Aborigines and the criminal law in Victoria, South Australia and Western Australia.* Canberra: Australian National University Press.

Fitzgerald, J. (2009). Why are indigenous imprisonment rates rising? *Crime and Justice Statistics Issues Paper, 41*, 1–6.

Fitzgerald, J. (2008). Does circle sentencing reduce aboriginal offending? *Crime and Justice Bulletin: Contemporary Issues in Crime and Justice, 115*, 1–12.

Gaykamangu, J. (2012). Ngarra law: Aboriginal customary law from Arnhem Land. *Northern Territory Law Journal, 2*(4), 236–248.

Gaymarani, G. (2011). An introduction to the Ngarra Law of Arnhem Land. *Northern Territory Law Journal, 1*, 283–304.

Gondarra, D. (2006). *Traditional law is keeping the peace on aboriginal lands.* Media Release. Aboriginal Resource and Development Services, http://www.supremecourt.nt.gov.au/media/docs/commonwealth_intervention.pdf. Accessed June 25, 2007.

Gondarra, D. (2011, March 3). Assent law of the first people: Views from a traditional owner. *National Indigenous Times*, p. 24.

Hannah-Moffat, K., & Maurutto, P. (2010). Recontextualising pre-sentence reports: Risk and race. *Punishment and Society, 12*(3), 262–286.

Hannam, H. (2013, July 18). *Current issues in delivering indigenous justice: Challenges for the courts.* Paper presented to the Australian Institute of Judicial Administration Conference, Adelaide. Melbourne: Australian Institute of Judicial Administration.

Harris, C. (1993). Whiteness as property. *Harvard Law Review, 106*(8), 1707–1791.

Hasluck, P. (1953). *Native welfare in Australia.* Perth: Patterson Brokenshaw.

Hasluck, P. (1988). *Shades of darkness: Aboriginal affairs 1925–1965.* Melbourne: Melbourne University Press.

Haswell, M., Williams, M., Blignault, I., Grand Ortega, M., & Jackson Pulver, L. (2014). *Returning home, back to community from custodial care: Learnings from the first year pilot project evaluation of three sites around Australia.* Sydney: Muru Marri, UNSW Australia School of Public Health and Community Medicine.

Hinton, R., Kavanagh, D. J., Barclay, L., Chenhall, R., & Nagel, T. (2015). Developing a best practice pathway to support improvements in Indigenous Australians' mental health and well-being: A qualitative study. *BMJ Open,*. doi:10.1136/bmjopen-2015-007938.

Hogg, R. (2001). Penality and modes of regulating indigenous people in Australia. *Punishment and Society, 3*(3), 355–379.

Hudson, B. (2006). Punishing monsters, judging aliens: Justice at the borders of community. *Australian & New Zealand Journal of Criminology, 39*(2), 232–247.

Hunyor, J. (2015). Imprison Me NT: Paperless arrests and the rise of executive power in the Northern Territory. *Indigenous Law Bulletin, 8*(21), 3–9.

Jeffries, S., & Bond, C. (2009). Does indigeneity matter? Sentencing indigenous offenders in South Australia's higher courts. *Australian & New Zealand Journal of Criminology, 42*(1), 47–71.

Jeffries, S., & Stenning, P. (2014). Sentencing aboriginal offenders: Law, policy, and practice in three countries. *Canadian Journal of Criminology and Criminal Justice, 56*, 447–494.

Karp, P. (2016, March 19). Indigenous organisations have been "disadvantaged" by grants program. *The Guardian.*

Kurdiji—Lajamanu Law and Justice Group. (2014). *Kurdiji.* Online report. Lajamanu Visitor Guide http://www.clc.org.au/files/pdf/KurdijiNEbook-6.pdf.

Lockwood, K., Hart, T. C., & Stewart, A. (2015). First nations peoples and judicial sentencing: Main effects and the impact of contextual variability. *British Journal of Criminology, 55*(4), 769–789.

Loy, D. (2010). *Bush law. Message Stick [Television programme].* Sydney, NSW: Australian Broadcasting Corporation.

Luke, G., & Cunneen, C. (1998). *Sentencing aboriginal people in the Northern Territory: A statistical analysis.* Sydney: Institute of Criminology, Sydney University Law School.

Marchetti, E. (2010). Indigenous sentencing courts and partner violence: Perspectives of court practitioners and elders on gender power imbalances during the sentencing hearing. *Australian & New Zealand Journal of Criminology, 43*(2), 263–281.

Marchetti, E., & Daly, K. (2007). Indigenous sentencing courts: Towards a theoretical and jurisprudential model. *Sydney Law Review, 29*(3), 416–443.

Marchetti, E., & Daly, K. (2012). Innovative justice processes. In M. Marmo, W. de Lint, & D. Palmer (Eds.), *Crime and justice: A guide to criminology* (pp. 455–481). Sydney: Thompson Reuters.

Marchetti, E., & Ransley, J. (2015). Applying the critical lens to judicial officers and legal practitioners involved in sentencing indigenous offenders: Will anyone or anything do? *University of New South Wales Law Journal, 37*(1), 1–33.

Methven, E. (2014). A very expensive lesson: Counting the costs of penalty notices for anti-social behaviour. *Current Issues in Criminal Justice, 26*(2), 249–257.

Moreton-Robinson, A. (2003). I still call Australia home: Indigenous belonging and place in a white postcolonising society. In S. Ahmed, C. Cataneda, A. M. Fortier, & M. Shellyey (Eds.), *Uproot-ings/regroupings: Questions of postcoloniality, home and place* (pp. 23–40). Oxford: Berg.

Morgan, A., & Louis, E. (2010). *Evaluation of the Queensland Murri Court: Final report*. Canberra: Australian Institute of Criminology.
O'Shane, P. (1992). Aborigines and the criminal justice system. In C. Cunneen (Ed.), *Aboriginal perspectives on criminal justice*. Sydney: Institute of Criminology, University of Sydney.
Pilkington, J. (2009). *Aboriginal communities and the Police's Taskforce Themis: Case studies in remote aboriginal community policing in the Northern Territory*. Darwin: North Australian Aboriginal Justice Agency and Central Australian Legal Aid Service.
Pugliese, J. (2007). The event-trauma of the carceral post-human. *Social Semiotics, 17*(1), 63–86.
Quinn, J. R. (2016, March 17). *Cultivating sympathy and reconciliation: The importance of sympathetic response in the uptake of transitional justice*. Paper presented to the Annual Convention of the International Studies Association, Atlanta.
Regan, P. (2010). *Unsettling the settler within Indian residential schools, truth telling, and reconciliation in Canada*. Vancouver: UBC Press.
Royal Commission into Aboriginal Deaths in Custody. (1991). *Final report*. Canberra: Australian Government Publisher.
Sherwood, J. (2013). Colonisation—It's bad for your health: The context of Aboriginal health. *Contemporary Nurse, 46*(1), 28–40.
Snowball, L., & Weatherburn, D. (2006). Indigenous over-representation in prison: The role of offender characteristics. *Contemporary Issues in Crime and Justice: Crime and Justice Bulletin, 99*, 1–20.
Snowball, L., & Weatherburn, D. (2007). Does racial bias in sentencing contribute to indigenous overrepresentation in prison? *Australian and New Journal Criminology, 40*(3), 272–290.
Steele, L., Dowse, L., & Trofimovs, J. (2016). Who is diverted?: Moving beyond diagnosed impairment towards a social and political analysis of diversion. *Sydney Law Review, 38*(2), 179–206.
Sutherland, J. (2002). *Colonialism, crime, and dispute resolution: A critical analysis of Canada's aboriginal justice strategy*. Online article. Mediate.com. http://www.mediate.com/articles/sutherlandJ.cfm.
Thomas, B. (1999). *Circle sentencing: Involving aboriginal communities in the sentencing process*. Discussion Paper. Sydney: New South Wales Aboriginal Justice Advisory Council.
Thorpe, B. (1992). Aboriginal employment and unemployment: Colonised labour. In C. Williams & B. Thorpe (Eds.), *Beyond industrial sociology: The work of men and women* (pp. 88–107). Sydney: Allen & Unwin.
Wahlquist, C. (2016, February 25). 'It's the same story': How Australia and Canada are twinning on bad outcomes for Indigenous people. *The Guardian*, https://www.theguardian.com/world/2016/feb/25/indigenous-australians-and-canadians-destroyed-by-same-colonialism.
Watson, J. (1995). "We couldn't tolerate any more": The Palm Island Strike of 1957. *Labour History, 69*, 149–170.

Chapter 16
What Is at Stake in Constitutional Recognition?

Adrian Little

Abstract Australia is currently involved in a national debate about the possibility of constitutional recognition of Aboriginal and Torres Strait Islander people. Since 2010 both of the major political parties have supported a process that leads to constitutional recognition but, beneath the surface, it remains an issue that engenders considerable political division. It is a matter of concern that no clear process for dealing with the issue has been articulated by political leaders and the future of Indigenous-settler relations after a referendum—whether the constitution is amended or not—is deeply contested. Amidst all of this uncertainty, this chapter contends that it is beneficial to seek guidance from the experiences of other societies that have attempted to formalize and institutionalize modes of conflict transformation. In particular, it discusses the processes in South Africa and Northern Ireland to evaluate the extent to which they are instructive in the decisions that face Australia. Ultimately, I argue that there are valuable lessons about the processes—albeit in different contexts—which are not being heeded by Australia's failure to understand its process and the implications of current decisions for the future of Indigenous-settler.

Keywords Recognition · Comparative political theory · Australia · South Africa · Northern Ireland

Introduction

For much of the last 10 years, the idea of constitutional recognition of Aboriginal and Torres Strait Islander peoples has been on the political agenda in Australia. Following the reconciliation process that developed in the 1990s with the establishment of the Council for Aboriginal Reconciliation and the Apology to the Stolen Generations by the Rudd government in 2008, the idea of constitutional

A. Little (✉)
University of Melbourne, Parkville, Australia
e-mail: little@unimelb.edu.au

S. Maddison et al. (eds.), *The limits of settler colonial reconciliation*,
DOI 10.1007/978-981-10-2654-6_16

recognition came to the fore as a means of continuing discussion about the 'unfinished business of justice for Indigenous people' (Calma 2008). Following the 2010 Federal election, the Australian Labor Party (ALP) under Julia Gillard had to seek support from independents to form government and part of the deal that was struck was that the government would initiate a process leading to a referendum on constitutional recognition during the 43rd parliament. In the intervening 6 years we have witnessed bipartisan support amongst Australia's largest political parties for a process towards a referendum on constitutional recognition and a massive, publically funded campaign to persuade people of the benefits of such an initiative. The proposal to hold a referendum in May 2017 remains on the table, but progress towards this proposition has been painfully slow.

A number of significant questions sit behind all of these political developments. In no particular order, we could ask whether constitutional recognition is a positive development for Indigenous peoples in Australia? What would constitutional recognition look like and what would its implications be? Would it help to facilitate debate about a further initiative towards a treaty which many Indigenous people desire or would it inhibit moves towards further political and constitutional reform? How should we ascertain that there is support for constitutional recognition and how should we expect initiatives for further reform in Australian Indigenous political relations to be continued in the future if constitutional recognition was approved? This chapter will touch on most of these questions in one way or another but the key focus here is on the question of what is at stake in constitutional recognition for the different parties to the debate. The major focus will be on the stakes for Aboriginal and Torres Strait Islander peoples but, in the course of the discussion, reference will also be made to the different stakes at play for non-Indigenous people as well as the Australian government and the settler-colonial state.

The chapter proceeds through three main sections. The first sets out the theoretical and methodological foundations of the argument by examining the emergence of comparative political theory in recent years. It delineates the benefits of examining the conceptual underpinnings of transformational processes aimed at grappling with historical and structural injustice such as that taking place in Australia in a comparative light. The second section evaluates the very different experiences of South Africa and Northern Ireland in recent years as they have emerged from protracted political conflicts. The variations between these examples help to make clear that Australia faces political choices over the forms of institutional processes that are employed to pursue social and political justice for Aboriginal and Torres Strait Islander people.

Despite some similarities, the contrasts between the processes in South Africa and Northern Ireland alongside the continuation of political conflict after transitional processes in both cases, demonstrate some of the limitations in the dominant modes of conflict transformation around the world. In particular, we can see that largely political forms of accommodation focused on governing institutions as in Northern Ireland have failed to pay sufficient attention to legacy issues and their capacity to undermine peace agreements. In the case of South Africa, we can suggest that the more reconciliatory process focused on engagement between individual victims and individual perpetrators became too burdened with the hopes of a nation. Attempts to address structural inequalities and collective forms of injustice could not be accommodated within a process focused on individuals. Thus, it becomes clear that in both transitions, there were significant limitations in the processes that have been employed. This implies that political actors in any society wishing to transform its conflicts need to think very clearly about the types of institutions and mechanisms that are established (including the capacity of, and limitations on, what those bodies are able to achieve).

In light of these comparative experiences elsewhere, the third section of the chapter addresses directly the question of what is at stake for various groups in Australia in debates over constitutional recognition of Indigenous people and the implications of these stakes for the ways in which the requisite political processes are imagined. Thus, given the diversity in the stakes that are held between different groups, it becomes clear that the types of institutions that are developed and the political techniques that are deployed will cater better for some groups than others. It is evident that there are limitations on all potential mechanisms from one perspective or another. This means that the question of *how* the issues of structural injustice in the Australian case are tackled becomes incredibly politically loaded. It is not just a matter of choosing mechanisms and then letting the process begin. The nature of the mechanisms and institutions that are developed to manage the transformation of Indigenous-settler relations in Australia is a part of the conflict to be addressed.

The chapter concludes with a critical assessment of the debate on constitutional recognition since 2010 and an outline of potential ways in which a future-oriented process of addressing injustice towards Indigenous people might look radically different. It makes clear that the failure to take account of processes elsewhere (and their shortcomings) is a major failing of the Australian debate thus far. Moreover, this introspection and myopia has been compounded by a failure to debate the appropriate political processes for governing Indigenous-settler relations with all of those that have a stake in the issue. The upshot is the possibility of a referendum without a proper political process before or after the point of decision and that seems unlikely to deliver the kind of transformational moment that the advocates of constitutional recognition aspire to.

Comparative Approaches to Reconciliation and Conflict Transformation

In the first section I consider the emergence of comparative political theory in the last 20 years and the specific form of comparative political theory that is valuable in using analysis of other societies to make sense of contemporary political debates in Australia. While no two conflicts are the same, the methods that are employed to manage and transform them are almost inevitably based on experiences in other settings and the outcomes that ensued (McGarry 2001). It is also the case that particular forms of transformation such as transitional justice can become politically 'fashionable' as the growth of truth and reconciliation processes since the mid-1990s made clear (Goodman 2009; Minow 2009; Moon 2008) after the presumed success of the South African model. However, there was great variety in these processes. The ensuing debates between transitional justice advocates and their critics suggest that it is perilous to simply deploy experiences from one context onto another (Hayner 2010; McEvoy 2007). In light of this, it is pertinent to ask what the value of a comparative mode of political theory might be in understanding the conceptual underpinnings of transformational processes in different social and political settings?

In the last 20 years comparative political theory has emerged as a distinctive strand of political thought that may have something to offer in answering this question. Key advocates and commentators including Dallmayr (2010a, b), Euben (1997), Godrej (2011), Jenco (2007, 2016), March (2009) and Parel and Keith (2003) have been instrumental in the development of a perspective that attempts to relocate the canon of political theory within a wider paradigm of non-Western and post-colonial traditions. This approach has been articulated and analysed as a distinctive and at times coherent outlook on political theory more generally. As this perspective has matured however, debates have emerged about the range of different ideas that are promoted under the rubric of comparative political theory and, in particular, the widely varying methodologies that have been employed by its advocates (Freeden and Vincent 2013).

There are many variants within comparative theory and Freeden (2007) identifies at least five ways in which political theories can be compared. Two in particular are relevant for the forthcoming argument. Firstly, Freeden (2007: 5) identifies the approach focused on concepts as a perspective that concentrates on the analysis of a unit—the concept—that is of a 'sufficiently microscopic scale' to enable comparison of how it plays out in multiple contexts. This is undoubtedly a viable way in which comparative political theory can be conducted insofar as it enables analyses that grasp 'the subtlety of semantic differences resulting from minor shifts in argumentative architecture and ideational context' (Freeden 2007: 5). Secondly, however, it is also important to understand the contextual dimension of comparative political theory that focuses on identifying shared patterns of language in which we are able to single out 'both the unique and the overlapping in diverse cultural and ideological contexts' (Freeden 2007: 4). The ensuing argument marries these approaches in a comparative theoretical method that is both conceptual and contextual. This enables an analysis that evaluates framing concepts in conflict transformation—e.g. reconciliation and recognition—and the means by which they can be operationalized *in different ways* according to the contexts in which they are applied.

Comparative conceptual analysis has value in demonstrating the ways in which political concepts are malleable and indeterminate. Therefore, depending on the things to which they are applied and the manner of this application, the same political concepts can mean rather different things in practice. This is why it is important to couple conceptual analysis with rich and deep understandings of their political context. It enables an account of political concepts that recognises the impact of context on their practical ramifications as well as the multiple interpretations that all concepts are subject to. Following Freeden (2007: 7) this approach can alternatively be described as one that highlights that concepts are both 'constraints on' and 'enablers of' political action (Freeden 2007: 6).

Unlike those who seek to position comparative political theory as primarily a means of increased engagement between Western and non-Western traditions in political thought, Andrew March (2009: 537) makes a much more methodological point when he contends that comparative political theory needs '*a specific common object of inquiry*' and '*distinction*' between cases. In methodological terms then, there is nothing inherently comparative about broadening the canon; *what matters is how that broadening is able to make better sense of the concepts we use in similar but different contexts through comparison*. Comparative political theory is not just an exercise in filling in the gaps created by the myopia of dominant traditions or an exercise in parallelism (Browers 2003); it is also concerned with understanding the morphology of the dominant interpretations of the concepts we employ and thus the ways in which semantic and structural constraints affect the manner of translation into practical politics and hence the empirical evidence which is subsequently observable (Freeden 2007).

March's point is reinforced by Williams and Warren (2013: 11) who contend that '*comparative* political theory … is nothing other than the representation and reconstruction of systems of ideas that have arisen in cultures or civilizations different from our own'. By this definition, comparative analysis need not be between Western and non-Western societies at all but could be focused on the comparison of ideas that may now share the same geographical space. Indeed, one of the most interesting examples that could be employed in comparative political theory is the differential understandings of concepts between Indigenous and non-Indigenous groups that have co-existed in the same space over decades or centuries. This example implies that completely self-contained conceptions of political ideas in particular spaces are rare although there may be particular cultural or religious connotations in the way they are deployed. More frequently, the interpretations of concepts have been formed in interactions between alternative views and traditions. In short, comparative political theory is best considered as a mean of shedding light on the relationship between political ideas and different contexts rather than viewing it as a means of comparing bounded traditions containing hermetically sealed systems of political meaning.

To conclude this section, my contention here is that the conceptual-contextual approach is a valuable form of comparative political theory because the grounding of conceptual analysis in empirical contexts makes clear the key variables that are at stake and assists us in understanding the morphology of political concepts. Moreover, it brings a new dimension to understanding this morphology by tracing the evolution of concepts in different contexts, which makes clear the political choices that are available and unavailable when problems are framed in particular contextual circumstances. In other words, it sheds light on the malleability of political concepts but also their partial dependence on social structures and interpretations of the structural constraints within which they are understood and translated into courses of political action.

In the remainder of the Chap. 1 deploy this conceptual-contextual approach to evaluate the politics of debates on reconciliation and constitutional recognition and argue that a comparative approach helps to make clear both the ambiguities of the concept of reconciliation as well as the ways in which this conceptual indeterminacy can lead to very different practical implications in varied conflictual circumstances. Therefore, this comparative approach helps to make clear how political concepts can be operationalised in multiple ways and how possibilities for political action can be constrained and/or enabled by our interpretations of political concepts in particular contextual circumstances.

Conflict Transformation Processes in South Africa and Northern Ireland

While there are obviously many examples that could be used as comparators to make sense of Australia's recent debates on constitutional recognition, the cases for comparison here were selected on the basis of March's criteria above, namely, '*a specific common object of inquiry*' and '*distinction*' between cases (March 2009). Australia, South Africa and Northern Ireland are all societies that engaged with the idea of reconciliation after historical injustice and conflict in the 1990s only to pursue very different political strategies as a means of transforming conflict for the future. Thus, South Africa and Northern Ireland are useful comparators for Australia as, despite employing similar discourse and at the same temporal juncture, the three countries pursued very different pathways on the question of reconciliation in terms of political institutions and practices.

Reconciliation was at the forefront of the political rhetoric in the South African transition and played a pivotal role in the 'moral imagination' of what a new South Africa would look like (du Toit 2017). Of course, it also translated into practical politics with the institutional formation of the Truth and Reconciliation Commission. In Northern Ireland however, after the contentious nature of reconciliation became clear in the mid 1990s, the peace process that subsequently took place occurred without direct reference to reconciliation. Indeed, to this day, Northern Ireland continues to struggle to address what are euphemistically referred to as 'legacy issues' and there is no agreed process for doing so. These different approaches have varying implications for the choices that Australia faces at the current time and they highlight the importance of those decisions for the shape of the debate about the past, present and future in contemporary Australian politics.

Among the most important contextual factors in this comparison is the significant variety in the compositional constituencies in the three cases. In South Africa, the transitional process was primarily about achieving justice for the significant non-White majority that had suffered under the Apartheid regime. In Northern

Ireland, the civil rights movement of the 1960s that inadvertently sparked the Troubles had been about rights for a significant minority of around 40 % of the population who identified as Catholics and/or nationalists. In Australia however, the case for reconciliation with or recognition for Aboriginal and Torres Strait Islander people is a case focused on less than 3 % of the population.

Therefore, in Australia, not only is there an absence of violent resistance to the established regime that characterised South Africa and Northern Ireland, but there is also a situation where the 'problem' that needs to be addressed can be construed as less pressing because the number of people suffering injustice is relatively insignificant compared to other countries. Moreover, the relatively small number of people affected by these injustices in comparative terms, assists the perception that the relationship between Indigenous and non-Indigenous people in Australia is not a conflictual one (Little and Macmillan 2016). Likewise, the small proportion of people involved in the experience of injustice in Australia has meant that it has not garnered the same degree of international interest compared to the other two countries in the study. For example, South Africa became an international pariah and suffered sanctions while the United Kingdom had to deal with a situation of considerable unrest within its own borders with substantial pressure from the outside (particularly the United States and, to a lesser extent, the European Union) to resolve the situation. These compositional dynamics have quite profound implications for stakeholders in the debate on constitutional recognition in Australia as they place Indigenous people in a much less powerful position than was the case for those pursuing justice in the other comparator countries.

So this chapter is less concerned about whether the conflicts are directly comparable and more focused on the comparative lessons that might be harnessed from the kinds of *processes* that have been undertaken to transform these situations. Of course, these are related to the specific contexts in which they operate but they also shed light on the choices ahead of Australia in the debate on constitutional recognition. From this perspective, there is not a *single* debate on constitutional recognition (and/or reconciliation) in Australia but rather a series of choices about how we pursue the debate that relate to and help to shape the nature of the debate itself. Put simply, the nature of the process matters and the experiences of other contexts are valuable in clarifying the kinds of decisions that need to be taken about processes and institutions.

South Africa

Not surprisingly, in examining many conflict transformation processes from the outside, the role of domestic leadership is often given a higher priority in political analysis than the structures and processes that were agreed. In the South African case, there is considerable focus on Mandela, De Klerk, Tutu, Ramaphosa and so forth and undoubtedly these actors were pivotal to change in different ways (Glad and Blanton 1997). Indeed, all political leaders are significant in this respect whether they agree with transitional processes or not. Quite often, the transitional process requires a simultaneous rhetoric and performance of war and peace. There are multiple audiences to speak to and they often want to hear different things. The capacity to speak to multiple audiences simultaneously—or what in the Northern Irish case has been alluded to as 'constructive ambiguity' (Aughey 2005)—is a precise skill, but agents require a structure and a process that enables them to do so. Political actors by themselves cannot create the structural conditions that facilitate this degree of rhetorical acumen and so it is vital to attend to those conditions as well as trying to encourage the 'right' kinds of interlocutors.

The focus on individual actors as the midwives of transition also draws attention away from the fact that all conflict transformation processes are full of setbacks and failures. While individual actors can enhance transformational processes, the *longue durée* of the processes themselves extends well beyond the capacity of one set of individuals in a given point of time to bring about lasting change. There are many similarities between South Africa and Northern Ireland in this respect. In South Africa there were two failed constitutional conventions preceding the final negotiated settlement and constitution as well as many preliminary events that have not been as prominent in the historical account of the transition, such as the National Peace Accord in 1991 (du Toit 2017). The National Peace Accord was a major multi-organisation event involving a range of civil society actors as well as many political parties. Its significance is not so much concerned with what it achieved directly but more in terms of how it enabled a rhetorical process of agenda-setting that fashioned a sense of commonality and inclusivity. This points to the importance of engendering the rhetorical space for change through a process of engagement rather than through attempting to forge an agreement that precedes such rhetorical space. In short, processes of engagement across difference and conflict create the imaginative space to bring about change rather than it being agreed upon before such processes take place.

The Truth and Reconciliation Commission in South Africa has generated a substantial literature. However, perhaps a little too much emphasis—at least in international circles—has been placed on the Truth and Reconciliation Commission (TRC) as an institutional manifestation of reconciliation and conflict transformation in South Africa with less attention to the problems of this kind of approach (Norval 1998; Moon 2008). While the TRC was undoubtedly highly significant in the transitional process, it was clearly incapable of delivering 'justice' of the kind that Mandela advocated for a subordinated group of people. Rather the TRC was concerned with delivering truth and reconciliation between individual perpetrators and their victims—and dealt with them in precisely these terms as 'perpetrator' and 'victim'—instead of being capable of delivering a broader sense of social justice that was attendant to the structural injustices that had been experienced by non-Whites under the Apartheid regime. The perceived shortcomings of the TRC are not necessarily reflective of what it was established to do and we need to be wary of expecting institutions to achieve things that cannot possibly be part of their mandate (Wilson 2001). Part of the reason for focusing on processes in phases of transition is to have a clearer understanding of what we can expect institutions to achieve and the impediments to their capacity to meet their objectives.

Regardless of the precise institutional architecture used to facilitate change, I contend that a sense of process helps to overcome the inevitable failures and setbacks of transitional initiatives. It engenders the perception of a shared dynamic of continued engagement even when processes do not seem to be progressing and it also facilitates discussion of alternative options. What this requires of political actors—especially political leaders—is a sense of the long game. While action is always required in the political present, the broader sense of a process of negotiating the terms of our togetherness across difference—or the degree of acceptable apartness—and the 'moral imagination' it can create leaves space for understanding the emergence of alternative forms of working through political conflicts. Ultimately, as Doxtader (2009) makes clear, reconciliation meant many things in South Africa and it required acts of political creativity to enable it to develop alongside the processes it invoked.

Northern Ireland

The actual process in Northern Ireland (as opposed to its content or the precise choreography) bears some remarkable similarities to the transitional process in South Africa. While Northern Ireland's peace process is usually associated with the decade of change in the 1990s, it is clear that there was a 'process' before the official peace process and it continued after the 1998 Good Friday Agreement (GFA) (Wilford 2001; Aughey 2005). Like South Africa, Northern Ireland's experience was a stop-start affair with periods of considerable progress punctuated by setbacks and failures. Ceasefires broke down. Political events in Westminster changed the context in which decisions on Northern Ireland could be taken. Forms of engagement between conflicting parties endured walk-outs and withdrawals. All the while, however, the process continued, shored up by high profile and highly symbolic international visits from the likes of the then president of the United States, Bill Clinton. Even the basic fact of getting the parties in a room to talk to each other involved a choreographed process of phases including the initial refusal to talk, 'talks about talks' (parties discussing whether they were prepared to talk to each other), and 'proximity talks' (where parties agreed to attend the same building but sit in different rooms while officials shuttled between them). As such, the 'process' was not linear, sequential and progressive as the post-1998 period demonstrates. Instead, it should be viewed as a series of interlinked phases which included the major 'event' of the GFA, but which had to continue after 1998 and still evolves today (Little 2009a, b). Despite many setbacks however, a sense of a broader process of governing with conflict has maintained momentum.

The 1998 Agreement has been described as an exercise in constructive ambiguity (Dixon 2002; McVeigh and Rolston 2007; Wilford 2001). It offered sufficient safeguards to all sides of the political landscape while also containing potential promise that agreement would eventually lead to favourable outcomes for their particular viewpoints. However, some care should be exercised in treating the 1998 Agreement as *the* 'event' without comprehending the surrounding end ensuing developments within which it was operationalised. Of course, the Agreement itself was symbolically important but it was also subject to referenda on both sides of the border with a majority in both Northern Ireland and the Republic of Ireland needed for its further passage. Furthermore, the referendum in Northern Ireland required majority support on both sides of the ethno-national divide. While the Agreement passed the referendum in the Republic easily (94 % support) and was widely supported among the Catholic-Nationalist minority in the North, it is estimated to have only mustered 57 % support among Protestant-Unionists (Hayes and McAllister 2001). While this constituted success, it also meant that there was considerable opposition from the outset.

This opposition was immediately obvious in the delay in implementing the Agreement. For 2 years after it was passed, there was an impasse based on the provision about the decommissioning of paramilitary weapons. Opponents asked a series of questions about whether paramilitary weapons had been decommissioned. How could we tell if they had been? What sort of proof would be required? How would we know if *all* of them had been decommissioned? Couldn't paramilitaries just acquire more weapons? This period after the Agreement required an intensive and extended period of shuttle diplomacy by Senator George Mitchell travelling weekly from Washington to Belfast to encourage interlocutors to move beyond the impasse to the implementation of the GFA's institutions (Schulze and Smith 2000). It should be obvious from this example that the process did not end with the 'event' of the Agreement. Rather it was just the latest staging post or punctuation mark in a process that must be ongoing.

As the Northern Ireland process has evolved after the Agreement, there have continued to be blockages and setbacks that at times have seemed to bring it close to an ongoing return to Westminster rule, if not a return to the violence of the past. Two further agreements at St. Andrews and Hillsborough have been required to prevent the Agreement's institutions from collapsing. Northern Ireland seems as far away as ever on being able to agree processes to manage 'legacy' issues including moving beyond a hierarchy of victimhood, discussing collusion between the state and loyalist paramilitaries in unsolved murders, and dealing with the victims of republican paramilitaries known as the 'disappeared' (Lundy and McGovern 2008).

The case of Northern Ireland since the 1998 Agreement demonstrates that processes continue long after the 'event' and that, despite key initiatives such as the signing of agreements or constitutional changes, everyday life in divided polities remains deeply contentious (Little 2014). There is considerable evidence that Belfast is a more divided city in sectarian terms than it was during the Troubles. For example, the number of peace lines, walls and fences dividing communities in the city has increased by at least 50 % since 1998 (Gormley-Heenan et al. 2013). Moreover, the institutions created by the GFA were designed in such a way that they enshrined sectarian divisions by requiring power sharing (Wilford 2001). Therefore, the consociational structures established by the GFA helped to perpetuate the divisions it was designed to address and sectarian division remains a defining motif of Northern Irish politics and society today (Taylor 2009).

Like South Africa, the experience of Northern Ireland is one of a constant process of negotiating the terms of living together (and, in some cases, 'managing apartness'). This makes clear that attentiveness to the enduring nature of conflicts and the need for continuing processes of managing and transforming them is paramount. The question remains as to what the lessons are from the comparison of the processes in South Africa and Northern Ireland for the current debate on constitutional recognition in Australia. One of the key points to highlight here is that the different participants and interlocutors in the transformative processes in South Africa and Northern Ireland had very different stakes in the debate. Certainly, in both examples, there was broad support in society for social and political change (not least to end political violence) but it is important to recognise that there were also considerable pockets of opposition to the processes that were initiated. This was a clear indicator that the participants in the debate had very different stakes and they influenced the political outlooks of some groups differently than others. Political choices had to be made which assessed this variety of claims and placed particular emphasis on some claims more than others in the processes that were eventually followed. However, these decisions were taken as part of the process rather than pre-emptively before a process could begin. Understanding the stakes in play is vital to political advancement and is pivotal to developing a process of engagement between competing perspectives. In the next section, I extend these comparative insights to Australia by asking what is at stake in recent debates around constitutional recognition of Indigenous peoples and what implications might they have for the political processes that are designed to address historical and contemporary injustices.

What is at Stake in the Australian Constitutional Recognition Debate?

In South Africa and Northern Ireland the stakes were clearly very high and widely understood. Both conflicts were characterised by political violence and it was evident that long-term stability and a move toward less violent forms of conflict was going to require substantial political change, with key concessions required from all participants in the process. The stakes in the Australian constitutional recognition debate have not been as widely discussed or understood. However, this section attempts to plot these stakes to make clear how they may influence the dynamics of the process and the design of institutions whether constitutional recognition is achieved or not.

Since the election of the Gillard government in 2010, with its reliance on the support of independents, the issue of constitutional recognition of Aboriginal and Torres Strait Islander people has been part of the national agenda and has, for the most part, received bipartisan support. The Gillard government subsequently appointed an Expert Panel (comprised of both Indigenous and non-Indigenous members) to consult and then formulate a proposal for a constitutional amendment. Following the debate over the proposed wording of an amendment after the Expert Panel's recommendations, the Abbott Coalition government sent the recommendations to a Joint Select Committee for further consideration and review. In 2015, the Abbott government consulted with four key Indigenous leaders: Megan Davis, Pat Dodson, Kirstie Parker and Noel Pearson and Abbott also invited forty Indigenous leaders to Kirribilli House to meet him and the leader of the Australian Labor Party, Bill Shorten. At that meeting, the importance of a 'black process' was reiterated by the Indigenous leadership with an appeal to Abbott and Shorten to provide the requisite resources. Shorten was much quicker than Abbott to accede to this demand before, in September 2015, Abbott was deposed as leader of the Liberal Party in his own party room by Malcolm Turnbull.

After three months of inactivity (in public at least), Turnbull eventually announced the formation of a Referendum Council (comprised of Indigenous and non-Indigenous members) in December 2015 tasked with smoothing the way to constitutional recognition. This has meant that a process that was initially slated to take place by 2013 is now being directed towards a referendum in May 2017 to mark the 50th anniversary of the 1967 referendum. The process has been unplanned and haphazard, with the numerous changes of direction implying that there is much at stake in getting this right but little rigorous planning as to how to achieve the key objectives. Indeed, there appear to be rather conflicting objectives in contemporary Indigenous and non-Indigenous Australia and few political mechanisms designed to enable their expression. Without such an engagement between conflicting parties, it is difficult to see how such a disorganised approach to the process of constitutional recognition could deliver outcomes that would satisfy key stakeholders. In the sections below I discuss what these various stakes might be for different stakeholders.

The Stakes for Aboriginal and Torres Strait Islander People

The stakes for Aboriginal and Torres Strait Islander peoples in the debate on constitutional recognition are incredibly high with pressure being place on them to understand and accept that this is a 'once in a generation' opportunity (Recognise 2014). However, the stakes are equally high in accepting a diluted proposition that is designed to attain consensus. After all, Indigenous people have lived without constitutional recognition for a very long time and, for those who see value in such recognition, anything short of a reconstituted 'lawful relationship' between the state and Aboriginal and Torres Strait Islander people remains a very dangerous proposition. In this pursuit the racial provisions in the constitution are significant and promise to be a major stumbling block with constitutional conservatives. However, equally important and potentially just as controversial, is the need to improve the institutional recognition of Indigenous people and their capacity for some form(s) of self-government. For Indigenous supporters of constitutional recognition, it is vital as Pat Dodson has argued that any change leaves open the possibility of further discussion about a treaty (The Guardian 2016).

Importantly, for many Aboriginal and Torres Strait Islander people, the debate needs to be framed around their relationship with *the state and its laws,* which is not necessarily how the mainstream debate is being pursued where the focus is more on relations between Indigenous and non-Indigenous *people* (Recognise no date). Moreover this confusion leads to a further *conceptual* blurring of discussions about what a referendum may be about. For non-Indigenous Australians, the conversation appears to be about formal equality in strictly legal terms, whereas, for Indigenous people, the discussion is more about recognition of their difference. The Constitution already treats Indigenous people differently so the discussion is about trying to right the injustices of the recognition of difference that already exists rather than promoting an agenda of sameness. Indeed, a discussion based on the idea of sameness (and mere equal treatment) would be anathema to many Indigenous activists (Little and Macmillan 2016).

The other major issue at stake is of course for those Aboriginal and Torres Strait Island activists who seek to preserve longer-term aspirations towards a treaty and a clearer recognition of sovereignty. While it could be argued that constitutional recognition could be viewed as another stepping stone on the way to a more substantive engagement with Indigenous peoples (The Guardian 2016), it is equally likely that a process of constitutional recognition could lead to marginalization of more substantive demands. It is impossible to judge on this point until we are clear about what it is that we might be asked to vote on, but there is growing evidence that the pursuit of consensus might dampen a form of wording that would allow for the need for more radical engagement in the future. This points to the possibility of cracks emerging in the bipartisan agreement over what recognition is designed to achieve (Sydney Morning Herald 2016). This constantly raises the stakes for Indigenous opponents of constitutional recognition. Moreover, constitutional recognition might reduce the appetite for more substantive change in the future and effectively defer discussions of a treaty. In this sense, there is likely to be considerable opposition from Aboriginal and Torres Strait Islander people, as has been signalled in early consultations on the matter in Victoria (Victorian Government 2016).

This raises one final issue in terms of the stakes for Indigenous people. This is the stake of rejecting the process until something more substantive has been agreed and established. This approach would reject the arbitrary timelines that have been established so far and seek to establish proper grounds for engagement about all of the issues. This approach raises the issue of timing because there is likely to be no means of actually establishing whether Indigenous people as a group are in favour of any proposed form of recognition in the actual referendum (if it takes place in 2017). After all, as only 3 % of the population, Aboriginal and Torres Strait Islanders people could vote 'No' *en masse* and it would be barely identifiable. Consultation mechanisms on constitutional recognition that have been mentioned fall well short of what could be construed as a representative sample (The Australian 2016). In other words, as a matter of strategy, any Indigenous opposition to the process as a whole needs to start long before we get to the actual point of a referendum. While it is likely that many progressive non-Indigenous Australians would not vote 'Yes' if they knew there was little Indigenous support, there may well be no actual means of identifying this opposition unless it is clearly articulated and various media are active in enabling the articulation of oppositional voices.

The Stakes for Non-Indigenous Australia

The situation is different for a wide range of non-Indigenous Australians. Those most opposed to constitutional recognition are constitutional conservatives and, more worryingly, others associated with a range of relatively small right wing groups who oppose the terms in which it might even be deemed necessary to deal with these questions. The greatest fear of both of these constituencies is that a large consensus is generated around very benign forms of constitutional recognition in a referendum but which leave open the door for more radical developments towards discussions of a treaty in the future. As indicated above, this looks unlikely to be the case while Treaty discussions remain on the margins of the mainstream debate, which means that the right has very little skin in the game as it stands. This is partly deliberate on the part of consecutive governments that do want to unleash the forces of opposition by encouraging more substantive demands. Nonetheless it is likely that the far right as well as constitutional conservatives will mount forms of opposition regardless of what is actually proposed. To this extent, it seems that the stakes are largely symbolic for these groups.

However, the stakes seem higher for progressives who recognise historical and contemporary injustices against Aboriginal and Torres Strait Islander people. For many of these non-Indigenous Australians, unable to actually ascertain whether Indigenous people support the proposed referendum question (given we don't know what it will be) and encouraged by public campaigns (e.g. Recognise) that we should support it (regardless of what it actually might be), it is difficult to maintain an oppositional perspective. At the time of writing, it looks likely that some of the faultlines may be beginning to open with more coverage of Indigenous opposition to constitutional recognition and this may create obstacles to the shepherding of non-Indigenous support around a Yes vote in a referendum. However, one of the risks for non-Indigenous progressives is that their 'white guilt' (Maddison 2011) will not be assuaged given that the degree of opposition to constitutional recognition from Indigenous people may not actually become apparent until after a referendum has been held.

A third group (and probably much the largest) is comprised of those who are not particularly aligned but will have to vote on the matter. Many of these people will potentially be swayed by campaigns in favour of recognition and, if it is a fairly benign and insubstantial constitutional amendment, will have nothing to lose from their 'Yes' vote. However, this group has relatively little at stake in the issue and could be dragged to the right by scaremongering about more substantive change. While the stakes are not high for this group themselves, there is a distinct possibility that they will turn around to Indigenous peoples and say 'we gave you what you want and still you ask for more' if there is a Yes vote that subsequently triggers Indigenous activism for a treaty. Therefore, while the stakes might not be high at the time of a referendum, they may well get very much higher in the future and that is a ripe breeding ground for the political right. Therefore, the process of understanding the stakes of recognition needs to be understood within a longer timeframe than the period leading up to a referendum.

The Stakes for the Australian Government

It is well documented that the stakes for any government in going to a referendum are high as it is not generally advisable to lose a referendum vote in such a short electoral cycle as occurs in Australia. As such, Australian governments need to be very confident that they are going to win should they support a proposed change to constitutional arrangements. This is compounded by the fact that successful referenda are notoriously difficult to achieve because of the constitutional requirements in Australian law (AHRC no date). Moreover, in terms of Indigenous affairs, no government wants to be seen as one that oversaw a failed attempt to recognise Aboriginal and Torres Strait Islander people. Therefore, the process appears to be have been designed to find the path of least resistance to a minimal form of recognition that will be so anodyne that it will not generate any visceral opposition from most Australians. Success in a referendum would be construed as a major achievement and presented as an act of reconciliation. However, it could also further reduce the prominence of Indigenous affairs in Australian public debate and enable governments to focus on much more practical—though difficult—matters such as 'closing the gap' (ABC 2016).

In the campaign for the 2016 Federal election there was evidence that the bipartisan support for constitutional recognition was beginning to fray. The ALP leader, Bill Shorten, indicated his support for the argument advanced by the Indigenous ALP Senator, Pat Dodson, that constitutional recognition could be a precursor to treaty discussions. This generated a hostile reaction from the Liberal Party including the Prime Minister, Malcolm Turnbull, who indicated that Shorten was threatening the bipartisan support for recognition because the Liberals did not support a treaty (Chalmers 2016). This echoed the sentiments of former leader, John Howard, who suggested that it was absurd for a country to establish a treaty with its own people (Bennan et al. 2004). Although this debate was a footnote in an election campaign where Indigenous affairs did not feature prominently, it does highlight a broader schism in Australian politics that the bipartisan approach to constitutional recognition has papered over. Given that a Yes vote would be unlikely to end campaigns for more substantive change in Australian society and a move towards a treaty, the bipartisan approach seems to only go as far as a fairly minimalist approach to constitutional recognition and could dissipate soon after a successful Yes campaign.

Conclusion: Why Australia is Getting it Wrong

The post-conflict experiences of Northern Ireland and South Africa are sobering and point to the need for a continuing process after landmark events have taken place. However, Australia has struggled to imagine a debate where the different stakes and opposing arguments alluded to above are given proper ventilation. The current debate on constitutional recognition in Australia is taking place:

- without an agreed process
- with a highly problematic and rushed timeline (forced by the proposal of an arbitrary deadline) which does not allow for a proper process
- with considerable expenditure on a campaign to get people to vote in favour of something that has not yet been decided and where we do not know if it has widespread Aboriginal and Torres Strait Islander support
- based on an ill-considered pursuit of consensus above a proper process of dialogue
- and with huge political stakes (that vary considerably between different groups).

This points to the fact that in the Australian debate we are failing to engage with the normal processes of this kind of conflict transformation including the attendant expectations of failure, setbacks and disappointment (Little 2017). Arguably, these kinds of setbacks are the major drivers of continuing processes of change, and yet we are not prepared to countenance them in the Australian debate. Instead, proposals are likely to be diluted by an artificial consensus designed not to agitate constitutional conservatives. This suggests that there is little understanding of the process of change and little consideration of the benefits that might accrue from a dialogue with dissenting voices be they from constitutional conservatives or Indigenous activists pursuing treaty and a more substantive sense of justice. This failure to establish a process of dialogue with dissenting views is compounded by the unwillingness to ascertain that there is in fact widespread Indigenous support for the process let alone the final referendum question. To date, the engagement has mainly been between various Prime Ministers and handpicked 'representatives' of Aboriginal and Torres Strait Islander peoples. Latterly, there has been more engagement with Indigenous communities and their leadership but to a very limited extent despite the claims of the Referendum Council that consultations will be 'thorough and inclusive' (DPMC 2016). Therefore, there has been limited capacity for these people to select their own representatives for their voices and hence arguments for treaty and discussions of sovereignty and justice have not made it on to the mainstream political agenda.

As things stand then, we have the possibility of a vote on a minimalist proposal that gains majority support because (a) it poses no threat to White Australia so the stakes are low, and (b) we do not know the degree of support from Indigenous peoples.

Beyond trying to assuage white guilt, the merits of such a process are limited and they offer little in trying to continue the debate that many Aboriginal and Torres Strait Islanders want about a treaty (or a series of agreements between a variety of Indigenous groups and the state). On the contrary, we need to make the case for a more open discussion about the process itself, representation therein, and the topics that are on the table for discussion. A more inclusive discussion would not only engage Indigenous opponents of constitutional recognition but also constitutional conservatives. Such a process is much more arduous and various groups may withdraw from and then return to the conversation over the course of time. However, the experiences of South Africa and Northern Ireland tell us that a sense of momentum is important in any such process of change. In other words, people may withdraw from time to time but they do so knowing that the conversation and the process is going to continue regardless.

Put quite simply, until we get to the starting line of imagining this kind of engagement, we haven't even started a proper conversation, let alone established a meaningful process towards constitutional recognition. That a 'Yes' vote in a referendum might happen without such a process occurring, points to the likely failure of constitutional recognition to meet any of the aspirations of transforming relations in Australian society. Moreover, the demands of Aboriginal and Torres Strait Islander peoples for a lawful relationship that reflects historical injustices against them and the need to recognise their difference in the future will remain unfulfilled through constitutional recognition.

References

Aughey, A. (2005). *The politics of Northern Ireland: Beyond the Belfast Agreement*. London: Routledge.

Australian Broadcasting Corporation (ABC). (2016). *Closing the gap: Australia is failing to close the gap on indigenous disadvantage*. http://www.abc.net.au/news/2016-02-10/australia-failing-to-close-the-gap-on-indigenous-disadvantage/7153234. Accessed July 13 2016.

Australian Human Rights Commission (AHRC). (no date). *Historical lessons for a successful referendum*. https://www.humanrights.gov.au/publications/constitutional-reform-fact-sheet-historical-lessons-successful-referendum. Accessed 13 July 2016.

Bennan, S., Gunn, B., & Williams, G. (2004). 'Laws, J. 2000, Interview with John Howard, Prime Minister of Australia (Sydney, 29 May 2000), quoted in Bennan, S. Gunn, B. and Williams, G. 2004, "'Sovereignty' and its Relevance to Treaty-Making Between Indigenous Peoples and Australian Governments", in the *Sydney Law Review*, Volume 26, Number 3, p. 308.

Browers, M. (2003). The reconciliation of political theory and comparative politics. In J. S. Holmes (Ed.), *New approaches to comparative politics: Insights from political theory*. Lanham, MD: Lexington.

Calma, T. (2008). *Let the Healing Begin: Response to Government to the National Apology to the Stolen Generations*. Sydney: Human Rights and Equal Opportunities Commission, February 13.
Chalmers, M. (2016). Turnbull attacks shorten on treaty, contradicts government's own 'recognise' campaign. *New Matilda*, https://newmatilda.com/2016/06/14/turnbull-attacks-shorten-on-treaty-contradicts-governments-own-recognise-campaign/. Accessed 13 July 2016.
Dallmayr, F. (ed.) (2010a). Introduction. In *Comparative political theory: An introduction*. London: Palgrave Macmillan, pp. 3–6.
Dallmayr, F. (ed.) (2010b). Beyond monologue: For a comparative political theory. In *Comparative political theory: An introduction*. London: Palgrave Macmillan, pp 7–20.
Department of Prime Minister and Cabinet (DPMC). (2016). *Referendum Council Communique, 10 May 2016*. https://www.dpmc.gov.au/sites/default/files/publications/referendum-council-communique-10-may-2016.pdf. Accessed 15 July 2016.
Dixon, P. (2002). Political skills or lying and manipulation? The choreography of the Northern Ireland peace process. *Political Studies, 50*(4), 725–741.
Doxtader, E. (2009). *With faith in the works of words: The beginnings of reconciliation in South Africa, 1985–1995*. Cape Town: David Philip.
du Toit, F. (2017). A broken promise? Evaluating South Africa's reconciliation process twenty years on. *International Political Science Review* (forthcoming).
Euben, R. (1997). Comparative political theory: An islamic fundamentalist critique of rationalism. *The Journal of Politics, 59*(1), 28–55.
Freeden, M. (2007). Editorial: The comparative study of political thinking. *Journal of Political Ideologies, 12*(1), 1–9.
Freeden, M., & Vincent, A. (Eds.). (2013). *Comparative political thought: Theorizing practices*. London: Routledge.
Glad, B., & Blanton, R. (1997). FW de Klerk and Nelson Mandela: A study in cooperative transformational leadership. *Presidential Studies Quarterly, 27*(3), 565–590.
Godrej, F. (2011). *Cosmopolitan political thought: method, practice, discipline*. Oxford: Oxford University Press.
Goodman, T. (2009). *Staging solidarity: Truth and reconciliation in a new South Africa*. Boulder, CO: Paradigm.
Gormley-Heenan, C., Byrne, J., & Robinson, G. (2013). The Berlin walls of Change to Belfast. *British Politics, 8*(3), 357–382.
Hayes, B. C., & McAllister, I. (2001). Who voted for peace? Public support for the 1998 Northern Ireland agreement. *Irish Political Studies, 16*(1), 73–93.
Hayner, P. B. (2010). *Unspeakable truths: Transitional justice and the challenge of truth commissions*. London: Routledge.
Jenco, L. (2007). "What does heaven ever say?" A methods-centered approach to cross-cultural engagement. *American Political Science Review, 101*(4), 741–755.
Jenco, L. (2016). New pasts for new futures: A temporal reading of global thought. *Constellations* (forthcoming).
Little, A. (2009a). Sunningdale for slow learners: Towards a complexity paradigm. In R. Taylor (Ed.), *Consociational Theory*. London: Routledge.
Little, A. (2009b). The Northern Ireland paradox. In A. Little & M. Lloyd (Eds.), *The politics of radical democracy*. Edinburgh: Edinburgh University Press.
Little, A. (2014). *Enduring conflict: Challenging the signature of peace and democracy*. New York: Bloomsbury.
Little, A. (2017). Fear, hope and disappointment: The politics of reconciliation and the dynamics of conflict transformation. *International Political Science Review* (forthcoming).
Little, A., & Macmillan, M. (2016). Invisibility and the politics of reconciliation in Australia: Keeping conflict in view. *Ethnopolitics*. doi:10.1080/17449057.2016.1219473.
Lundy, P., & McGovern, M. (2008). Truth, justice and dealing with the legacy of the past in Northern Ireland, 1998–2008. *Ethnopolitics, 7*(1), 177–193.
Maddison, S. (2011). *Beyond white guilt*. Sydney: Allen & Unwin.
March, A. F. (2009). What is comparative political theory. *The Review of Politics, 71*, 531–565.

McEvoy, K. (2007). Beyond legalism: Towards a thicker understanding of transitional justice. *Journal of Law and Society, 34*(4), 411–440.
McGarry, J. (Ed.). (2001). *Northern Ireland and the divided world: Post-agreement Northern Ireland in comparative perspective*. Oxford: Oxford University Press.
McVeigh, R., & Rolston, B. (2007). From Good Friday to good relations: Sectarianism, racism and the Northern Ireland State. *Race and Class, 48*(4), 1–23.
Minow, M. (2009). *Breaking the cycles of hatred: Memory, law, and repair*. Princeton, NJ: Princeton University Press.
Moon, C. (2008). *Narrating political reconciliation: South Africa's Truth and Reconciliation Commission*. Lanham, Md: Lexington Books.
Norval, A. J. (1998). Memory, Identity and the (im)possibility of Reconciliation: The work of the Truth and Reconciliation Commission in South Africa. *Constellations, 5*(2), 250–265.
Parel, A. J., & Keith, R. C. (Eds.). (2003). *Comparative political philosophy: Studies under the upas tree*. Lanham, MD: Lexington.
Recognise. (2014). *Once in a generation opportunity*. http://www.recognise.org.au/blogs/once-in-a-generation-opportunity/. Accessed 13 July 2016.
Recognise. (no date). *Strengthening relations between Indigenous and non-Indigenous Australians*. http://www.recognise.org.au/wp-content/uploads/shared/downloads/c6fcbd6e605aa813d4e1.pdf. Accessed 13 July 2016.
Schulze, K. E., & Smith, M. L. R. (2000). Decommissioning and paramilitary strategy in Northern Ireland: A problem compared. *The Journal of Strategic Studies, 23*(4), 77–106.
Sydney Morning Herald. (2016, June 14). *Indigenous leaders push for treaty negotiations as Macolm Turnbull agrees with "invasion"*. http://www.smh.com.au/federal-politics/federal-election-2016/federal-election-2016-indigenous-leaders-push-for-treaty-negotiations-as-malcolm-turnbull-agrees-with-invasion-20160614-gpiwqg.html. Accessed July 13, 2016.
Taylor, R. (Ed.). (2009). *Consociational theory: McGarry and O'Leary and the Northern Ireland conflict*. London: Routledge.
The Australian. (2016, April 30). *Recognise the limits of constitutional recognition*. http://www.theaustralian.com.au/news/inquirer/recognise-the-limits-of-indigenous-constitutional-recognition/news-story/75f38b448ed42b91ba66ba2e027734cc. Accessed 13 July 2016.
The Guardian. (2016, May 9). *Labor's Patrick Dodson says Indigenous treaty should be an option*. https://www.theguardian.com/australia-news/2016/may/09/labors-patrick-dodson-says-indigenous-treaty-should-be-an-option. Accessed 13 July 2016.
Victorian Government. (2016, March 26). *Statement on self-determination*. http://www.premier.vic.gov.au/statement-on-self-determination. Accessed 13 July 2016.
Wilford, R. (Ed.). (2001). *Aspects of the Belfast agreement*. Oxford: Oxford University Press.
Williams, M. S., & Warren, M. E. (2013). A democratic case for comparative political theory. *Political Theory, 42*(1), 26–57.
Wilson, R. (2001). *The politics of truth and reconciliation in South Africa: Legitimizing the post-apartheid state*. Cambridge: Cambridge University Press.

Erratum to: The Poetics of Non-Indigenous Reflexive Self-awareness: Strategies of Embodiment and Delegation in Focus Group Discussions in Australia

Angélique Stastny, Sasha Henriss-Anderssen and Tom Clark

Erratum to:
Chapter 10 in: S. Maddison et al. (eds.), *The Limits of Settler Colonial Reconciliation*, DOI 10.1007/978-981-10-2654-6_10

The original version of the book was inadvertently published with chapter author names as keywords in Chapter 10. The erratum chapter has been updated with the correct keywords.

The updated original online version for this chapter can be found at 10.1007/978-981-10-2654-6_10

A. Stastny (✉)
University of Melbourne, Parkville, Australia
e-mail: a.stastny@student.unimelb.edu.au

S. Henriss-Anderssen · T. Clark
Victoria University, Melbourne, Australia
e-mail: Sasha.Henriss-Andersse@vu.edu.au

T. Clark
e-mail: Tom.Clark@vu.edu.au

S. Maddison et al. (eds.), *The limits of settler colonial reconciliation*,
DOI 10.1007/978-981-10-2654-6_17

Appendix
Research Methodology

Angelique Stastny, Sarah Maddison, Sasha Henriss-Anderssen, Ravi de Costa and Tom Clark

Background and Overview

Chapters 10, 12, and 14 of this collection, written by the editors and their associates, arise directly from a research project that explores non-Indigenous identities, attitudes, and understandings in relation to the prospects for 'Aboriginal reconciliation' in Australia. With support from the Australian Research Council's Discovery scheme, the project has used focus groups and one-to-one interviews to explore a highly complex and circumscribed public topic at the everyday level of non-Indigenous Australians living and working in their local communities. The project provided much of the impetus to convene the workshop that has produced this book. In this appendix, we summarize key points of the project's methodology, principally in order to offer a richer context for the origins of those three chapters.

The project is titled 'Non-Indigenous pathways to reconciliation in Australia.' It has drawn heavily on international evidence and new empirical data in an effort to contribute to local and international knowledge of reconciliation processes, including a focus on their capacity to create social change through a greater engagement among non-Indigenous people. It has been the first such research undertaken in Australia, although it builds on qualitative research that Tom Clark and Ravi de Costa undertook in Canada, combined with the agonistic orientation towards reconciliation that Sarah Maddison has developed over successive recent works. The culmination of that approach was to pose the question: how can public and less public versions of non-Indigeneity surface underlying conflicts that inhibit non-Indigenous engagement with reconciliation in Australia?

As all the contributions to this book attest, an important corollary for such research is a need to scrutinize the capacity for reconciliation processes to create opportunities for intercultural engagement intensely, examining the effects of policy initiatives and institutional developments that can arise through such processes and identifying the opportunities and constraints inherent to public discourse. The research project we describe here has actively considered how non-Indigenous identities and ideologies both prevent and enable genuine engagement (as distinct from superficial gestures of engagement) with reconciliation in a settler colonial society such as Australia. The project has brought empirically focused data to bear

S. Maddison et al. (eds.), *The limits of settler colonial reconciliation*,
DOI 10.1007/978-981-10-2654-6

on these questions, in order to scope the 'pathways to reconciliation' that may be latent in non-Indigenous Australians' understandings of their own situations.

Through the two interwoven strands of inquiry advanced in this project—reconciliation and discourse—the project has elaborated and deepened understandings of reconciliation in theory and practice. In particular, it has contributed substantially to the emerging field of reconciliation studies through two innovations. The first has been a systematic effort to demarcate and analyze non-Indigeneity as a category in its own right. To optimize that exploration, the project's second innovation has been to augment the semantic focus of critical discourse analysis with an expressly aesthetic or 'textural' frame of reference. This reflects a conviction that the form of language reveals much of its ideological intent, and that such revelations emerge as we analyze and compare varied settings for discourse about reconciliation. This approach resonates with the emerging interest in narrative and rhetoric that characterises much of the leading theory around reconciliation studies. It is an approach that has allowed the researchers to develop new insights into the influences affecting non-Indigenous engagement (or otherwise) with reconciliation work. We hope a better understanding of these issues inform political leaders and organisations across Australia—many of them right now deeply involved in campaigning to engage non-Indigenous Australians with the proposed referendum on constitutional recognition of Aboriginal and Torres Strait Islander peoples.

Thus, the project has asked how the process of reconciliation in Australia can connect to the attitudes of non-Indigenous people in ways that may prompt their engagement with Indigeneity, and will examine the potential for the Australian version of reconciliation to transform the relationships between Indigenous and non-Indigenous people.

Rationale for Focus Groups and Interviews

The chief research technique mobilized in the project has been the focus group. We are fundamentally interested in broad patterns of value among non-Indigenous people in settler societies. We believe this issue has been understudied in considerations of how to think about or improve Indigenous-settler relations. Broad theorisations of "whiteness" or "settler colonialism" are instructive, but do not invite us into the fissures within dominant structures that may contain more positive modes of reconciled, postcolonial, anti-colonial, or decolonized interaction. These potentials—where they exist—emerge most fruitfully during open conversations among groups of individuals.

This focus group approach is in contrast to quantitative approaches such as the survey techniques used in the Australian Reconciliation Barometer, or the survey of Canadians done by the Department of Justice in 2008 in relation to Indian Residential Schools and the Truth and Reconciliation Commission. It is not that such approaches cannot tell us about non-Indigenous commitments, but they are less useful in exploring the ways in which we might begin to think about non-Indigenous identities as collaborative and mutually reinforcing. It is our view that, whether we see the pursuit of justice as a matter of education or redistribution, non-Indigenous peoples must be engaged as conscious, reflective beings in the manner suggested by Habermas (1997).

The research team has undertaken a series of carefully facilitated focus groups, generating emergent discourses of groups with similar cultural characteristics (see below) on which we can fruitfully deploy the semantic and aesthetic analyses comprising our public poetics approach. Focus groups are an empirical tool with a particular capacity to reveal the formation and emergence of attitudes in group settings (Schensul 1998). Before this project's commencement, earlier work by the research team had shown that the focus group approach reveals core themes of cohesion and dissensus in non-Indigenous responses to the topic of reconciliation, especially within 'quotidian' (Lefebvre and Levich 1987), 'ordinary people's' (Brett and Moran 2006), or 'banal' (Baudrillard 1998) discursive frames.

Our working hypothesis has been that many non-Indigenous people feel their knowledge of the topic is very limited and that they feel profoundly reliant on opinion leaders to help them define the topic and its importance. Non-Indigenous people often show that reliance quite saliently by reusing and recycling language formulas from public discourse, reiterating, refining or contesting the ideas of public opinion leaders. In this respect, we have surmised that focus groups emulate quotidian ideology processes.

Design of Focus Groups and Interviews

Focus groups can replicate the ways communities generate opinions, and this has been the research project's primary interest. In 2014 we conducted eight focus groups in four locations around Australia: Parramatta in Sydney, Perth in Western Australia, Bega in southern New South Wales, and Gladstone in Queensland. Since the concept of locality is central to our research design, the four sites were chosen to represent a mixture of urban and rural populations with varying levels of non-Indigenous ethnic diversity, as well as varying Indigenous demographics.

Parramatta is a diverse neighbourhood in the Western suburbs of Sydney with a population of around 395,000 and an estimated Indigenous population of 0.8 %. The percentage of the population with parents born overseas is significantly higher in Parramatta than in the other focus group locations (CensusData 2013d). Perth's population of about 1,730,000 is primarily of European descent with a majority of the population's parents born overseas. There is an Indigenous population of around 1.6 % (CensusData 2013c). Bega has a population of about 32,000 people, of which 2.8 % identifies as Aboriginal—marginally above the national average of 2.7 %. The rest of the population is overwhelmingly of European descent with the majority of people and their parents born in Australia (CensusData 2013a). Gladstone's population of approximately 32,500 is also overwhelmingly of European descent with the majority born in Australia. The Aboriginal population is significantly higher in Gladstone than the national average at 4.1 % (CensusData 2013b). Although our intention had been to include a site with either a large Indigenous population or a majority Indigenous population, noting that the Canadian study found such communities housed quite distinctive non-Indigenous attitudes, limited funding meant this was not achievable. Despite this limitation, the pool of information gathered in the four sites mentioned provides us with a rich and varied basis to explore non-Indigenous attitudes and identities.

Focus groups in all locations were recruited by an independent agency, Jetty Media. Participants were given a small remuneration for their time. Two focus groups were conducted in each location. All groups consisted of exclusively non-Indigenous people, with specific questions asked during recruitment to exclude any potential participants who identified as Indigenous Australians. The first groups comprised people born in Australia while the second comprised people born overseas. Mindful of the Canadian comparison (RW.ERROR—Unable to find reference: 2932), one purpose of dividing the groups in this way was to ascertain whether there is any difference in the understanding of those who have been in the country longer or who might feel stronger ties to Australia. The groups in all locations were overwhelmingly of European descent, although the second groups were often slightly more ethnically diverse. The groups varied in size with between eight to twelve people in each group and with a good representation of ages and gender.

In each location focus groups were conducted in a room with one facilitator from Jetty Media. In Bega and Gladstone an observer from the research team was also present in the room. The facilities used in Perth and Sydney offered purpose-built market research rooms, and so the observer sat behind one-way glass. Discussions were held at tables with the facilitator sitting at the head and participants seated around the sides.

The independent facilitator enabled inclusive discussion; drawing out less vocal participants and creating an environment where participants felt safe to voice unpopular points of view. The purpose of having an observer from the research team present was to give them the opportunity to watch and note paralinguistic features, such as the body language of participants, as well as in changes in the mood of the room. These changes are not always apparent in recordings, nor especially in the subsequent transcripts, so having an observer on-site enabled a richer pool of knowledge than recordings alone. We did notice however that the presence of an observer in the focus group did affect the behaviour of participants, at least to the extent that we recorded two brief instances where the observer was drawn into the discussion. We do not believe this has in any way vitiated those discussions, but a reflexively self-aware reading of our own practices needs to understand that it has affected them.

Chapter 14 in this book (Maddison and Stastny) also draws on data from a series of interviews conducted for this project. In 2015, six participants from the focus groups were invited to take part in follow-up interviews. These six participants were selected on the basis of their contribution to the focus groups, targeting specifically those who had shown either a stronger or weaker sense of reconciliation and responsibility to engage in relationships with Indigenous people and cultures. The interviews attempted to gain a greater understanding of the factors that might stimulate a sense of responsibility to engage.

The interviews were semi-structured telephone conversations, lasting 30–60 minutes, which the research team also recorded as audio files and transcribed. Interviewees were asked to reflect upon the discourses of reconciliation they use, with a particular emphasis on four themes: (i) reconciliation now, its purpose and value; (ii) whether participation in the focus group had changed those views—and, if so, how; (iii) whether any public commentators have influenced their views about reconciliation (and if so, whom they have found most influential); and finally, (iv) inviting comparison between their focus group experience or personal conversations about reconciliation with media debates about reconciliation.

As the relevant chapters in this book make clear, the project team has conducted both semantic and aesthetic analyses of the reconciliation discourses that the focus groups and interviews have generated. It is not our intention to summarize those analytic steps here—the chapters can speak for themselves in that regard. However, a striking measure of this book's overall coherence—a strong indication that it has been timely to bring together these 19 authors in this collection—is the way similar analytic values play out in all 16 chapters. Scoping such an ambiguous and highly circumscribed political problem as this book addresses requires drawing on the richest possible information about how a given community may understand and respond to that problem.

The manufacturer's authorised representative in the EU is Springer Nature Customer Service Centre GmbH, Europaplatz 3, 69115 Heidelberg, Germany. If you have any concerns regarding our products, please contact ProductSafety@springernature.com

Printed and bound by CPI Group (UK) Ltd, Croydon, CR0 4YY
05/10/2026
02227652-0002